CERES™
Celestial Legend
Volume 9: Progenitor
Shôjo Edition

STORY & ART BY YÛ WATASE

English Adaptation/Gary Leach

Translation/Lillian Olsen
Touch-Up Art & Lettering/Melanie Lewis
Cover & Graphic Design/Hidemi Sahara
Editor/Avery Gotoh
Supervising Editor/Frances E. Wall

Managing Editor/Annette Roman
Editorial Director/Alvin Lu
Sr. Director of Licensing & Acquisitions/Rika Inouye
Director of Production/Noboru Watanabe
Vice President of Sales & Marketing/Liza Coppola
Executive Vice President/Hyoe Narita
Publisher/Seiji Horibuchi

© 1997 Yuu Watase/Shogakukan, Inc. First published by Shogakukan, Inc. in Japan as "Ayashi no Ceres."

New and adapted artwork and text © 2004 VIZ, LLC. The CERES: CELESTIAL LEGEND logo is a trademark of VIZ, LLC.
All rights reserved. No unauthorized reproduction allowed.
The stories, characters and incidents mentioned in this publication are entirely fictional.

Printed in Canada

Published by VIZ, LLC
P.O. Box 77010 • San Francisco CA 94107

Shôjo Edition

10 9 8 7 6 5 4 3 2 1

First printing, October 2004

VIZ GRAPHIC NOVEL

Ceres™

Celestial Legend

Vol. 9: Progenitor

Story and Art by
Yû Watase

AYA MIKAGE: Sixteen years old at the start of the story, Aya has since become a woman. Separated from Tôya but more in love with him than ever, she travels across Japan in search of the hagoromo, trying to reconcile her love for twin-brother Aki with her fear of the monster he's since become.

AKI MIKAGE: Aya's twin brother. While the consciousness of Ceres is taking over Aya, Aki is showing signs of bearing the consciousness of the founder (progenitor) of the Mikage family line. Placed under confinement by the Mikage family to keep him separated from Aya, still nothing will keep him from her....

CERES: Once upon a time...long, long ago...a ten'nyo named Ceres descended to Earth. Her hagoromo or "feathered robes" stolen, Ceres—unable to return to the heavens—was forced by the human thief to become his wife and bear his children...thus beginning the Mikage family line. Awakened after aeons of waiting—and anger—Ceres wants her hagoromo back and vows to use all her celestial powers to avenge herself against the descendants of the man who wronged her.

CHIDORI:
Awakened to her own, unsuspected celestial powers only after her younger brother was put in mortal danger, Chidori Kuruma was at  first another target of Kagami's, but was spared by the compassion of Tôya. Deceptively young in appearance (she looks like a grade-schooler but is actually in high school, just like Aya), Chidori has since decided to help Aya and the others in the search for Ceres' missing hagoromo.

TÔYA: Aya's mysterious lover; he must keep himself away from Aya as he tries to center himself after a long period of amnesia. Cruelly toyed with by Kagami and the false memories he implanted, Tôya is no longer sure who or even what he is. One thing is for sure, though—he still has strong feelings for Aya.

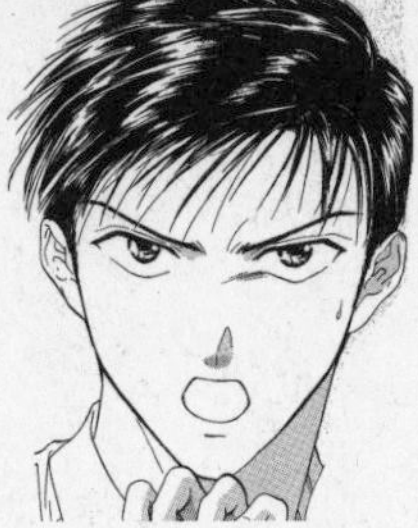

YÛHI: Sixteen-year-old brother-in-law to Suzumi. A skilled martial artist and aspiring chef, Yûhi has been asked (ordered, more like) to serve as Aya's watchful protector and guardian...his own feelings for her notwithstanding.

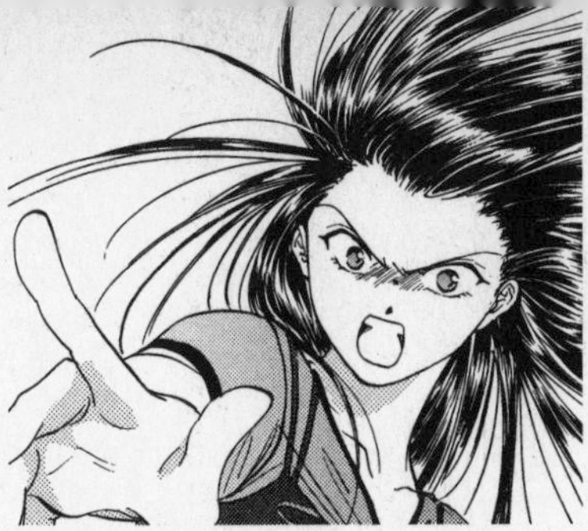

MIORI SAHARA: An innocent victim used by Kagami against Tôya (and also, therefore, against Aya), it turns out that Miori looks like Aya—and Ceres—for a reason: she herself is also a ten'nyo or "celestial maiden." Will her resentment against Aya for an inadvertent role in a family tragedy go too far?

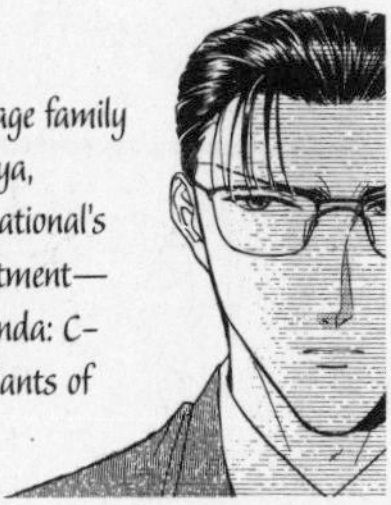

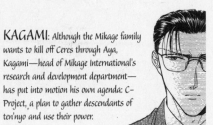

KAGAMI: Although the Mikage family wants to kill off Ceres through Aya, Kagami—head of Mikage International's research and development department—has put into motion his own agenda: C-Project, a plan to gather descendants of ten'nyo and use their power.

SHURO: Surviving member of the beautiful, androgynous Japan pop duo, GeSANG. A woman (with ten'nyo ancestry) passing as a man, her agent's urging prompts Shuro to consider a return to the pop-music scene, this time as a solo act.

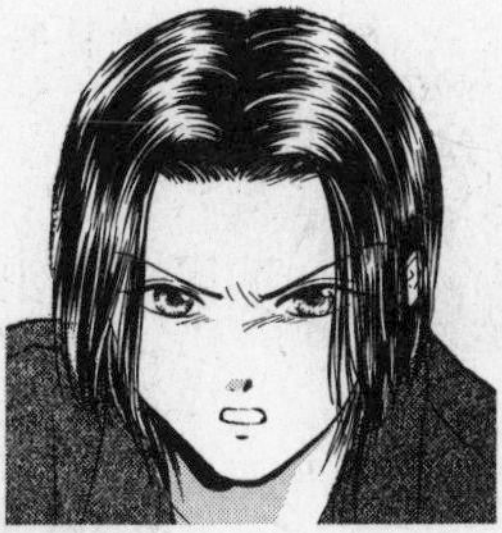

SUZUMI: Instructor of traditional Japanese dance and descendant of ten'nyo or "celestial maidens" herself. A big sister figure, Suzumi has welcomed Aya into her household and is more than happy to provide her with all the protection, assistance and support that she can.

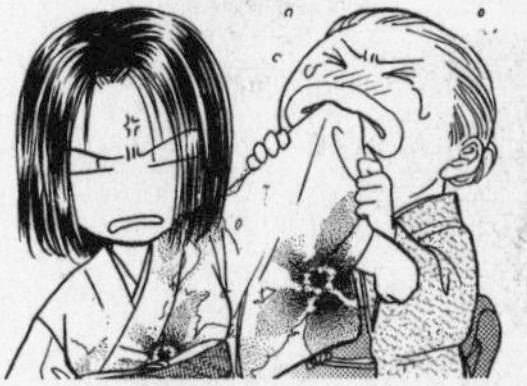

MRS. Q (ODA-KYÛ): Eccentric yet loyal-to-a-fault servant of the Aogiri household.

You may have noticed some unfamiliar people and things mentioned in CERES. VIZ left these Japanese pop-culture references as they originally appeared in the manga series. Here's an explanation for those who may not be so J-Pop savvy:

Page 69: "Senpai": A term of respect, similar in usage to the perhaps more commonly known "sensei." Unlike the former, however, "senpai" connotes an established junior-senior relationship, such as that between Watase (the published manga artist) and the students at her old high school (who maybe hope someday to become manga artists themselves).

Page 105: "Cutting hair after heartbreak": One of the things about being a fan of anime and manga is learning the little cultural "signifiers" that keep popping up. One of those—along with the giant drop of "sweat" to indicate nervousness or discomfort, and the "popping blood vessels" to show extreme anger and/or frustration—is the cutting of hair by female characters. Cutting your hair can mean sending the message that someone's broken your heart, or it can also signal your determination to "get on with your life" despite any possible tragedies you may have endured or may currently be enduring.

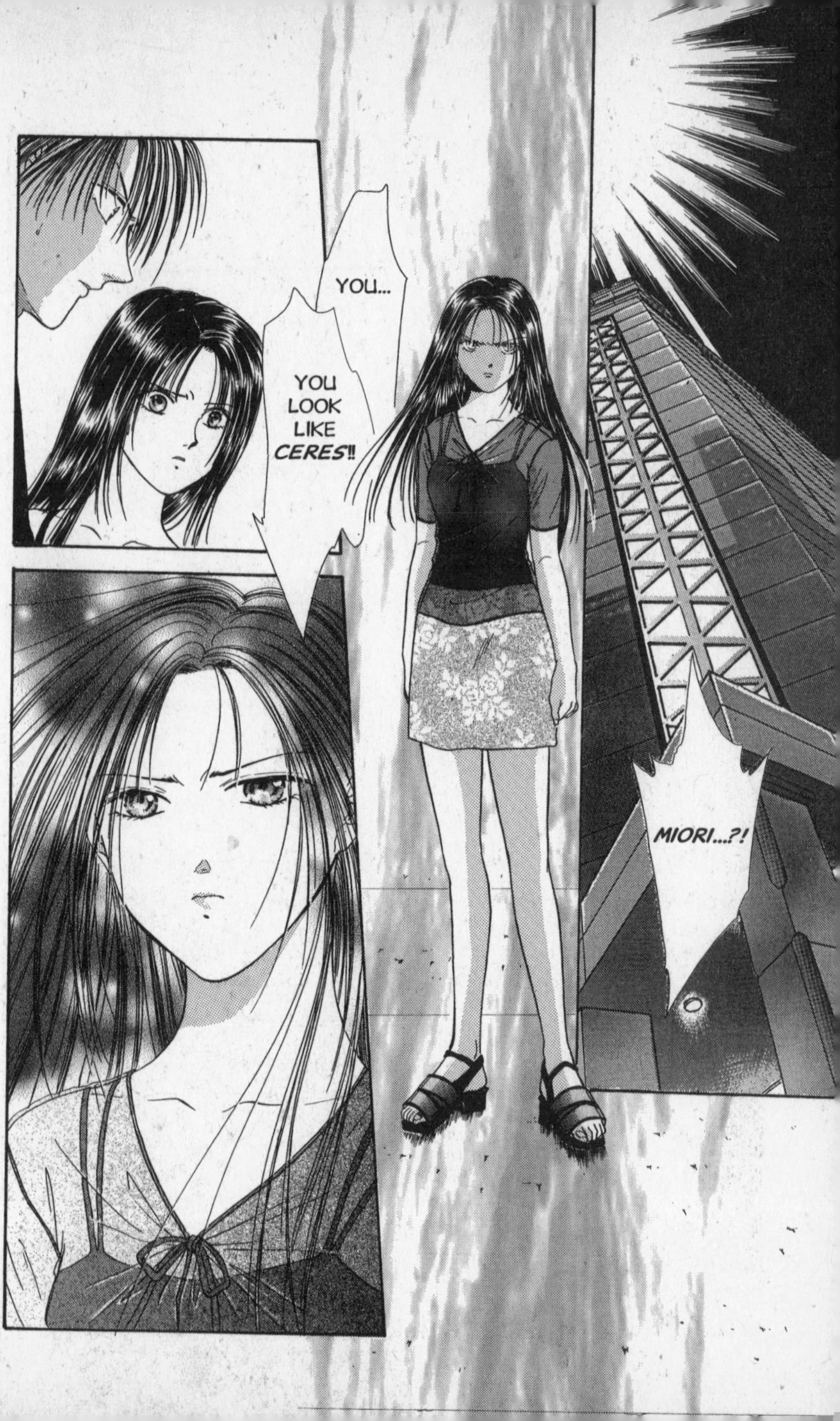
MIORI...?!
YOU...
YOU LOOK LIKE *CERES*!!

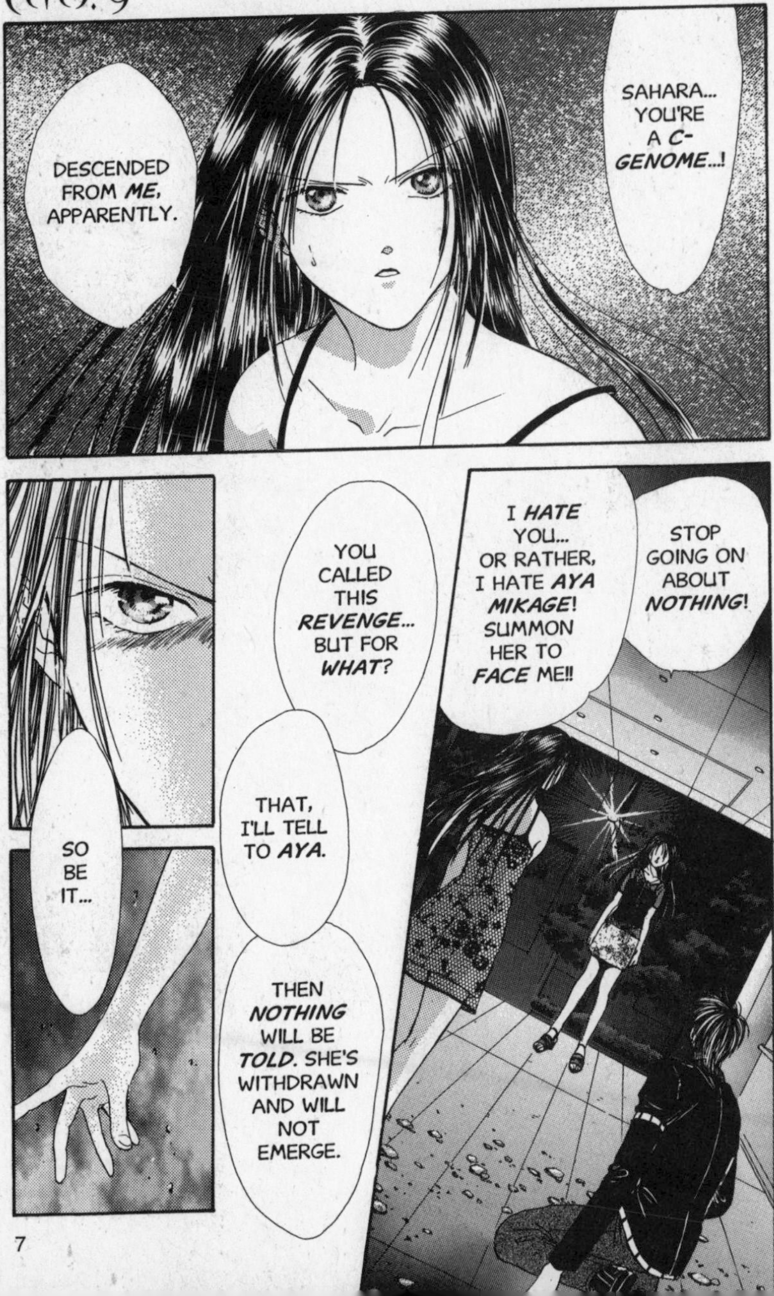
SAHARA... YOU'RE A C-GENOME...!
DESCENDED FROM ME, APPARENTLY.
STOP GOING ON ABOUT NOTHING!
I HATE YOU... OR RATHER, I HATE AYA MIKAGE! SUMMON HER TO FACE ME!!
YOU CALLED THIS REVENGE... BUT FOR WHAT?
THAT, I'LL TELL TO AYA.
THEN NOTHING WILL BE TOLD. SHE'S WITHDRAWN AND WILL NOT EMERGE.
SO BE IT...

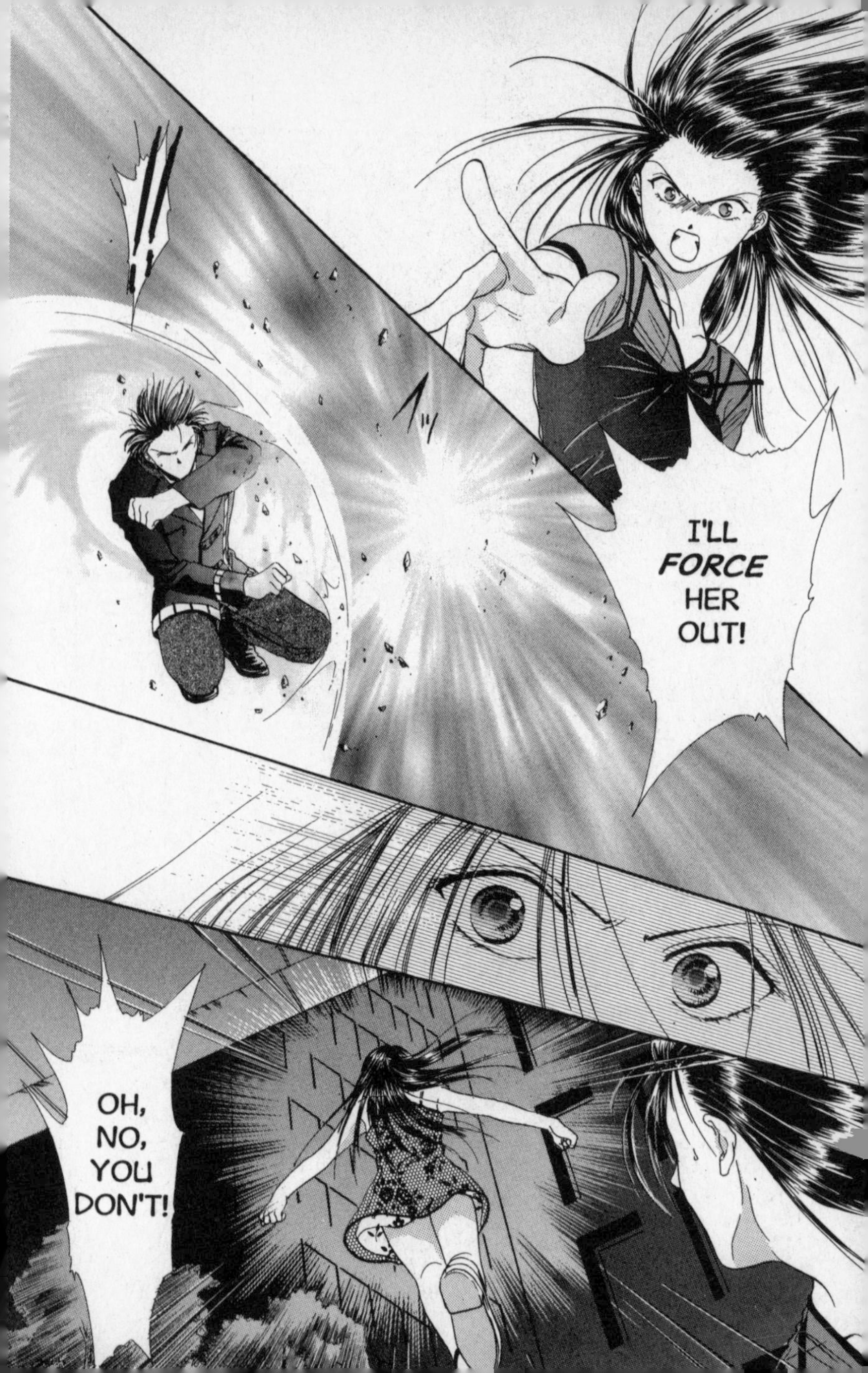
I'LL *FORCE* HER OUT!
OH, NO, YOU DON'T!

◆ Progenitor ◆

It's me, Watase! **Ceres** is in its 9th volume! And it's reached a climax.

First, though, I have to apologize and make a correction for Volume 8. A whole paragraph in the second panel, top right, on page 186 about Anime Expo was left out by mistake (what kind of mistake, you ask?). How it should have read was "...of **Galaxy Fraulein Yuna** fame, Jun'ichi Hayama, character designer for **JoJo's Bizarre Adventures**...all famous if you're 'in the know'! I've never felt like such a nobody." Sorry. While we're at it, in the third panel, page 138, the furigana for the kanji "Aki" had been (mistakenly) written "Akira," and the kanji for "him" became "after." Reminds me of the time people wrote in about the furigana for "Tasuki" showing up as "Hotohori" in "Nakago, Get a Hold of Yourself! 2," as printed in the book "Nanako the Matchmaker." Surprised? Actually, I'm the one who's surprised. (I mean, I wouldn't get the names wrong!) These are mistakes in the typesetting stage—I write the words in the balloons in pencil, someone else typesets, then the editor pastes them in. Each and every line is the product of many people's work. (When I was young, I figured the writer had to do it all, and so I practiced.) ☺ But we're all human, and mistakes happen. ...Okay, so maybe I make the mistakes to begin with, but I wouldn't get the **character** names wrong. ☺ The manga artist draws the manga on paper only and hands it in (though that itself takes a lot of effort), but there's lots of other people involved in the production, too, from the title-logo design, to the "look" of the text.

The mistakes mentioned above apply only to the first [Japanese] printing, BTW, and have been fixed for all subsequent printings.

CERES GOT AWAY!

DAMMIT, AND WE ALMOST *HAD* HER!

SWITCH CAMERAS AND FOLLOW THEM.

MASTER?!

I *WARNED* MIORI NOT TO DO THIS. WE'VE COME *TOO FAR* FOR HER TO SUCCUMB TO *PERSONAL FEELINGS.*

SIGH...

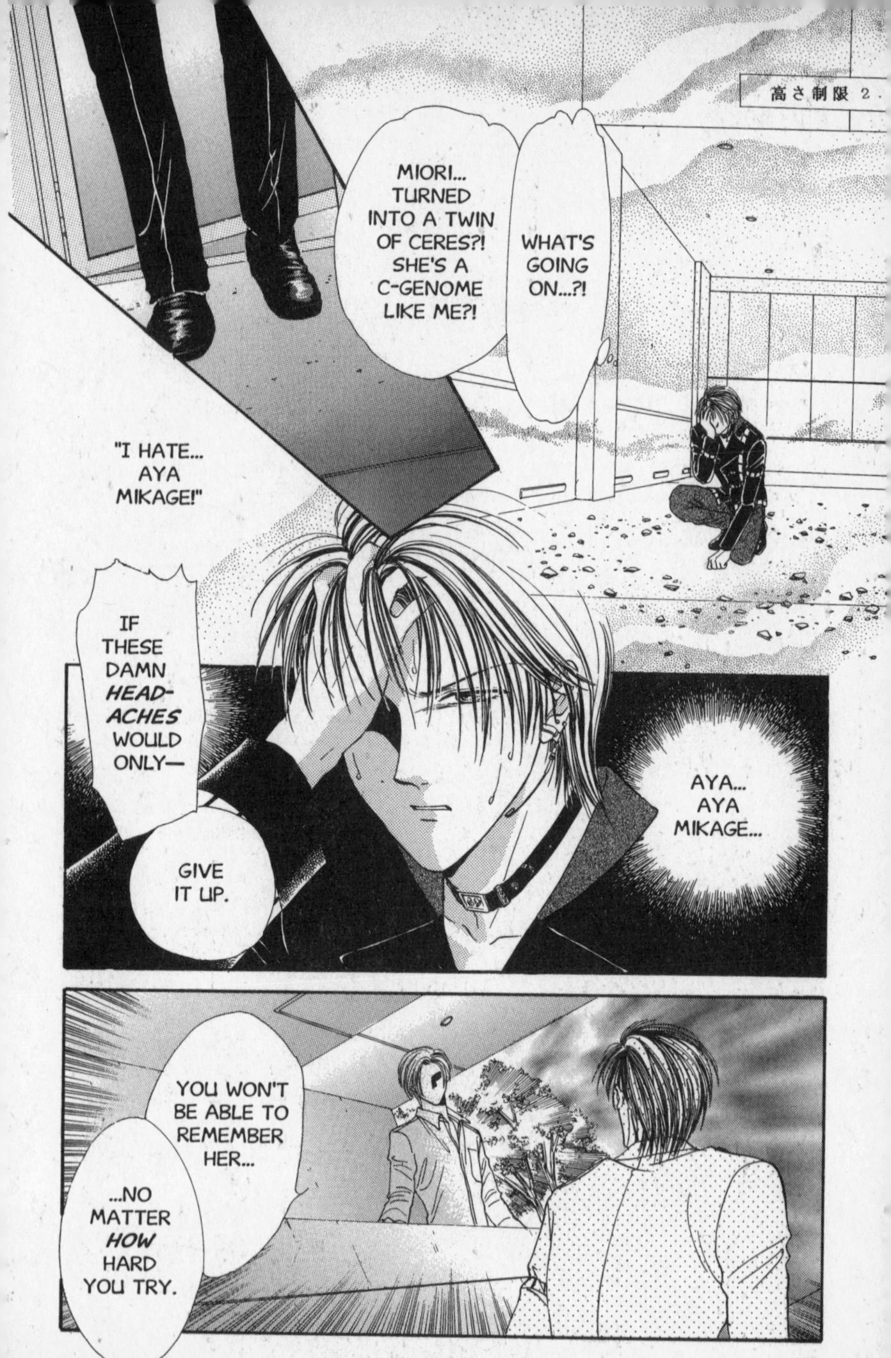

高さ制限 2
WHAT'S GOING ON...?!
MIORI... TURNED INTO A TWIN OF CERES?! SHE'S A C-GENOME LIKE ME?!
"I HATE... AYA MIKAGE!"
AYA... AYA MIKAGE...
IF THESE DAMN *HEAD-ACHES* WOULD ONLY—
GIVE IT UP.
YOU WON'T BE ABLE TO REMEMBER HER...
...NO MATTER *HOW* HARD YOU TRY.

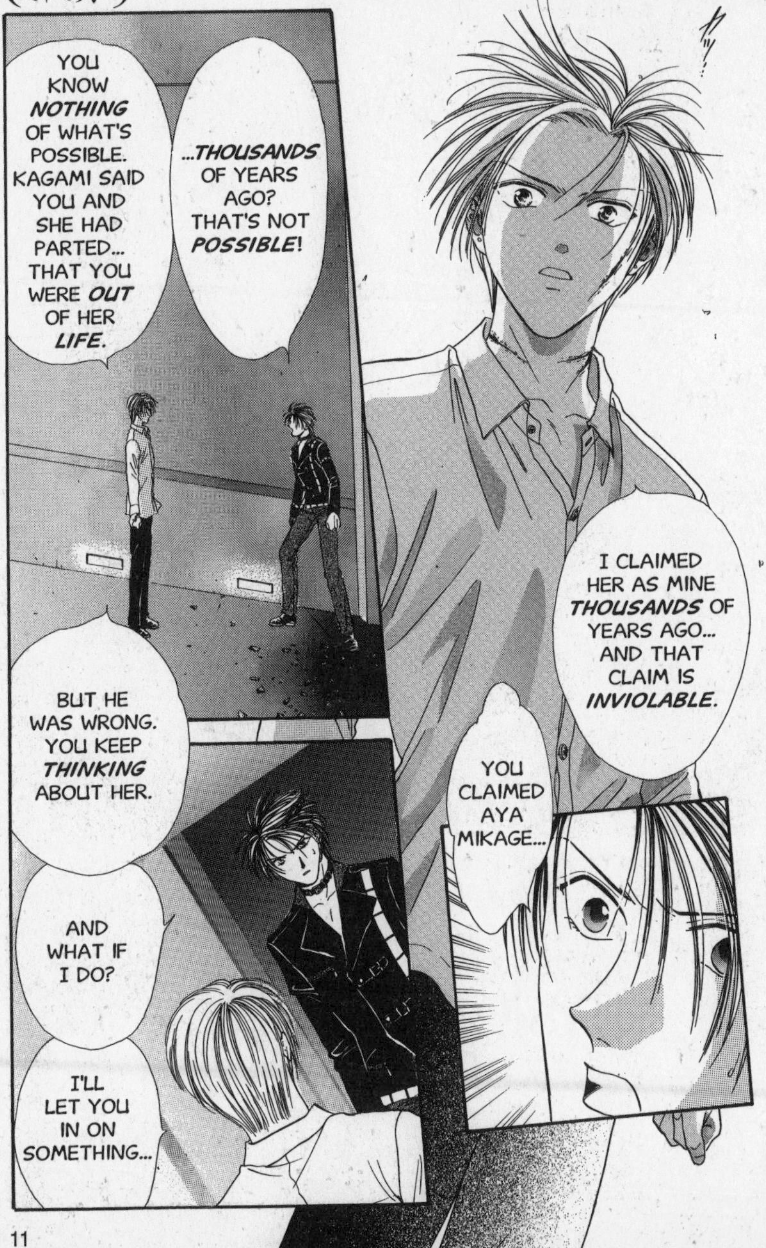
I CLAIMED HER AS MINE *THOUSANDS* OF YEARS AGO... AND THAT CLAIM IS *INVIOLABLE*.
YOU CLAIMED AYA MIKAGE...
...*THOUSANDS* OF YEARS AGO? THAT'S NOT *POSSIBLE*!
YOU KNOW *NOTHING* OF WHAT'S POSSIBLE. KAGAMI SAID YOU AND SHE HAD PARTED... THAT YOU WERE *OUT* OF HER *LIFE*.
BUT HE WAS WRONG. YOU KEEP *THINKING* ABOUT HER.
AND WHAT IF I DO?
I'LL LET YOU IN ON SOMETHING...

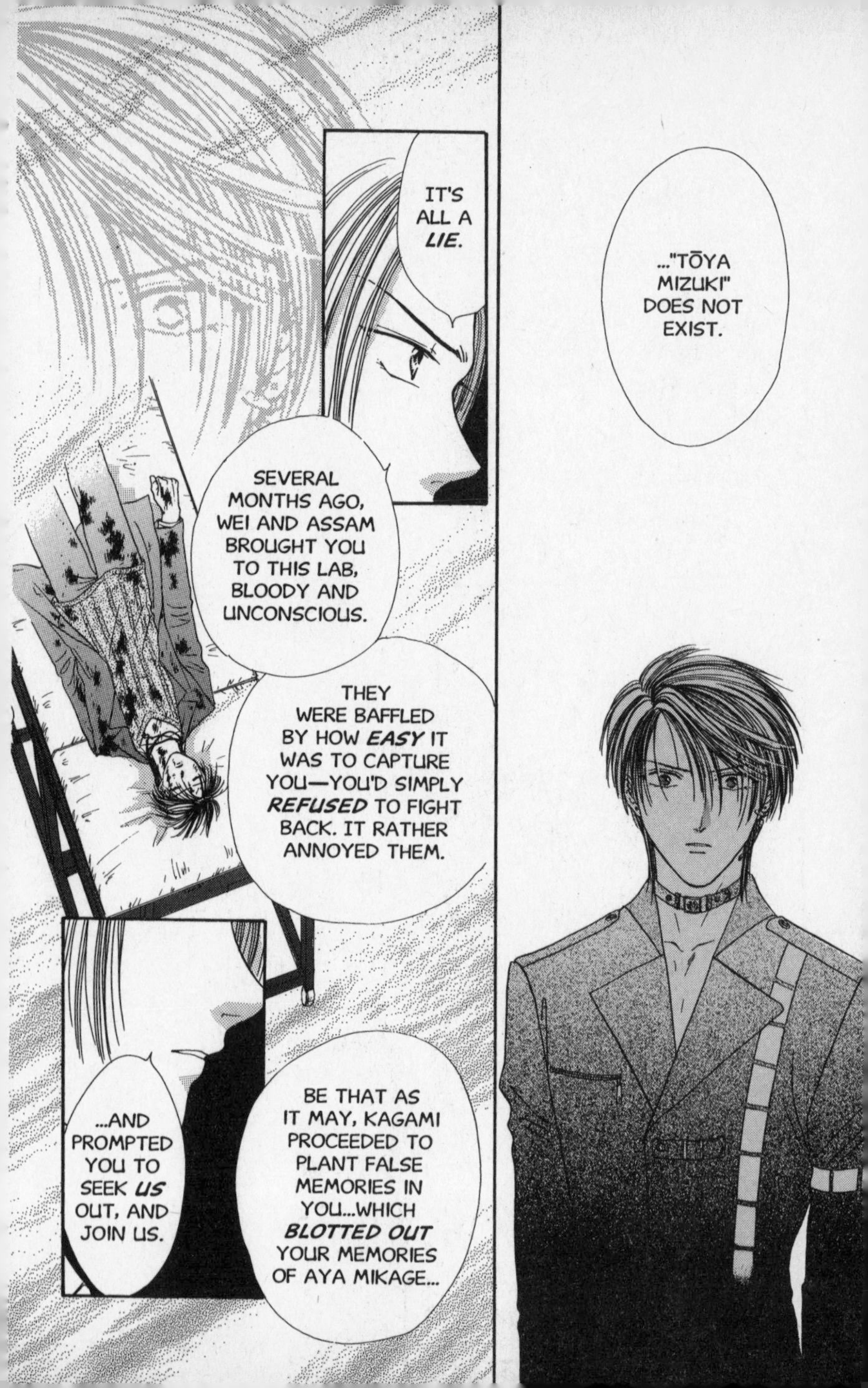
..."TŌYA MIZUKI" DOES NOT EXIST.
IT'S ALL A *LIE*.
SEVERAL MONTHS AGO, WEI AND ASSAM BROUGHT YOU TO THIS LAB, BLOODY AND UNCONSCIOUS.
THEY WERE BAFFLED BY HOW *EASY* IT WAS TO CAPTURE YOU—YOU'D SIMPLY *REFUSED* TO FIGHT BACK. IT RATHER ANNOYED THEM.
BE THAT AS IT MAY, KAGAMI PROCEEDED TO PLANT FALSE MEMORIES IN YOU...WHICH *BLOTTED OUT* YOUR MEMORIES OF AYA MIKAGE...
...AND PROMPTED YOU TO SEEK *US* OUT, AND JOIN US.

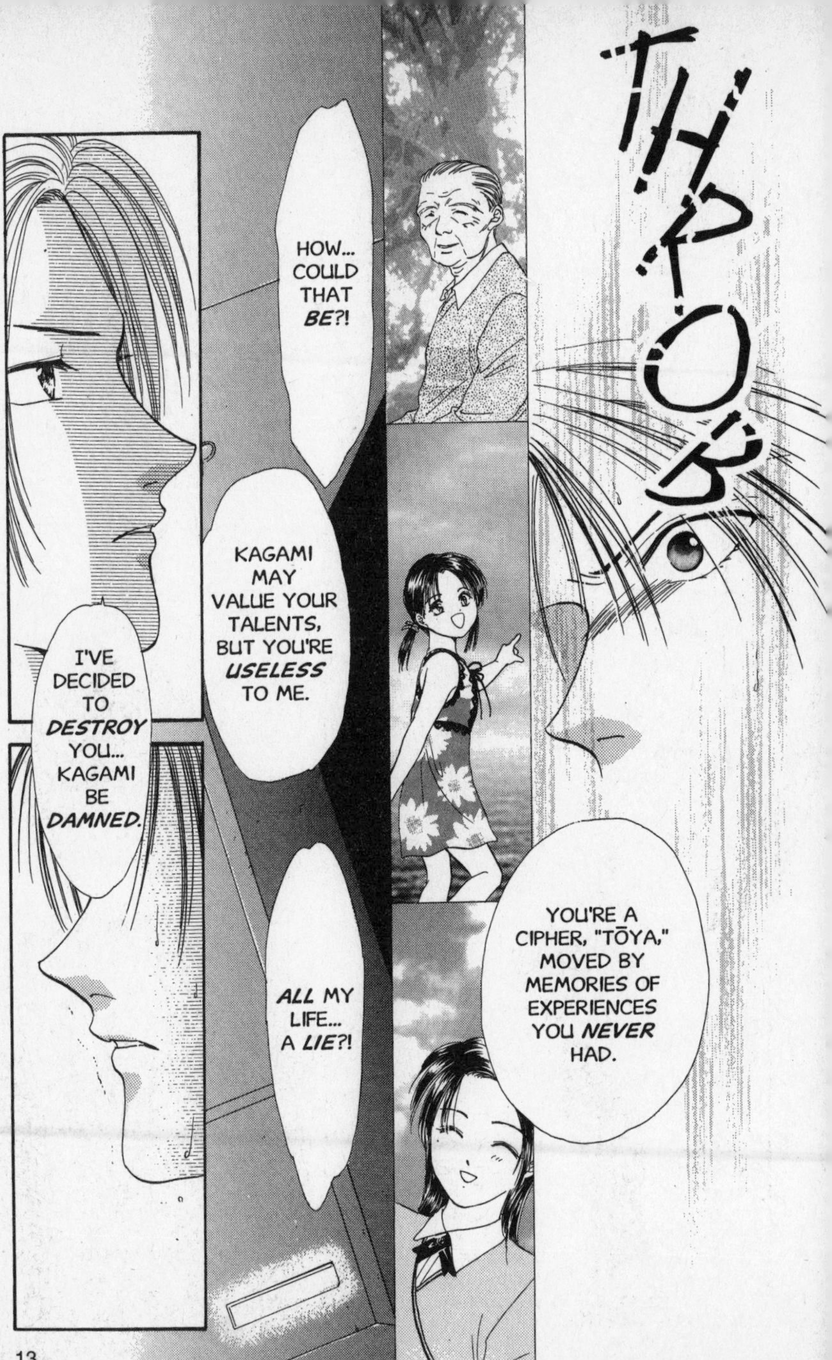
THROB
HOW... COULD THAT *BE*?!
KAGAMI MAY VALUE YOUR TALENTS, BUT YOU'RE *USELESS* TO ME.
YOU'RE A CIPHER, "TŌYA," MOVED BY MEMORIES OF EXPERIENCES YOU *NEVER* HAD.
ALL MY LIFE... A *LIE*?!
I'VE DECIDED TO *DESTROY* YOU... KAGAMI BE *DAMNED*.

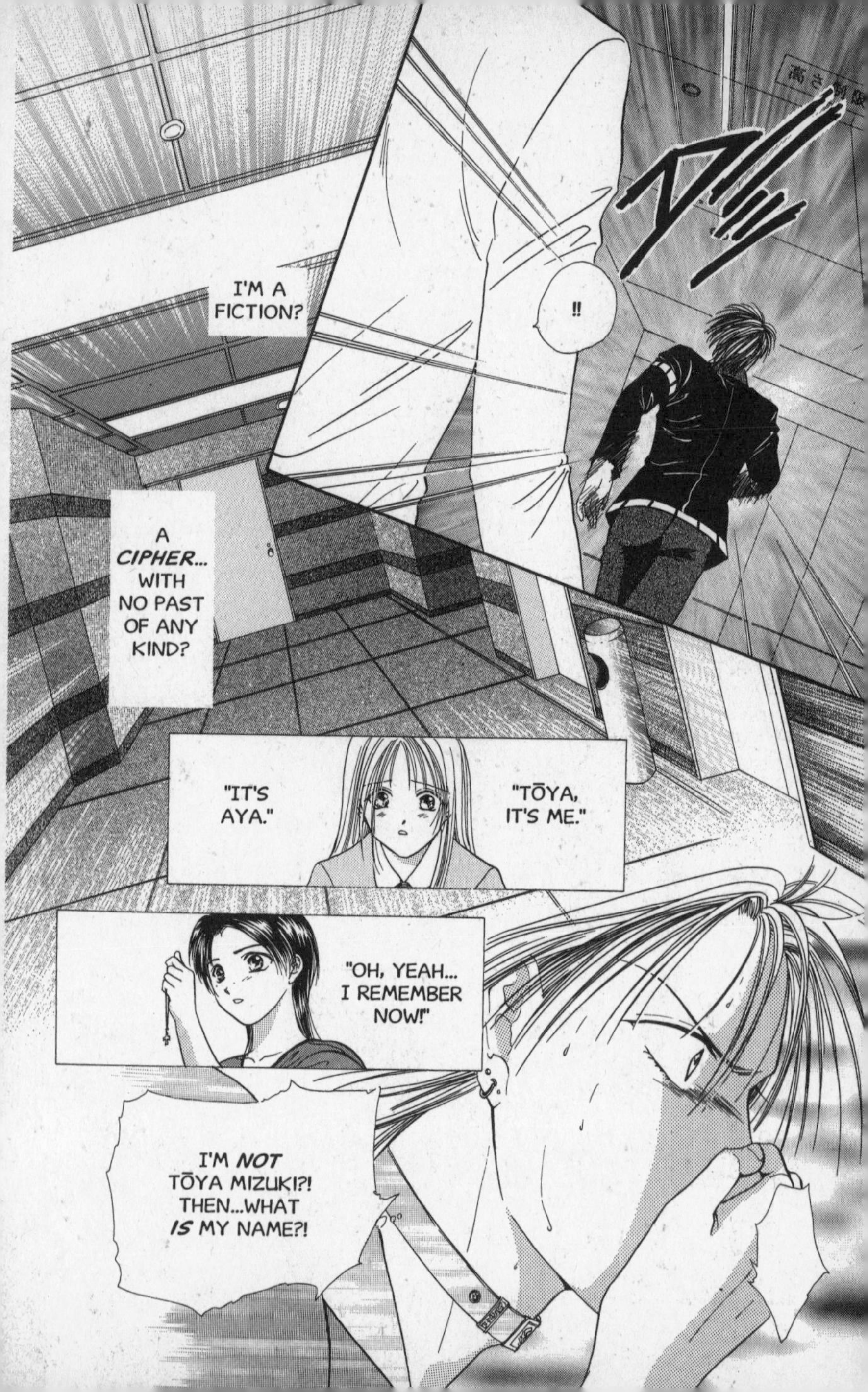
!!
I'M A FICTION?
A *CIPHER*... WITH NO PAST OF ANY KIND?
"TŌYA, IT'S ME."
"IT'S AYA."
"OH, YEAH... I REMEMBER NOW!"
I'M *NOT* TŌYA MIZUKI?! THEN...WHAT *IS* MY NAME?!

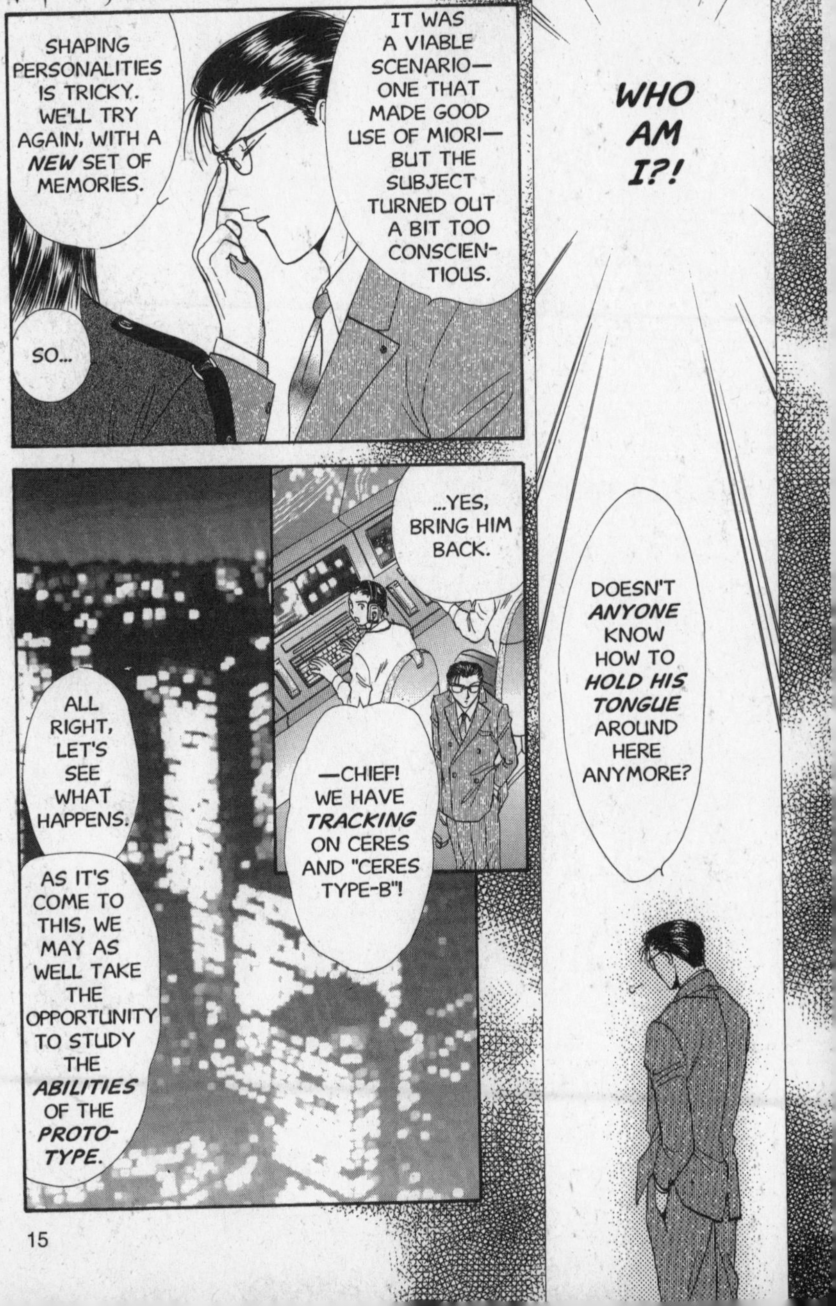
WHO AM I?!
DOESN'T ANYONE KNOW HOW TO HOLD HIS TONGUE AROUND HERE ANYMORE?
IT WAS A VIABLE SCENARIO—ONE THAT MADE GOOD USE OF MIORI—BUT THE SUBJECT TURNED OUT A BIT TOO CONSCIENTIOUS.
SHAPING PERSONALITIES IS TRICKY. WE'LL TRY AGAIN, WITH A NEW SET OF MEMORIES.
SO...
...YES, BRING HIM BACK.
—CHIEF! WE HAVE TRACKING ON CERES AND "CERES TYPE-B"!
ALL RIGHT, LET'S SEE WHAT HAPPENS.
AS IT'S COME TO THIS, WE MAY AS WELL TAKE THE OPPORTUNITY TO STUDY THE ABILITIES OF THE PROTOTYPE.

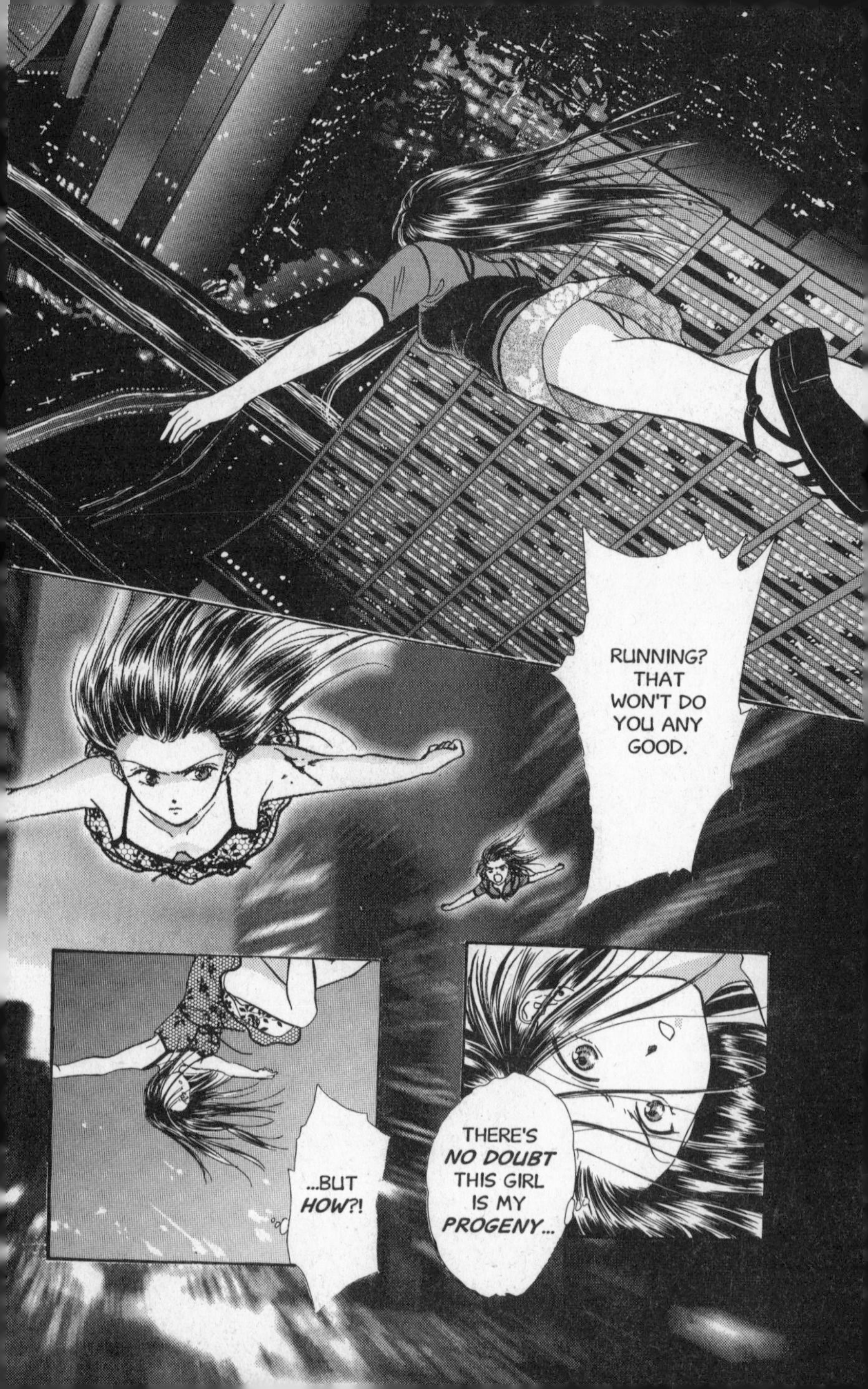
RUNNING? THAT WON'T DO YOU ANY GOOD.
THERE'S *NO DOUBT* THIS GIRL IS MY *PROGENY*...
...BUT *HOW?!*

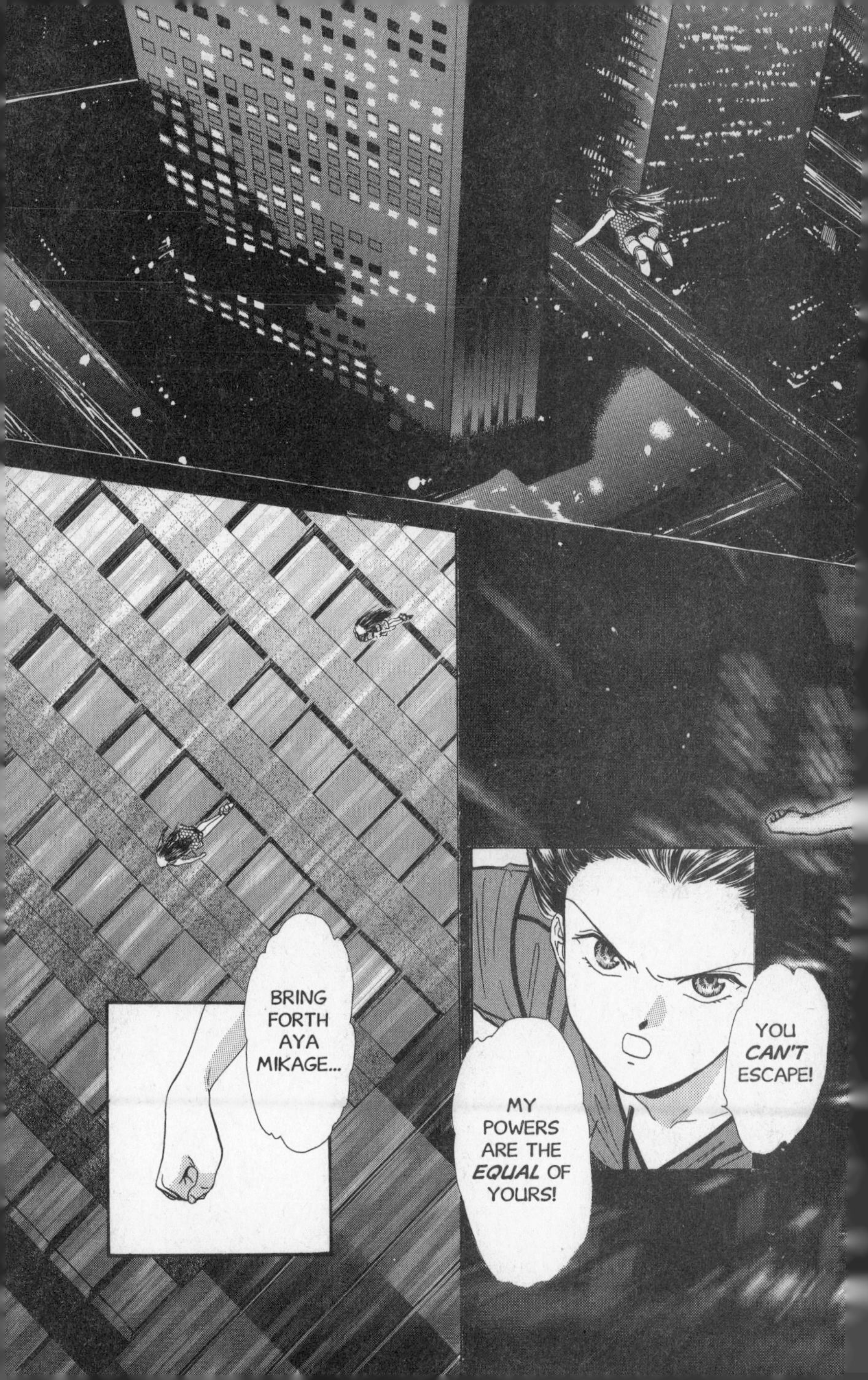
YOU *CAN'T* ESCAPE!
MY POWERS ARE THE *EQUAL* OF YOURS!
BRING FORTH AYA MIKAGE...

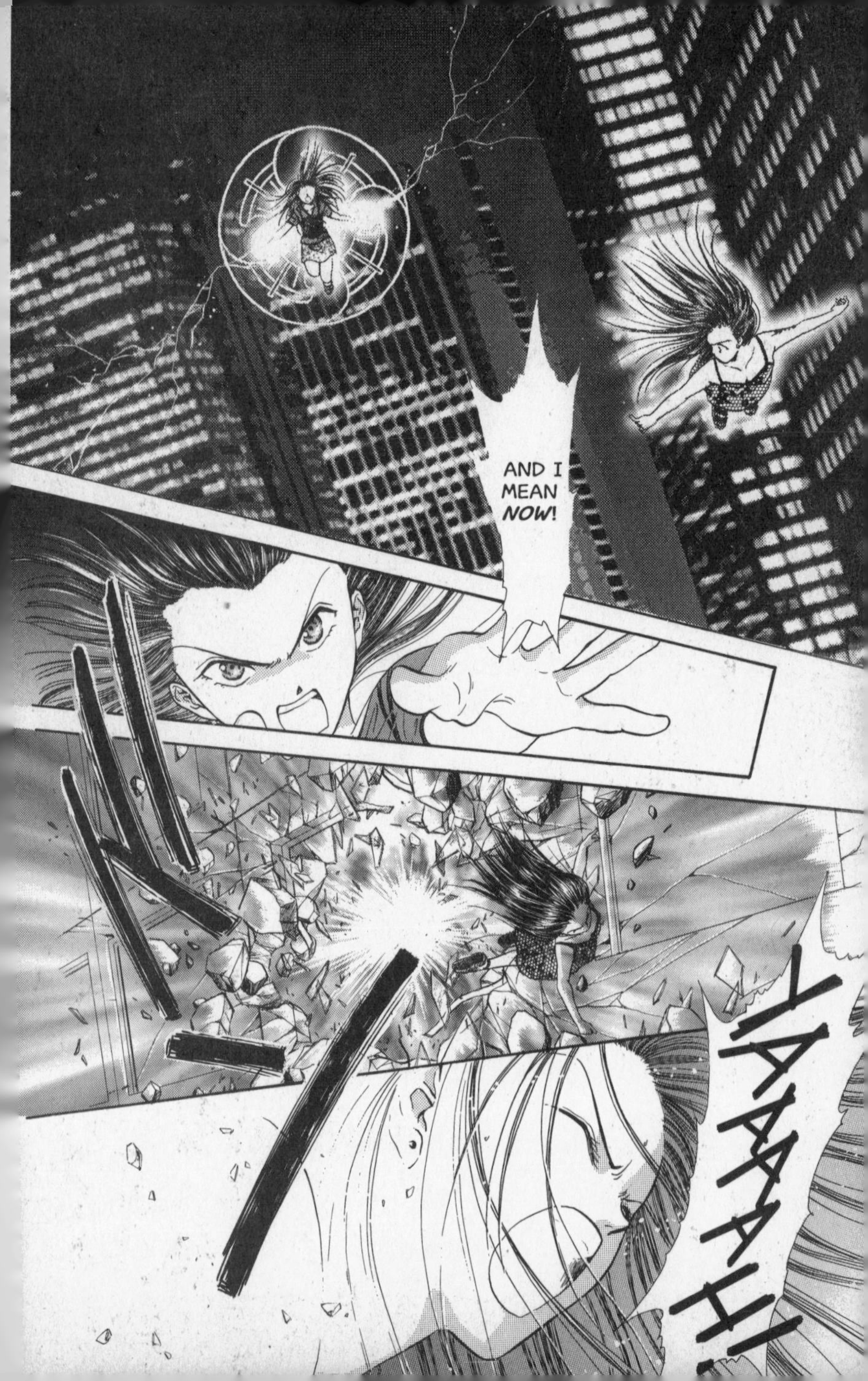
AND I MEAN NOW!
YAAAAAH!!

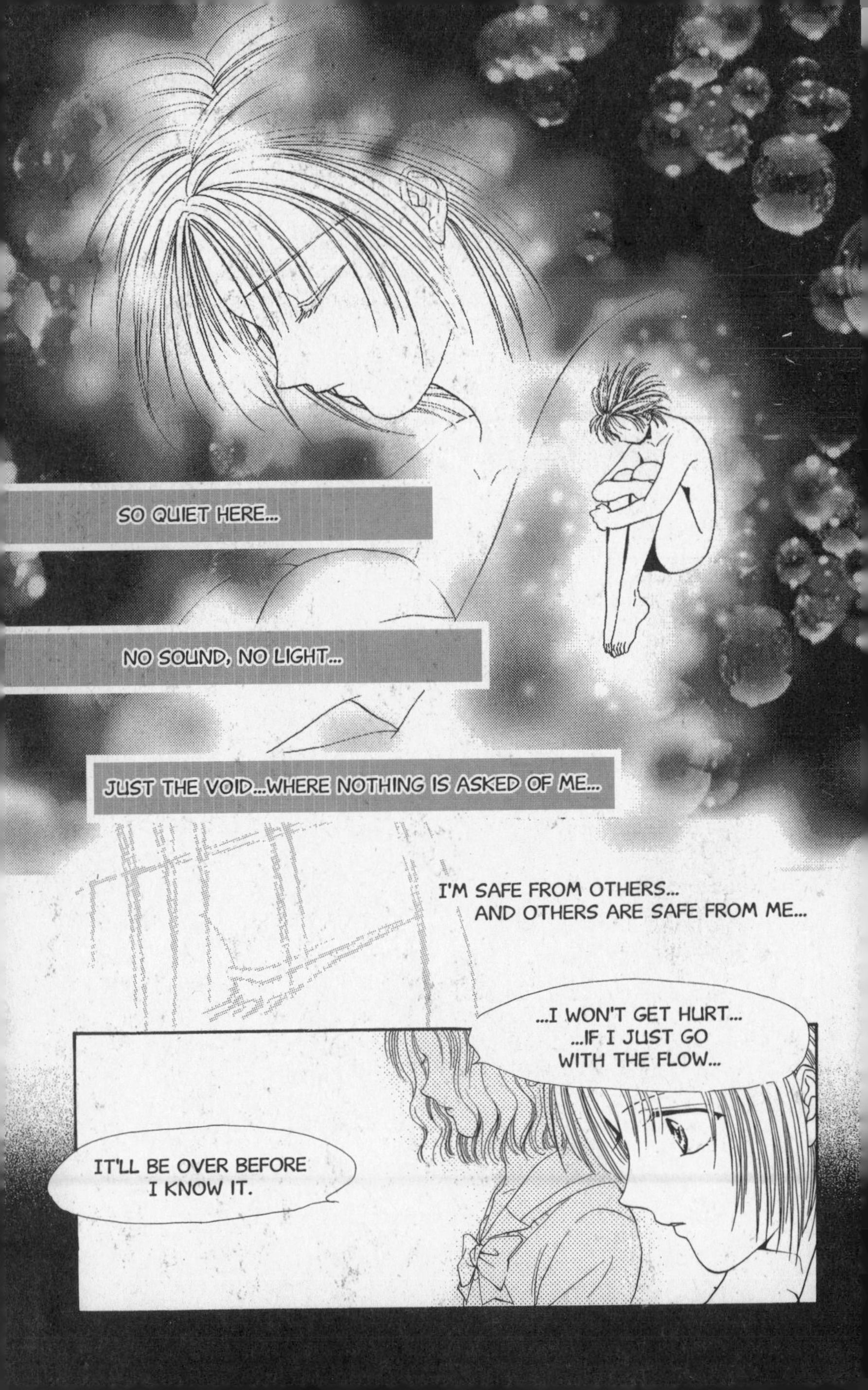
SO QUIET HERE...
NO SOUND, NO LIGHT...
JUST THE VOID...WHERE NOTHING IS ASKED OF ME...
I'M SAFE FROM OTHERS... AND OTHERS ARE SAFE FROM ME...
...I WON'T GET HURT... ...IF I JUST GO WITH THE FLOW...
IT'LL BE OVER BEFORE I KNOW IT.

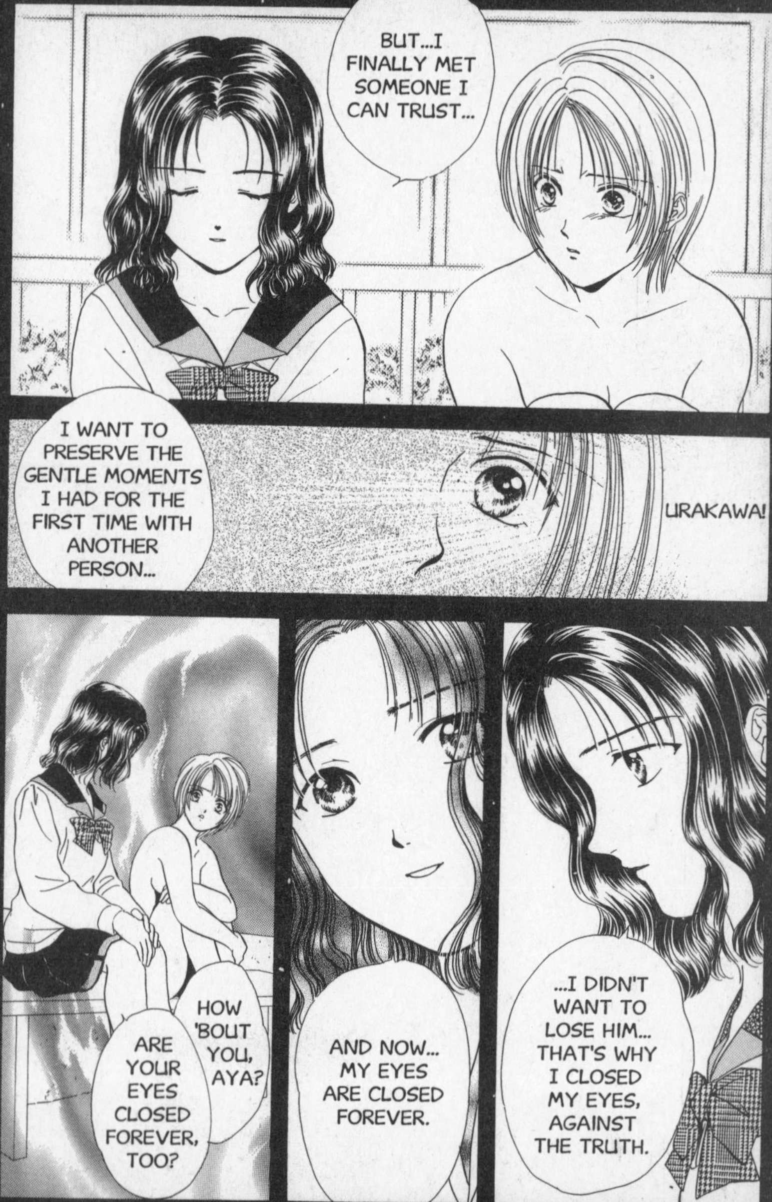
BUT...I FINALLY MET SOMEONE I CAN TRUST...
URAKAWA!
I WANT TO PRESERVE THE GENTLE MOMENTS I HAD FOR THE FIRST TIME WITH ANOTHER PERSON...
...I DIDN'T WANT TO LOSE HIM... THAT'S WHY I CLOSED MY EYES, AGAINST THE TRUTH.
AND NOW... MY EYES ARE CLOSED FOREVER.
HOW 'BOUT YOU, AYA?
ARE YOUR EYES CLOSED FOREVER, TOO?

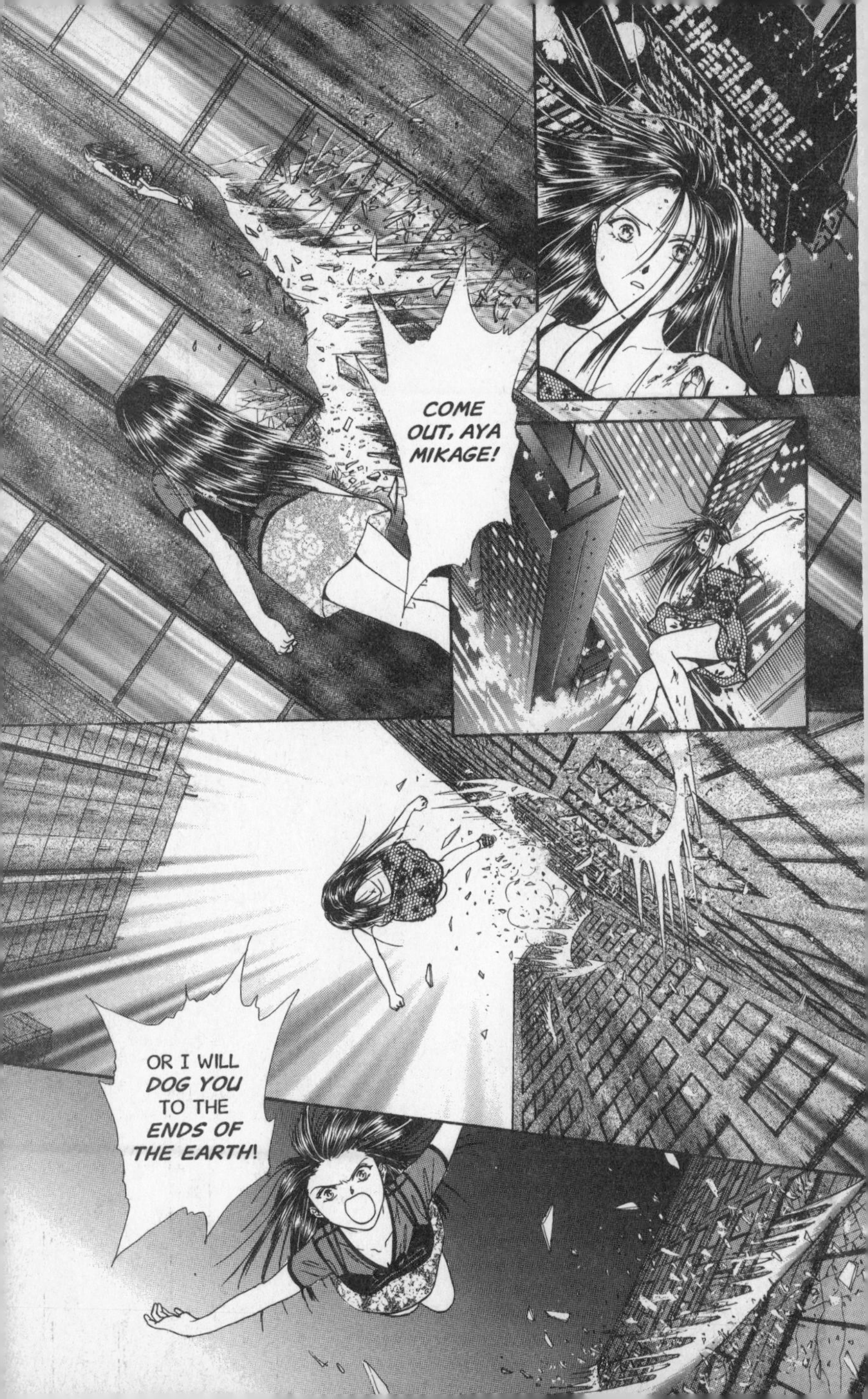
COME OUT, AYA MIKAGE!
OR I WILL DOG YOU TO THE ENDS OF THE EARTH!

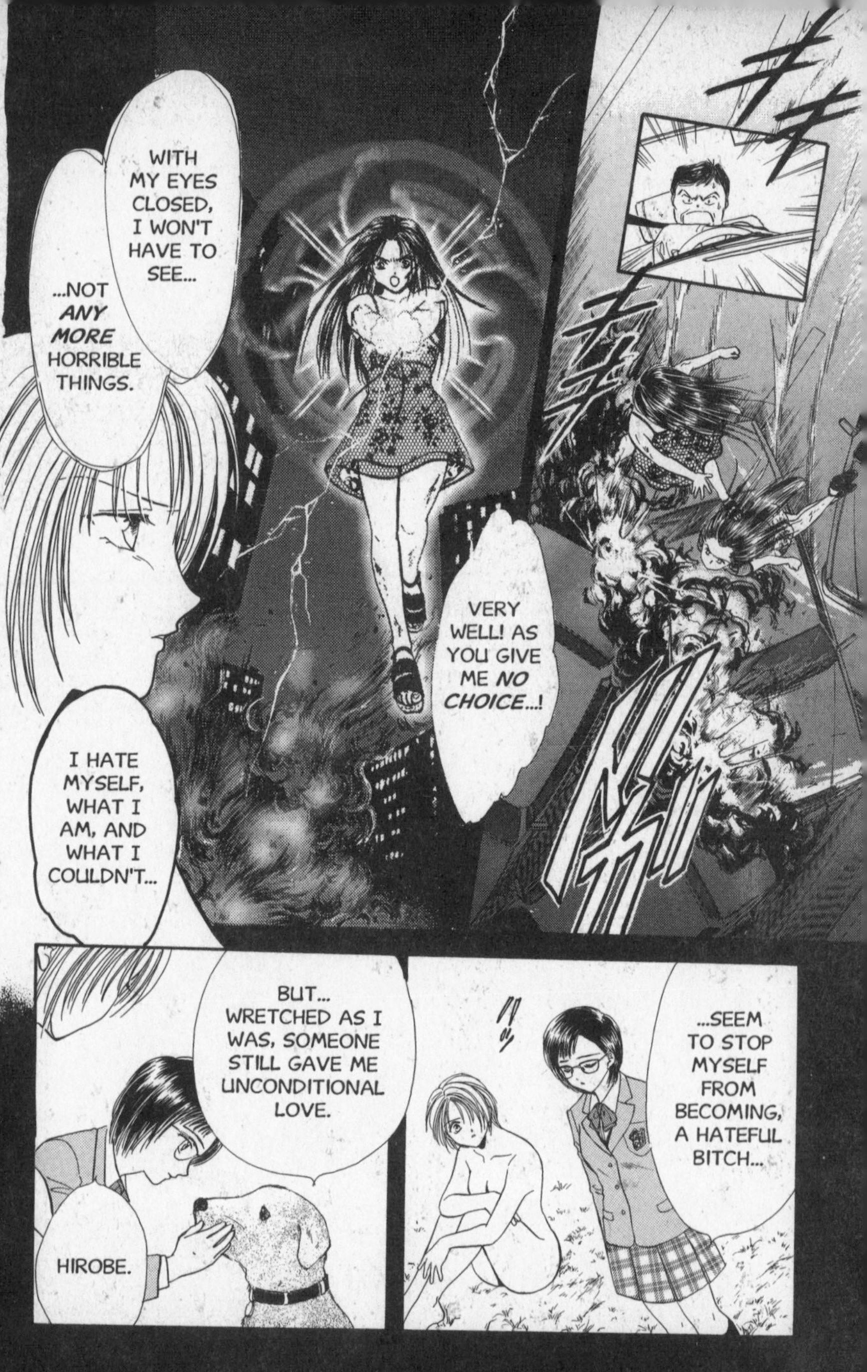
VERY WELL! AS YOU GIVE ME *NO CHOICE*...!
WITH MY EYES CLOSED, I WON'T HAVE TO SEE...
...NOT *ANY MORE* HORRIBLE THINGS.
I HATE MYSELF, WHAT I AM, AND WHAT I COULDN'T...
...SEEM TO STOP MYSELF FROM BECOMING, A HATEFUL BITCH...
BUT... WRETCHED AS I WAS, SOMEONE STILL GAVE ME UNCONDITIONAL LOVE.
HIROBE.

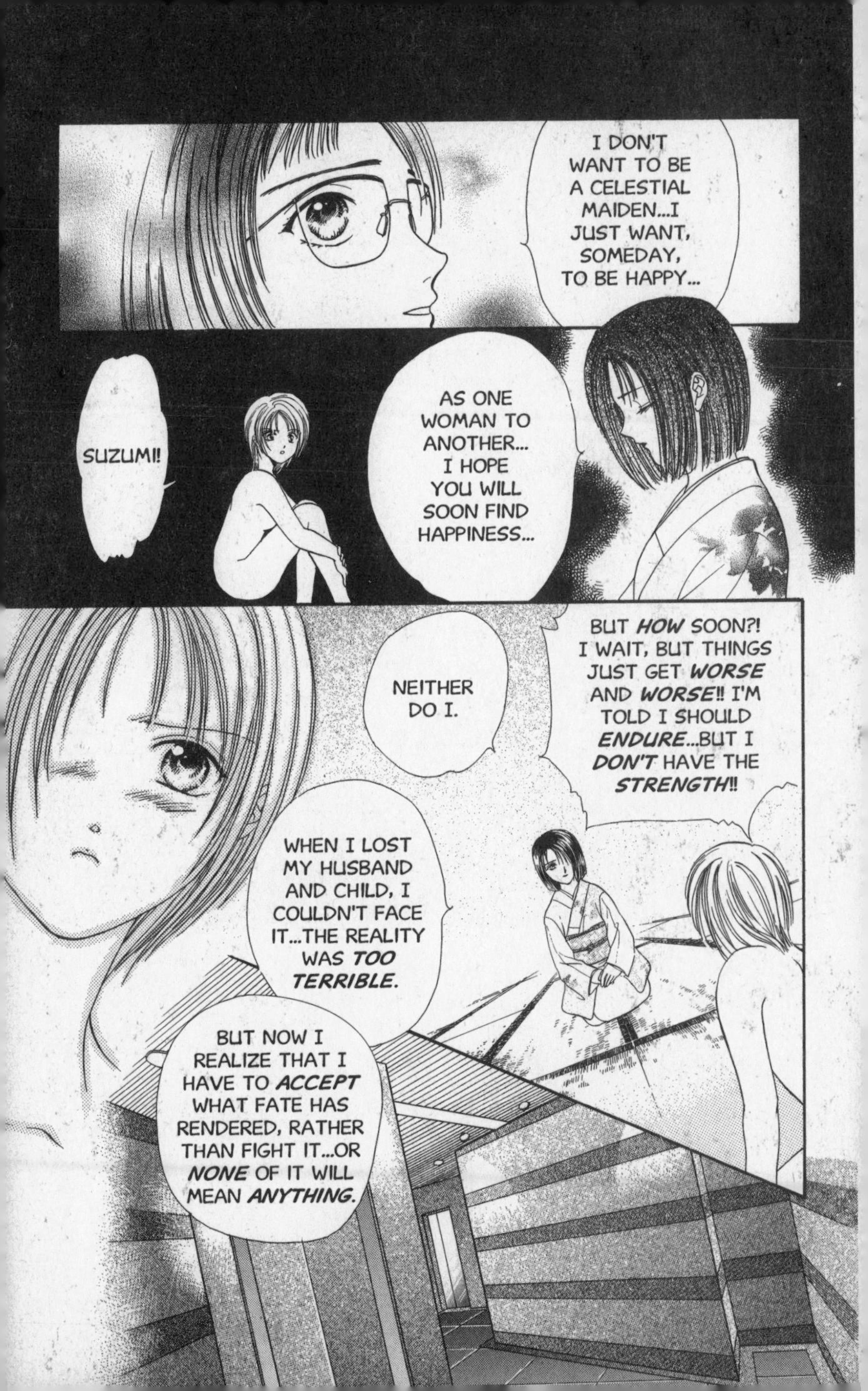

I DON'T WANT TO BE A CELESTIAL MAIDEN...I JUST WANT, SOMEDAY, TO BE HAPPY...
AS ONE WOMAN TO ANOTHER... I HOPE YOU WILL SOON FIND HAPPINESS...
SUZUMI!!
BUT *HOW* SOON?! I WAIT, BUT THINGS JUST GET *WORSE* AND *WORSE*!! I'M TOLD I SHOULD *ENDURE*...BUT I *DON'T* HAVE THE *STRENGTH*!!
NEITHER DO I.
WHEN I LOST MY HUSBAND AND CHILD, I COULDN'T FACE IT...THE REALITY WAS *TOO TERRIBLE*.
BUT NOW I REALIZE THAT I HAVE TO *ACCEPT* WHAT FATE HAS RENDERED, RATHER THAN FIGHT IT...OR *NONE* OF IT WILL MEAN *ANYTHING*.

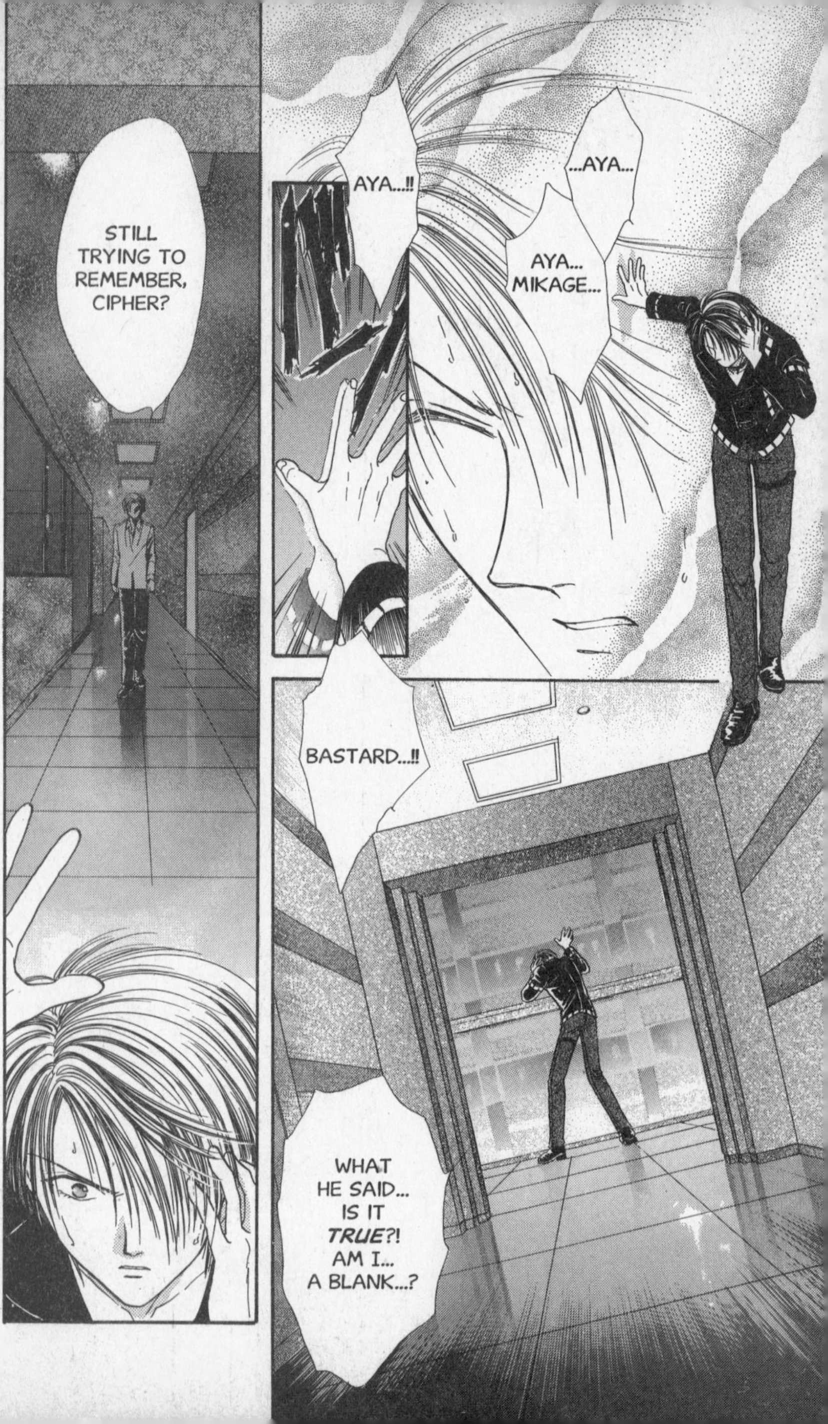
...AYA...
AYA... MIKAGE...
AYA...!!
BASTARD...!!
WHAT HE SAID... IS IT *TRUE*?! AM I... A BLANK...?
STILL TRYING TO REMEMBER, CIPHER?

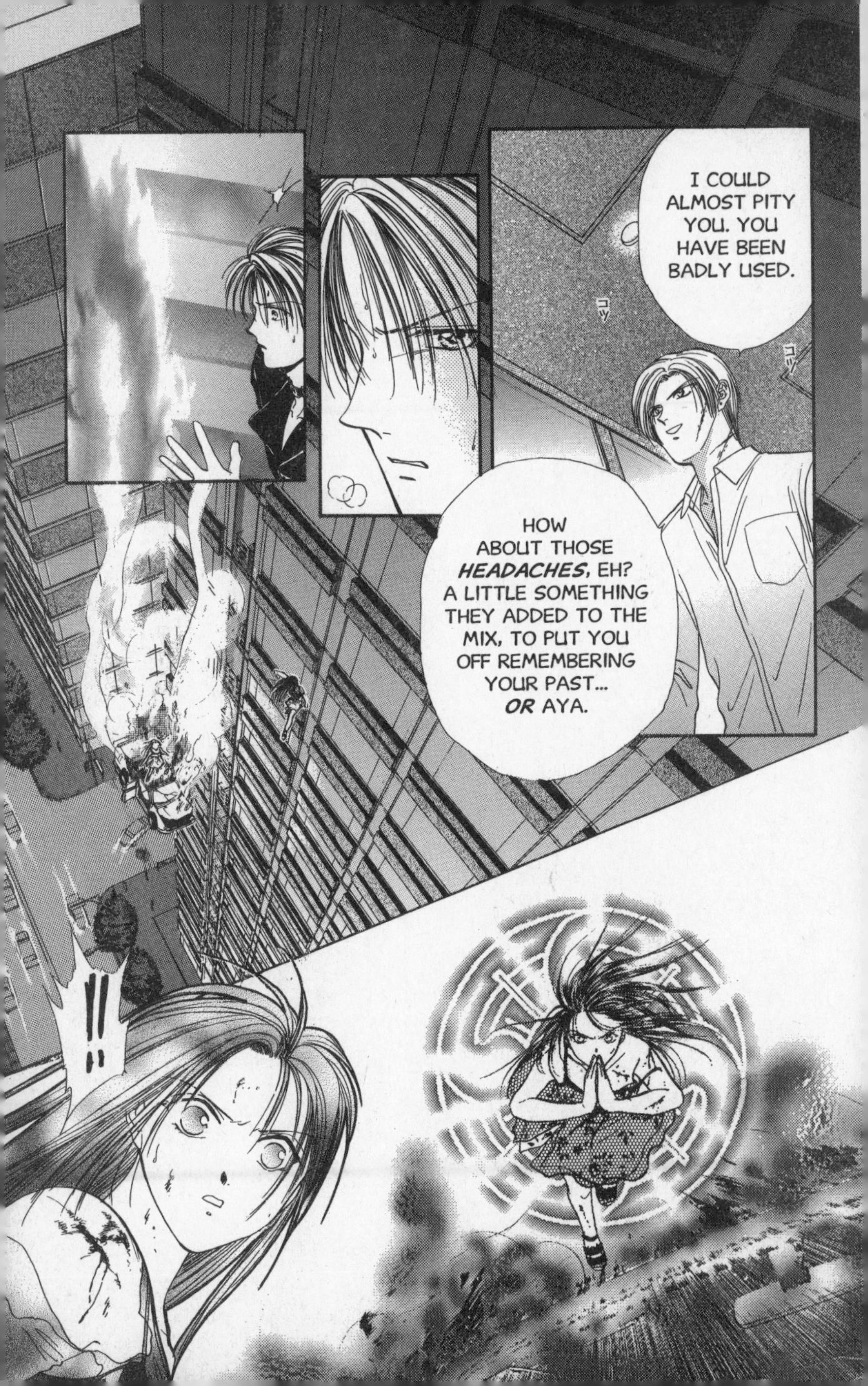
I COULD ALMOST PITY YOU. YOU HAVE BEEN BADLY USED.
HOW ABOUT THOSE *HEADACHES*, EH? A LITTLE SOMETHING THEY ADDED TO THE MIX, TO PUT YOU OFF REMEMBERING YOUR PAST... *OR* AYA.
!!

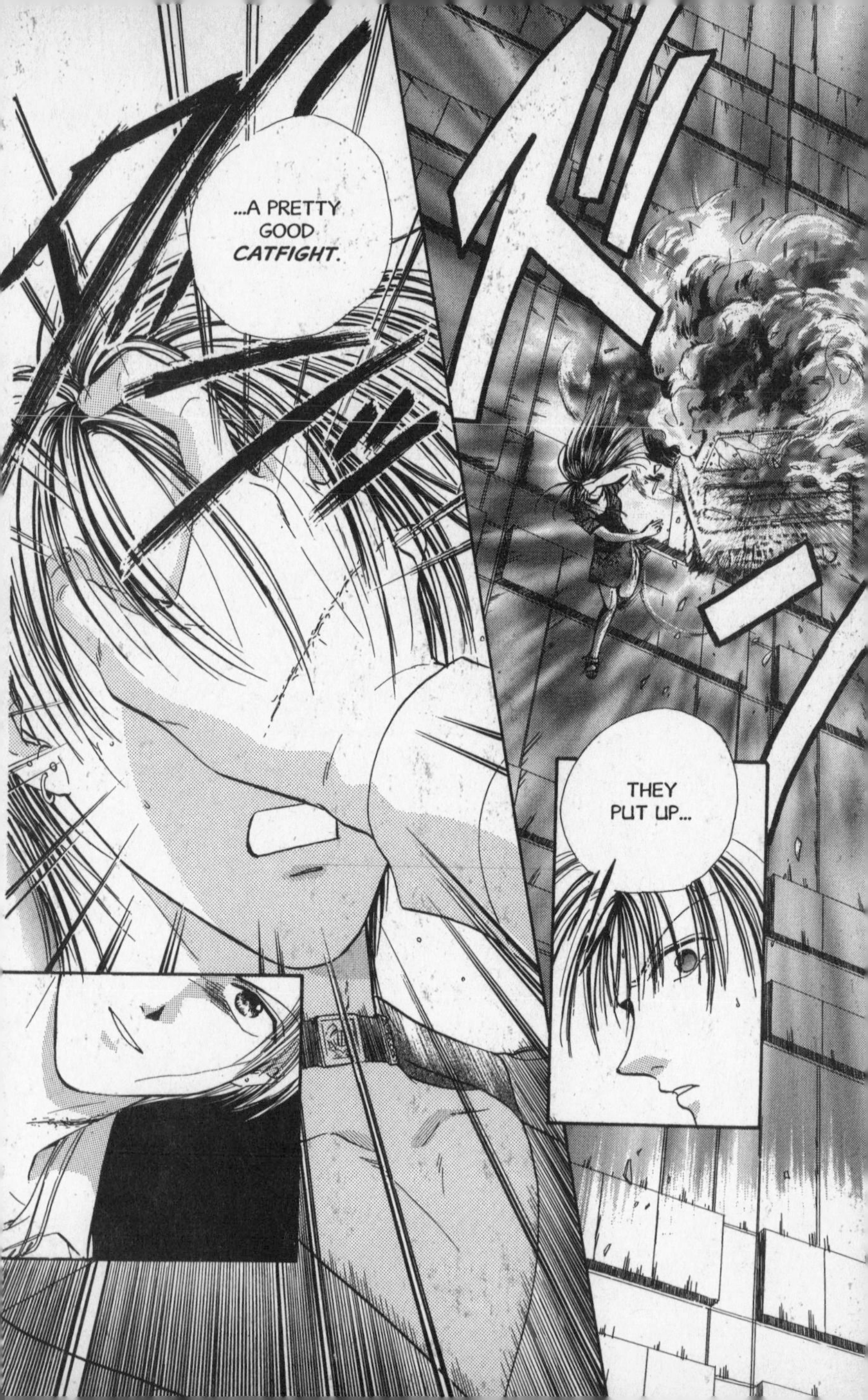
THEY PUT UP...
...A PRETTY GOOD *CATFIGHT*.

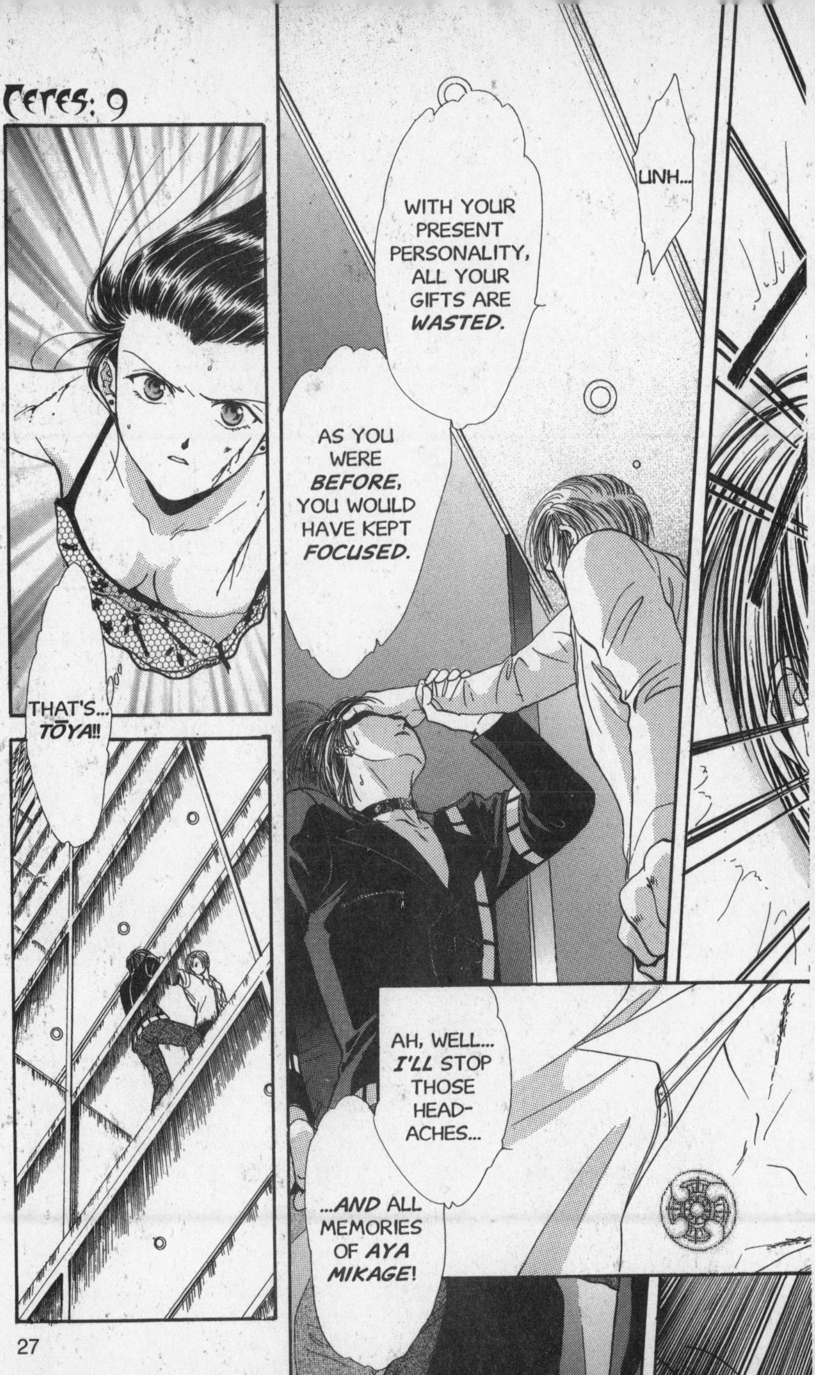
UNH...
WITH YOUR PRESENT PERSONALITY, ALL YOUR GIFTS ARE WASTED.
AS YOU WERE BEFORE, YOU WOULD HAVE KEPT FOCUSED.
THAT'S... TŌYA!!
AH, WELL... I'LL STOP THOSE HEAD-ACHES...
...AND ALL MEMORIES OF AYA MIKAGE!

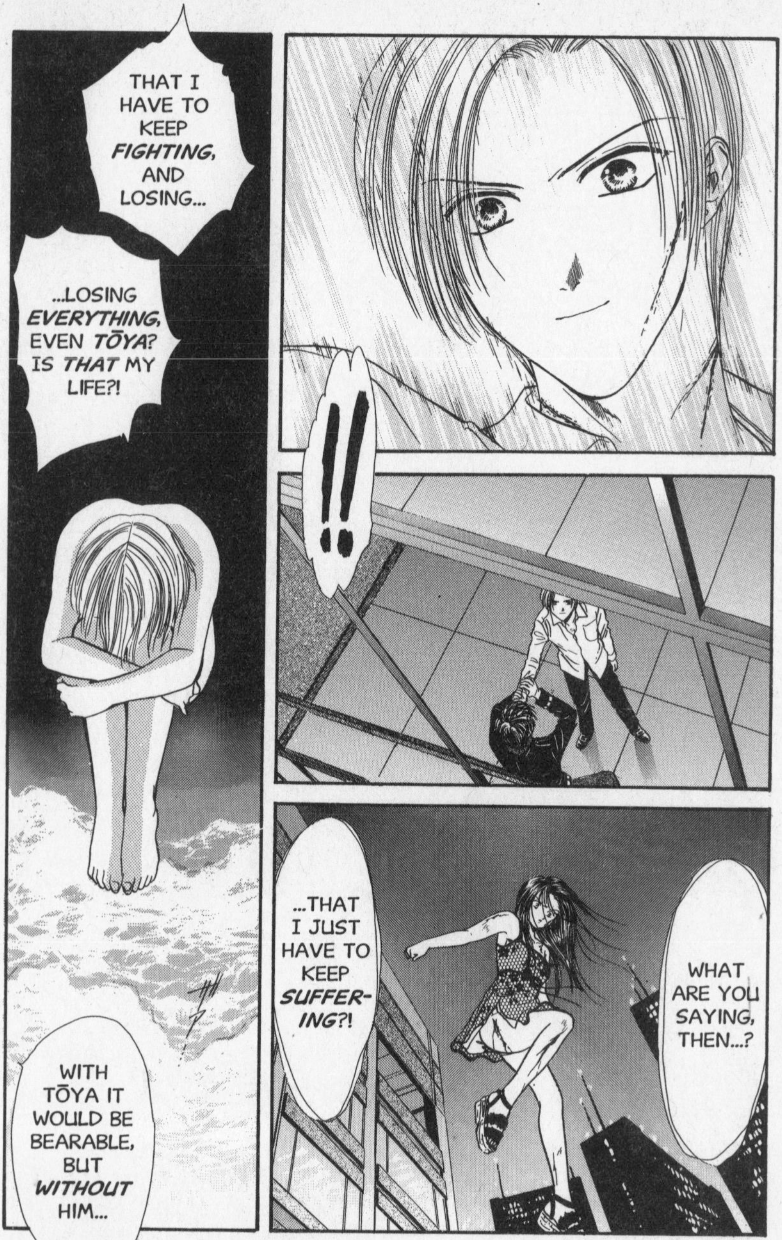
!!
WHAT ARE YOU SAYING, THEN...?
...THAT I JUST HAVE TO KEEP SUFFERING?!
THAT I HAVE TO KEEP FIGHTING, AND LOSING...
...LOSING EVERYTHING, EVEN TŌYA? IS THAT MY LIFE?!
WITH TŌYA IT WOULD BE BEARABLE, BUT WITHOUT HIM...

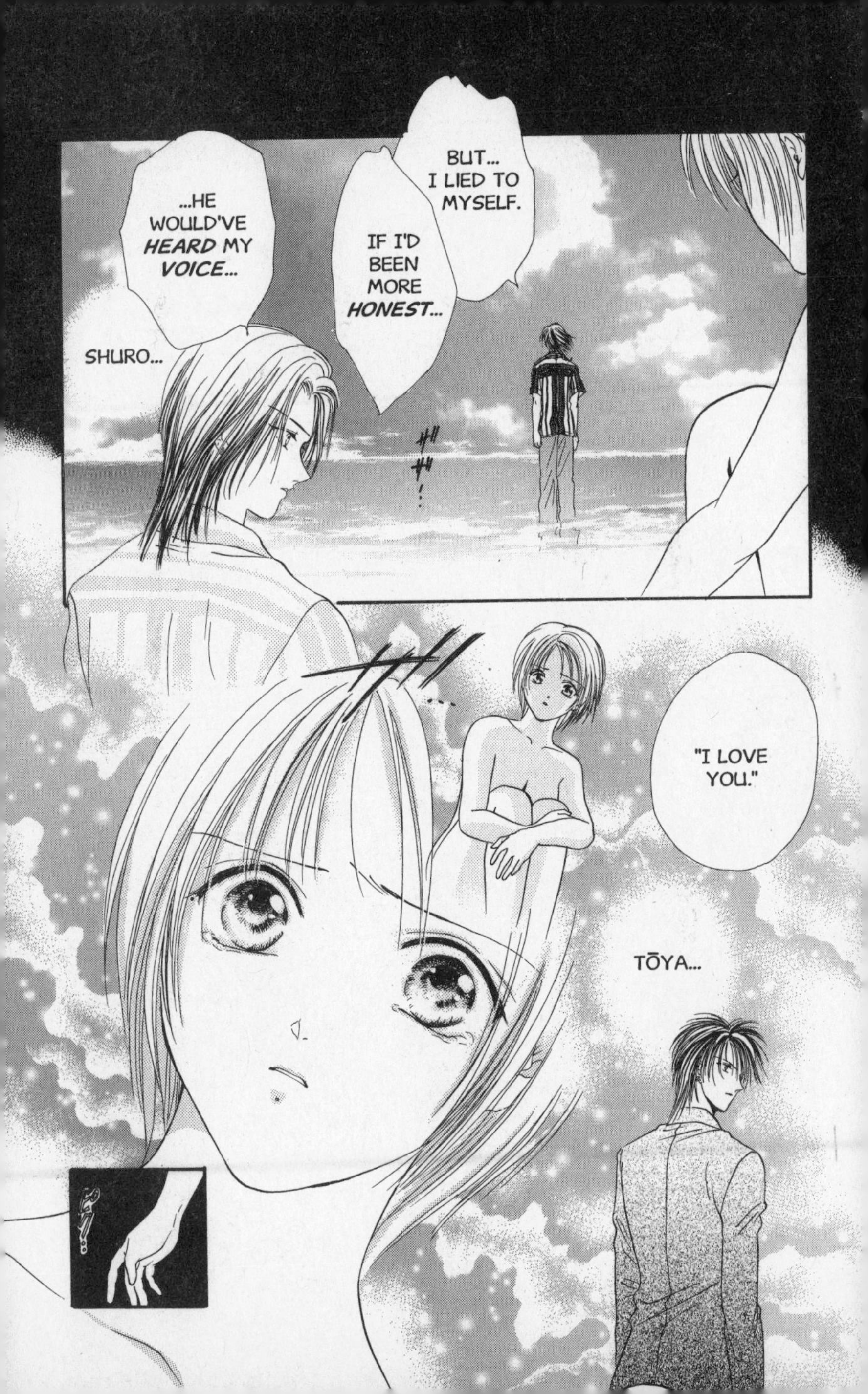
BUT... I LIED TO MYSELF.
IF I'D BEEN MORE **HONEST**...
...HE WOULD'VE **HEARD** MY **VOICE**...
SHURO...
"I LOVE YOU."
TŌYA...

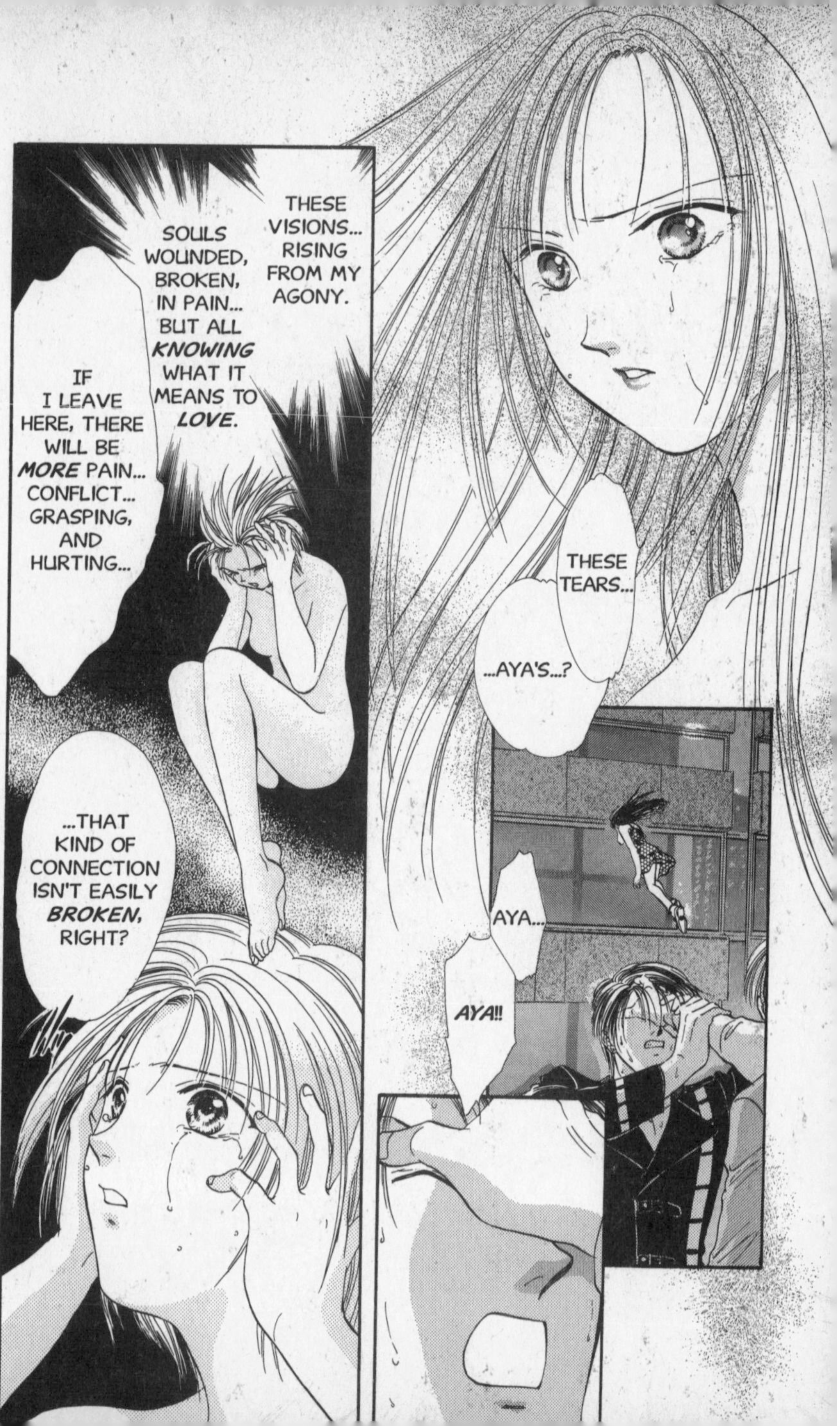
THESE TEARS...
...AYA'S...?
AYA...
AYA!!
THESE VISIONS... RISING FROM MY AGONY.
SOULS WOUNDED, BROKEN, IN PAIN... BUT ALL *KNOWING* WHAT IT MEANS TO *LOVE*.
IF I LEAVE HERE, THERE WILL BE *MORE* PAIN... CONFLICT... GRASPING, AND HURTING...
...THAT KIND OF CONNECTION ISN'T EASILY *BROKEN*, RIGHT?

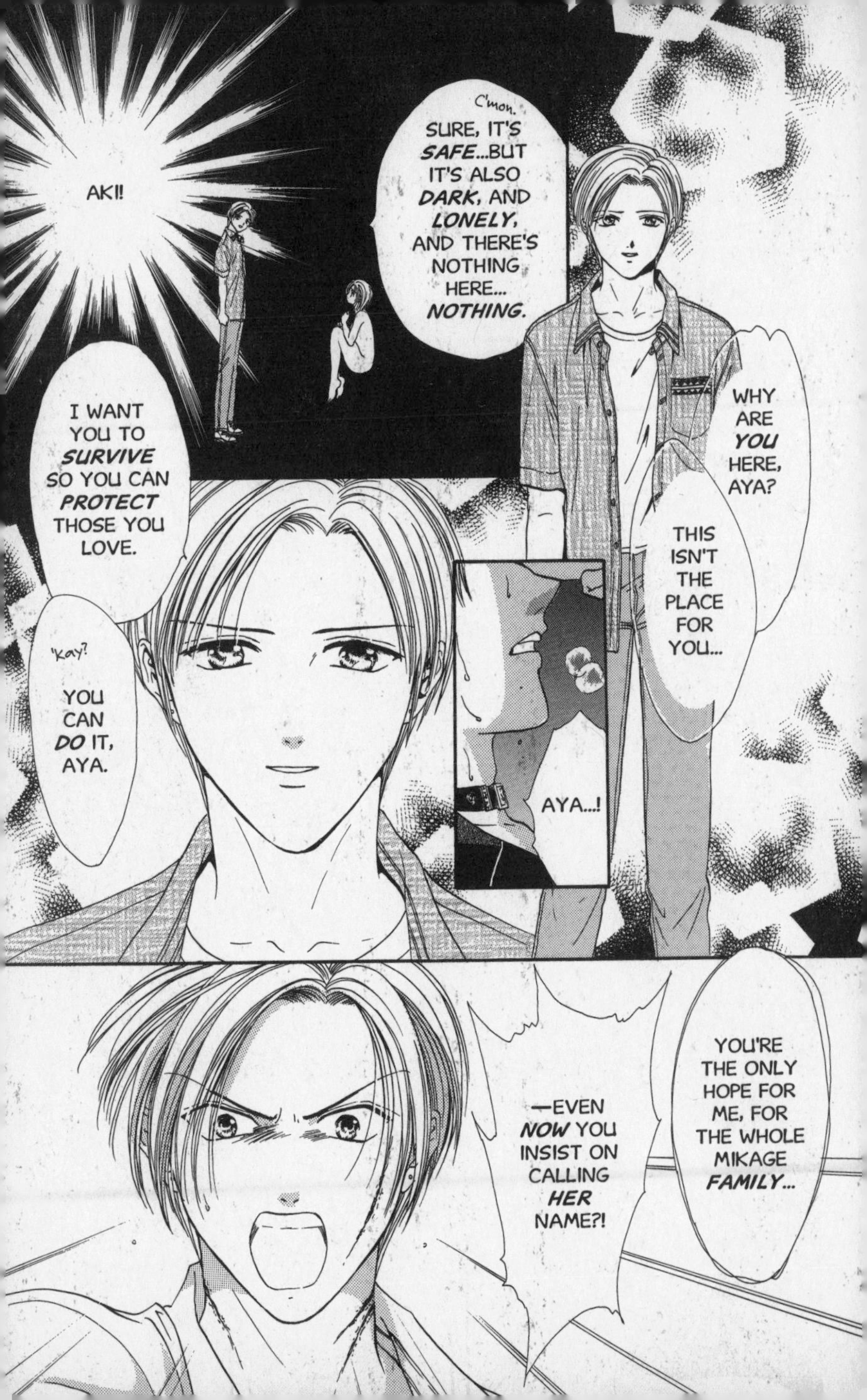
WHY ARE YOU HERE, AYA?
THIS ISN'T THE PLACE FOR YOU...
C'mon.
SURE, IT'S SAFE...BUT IT'S ALSO DARK, AND LONELY, AND THERE'S NOTHING HERE... NOTHING.
AKI!
I WANT YOU TO SURVIVE SO YOU CAN PROTECT THOSE YOU LOVE.
'Kay?
YOU CAN DO IT, AYA.
AYA...!
YOU'RE THE ONLY HOPE FOR ME, FOR THE WHOLE MIKAGE FAMILY...
—EVEN NOW YOU INSIST ON CALLING HER NAME?!

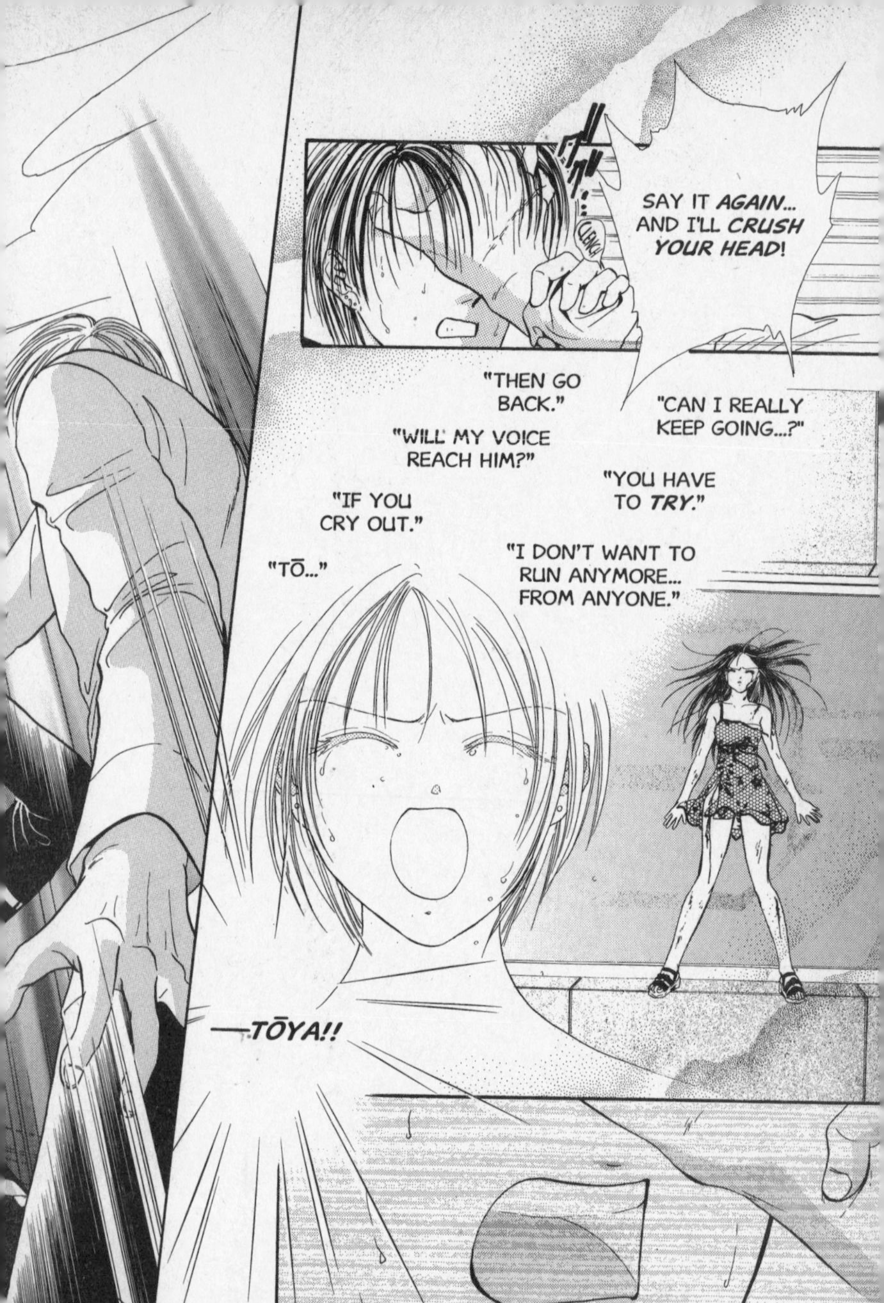

CLENCH
SAY IT *AGAIN*... AND I'LL *CRUSH YOUR HEAD*!
"CAN I REALLY KEEP GOING...?"
"THEN GO BACK."
"YOU HAVE TO *TRY*."
"WILL MY VOICE REACH HIM?"
"IF YOU CRY OUT."
"I DON'T WANT TO RUN ANYMORE... FROM ANYONE."
"TŌ..."
—*TŌYA!!*

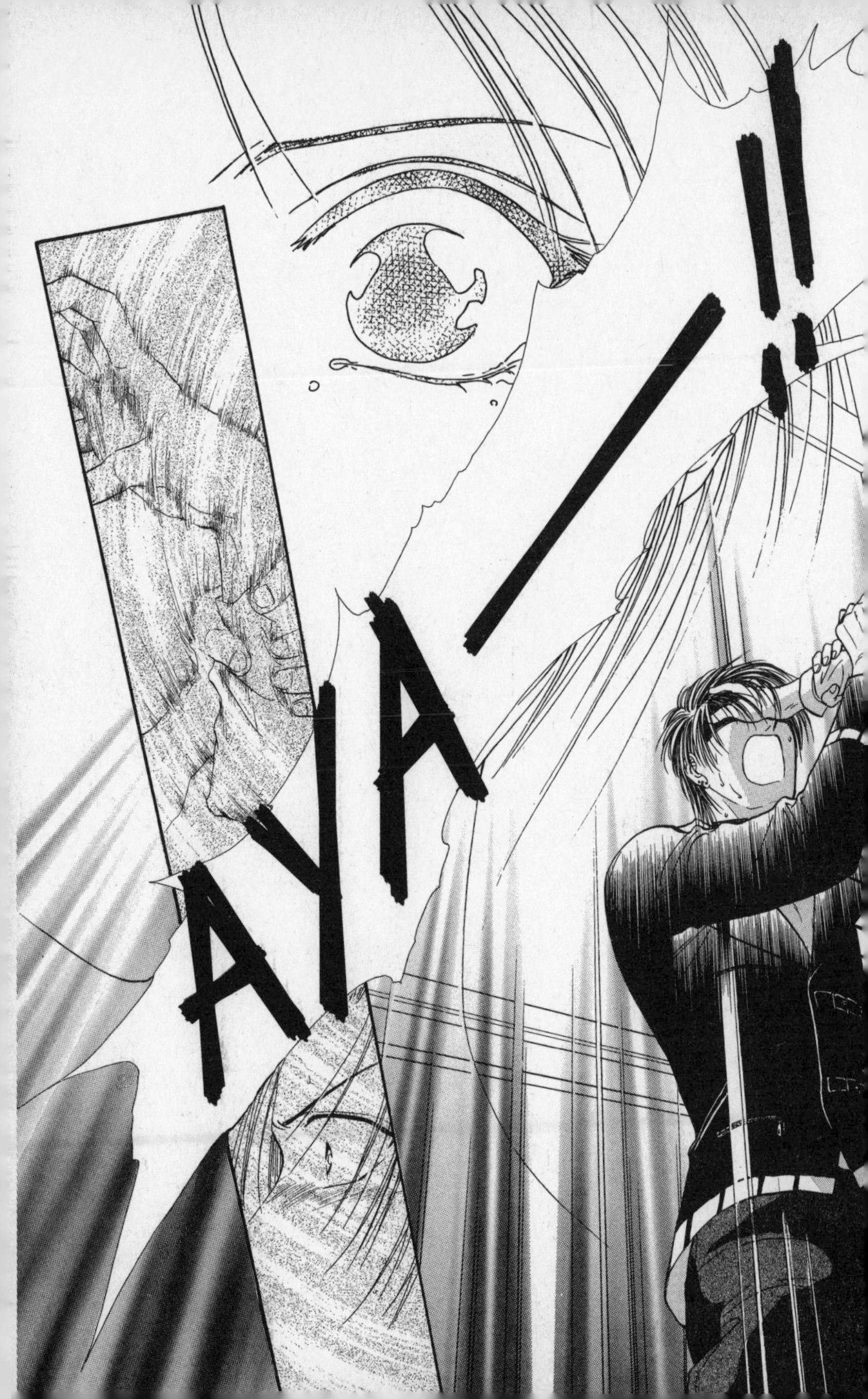
AYA—!!

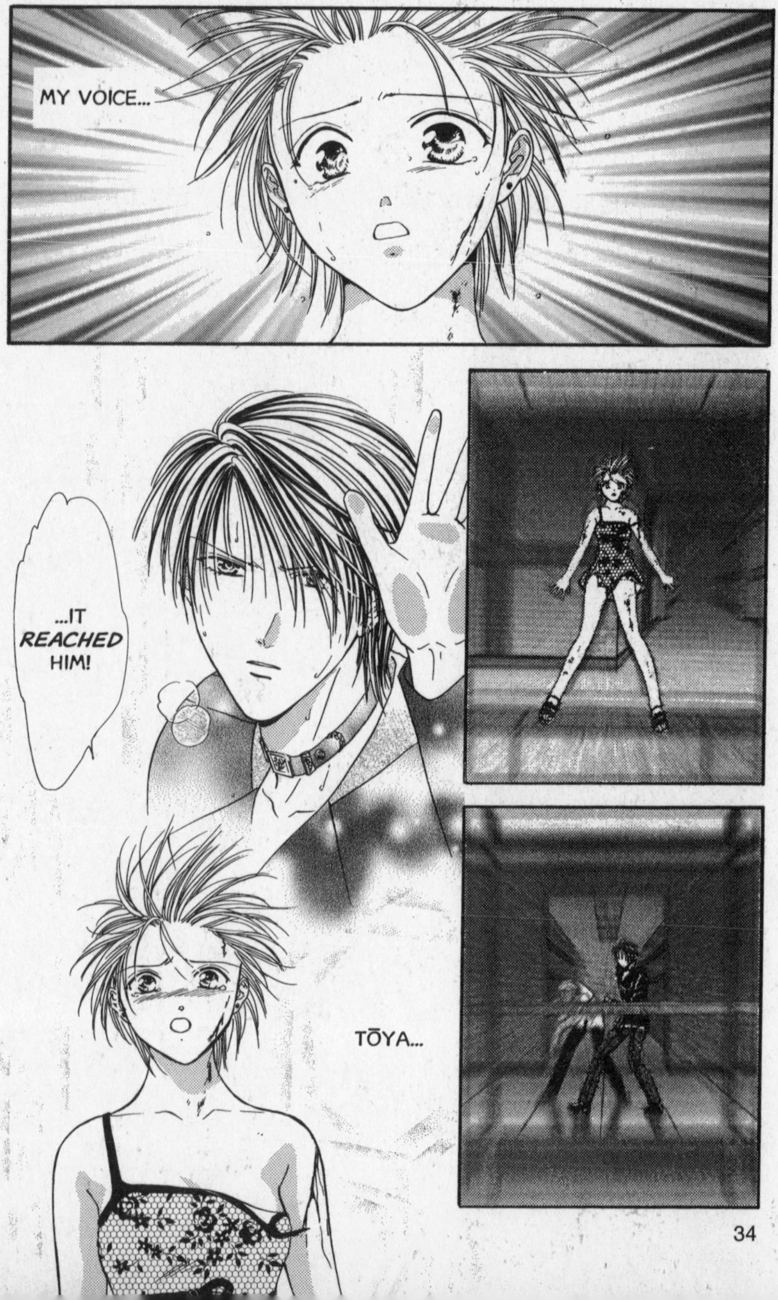
MY VOICE...
...IT *REACHED* HIM!
TŌYA...

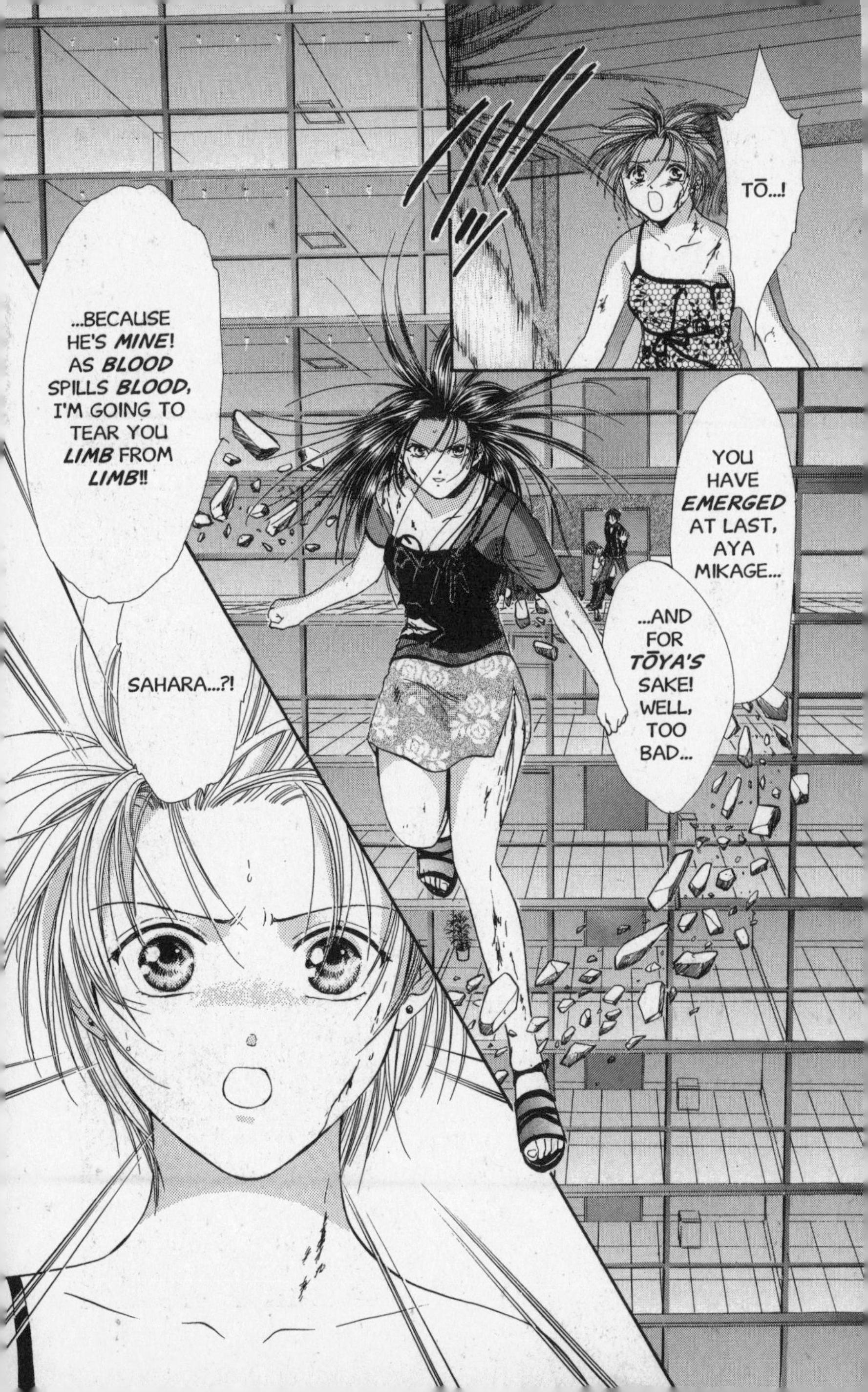

TŌ...!
YOU HAVE *EMERGED* AT LAST, AYA MIKAGE...
...AND FOR *TŌYA'S* SAKE! WELL, TOO BAD...
...BECAUSE HE'S *MINE*! AS *BLOOD* SPILLS *BLOOD*, I'M GOING TO TEAR YOU *LIMB* FROM *LIMB*!!
SAHARA...?!

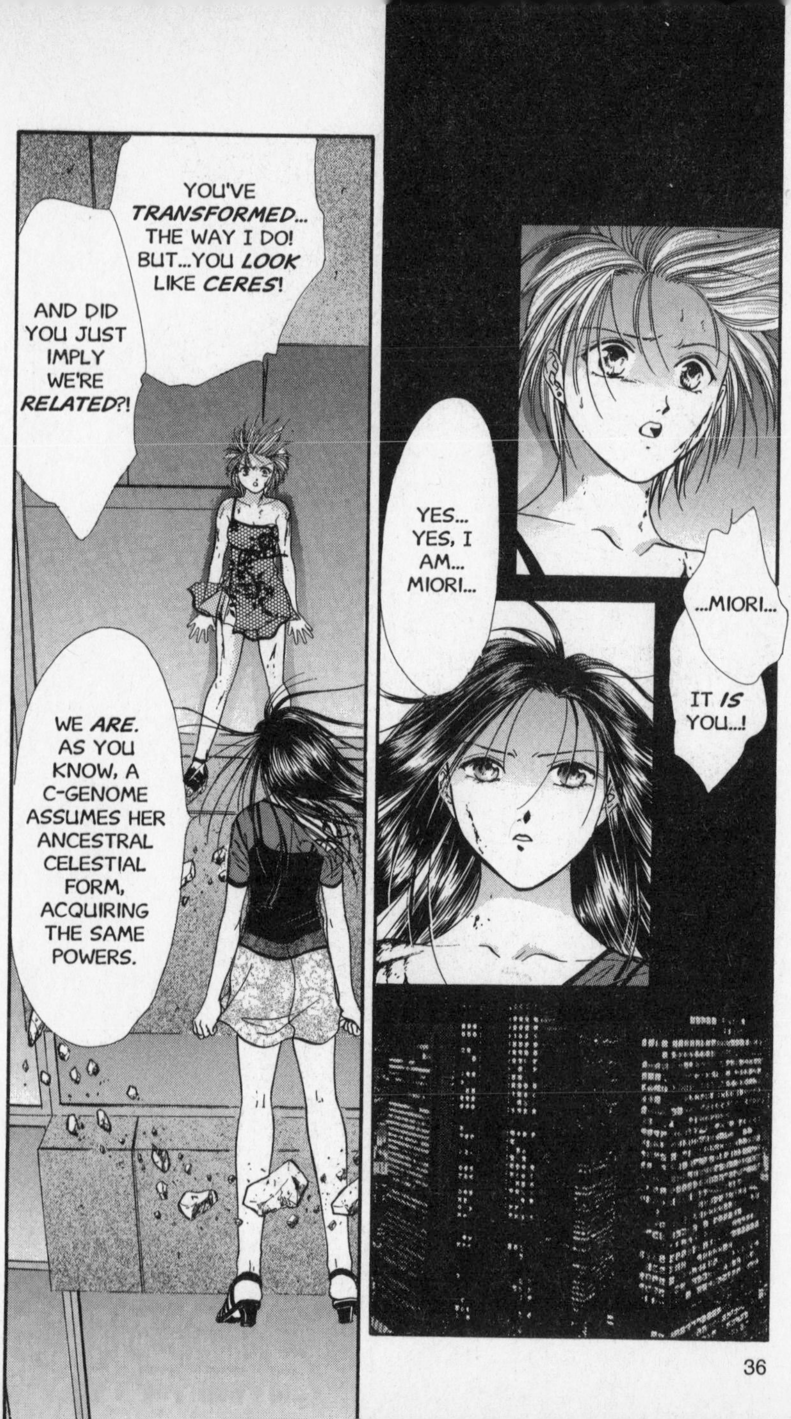
...MIORI...
IT IS YOU...!
YES... YES, I AM... MIORI...
YOU'VE TRANSFORMED... THE WAY I DO! BUT...YOU LOOK LIKE CERES!
AND DID YOU JUST IMPLY WE'RE RELATED?!
WE ARE. AS YOU KNOW, A C-GENOME ASSUMES HER ANCESTRAL CELESTIAL FORM, ACQUIRING THE SAME POWERS.

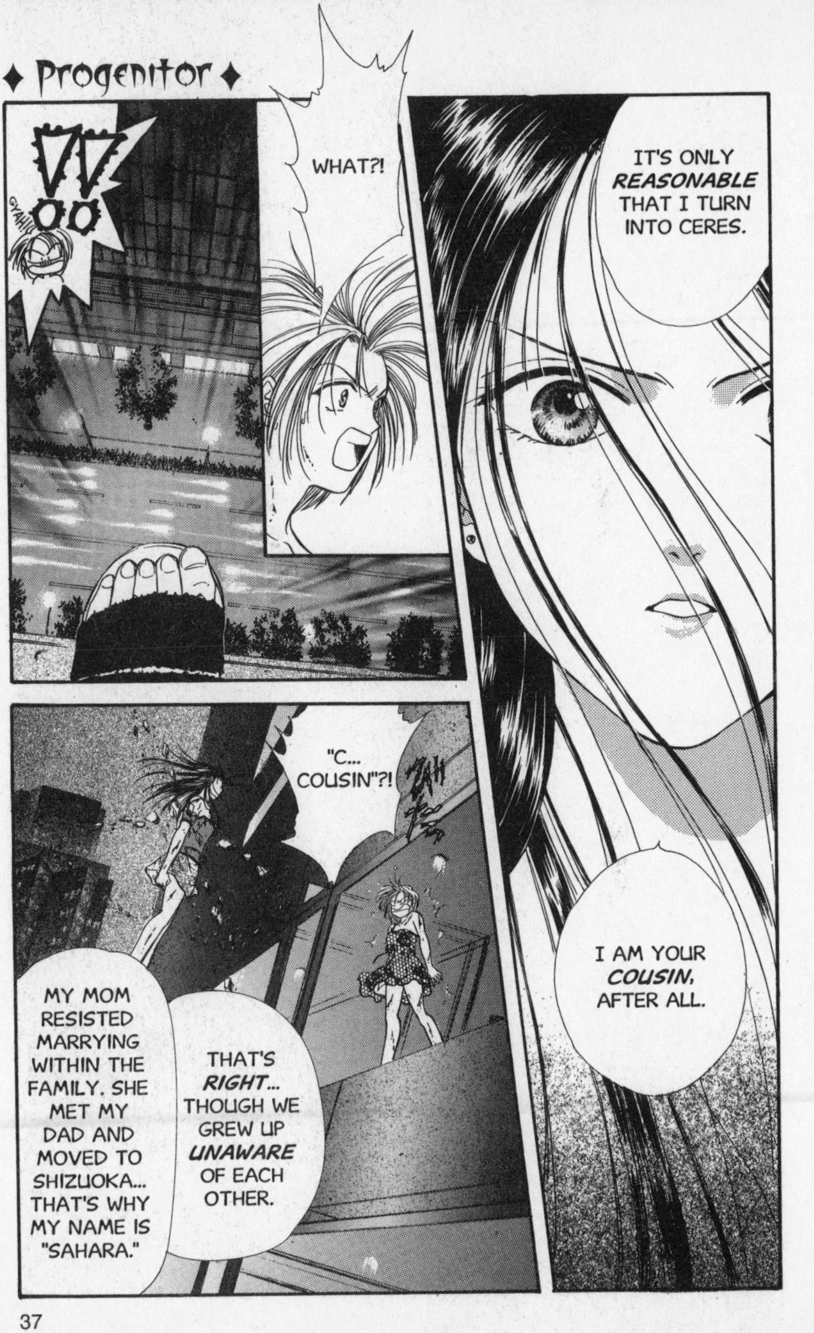
IT'S ONLY *REASONABLE* THAT I TURN INTO CERES.
I AM YOUR *COUSIN,* AFTER ALL.
WHAT?!
"C... COUSIN"?!
THAT'S *RIGHT*... THOUGH WE GREW UP *UNAWARE* OF EACH OTHER.
MY MOM RESISTED MARRYING WITHIN THE FAMILY. SHE MET MY DAD AND MOVED TO SHIZUOKA... THAT'S WHY MY NAME IS "SAHARA."

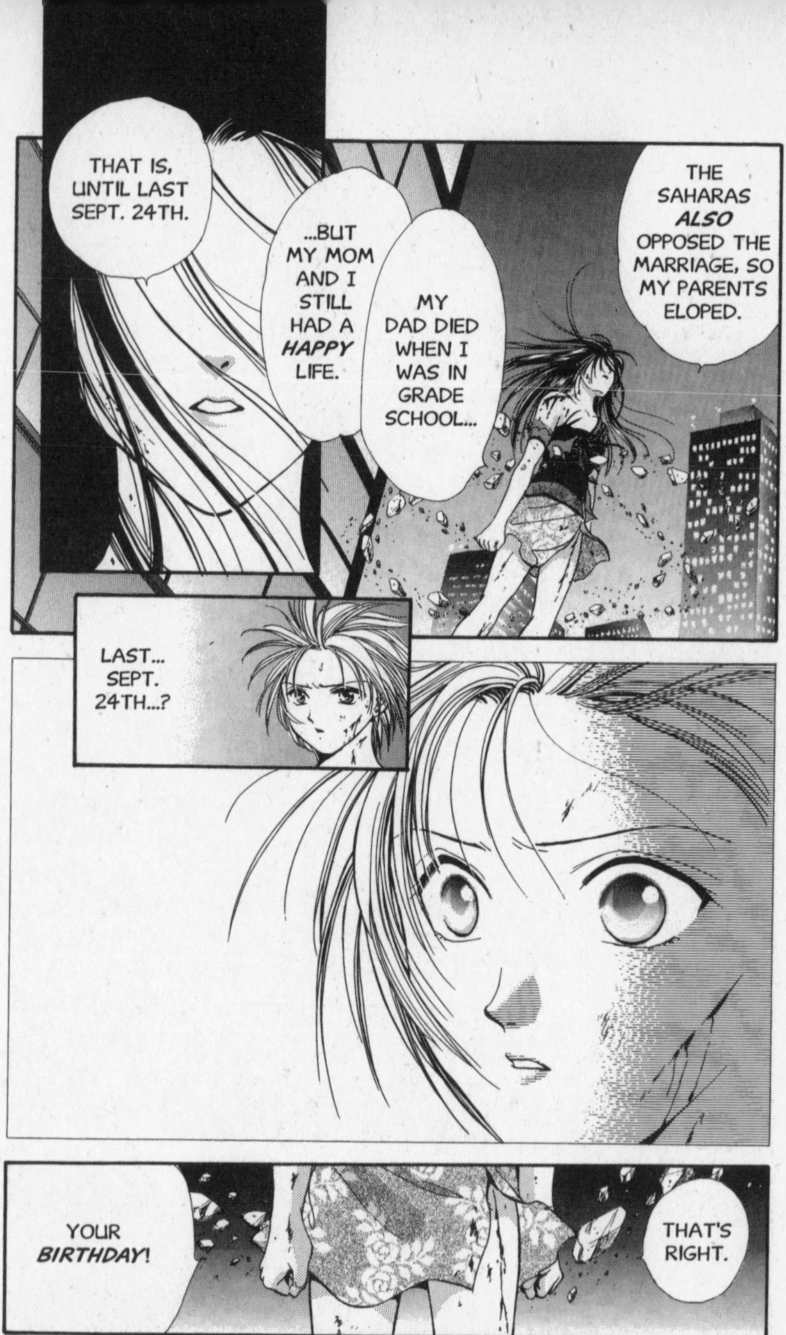
THE SAHARAS *ALSO* OPPOSED THE MARRIAGE, SO MY PARENTS ELOPED.
MY DAD DIED WHEN I WAS IN GRADE SCHOOL...
...BUT MY MOM AND I STILL HAD A *HAPPY* LIFE.
THAT IS, UNTIL LAST SEPT. 24TH.
LAST... SEPT. 24TH...?
THAT'S RIGHT.
YOUR *BIRTHDAY*!

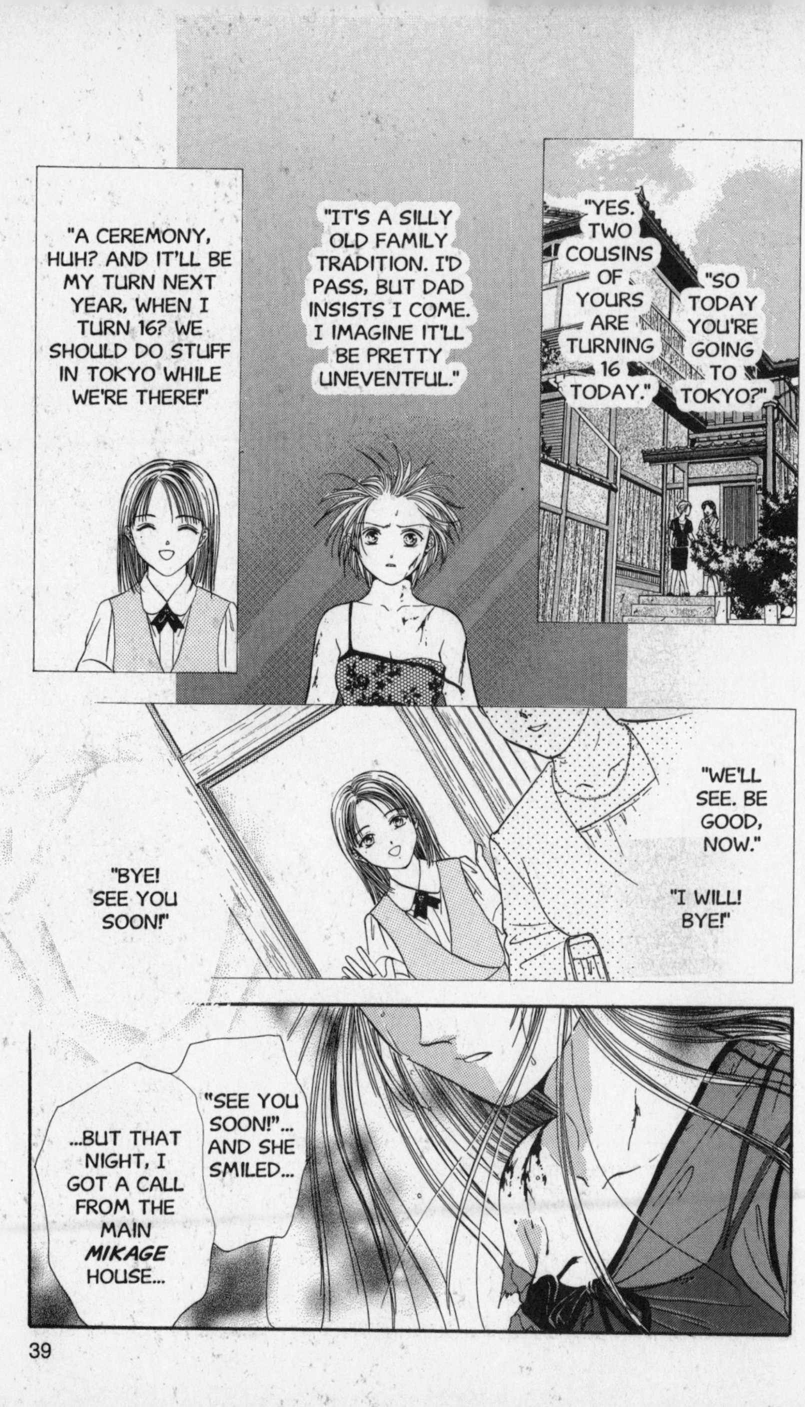
"SO TODAY YOU'RE GOING TO TOKYO?"
"YES. TWO COUSINS OF YOURS ARE TURNING 16 TODAY."
"IT'S A SILLY OLD FAMILY TRADITION. I'D PASS, BUT DAD INSISTS I COME. I IMAGINE IT'LL BE PRETTY UNEVENTFUL."
"A CEREMONY, HUH? AND IT'LL BE MY TURN NEXT YEAR, WHEN I TURN 16? WE SHOULD DO STUFF IN TOKYO WHILE WE'RE THERE!"
"WE'LL SEE. BE GOOD, NOW."
"I WILL! BYE!"
"BYE! SEE YOU SOON!"
"SEE YOU SOON!"... AND SHE SMILED...
...BUT THAT NIGHT, I GOT A CALL FROM THE MAIN *MIKAGE* HOUSE...

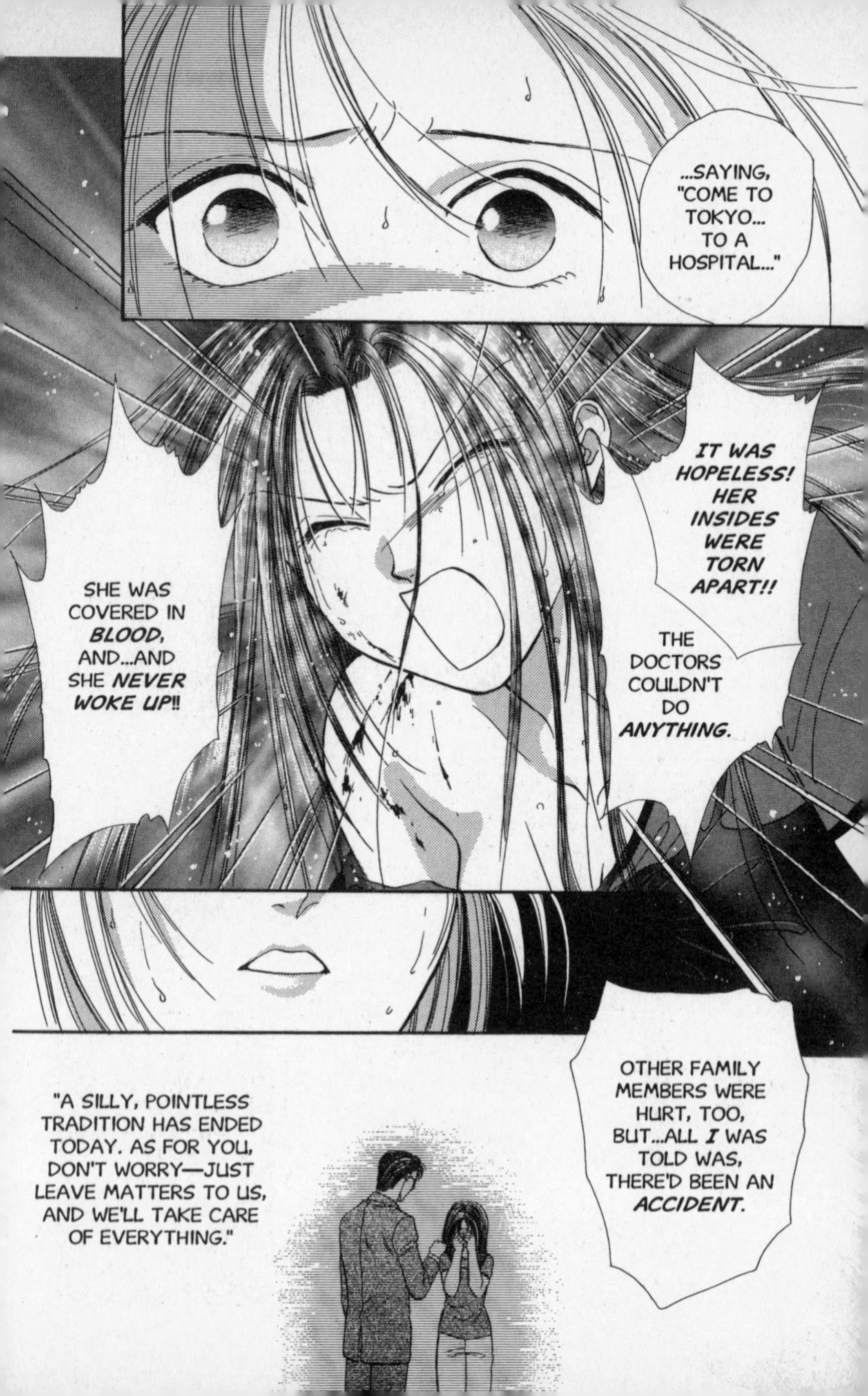
...SAYING, "COME TO TOKYO... TO A HOSPITAL..."
IT WAS HOPELESS! HER INSIDES WERE TORN APART!!
THE DOCTORS COULDN'T DO ANYTHING.
SHE WAS COVERED IN BLOOD, AND...AND SHE NEVER WOKE UP!!
OTHER FAMILY MEMBERS WERE HURT, TOO, BUT...ALL I WAS TOLD WAS, THERE'D BEEN AN ACCIDENT.
"A SILLY, POINTLESS TRADITION HAS ENDED TODAY. AS FOR YOU, DON'T WORRY—JUST LEAVE MATTERS TO US, AND WE'LL TAKE CARE OF EVERYTHING."

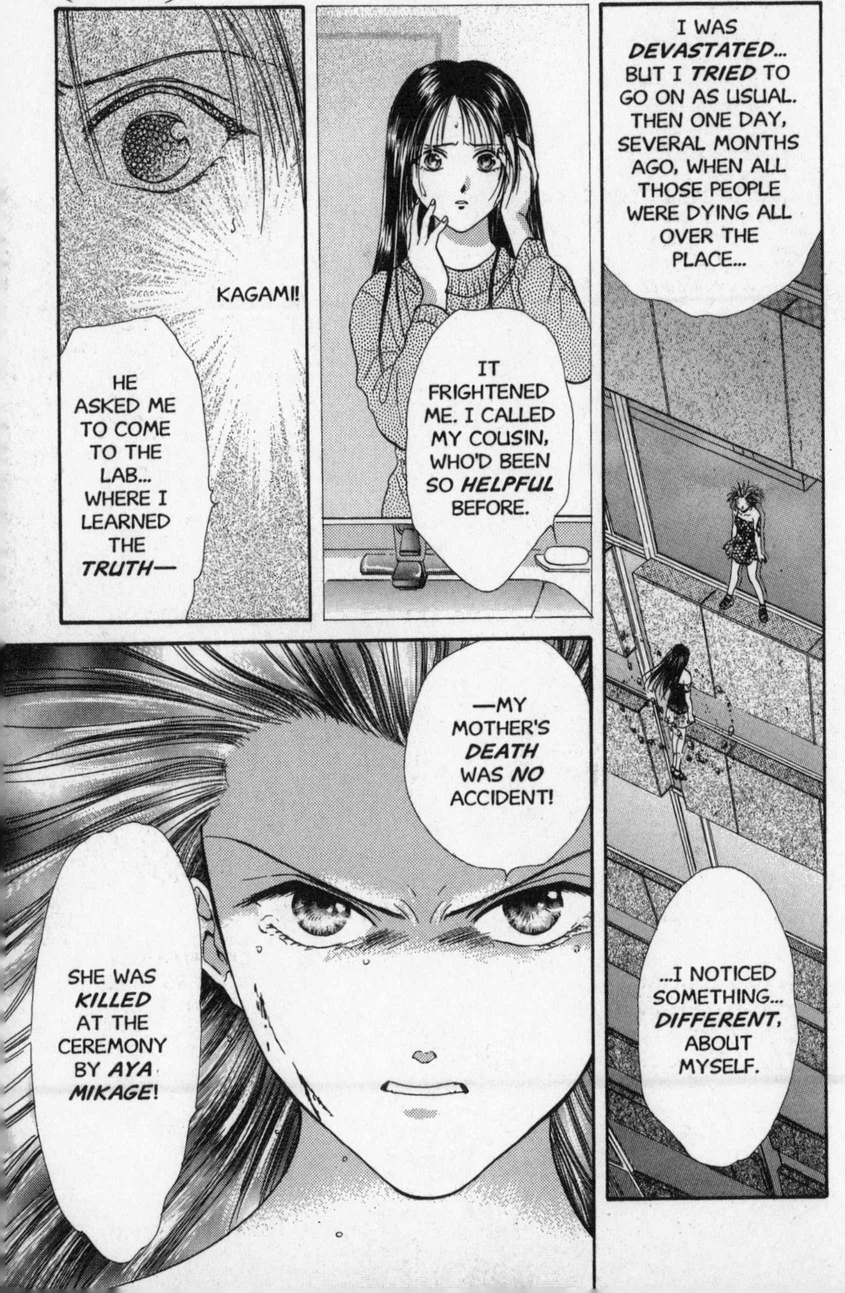
I WAS *DEVASTATED*... BUT I *TRIED* TO GO ON AS USUAL. THEN ONE DAY, SEVERAL MONTHS AGO, WHEN ALL THOSE PEOPLE WERE DYING ALL OVER THE PLACE...
...I NOTICED SOMETHING... *DIFFERENT*, ABOUT MYSELF.
IT FRIGHTENED ME. I CALLED MY COUSIN, WHO'D BEEN SO *HELPFUL* BEFORE.
KAGAMI!
HE ASKED ME TO COME TO THE LAB... WHERE I LEARNED THE *TRUTH*—
—MY MOTHER'S *DEATH* WAS *NO* ACCIDENT!
SHE WAS *KILLED* AT THE CEREMONY BY *AYA MIKAGE*!

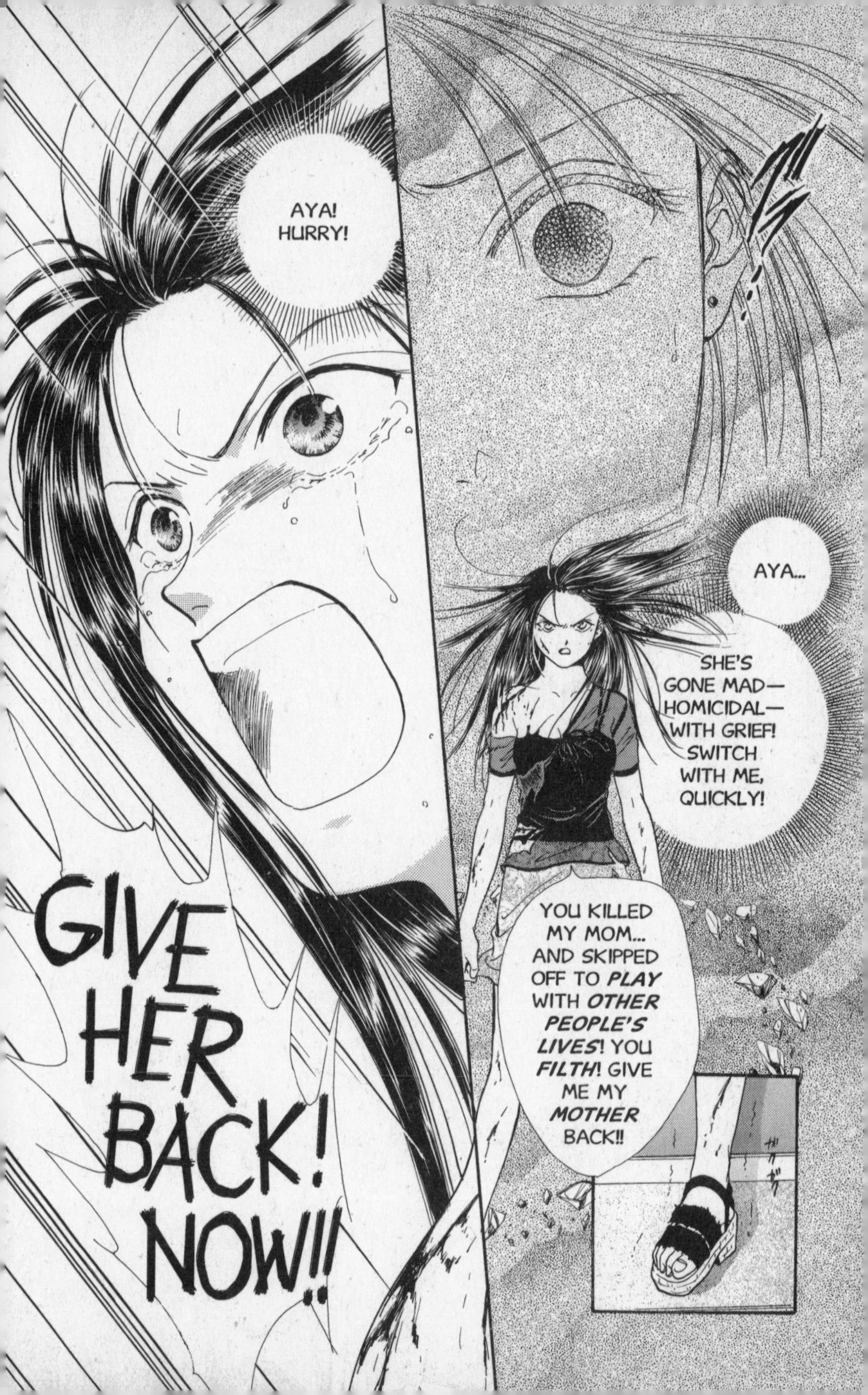
AYA...
SHE'S GONE MAD—HOMICIDAL—WITH GRIEF! SWITCH WITH ME, QUICKLY!
YOU KILLED MY MOM... AND SKIPPED OFF TO *PLAY* WITH *OTHER PEOPLE'S LIVES*! YOU *FILTH*! GIVE ME MY *MOTHER* BACK!!
AYA! HURRY!
GIVE HER BACK! NOW!!

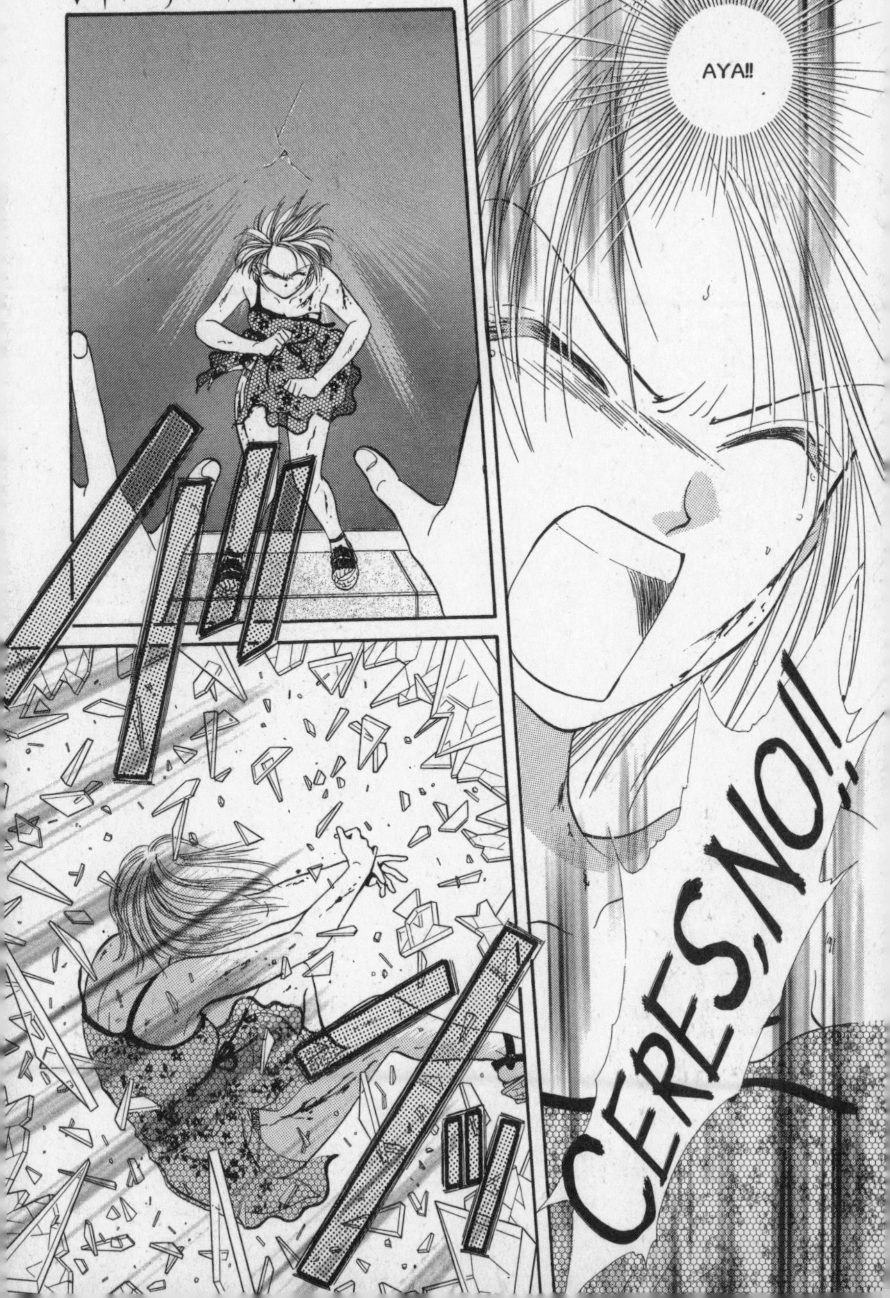
AYA!!
CERES, NO!!

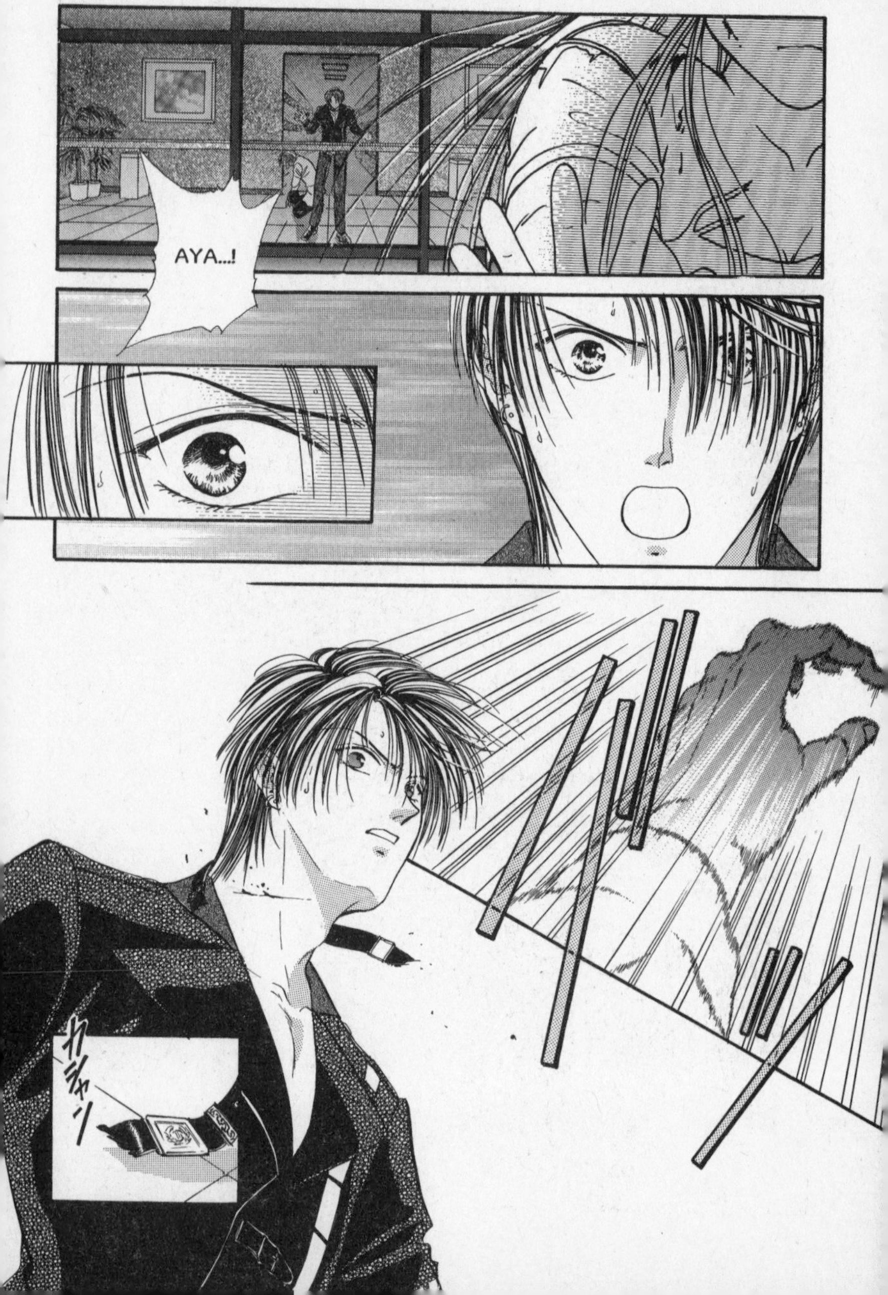
AYA...!
カシャン

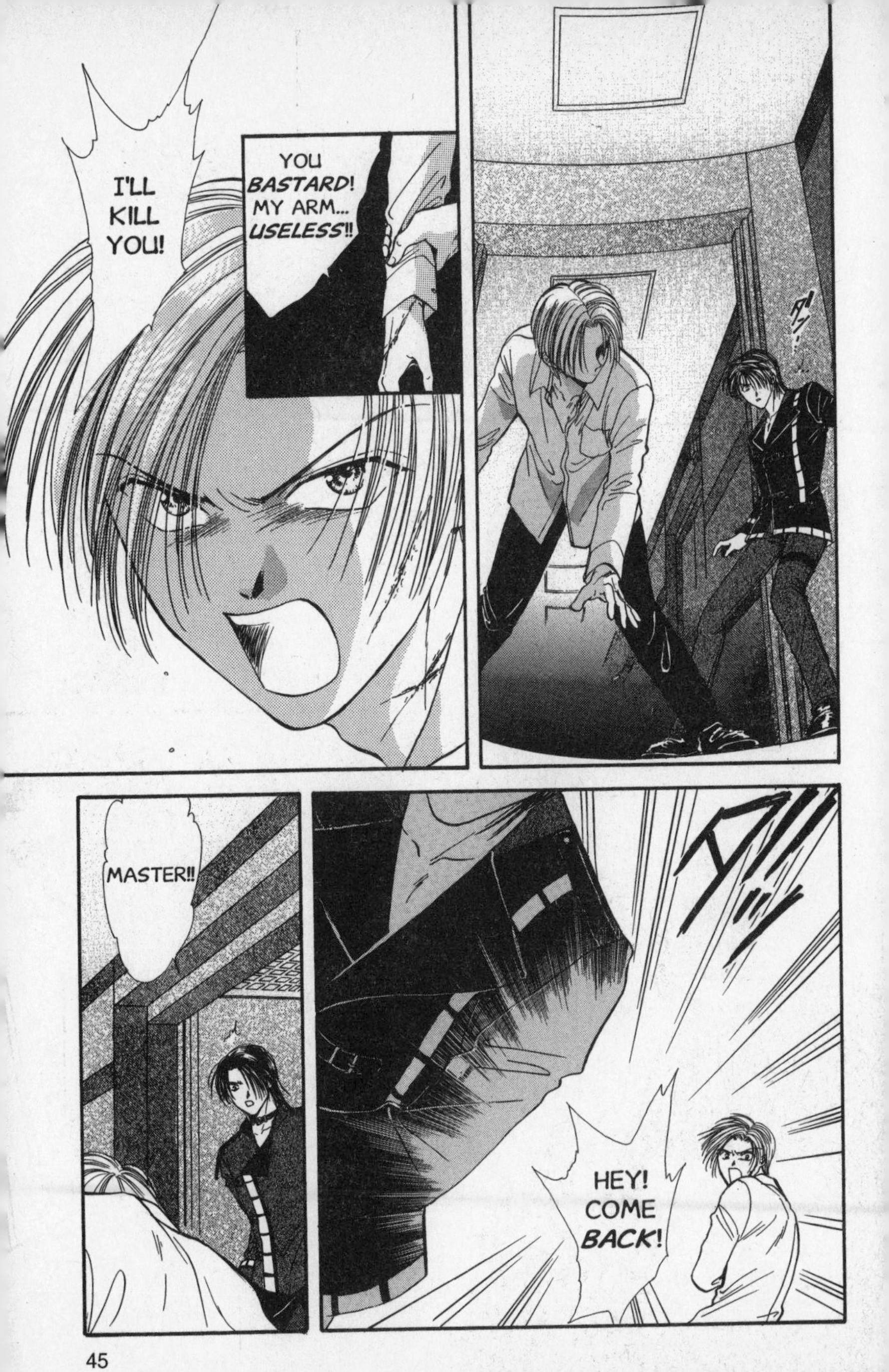
YOU BASTARD! MY ARM... USELESS!!
I'LL KILL YOU!
HEY! COME BACK!
MASTER!!

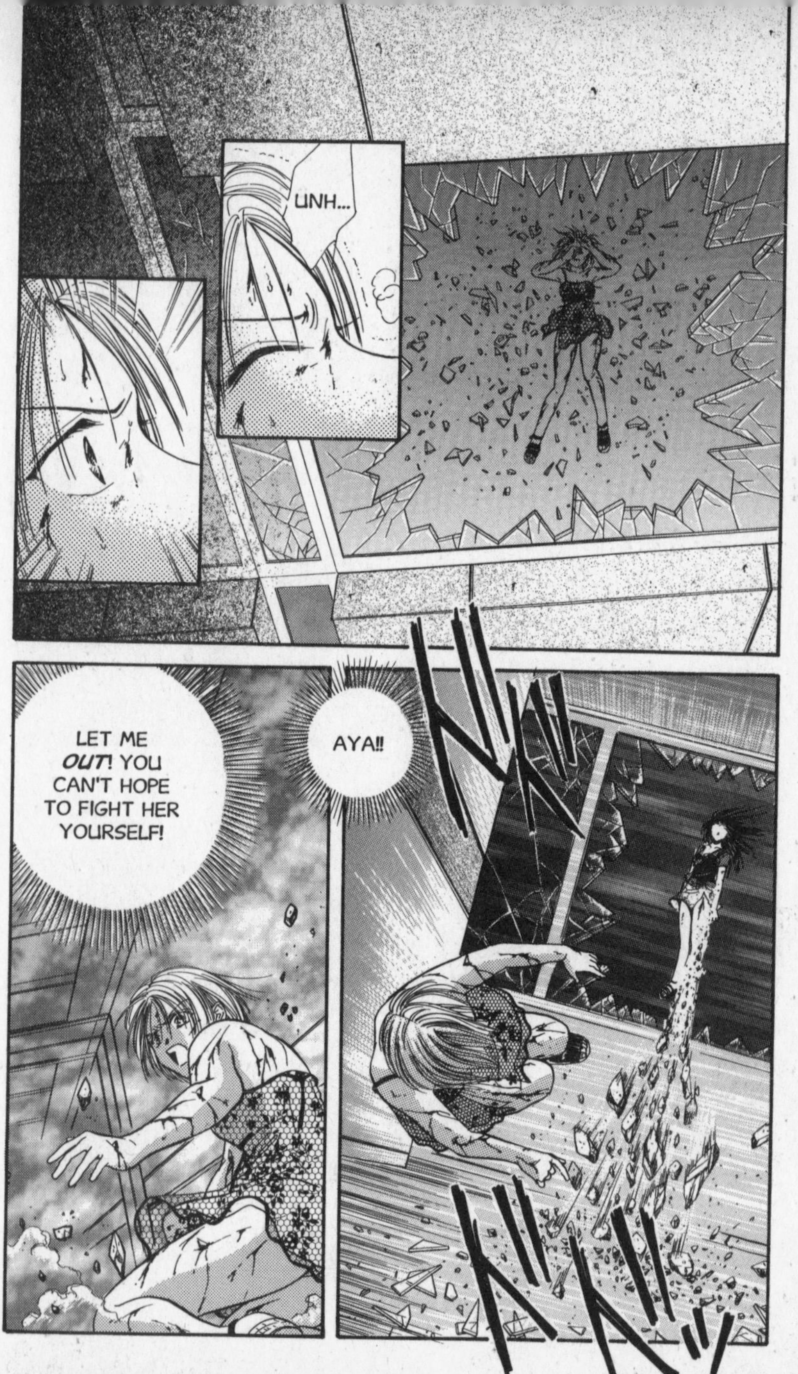
UNH...
AYA!!
LET ME OUT! YOU CAN'T HOPE TO FIGHT HER YOURSELF!

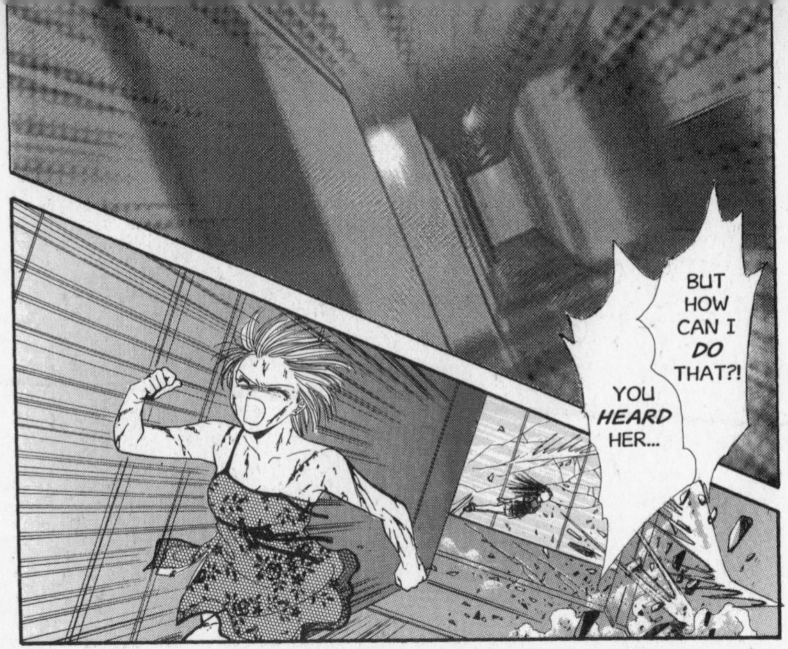
BUT HOW CAN I *DO* THAT?!
YOU *HEARD* HER...

SHE WAS TALKING ABOUT AKI'S AND MY *16TH BIRTHDAY*...
THE DAY YOU *AWAKENED* IN ME!

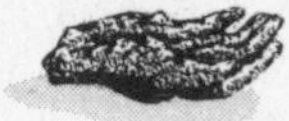

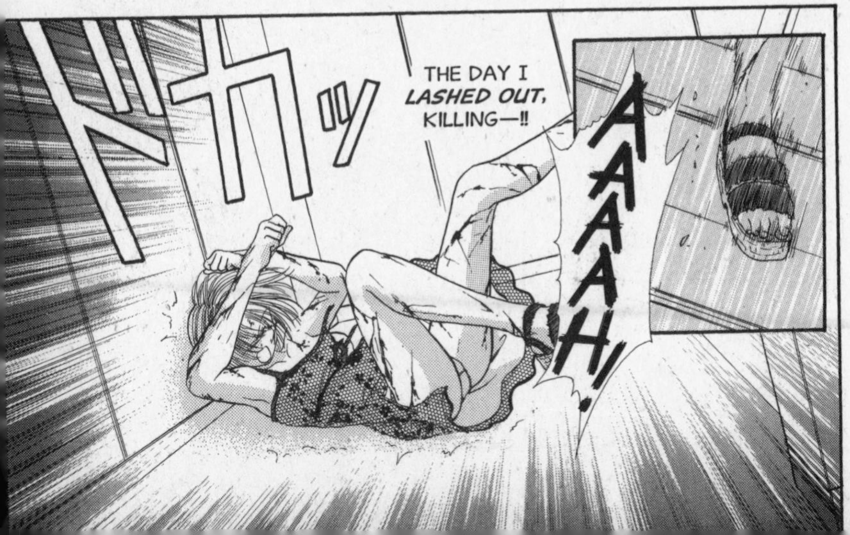
THE DAY I *LASHED OUT*, KILLING—!!
AAAAH!!

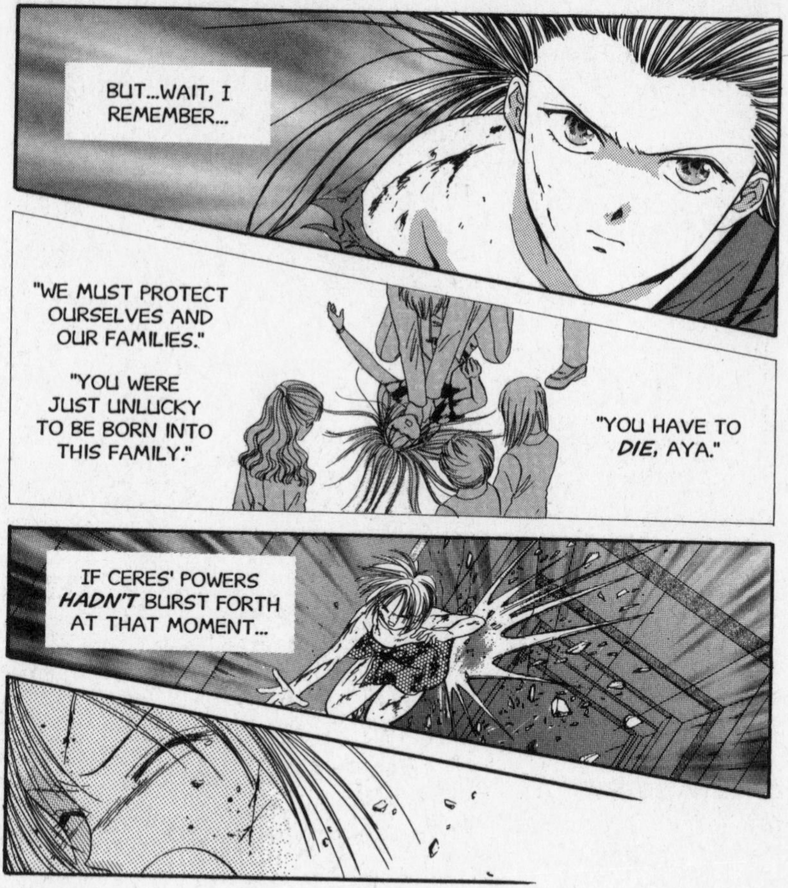
BUT...WAIT, I REMEMBER...
"WE MUST PROTECT OURSELVES AND OUR FAMILIES."
"YOU WERE JUST UNLUCKY TO BE BORN INTO THIS FAMILY."
"YOU HAVE TO *DIE*, AYA."
IF CERES' POWERS ***HADN'T*** BURST FORTH AT THAT MOMENT...

...THOSE I KILLED WOULD HAVE KILLED ***ME***! ***IN COLD BLOOD***!!

Ceres: 9

...Okay, so! More about corrections. For those of you who have first printings of Volume 3, in Tōya's line in the last panel on page 74 (and the first panel of page 95), the *furigana* over the *kanji* for "celestial maiden (ten'nyo)" reads "Ceres." That's a mistake...! It's really supposed to be just "celestial maiden." It's the descendants of **other** maidens who are the C-Genomes. (This was a misprint, too.) It might not be fixed even in the second or third printings; check your copies, and draw lines through if it's wrong. ◡̈ They're not **all** descended from Ceres. I'll have to be better about this. Nothing gets done about it if I don't pay attention.... I'd forgotten to write about it in here too.

Back to the characters. Ceres is admired by girl-readers, and thus is pretty popular—she's beautiful, strong, cool. She was mad and scary in the beginning, but she's also really feminine. She must have started out as a kind, generous woman...but women change according to the guys they go out with. ◡̈ My assistant said that, to her, Ceres seems "motherly." It's possible she hasn't even hit 20 yet, though! Ceres **could** be surprisingly young. People tend to think she and Aya are different, but really, they're the same person. Aya's dark side **is** Ceres! The mature woman...and the young self. The ego, and the superego. (Maybe I'm reaching.) Since Aya transforms, though, people assume it's into something (someone) else. ...Wait, is **Ceres** one of those "*henshin* (transformation)" shows?! (Just kidding.) ◡̈ How will the long history between Ceres and the Progenitor end...? It depends on what **really** happened between them, regarding the celestial robes.

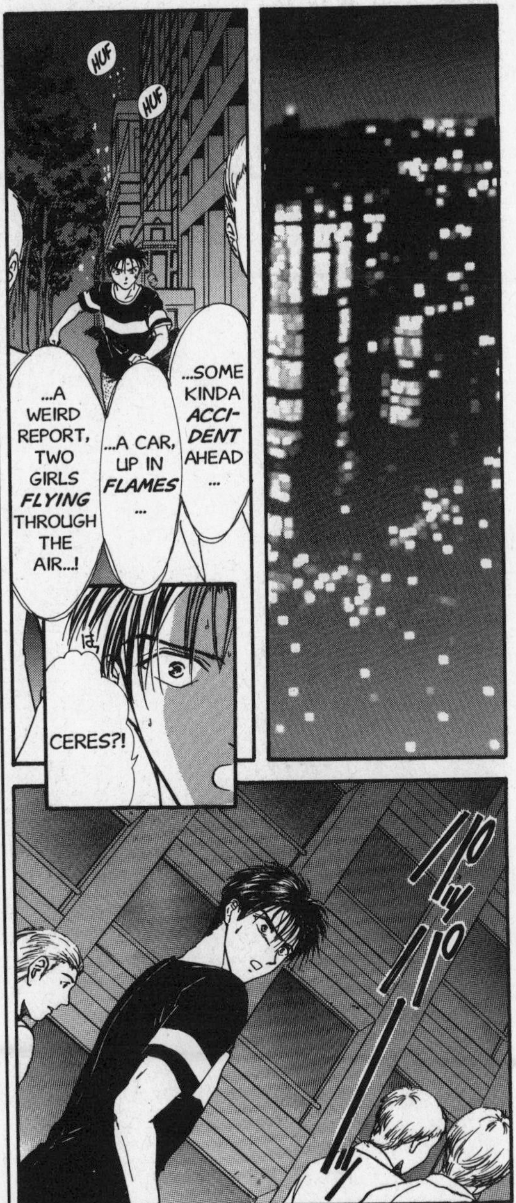
HUF
HUF
...SOME KINDA ACCIDENT AHEAD...
...A CAR, UP IN FLAMES...
...A WEIRD REPORT, TWO GIRLS FLYING THROUGH THE AIR...!
CERES?!

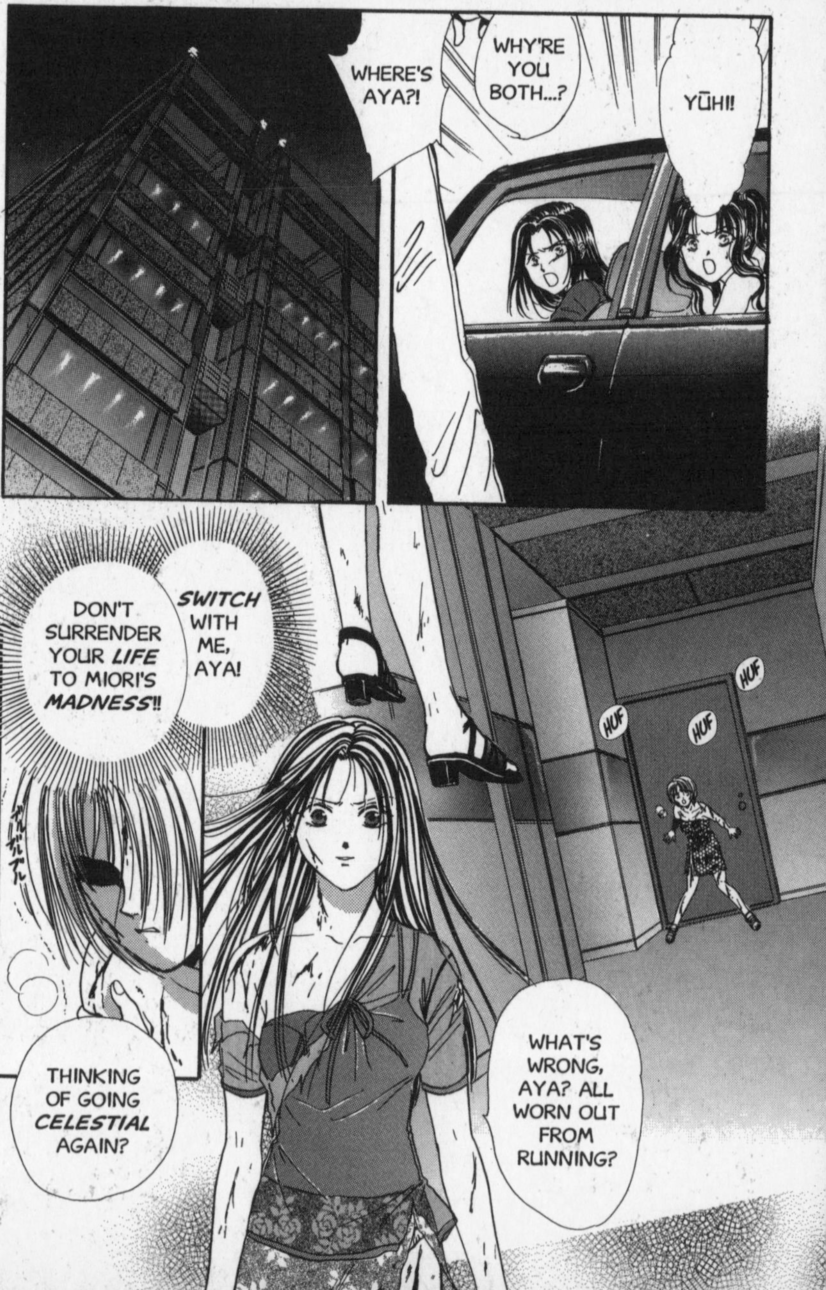
YŪHI!
WHY'RE YOU BOTH...?
WHERE'S AYA?!
HUF
HUF
HUF
SWITCH WITH ME, AYA!
DON'T SURRENDER YOUR LIFE TO MIORI'S MADNESS!!
WHAT'S WRONG, AYA? ALL WORN OUT FROM RUNNING?
THINKING OF GOING CELESTIAL AGAIN?

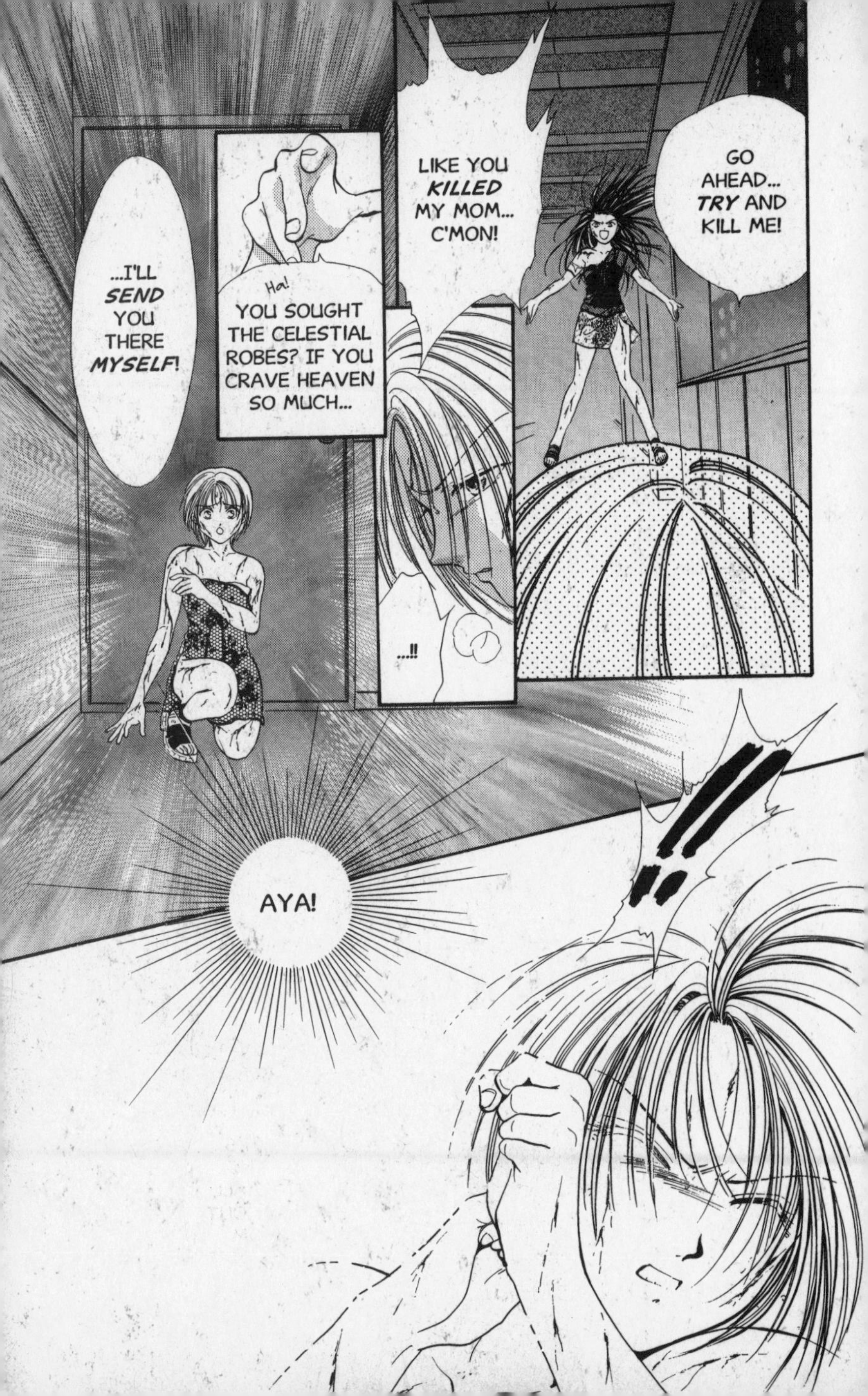
GO AHEAD... TRY AND KILL ME!
LIKE YOU KILLED MY MOM... C'MON!
...!!
Ha!
YOU SOUGHT THE CELESTIAL ROBES? IF YOU CRAVE HEAVEN SO MUCH...
...I'LL SEND YOU THERE MYSELF!
AYA!

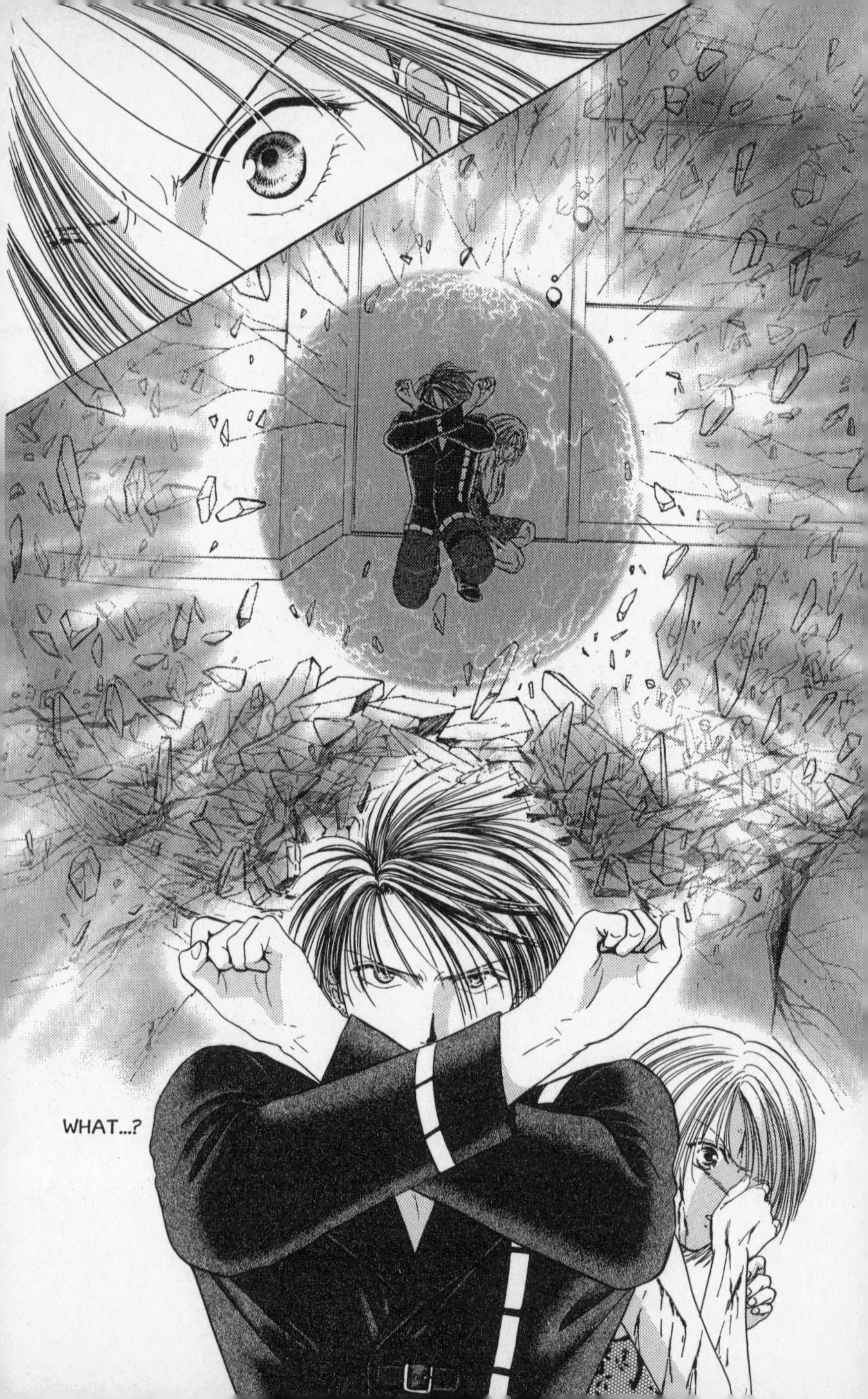
WHAT...?

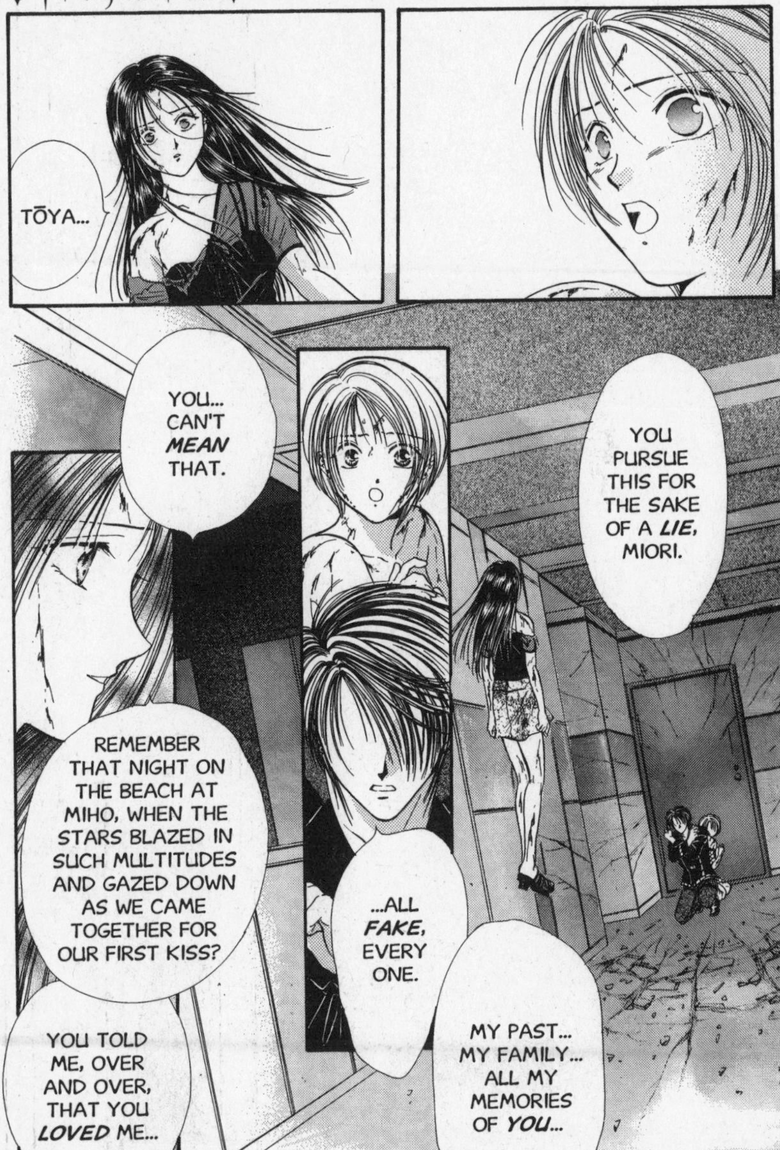
TŌYA...
YOU PURSUE THIS FOR THE SAKE OF A *LIE*, MIORI.
YOU... CAN'T *MEAN* THAT.
REMEMBER THAT NIGHT ON THE BEACH AT MIHO, WHEN THE STARS BLAZED IN SUCH MULTITUDES AND GAZED DOWN AS WE CAME TOGETHER FOR OUR FIRST KISS?
YOU TOLD ME, OVER AND OVER, THAT YOU *LOVED* ME...
MY PAST... MY FAMILY... ALL MY MEMORIES OF *YOU*...
...ALL *FAKE*, EVERY ONE.

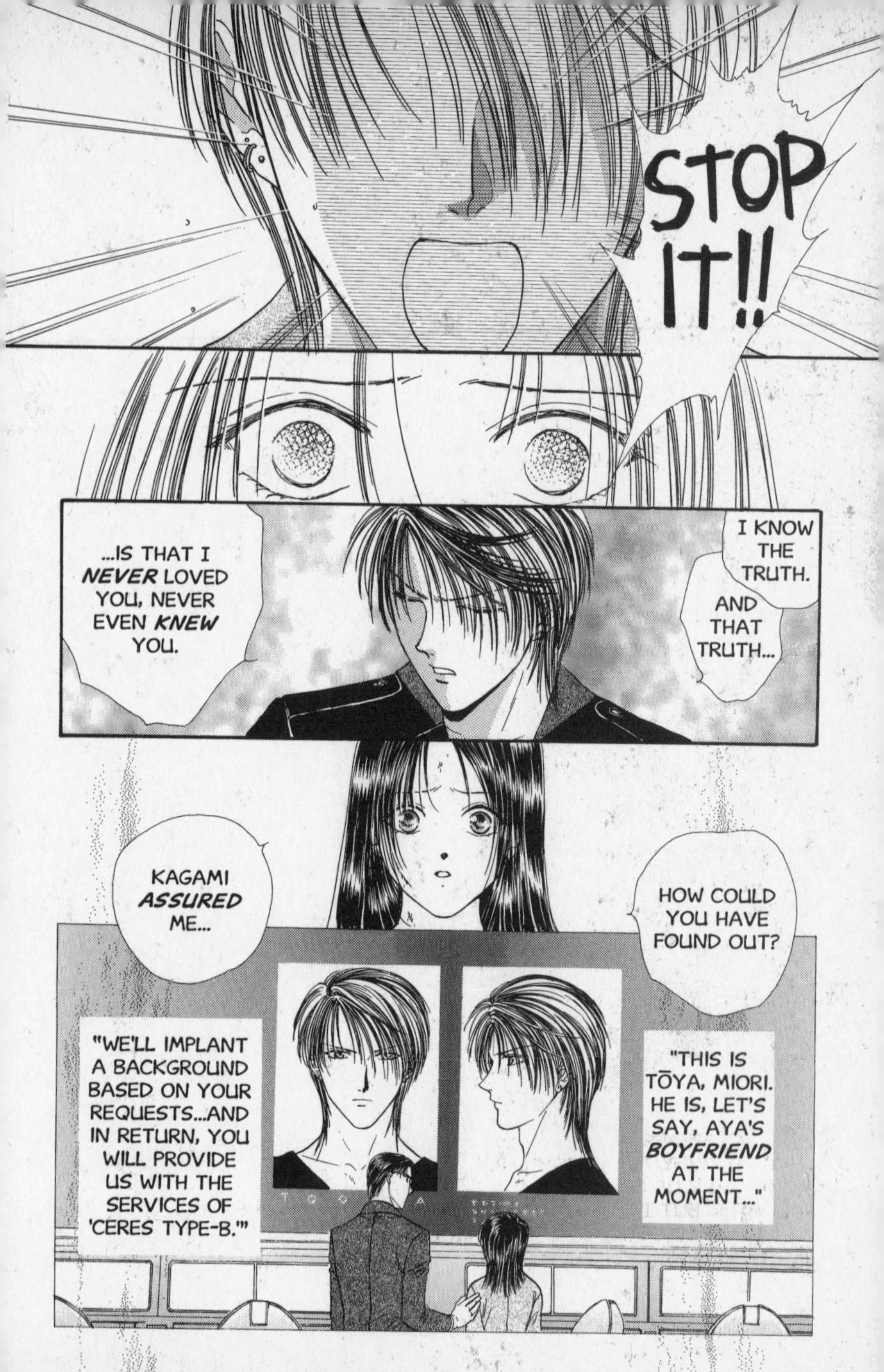
STOP IT!!
I KNOW THE TRUTH.
AND THAT TRUTH...
...IS THAT I *NEVER* LOVED YOU, NEVER EVEN *KNEW* YOU.
HOW COULD YOU HAVE FOUND OUT?
KAGAMI *ASSURED* ME...
"THIS IS TŌYA, MIORI. HE IS, LET'S SAY, AYA'S *BOYFRIEND* AT THE MOMENT..."
"WE'LL IMPLANT A BACKGROUND BASED ON YOUR REQUESTS...AND IN RETURN, YOU WILL PROVIDE US WITH THE SERVICES OF 'CERES TYPE-B.'"

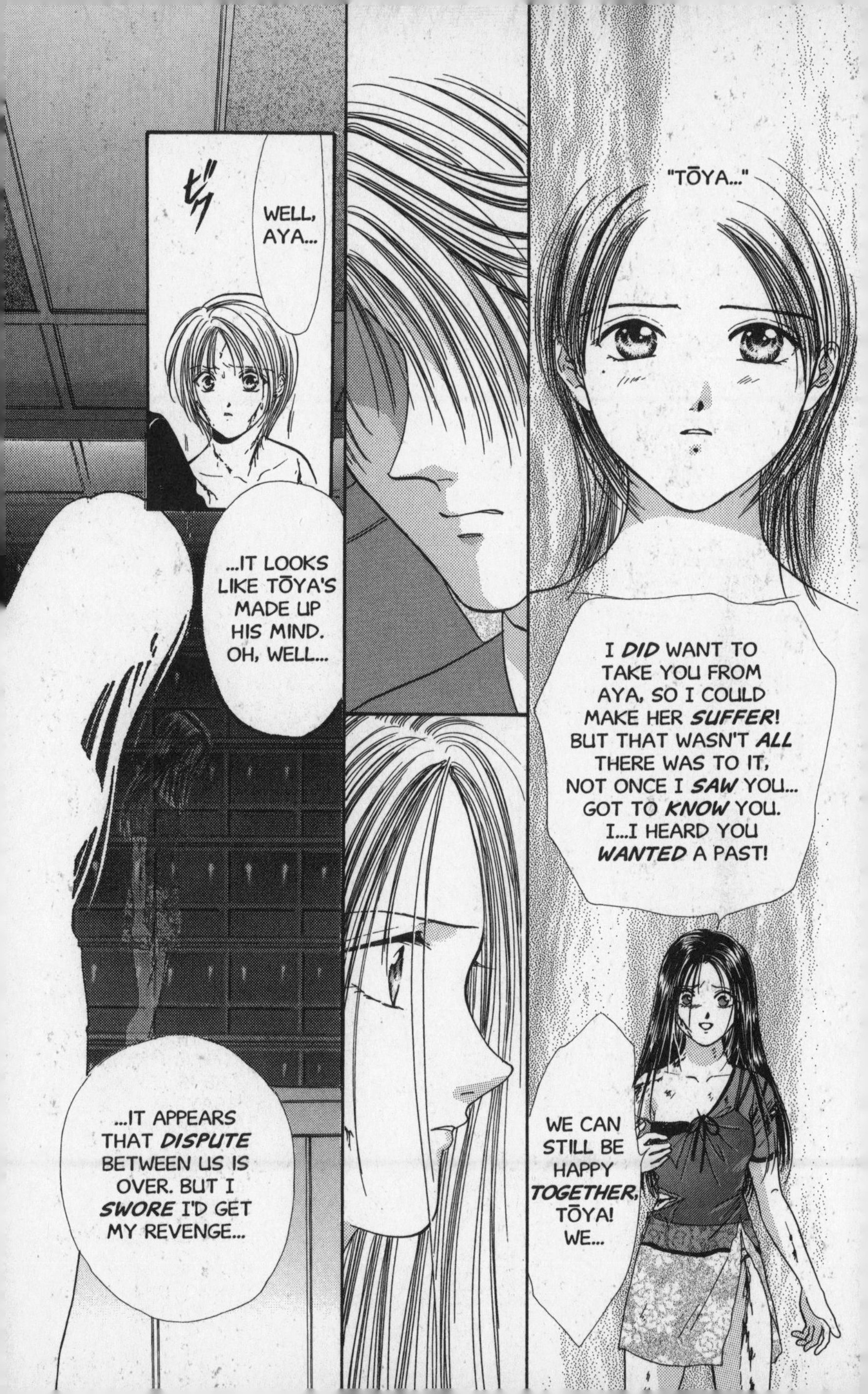
"TŌYA..."
I DID WANT TO TAKE YOU FROM AYA, SO I COULD MAKE HER SUFFER! BUT THAT WASN'T ALL THERE WAS TO IT, NOT ONCE I SAW YOU... GOT TO KNOW YOU. I...I HEARD YOU WANTED A PAST!
WE CAN STILL BE HAPPY TOGETHER, TŌYA! WE...
WELL, AYA...
...IT LOOKS LIKE TŌYA'S MADE UP HIS MIND. OH, WELL...
...IT APPEARS THAT DISPUTE BETWEEN US IS OVER. BUT I SWORE I'D GET MY REVENGE...

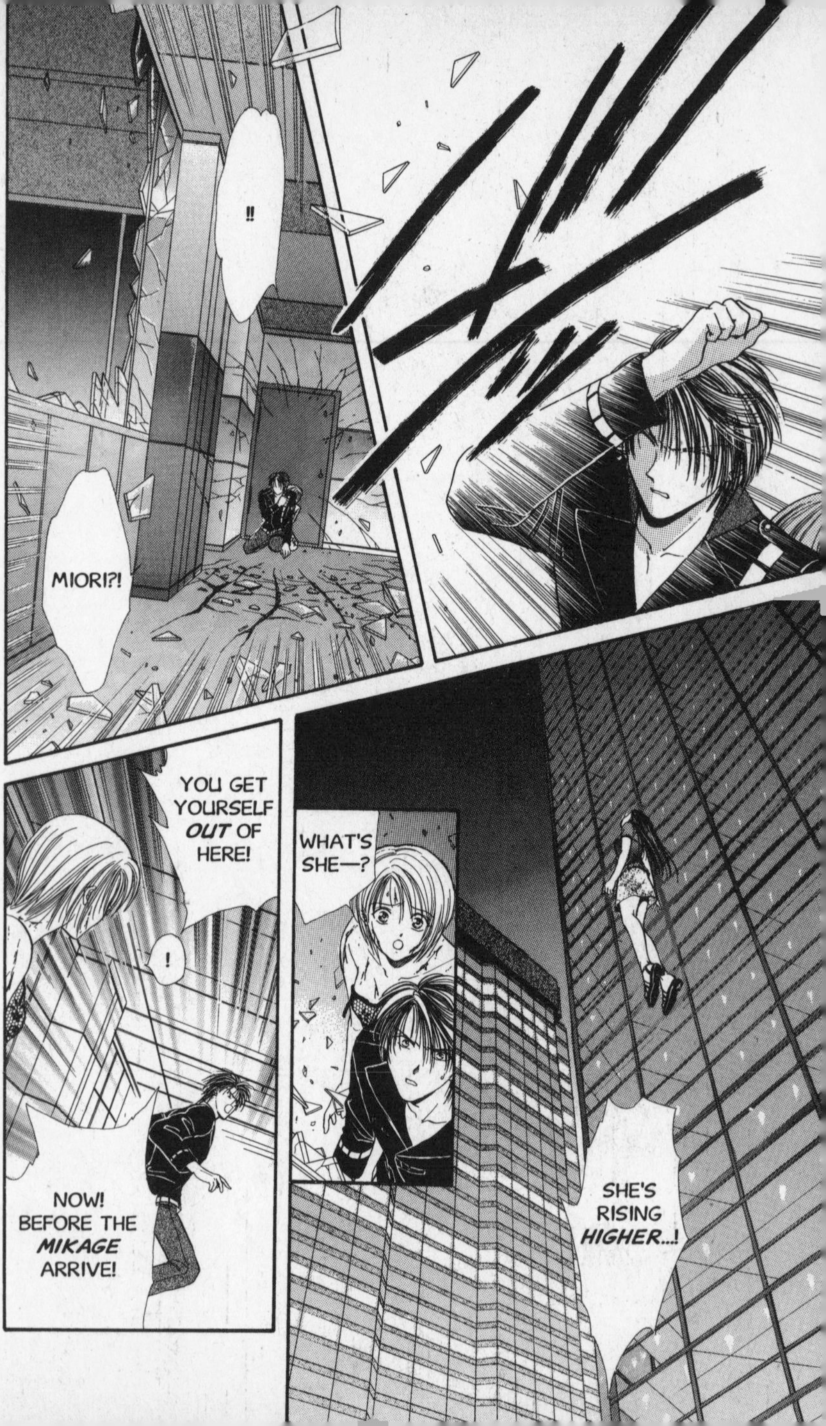
!!
MIORI?!
SHE'S RISING HIGHER...!
WHAT'S SHE—?
YOU GET YOURSELF OUT OF HERE!
!
NOW! BEFORE THE MIKAGE ARRIVE!

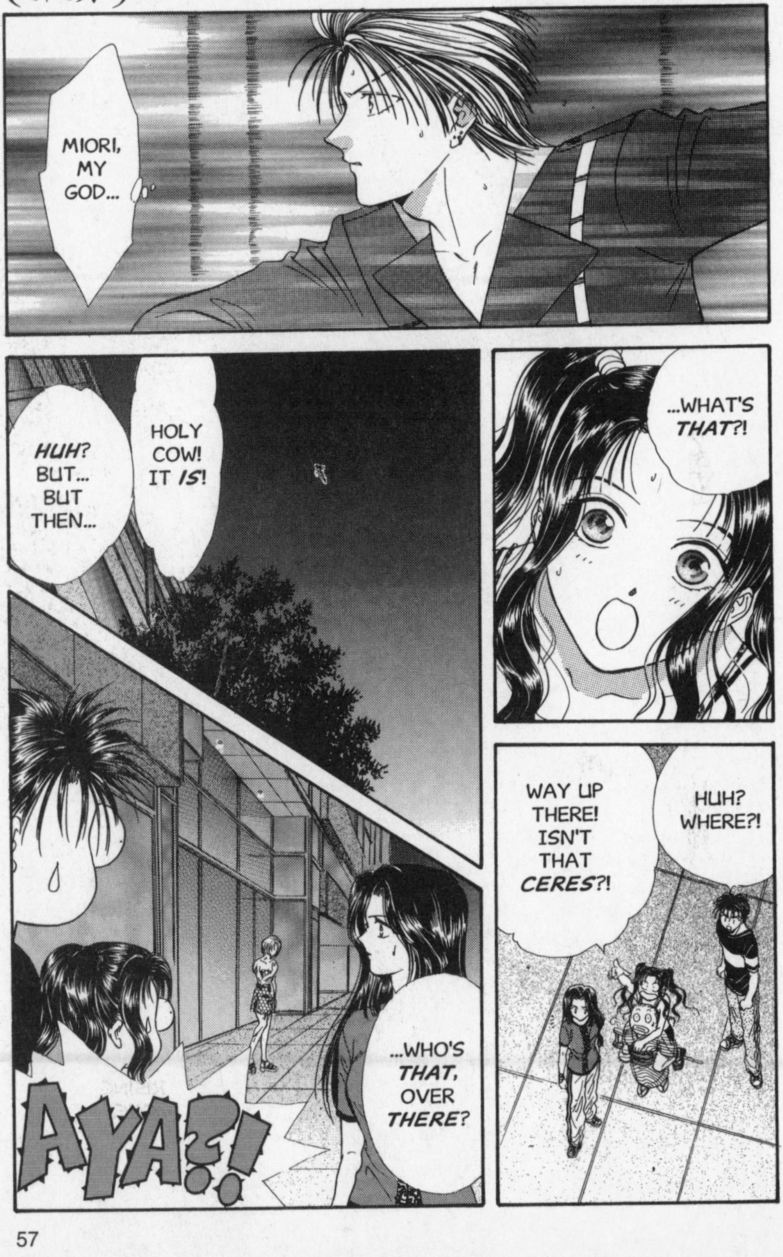
MIORI, MY GOD...
...WHAT'S *THAT*?!
HUH? WHERE?!
WAY UP THERE! ISN'T THAT *CERES*?!
HOLY COW! IT *IS*!
HUH? BUT... BUT THEN...
...WHO'S *THAT*, OVER *THERE*?
AYA?!

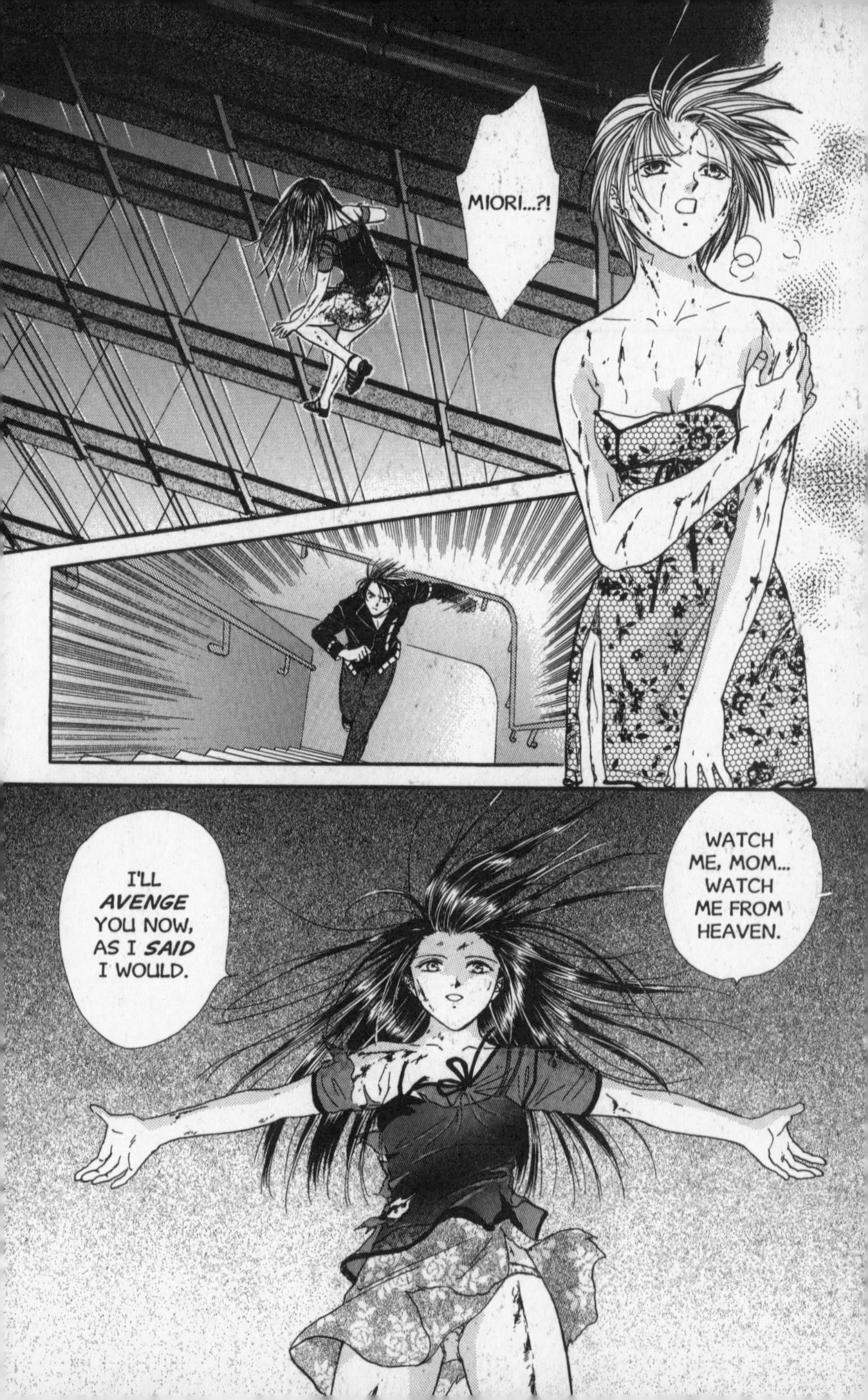
MIORI...?!
WATCH ME, MOM... WATCH ME FROM HEAVEN.
I'LL *AVENGE* YOU NOW, AS I *SAID* I WOULD.

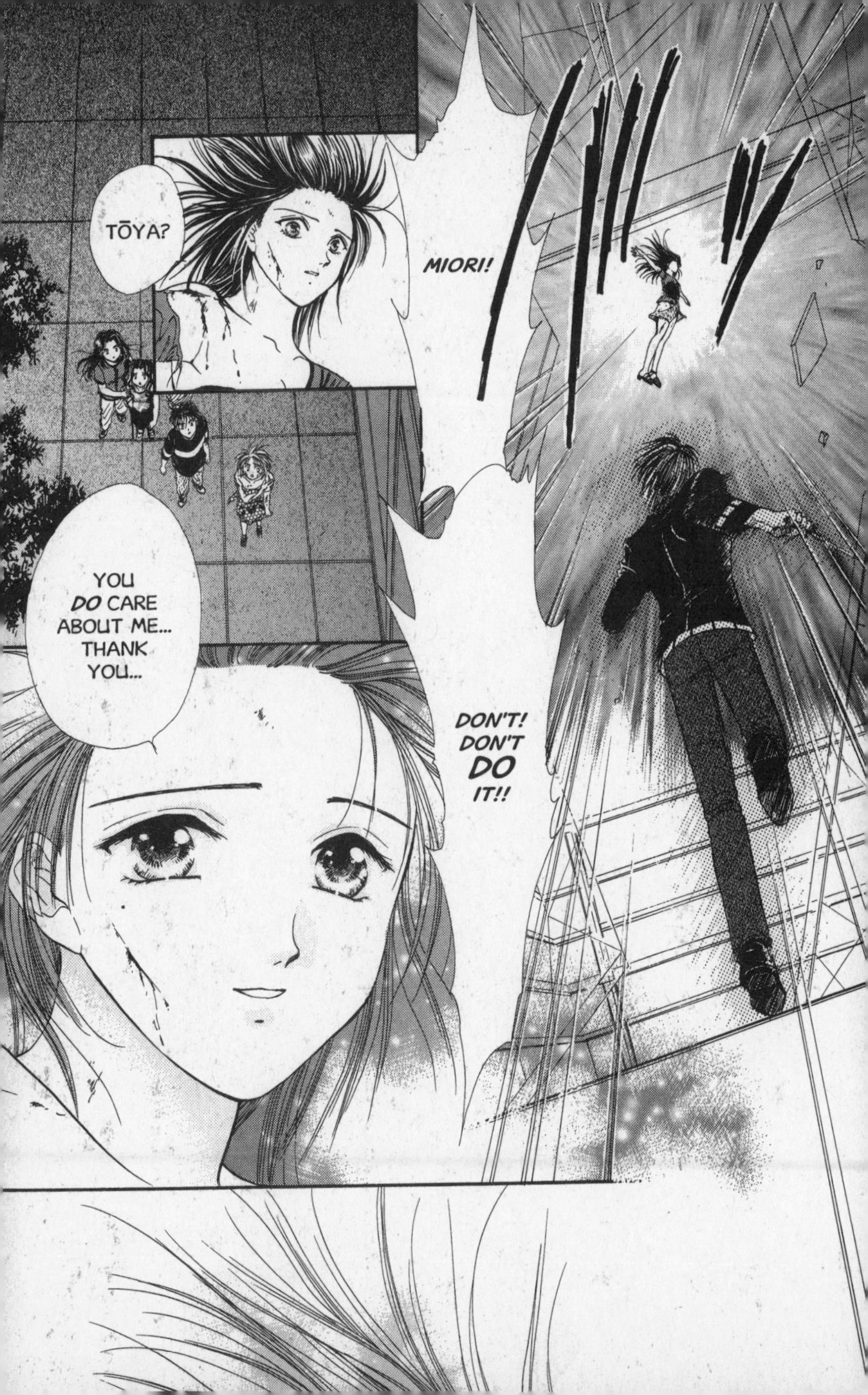
MIORI!
DON'T! DON'T DO IT!!
TŌYA?
YOU DO CARE ABOUT ME... THANK YOU...

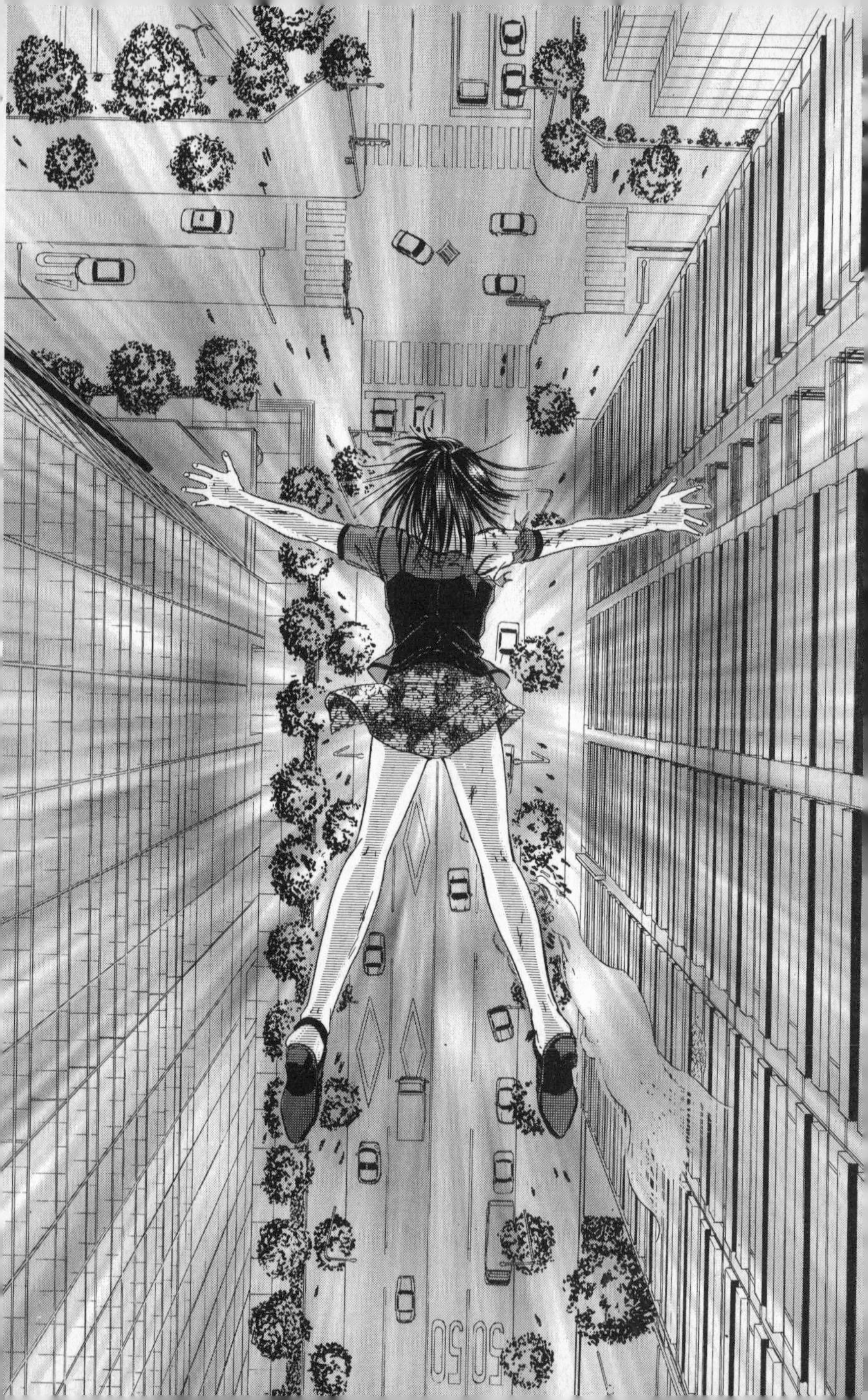

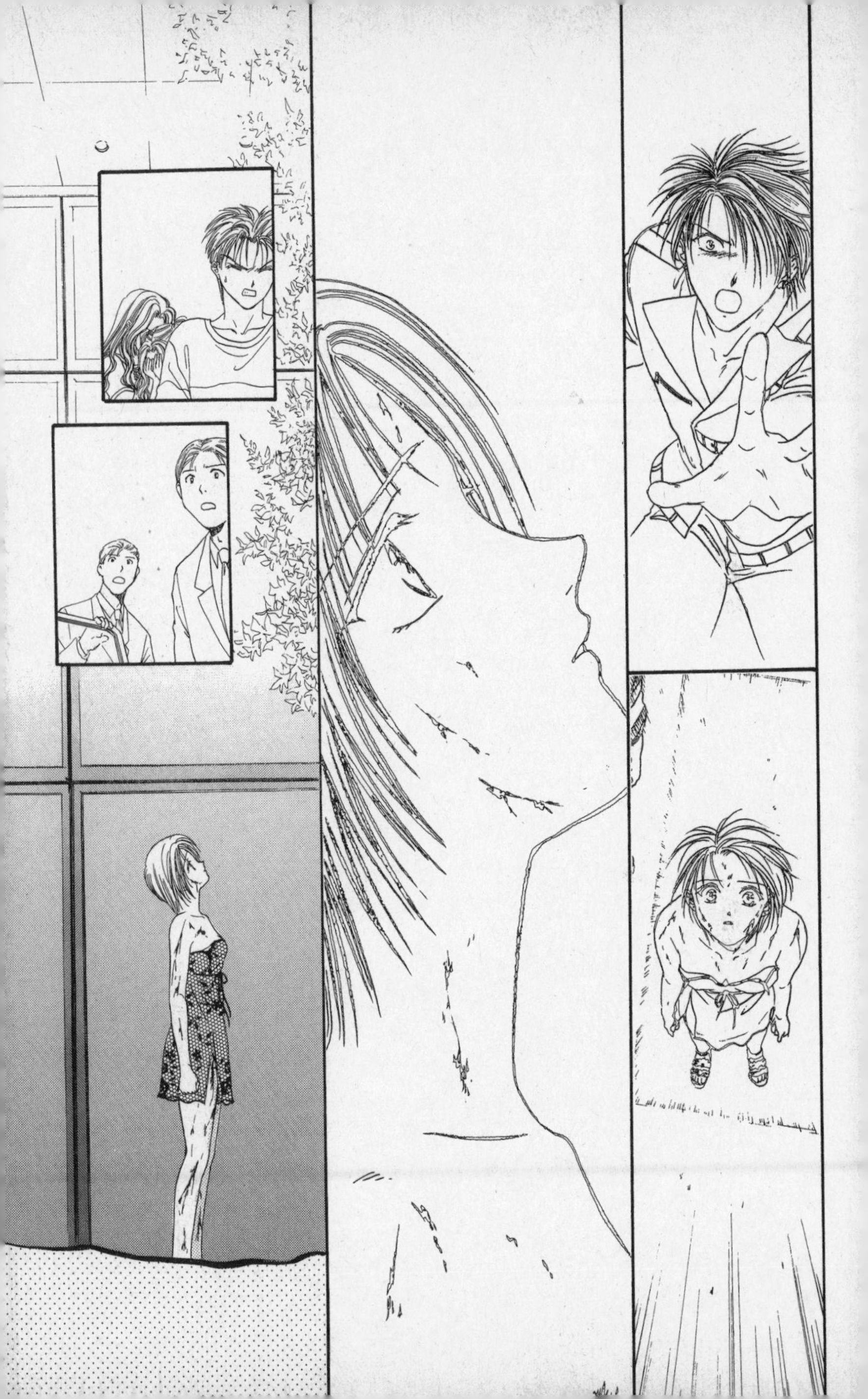

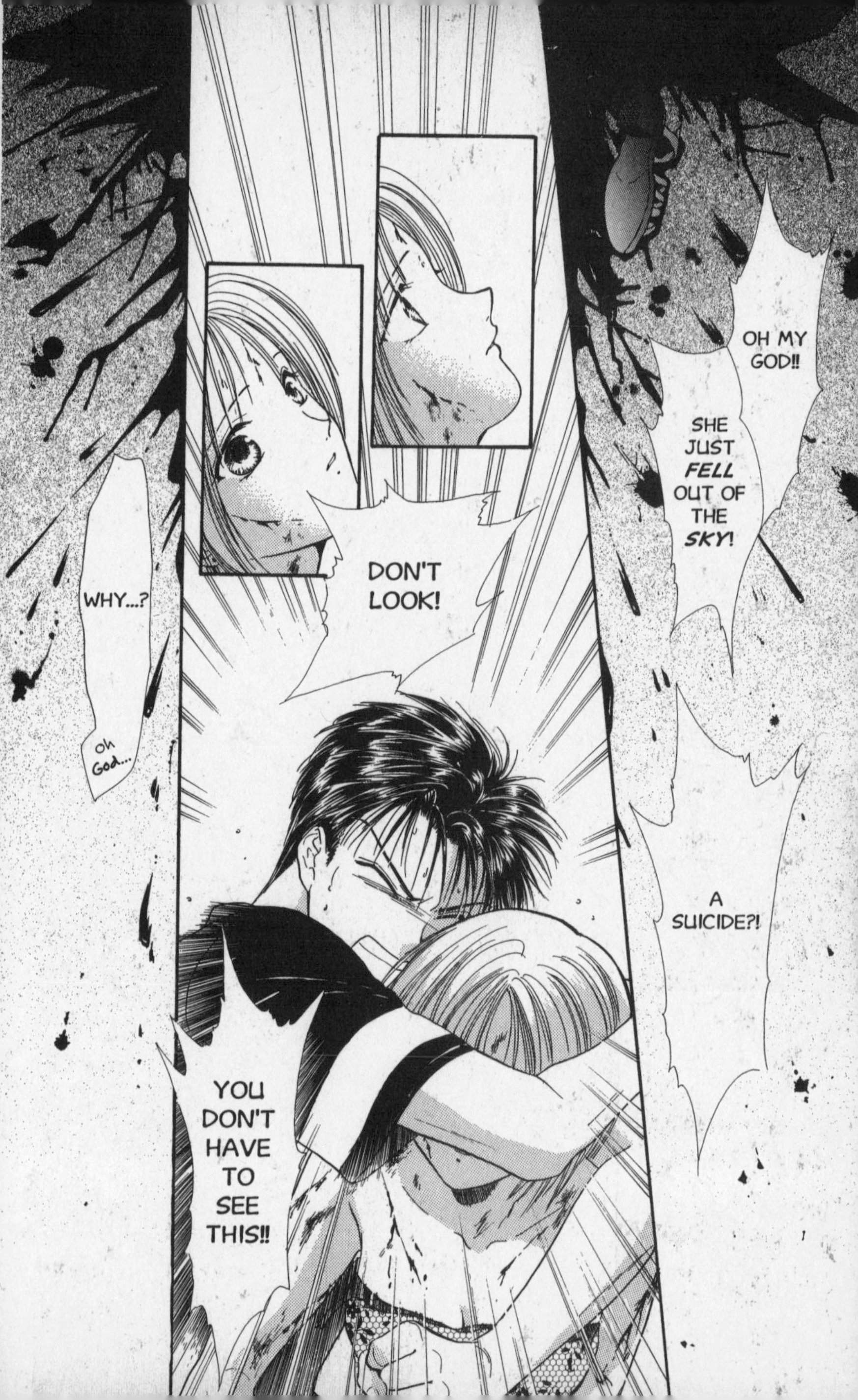
OH MY GOD!!
SHE JUST *FELL* OUT OF THE *SKY*!
A SUICIDE?!
DON'T LOOK!
YOU DON'T HAVE TO SEE THIS!!
WHY...?
oh God...

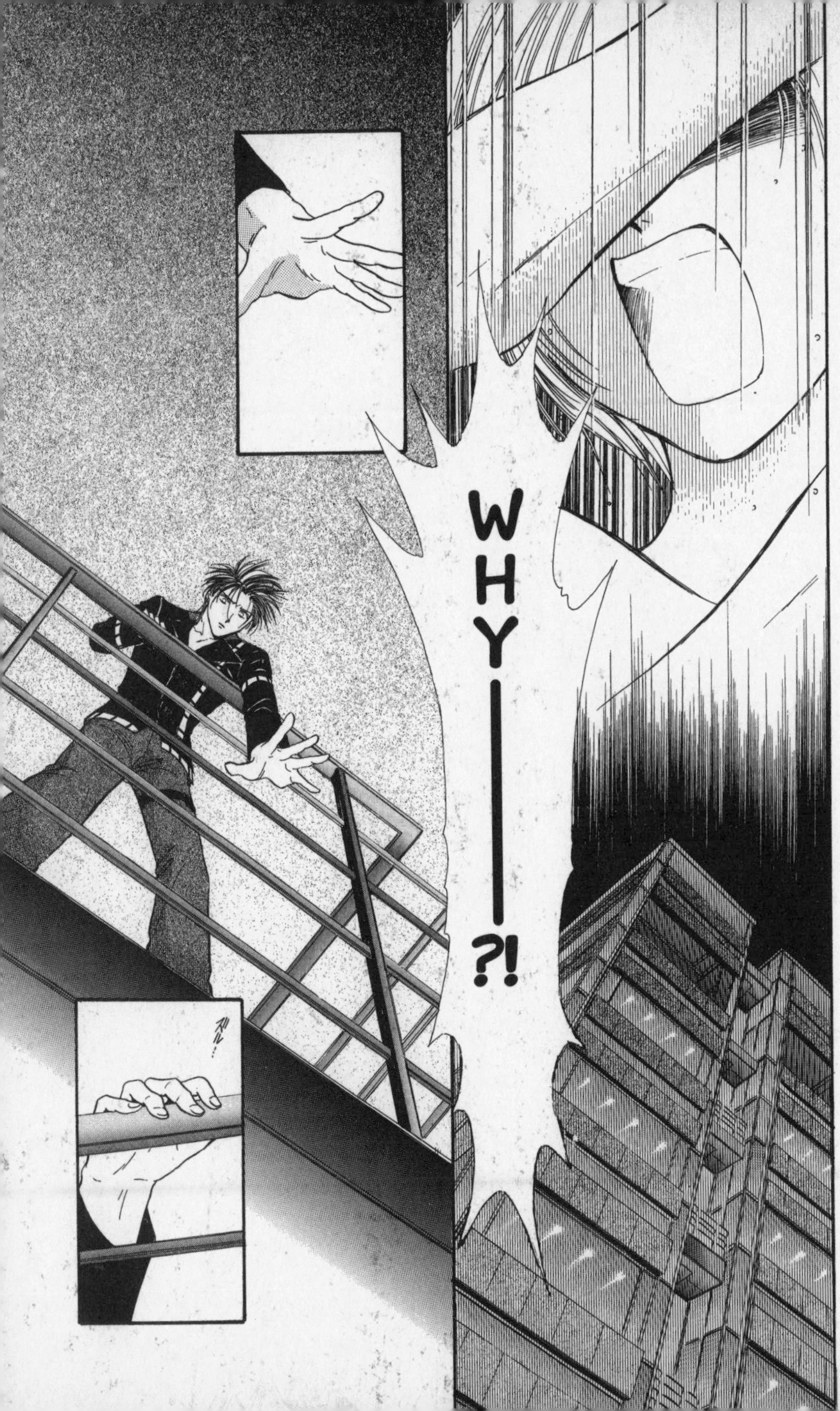
WHY——?!
ズル…

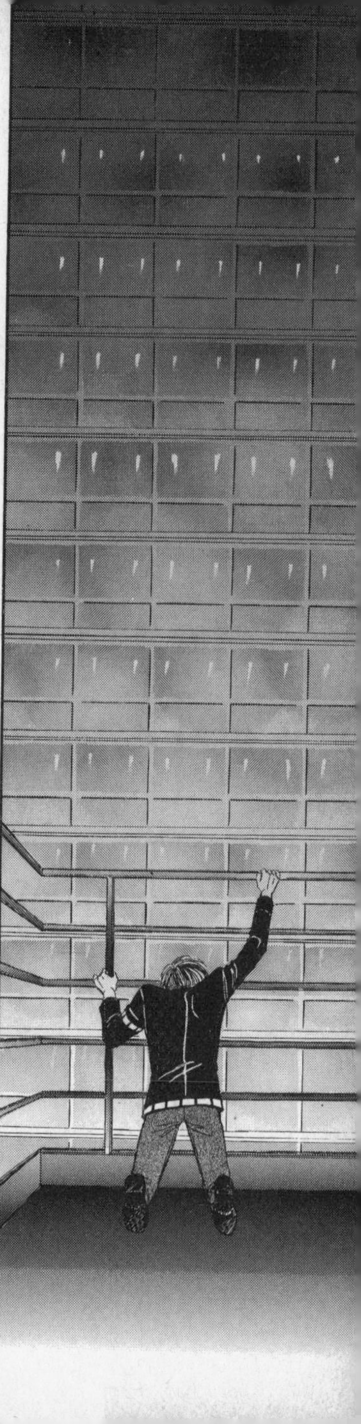

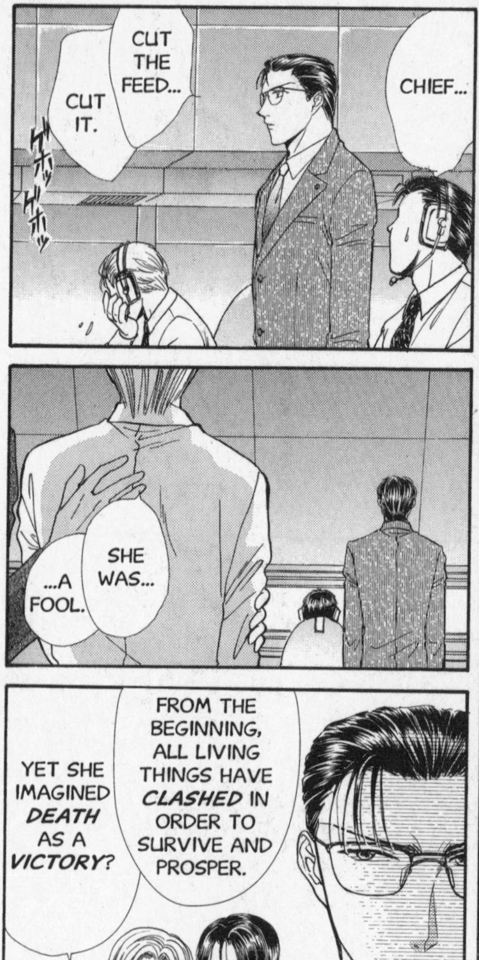
CHIEF...
CUT THE FEED...
CUT IT.
ゲホッゲホッ
SHE WAS...
...A FOOL.
FROM THE BEGINNING, ALL LIVING THINGS HAVE *CLASHED* IN ORDER TO SURVIVE AND PROSPER.
YET SHE IMAGINED *DEATH* AS A *VICTORY*?

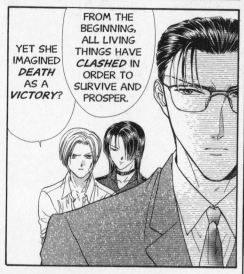

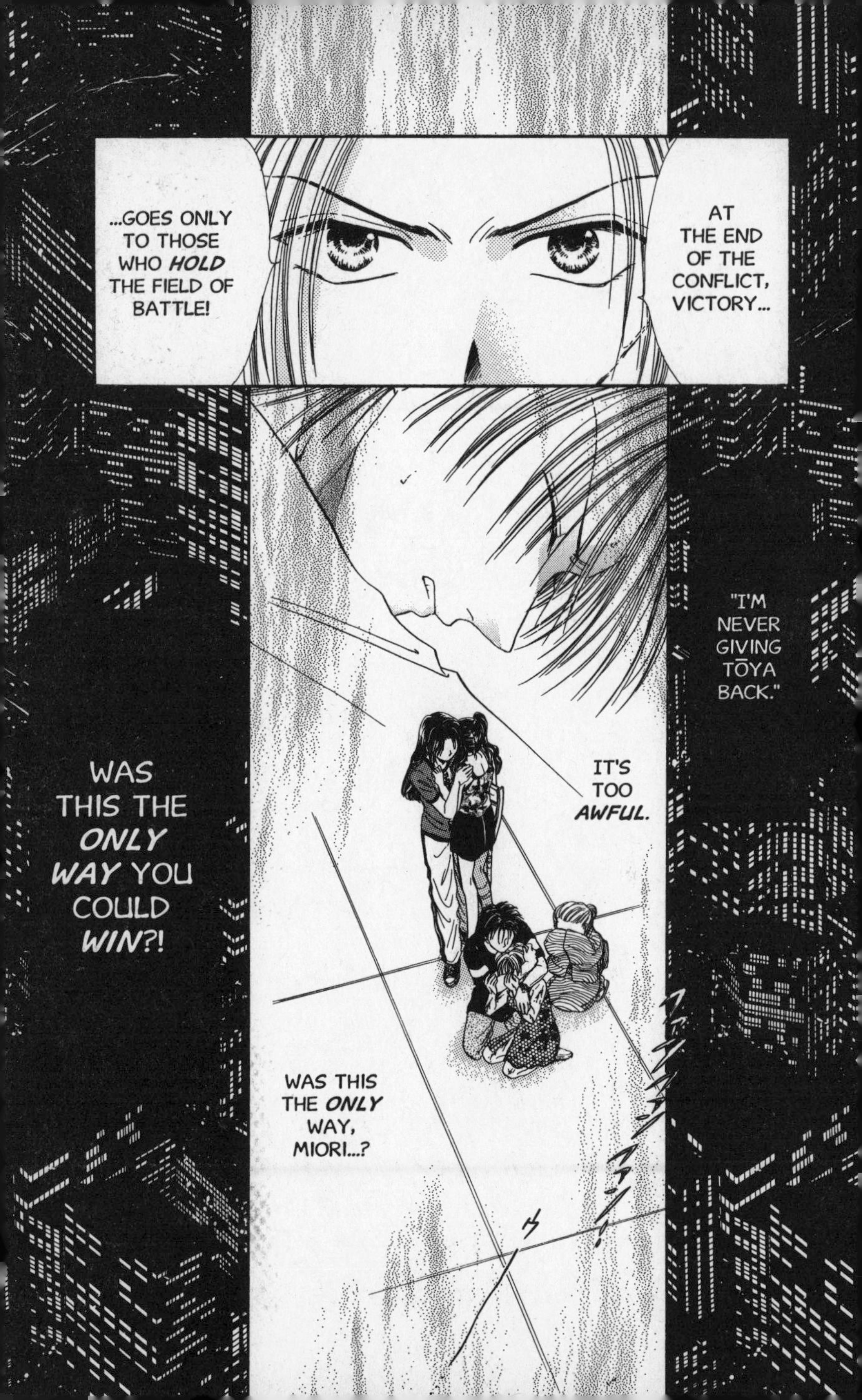
AT THE END OF THE CONFLICT, VICTORY...
...GOES ONLY TO THOSE WHO *HOLD* THE FIELD OF BATTLE!
"I'M NEVER GIVING TŌYA BACK."
IT'S TOO *AWFUL*.
WAS THIS THE *ONLY WAY* YOU COULD *WIN*?!
WAS THIS THE *ONLY* WAY, MIORI...?

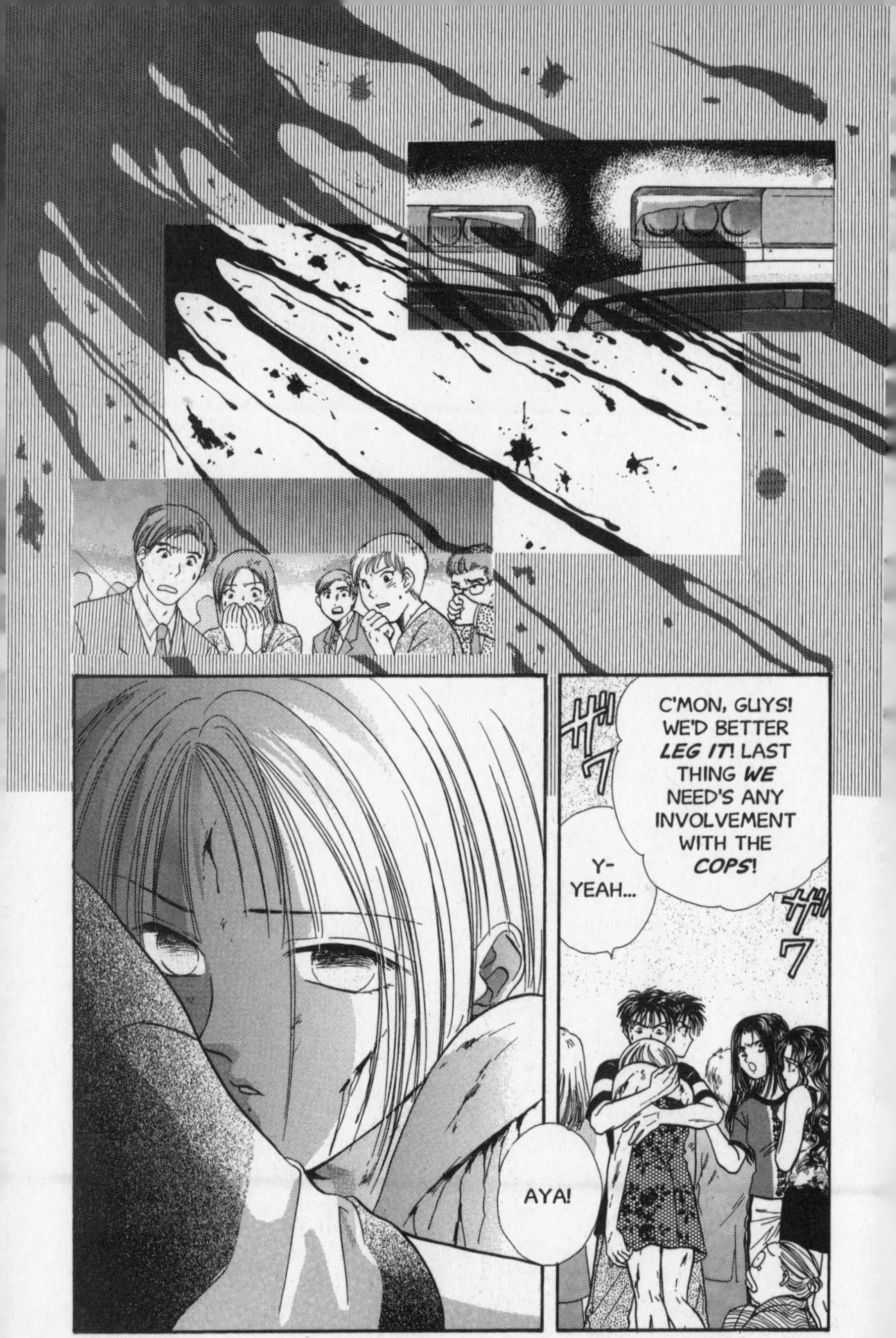

ザワ
C'MON, GUYS! WE'D BETTER ***LEG IT***! LAST THING ***WE*** NEED'S ANY INVOLVEMENT WITH THE ***COPS***!
ザワ
Y-YEAH...
AYA!

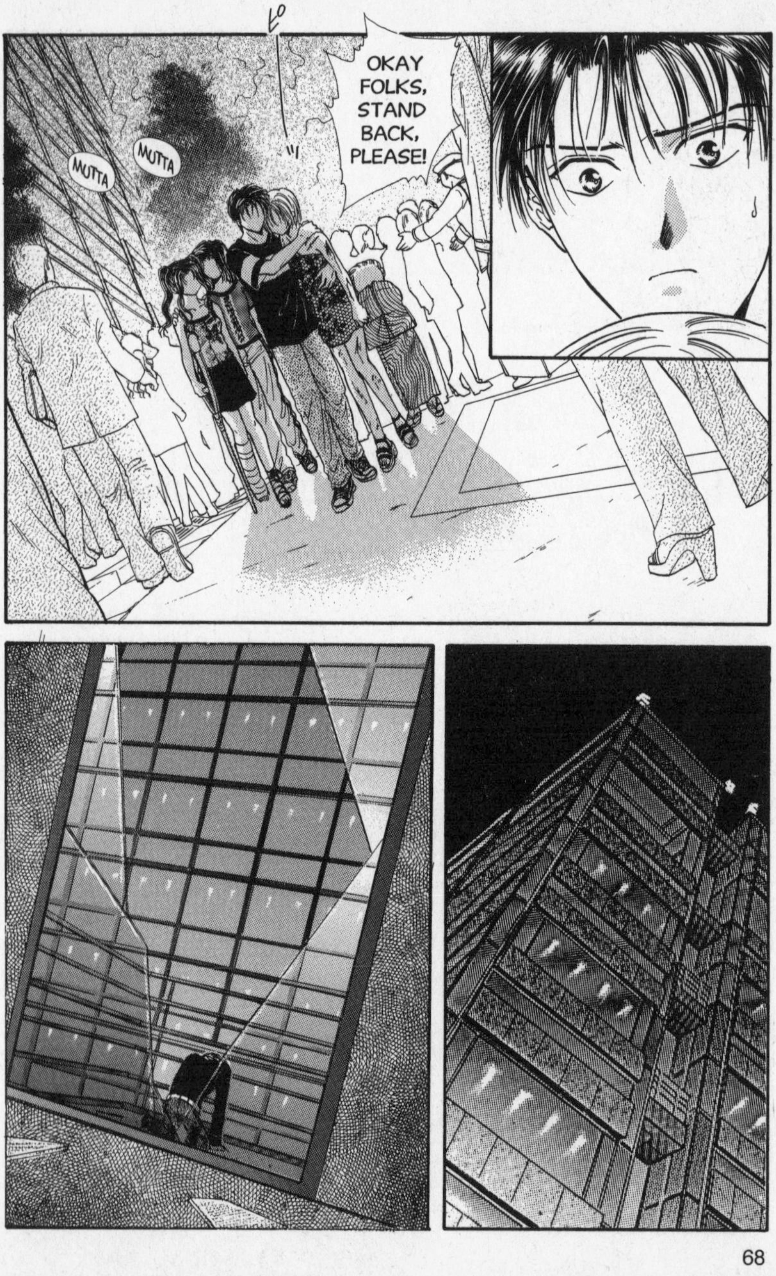
OKAY FOLKS, STAND BACK, PLEASE!
MUTTA
MUTTA

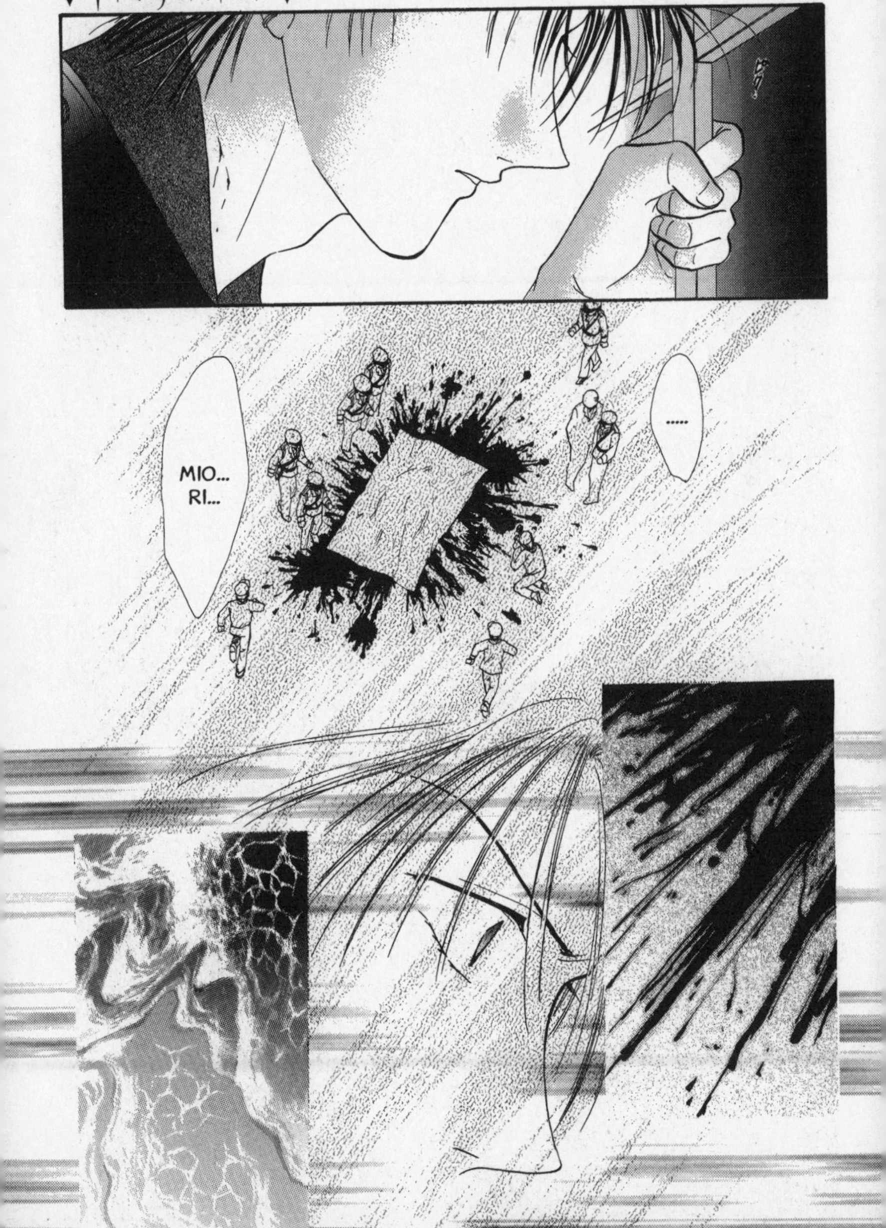
......
MIO... RI...

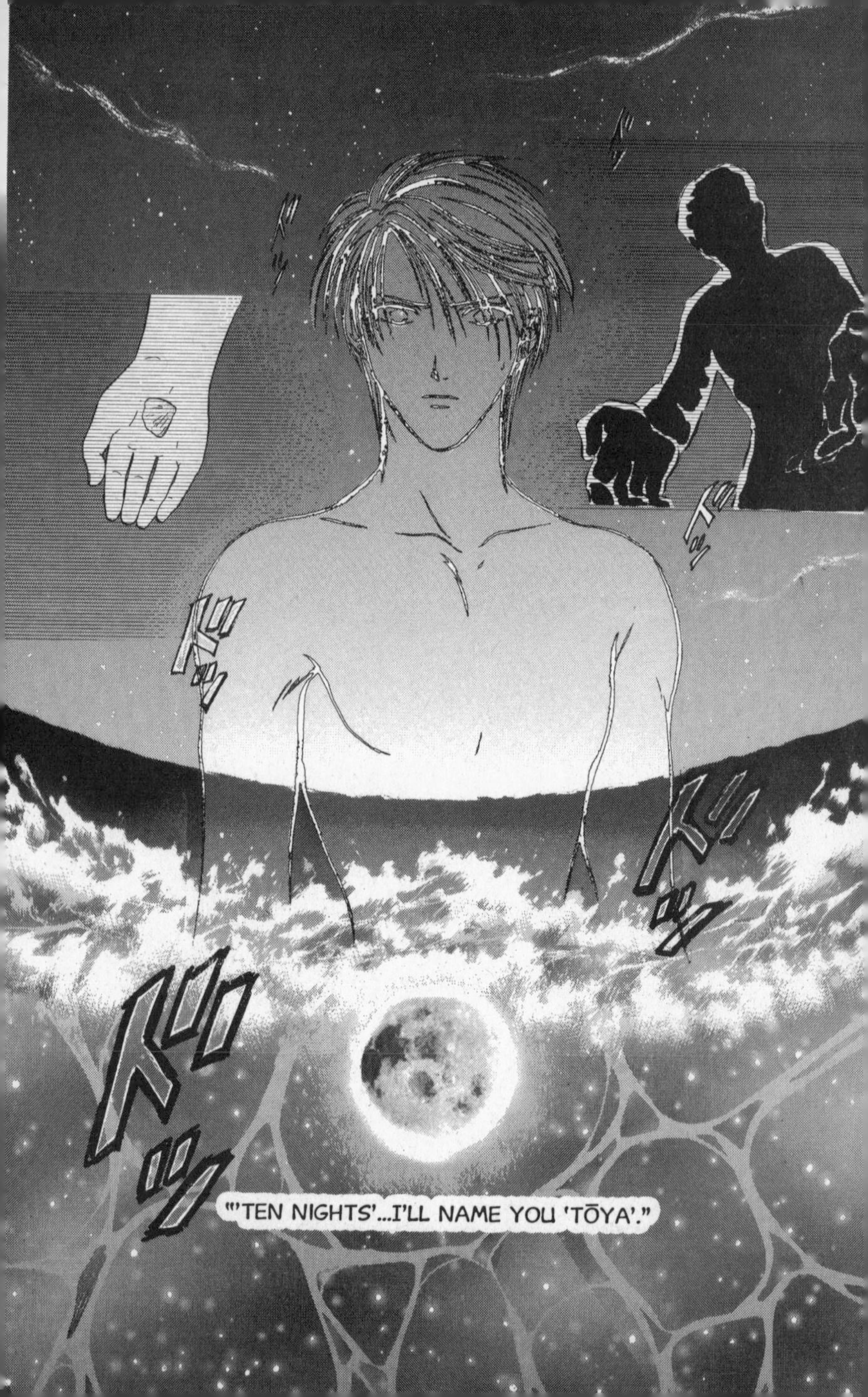
"'TEN NIGHTS'...I'LL NAME YOU 'TŌYA'."

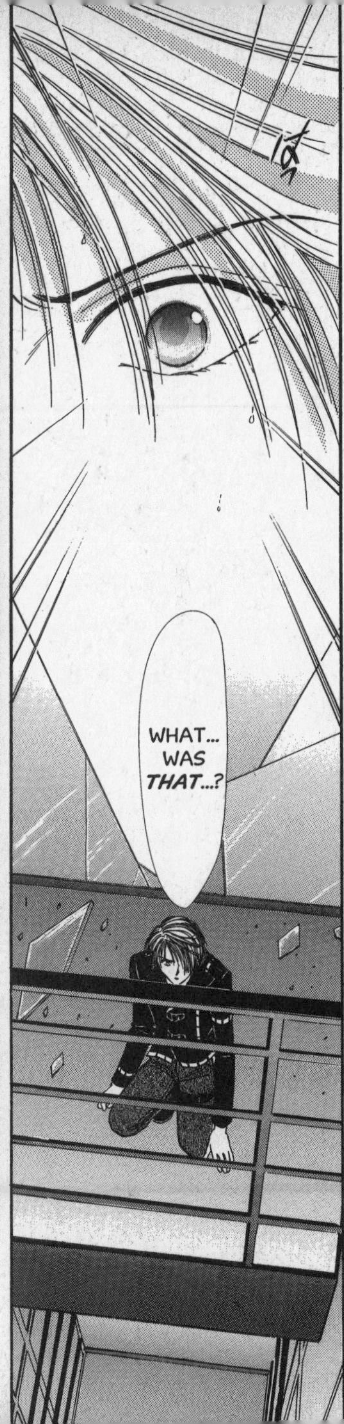
WHAT... WAS *THAT*...?

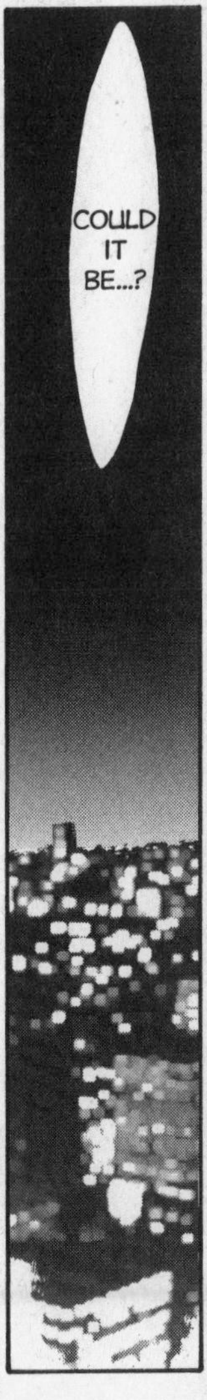
COULD IT BE...?

Ceres: 9

Onto a new subject, 'cause I talked about my high-school uniform on the last [Japan-published] volume's cover flap.... So, my alma mater invited me to their campus festival. I thought it would be something casual, since all alumni are free to attend, so I asked a friend to come along...but then they gave us the royal welcome, and we didn't know **what** to make of it. Really, doing the pamphlet wasn't a big deal. I'd been swamped with work, so it was a nice change of pace. (Yeah, and then things got even **more** hectic over the following two weeks.) The school is currently known as "Sakai Girls' High School." I hadn't been back in ages, and it hadn't changed. It did seem a bit brighter, though, a bit more cheerful, and the buildings more colorful—like a nice place. We arrived late, so we couldn't see much of the festival itself (darn it), but the students seemed excited to see me. I saw many of my former teachers, and it was great to see that they were doing well. There are just some things you don't appreciate when you're a student yourself, you know? Several girls recognized me as I was walking along (well, duh, my picture **was** in the pamphlet with the interview). I took pictures with them, shook their hands, felt a certain camaraderie.... Oh yeah, and I was pleased to hear one girl calling me "Senpai," rather than "Ms. Watase." For a time, I had been in the Film Club and the Visual Arts Club, so I peeked in and chatted with the current members. That was fun. I was surprised to hear that one of them had applied there (early decision, too) specifically because she was a fan of mine! Another girl started crying when she saw me. I hear that the band is doing well; I'm sorry I took so many pictures during your practice. And thanks to the girl who let me into the classrooms when I was taking reference pictures in the hallways! Most of all, big thanks go to the Chairman of the Board (a woman). My friend is a fan of hers now. It was such a friendly campus, and the faculty and students (they were all so cheerful) seemed to get along so well. You don't see schools like that often. Now I wish I could go back to school myself.... I even gave out some secret autographs. I wonder if I can get a copy of that group picture we took...?

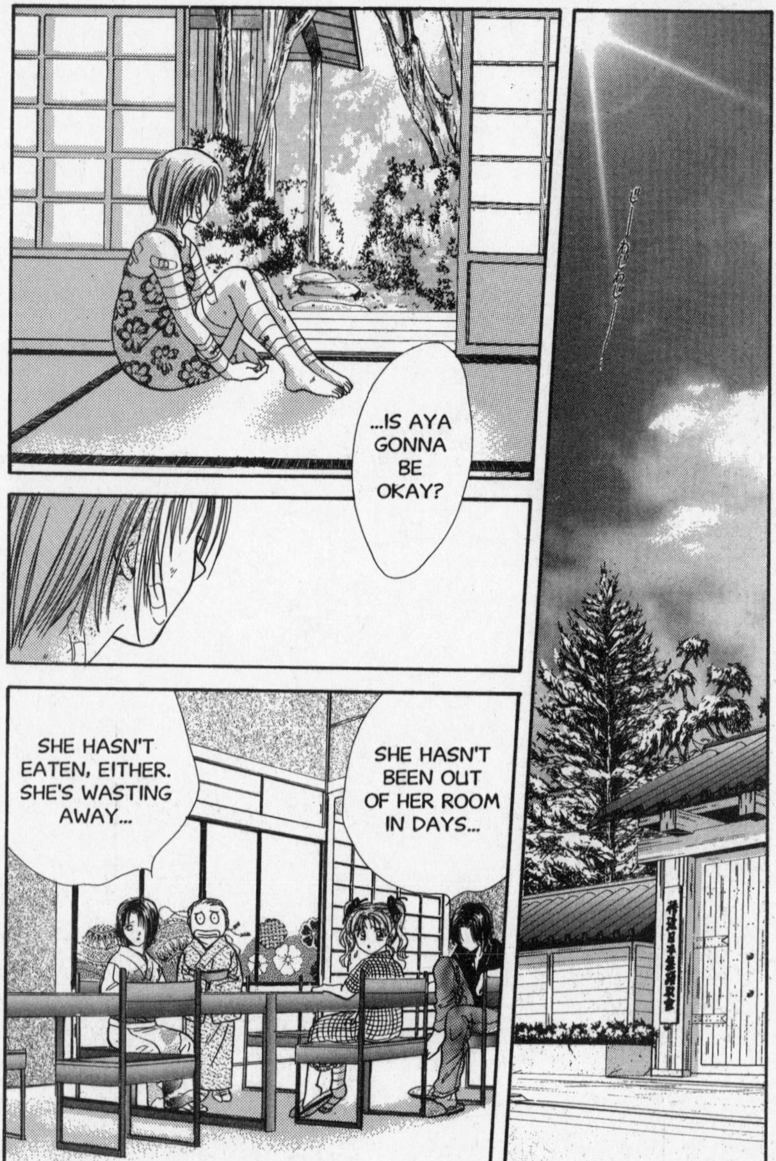
...IS AYA GONNA BE OKAY?
SHE HASN'T BEEN OUT OF HER ROOM IN DAYS...
SHE HASN'T EATEN, EITHER. SHE'S WASTING AWAY...

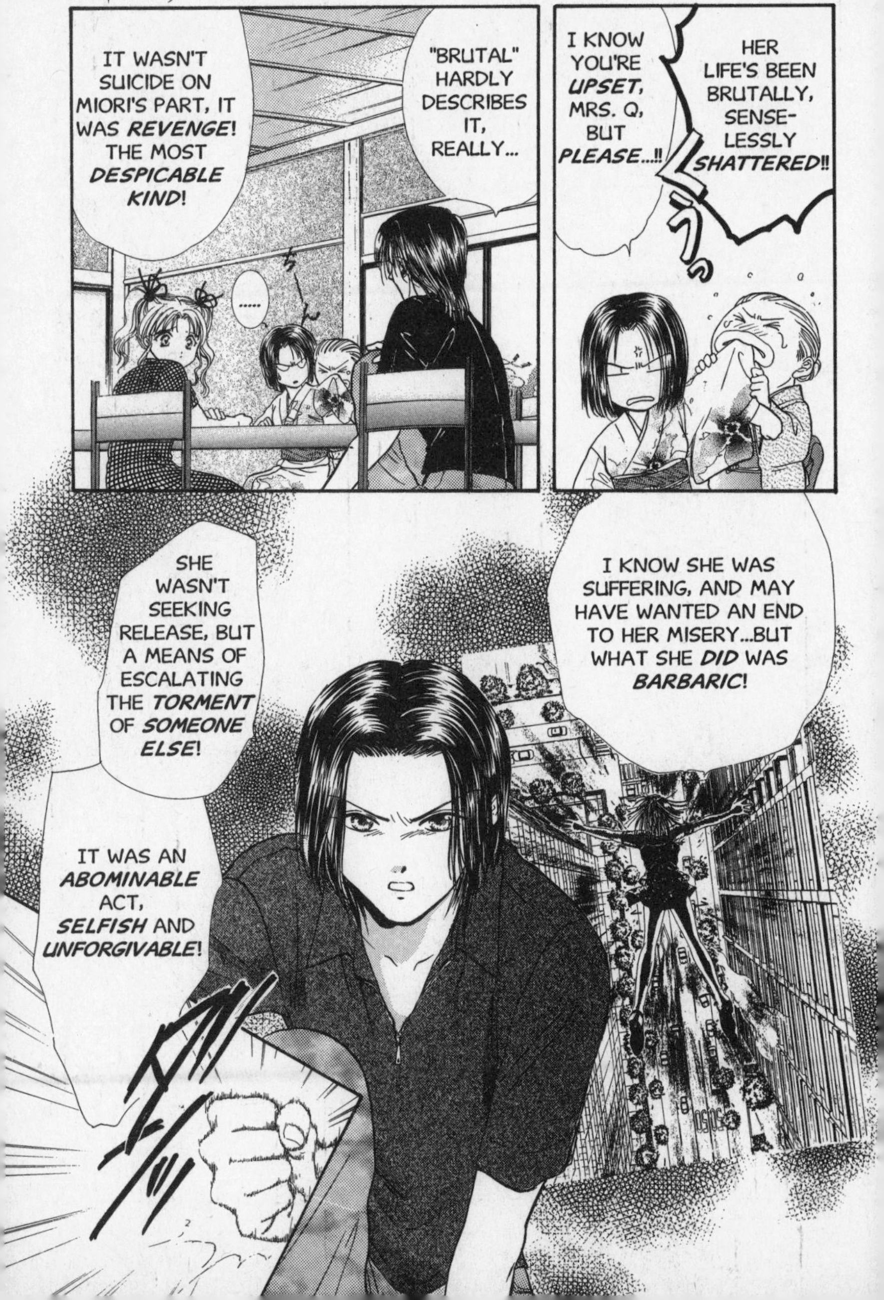
HER LIFE'S BEEN BRUTALLY, SENSE-LESSLY SHATTERED!!
I KNOW YOU'RE UPSET, MRS. Q, BUT PLEASE...!!
"BRUTAL" HARDLY DESCRIBES IT, REALLY...
IT WASN'T SUICIDE ON MIORI'S PART, IT WAS REVENGE! THE MOST DESPICABLE KIND!
......
I KNOW SHE WAS SUFFERING, AND MAY HAVE WANTED AN END TO HER MISERY...BUT WHAT SHE DID WAS BARBARIC!
SHE WASN'T SEEKING RELEASE, BUT A MEANS OF ESCALATING THE TORMENT OF SOMEONE ELSE!
IT WAS AN ABOMINABLE ACT, SELFISH AND UNFORGIVABLE!

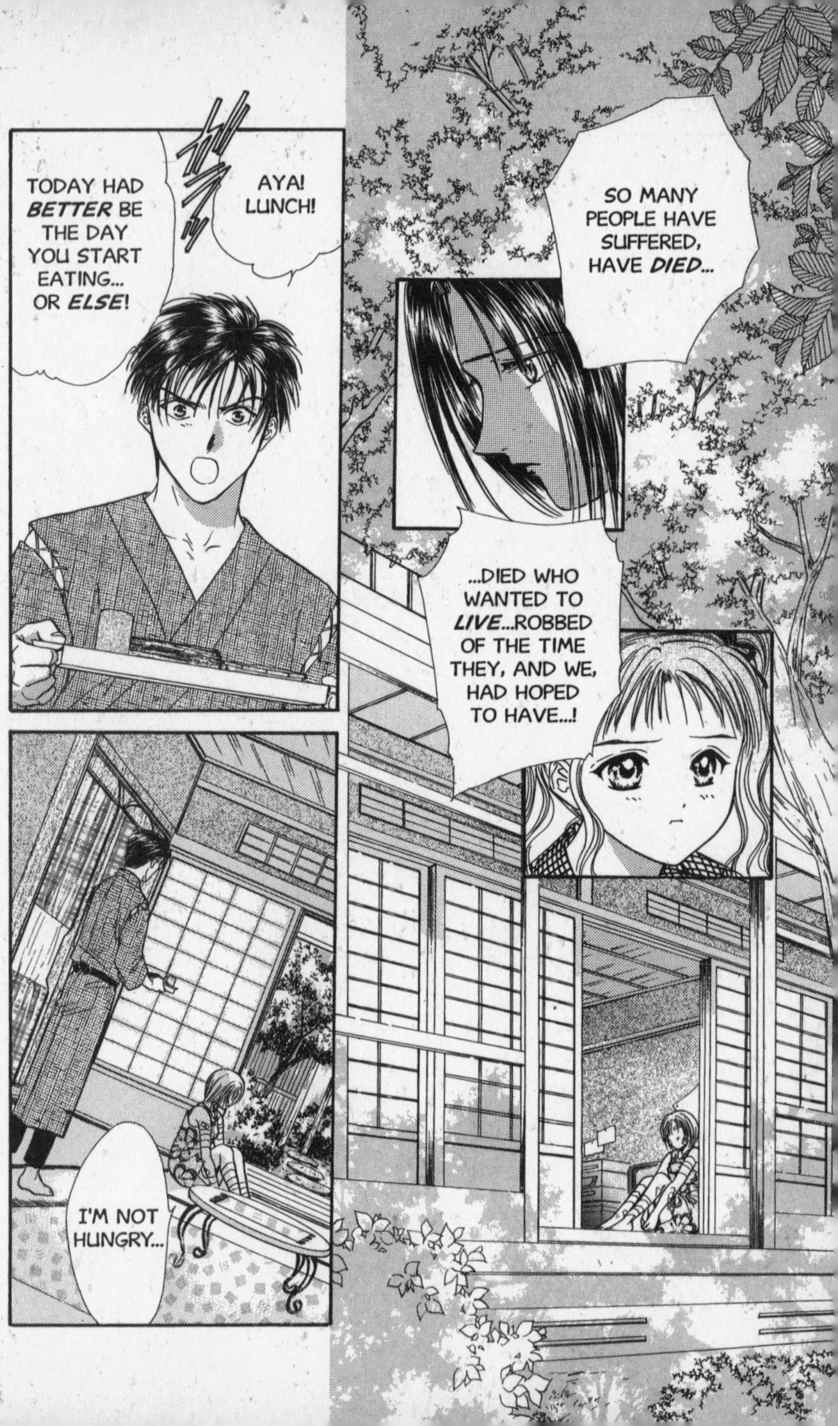
SO MANY PEOPLE HAVE SUFFERED, HAVE *DIED*...
...DIED WHO WANTED TO *LIVE*...ROBBED OF THE TIME THEY, AND WE, HAD HOPED TO HAVE...!
AYA! LUNCH!
TODAY HAD *BETTER* BE THE DAY YOU START EATING... OR *ELSE*!
I'M NOT HUNGRY...

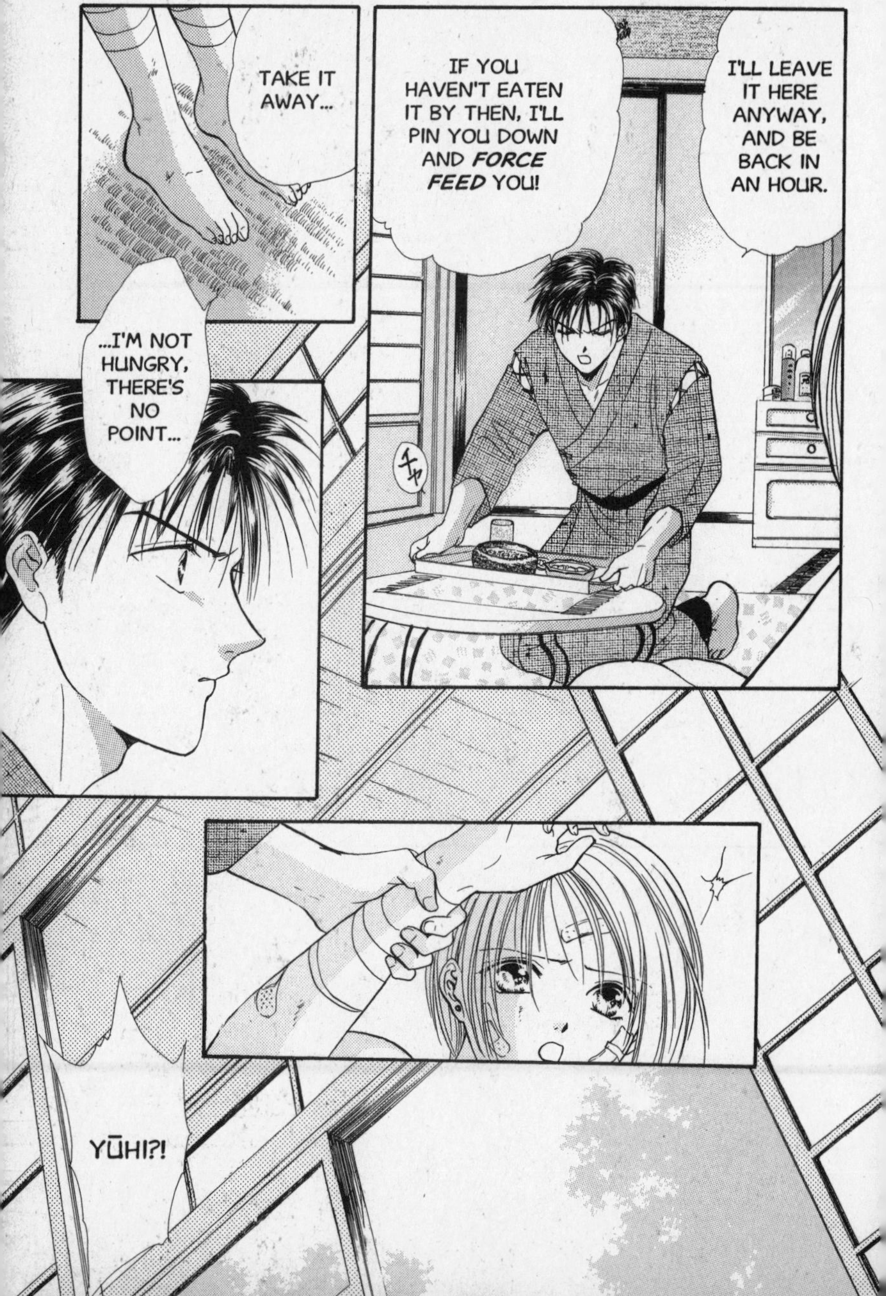
I'LL LEAVE IT HERE ANYWAY, AND BE BACK IN AN HOUR.
IF YOU HAVEN'T EATEN IT BY THEN, I'LL PIN YOU DOWN AND *FORCE FEED* YOU!
TAKE IT AWAY...
...I'M NOT HUNGRY, THERE'S NO POINT...
YŪHI?!

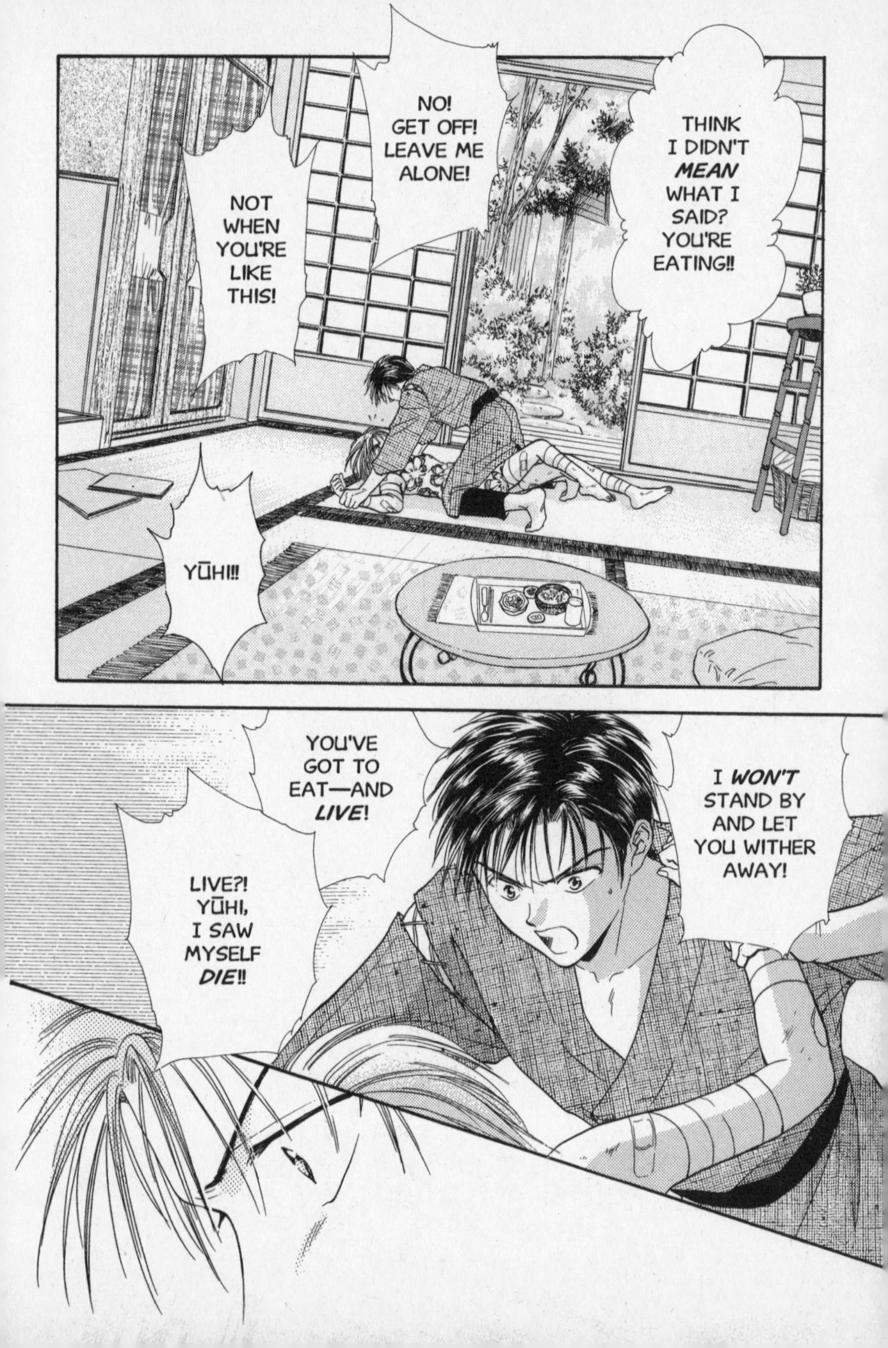
THINK I DIDN'T *MEAN* WHAT I SAID? YOU'RE EATING!!
NO! GET OFF! LEAVE ME ALONE!
NOT WHEN YOU'RE LIKE THIS!
YŪHI!!
I *WON'T* STAND BY AND LET YOU WITHER AWAY!
YOU'VE GOT TO EAT—AND *LIVE*!
LIVE?! YŪHI, I SAW MYSELF *DIE*!!

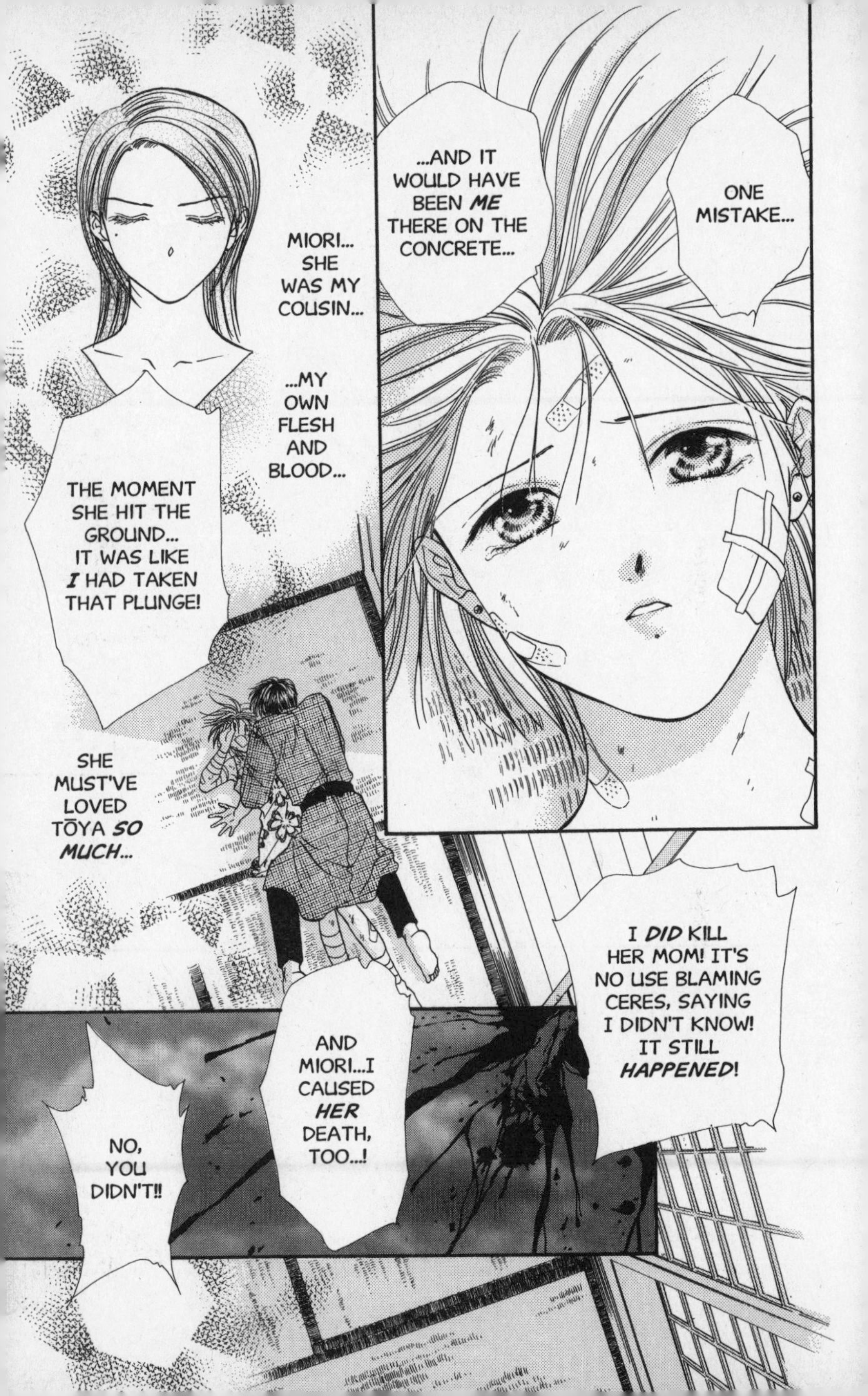
ONE MISTAKE...
...AND IT WOULD HAVE BEEN ME THERE ON THE CONCRETE...
MIORI... SHE WAS MY COUSIN...
...MY OWN FLESH AND BLOOD...
THE MOMENT SHE HIT THE GROUND... IT WAS LIKE I HAD TAKEN THAT PLUNGE!
SHE MUST'VE LOVED TŌYA SO MUCH...
I DID KILL HER MOM! IT'S NO USE BLAMING CERES, SAYING I DIDN'T KNOW! IT STILL HAPPENED!
AND MIORI...I CAUSED HER DEATH, TOO...!
NO, YOU DIDN'T!!

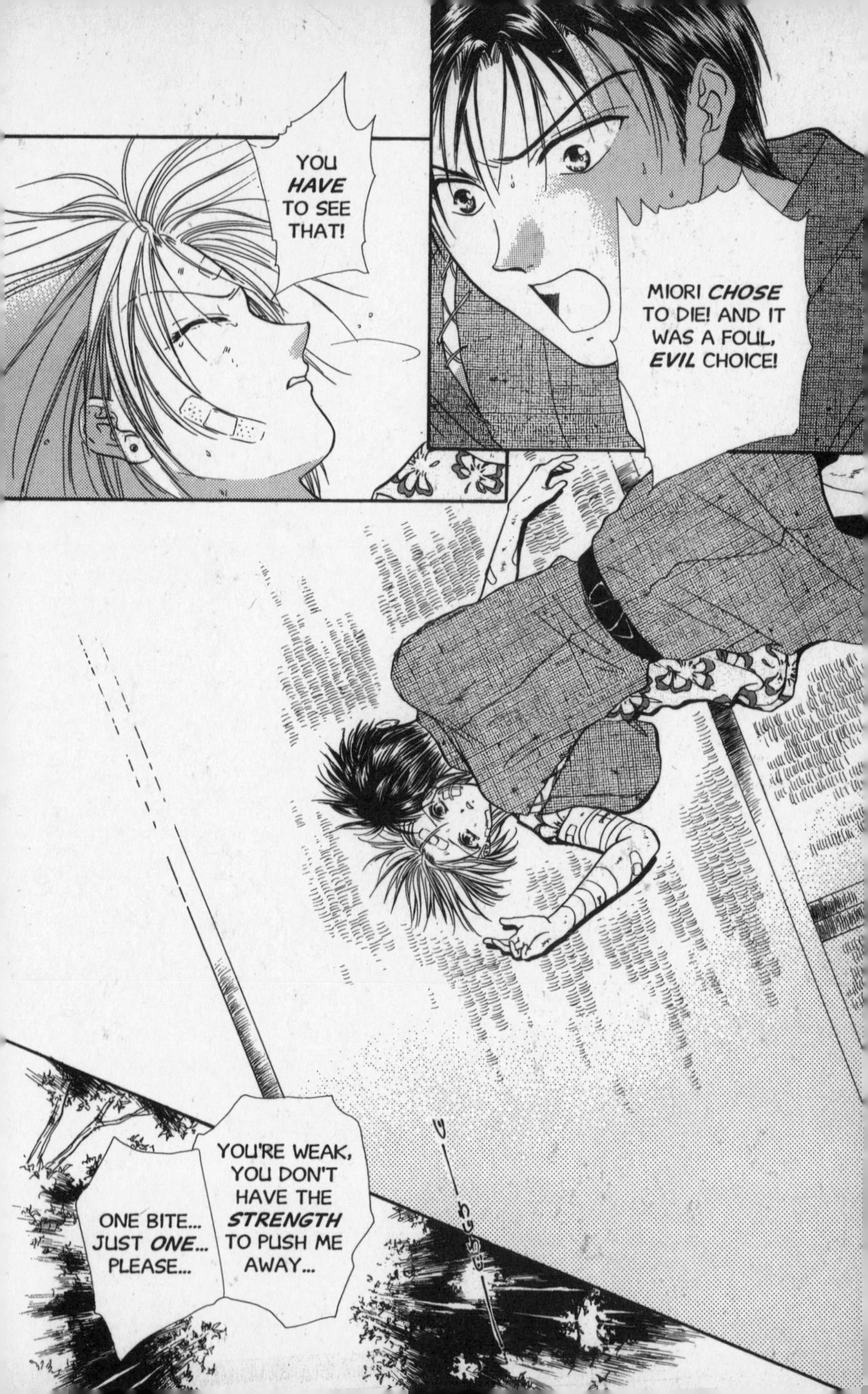
MIORI *CHOSE* TO DIE! AND IT WAS A FOUL, *EVIL* CHOICE!
YOU *HAVE* TO SEE THAT!
YOU'RE WEAK, YOU DON'T HAVE THE *STRENGTH* TO PUSH ME AWAY...
ONE BITE... JUST *ONE*... PLEASE...

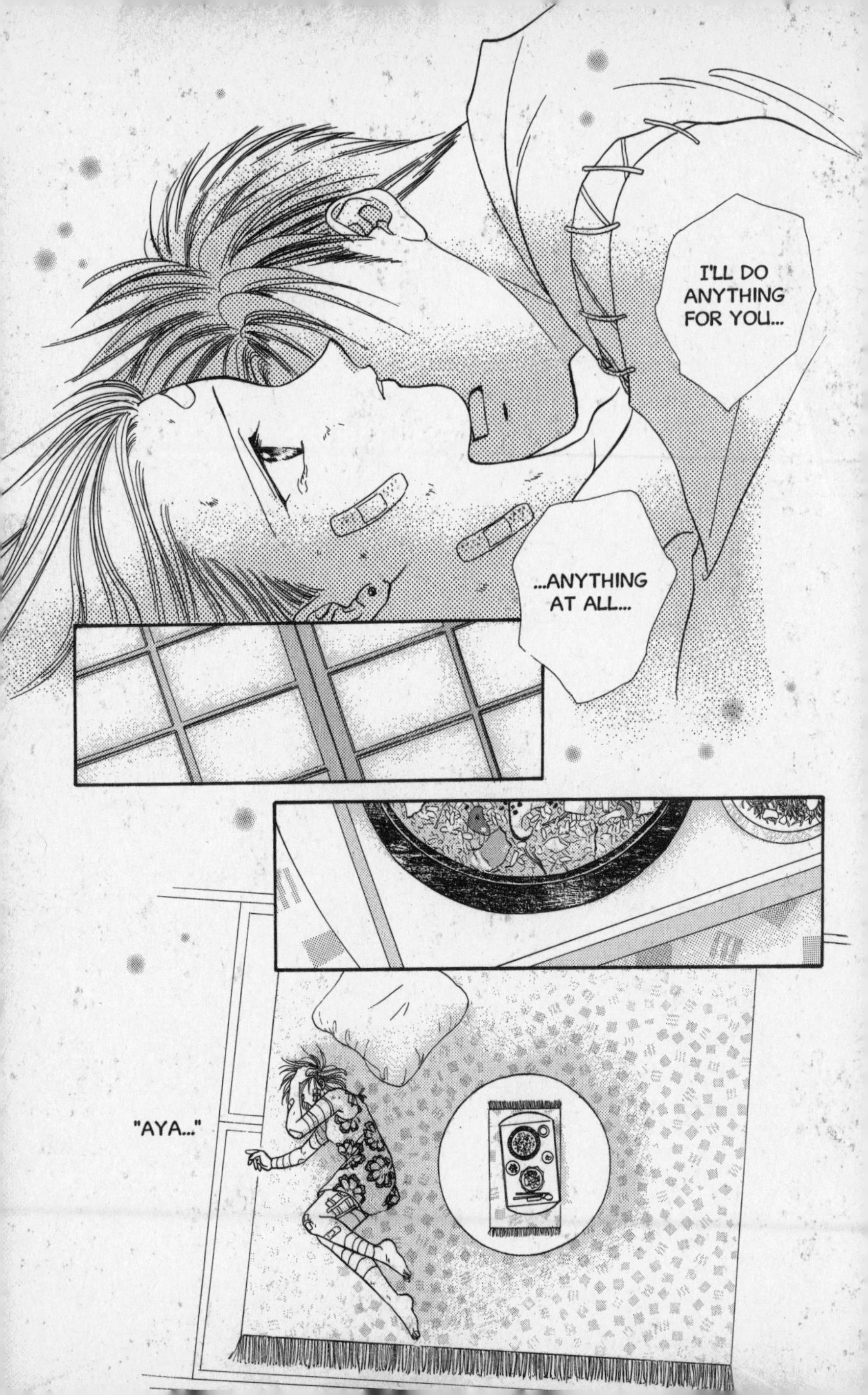
I'LL DO ANYTHING FOR YOU...
...ANYTHING AT ALL...
"AYA..."

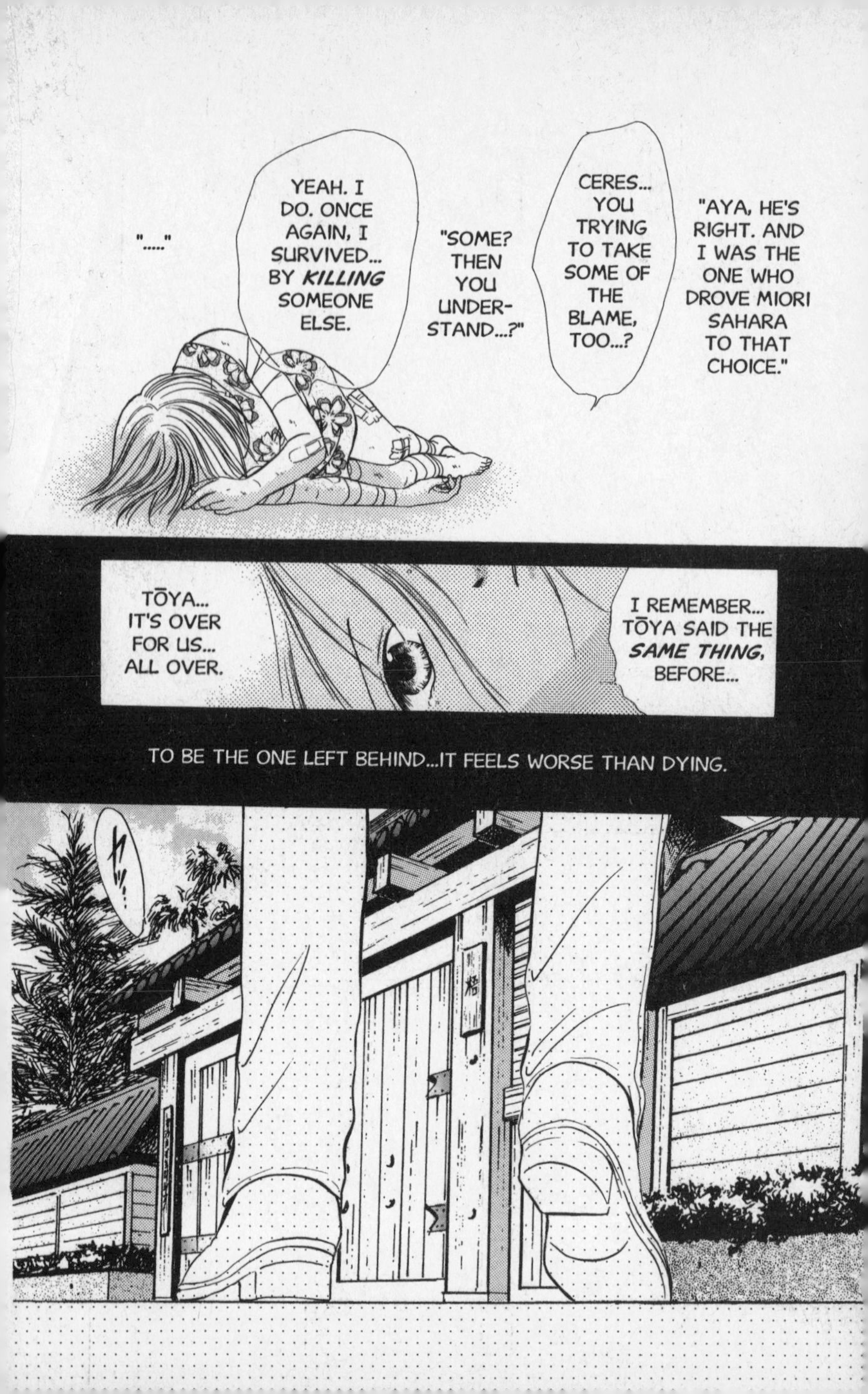
"AYA, HE'S RIGHT. AND I WAS THE ONE WHO DROVE MIORI SAHARA TO THAT CHOICE."
CERES... YOU TRYING TO TAKE SOME OF THE BLAME, TOO...?
"SOME? THEN YOU UNDERSTAND...?"
YEAH. I DO. ONCE AGAIN, I SURVIVED... BY *KILLING* SOMEONE ELSE.
"....."
I REMEMBER... TŌYA SAID THE *SAME THING*, BEFORE...
TŌYA... IT'S OVER FOR US... ALL OVER.
TO BE THE ONE LEFT BEHIND...IT FEELS WORSE THAN DYING.

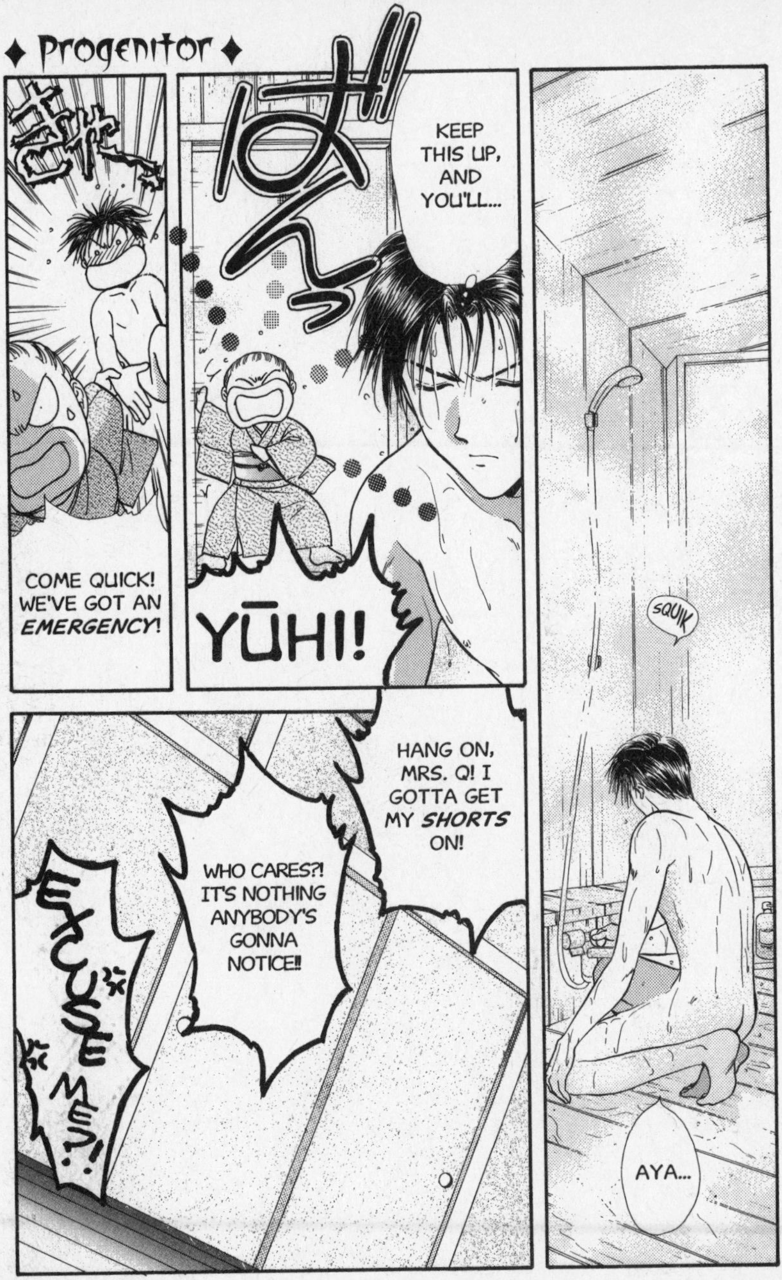
SQUIK
AYA...
KEEP THIS UP, AND YOU'LL...
YŪHI!
COME QUICK! WE'VE GOT AN *EMERGENCY*!
HANG ON, MRS. Q! I GOTTA GET MY *SHORTS* ON!
WHO CARES?! IT'S NOTHING ANYBODY'S GONNA NOTICE!!
EXCUSE ME?!

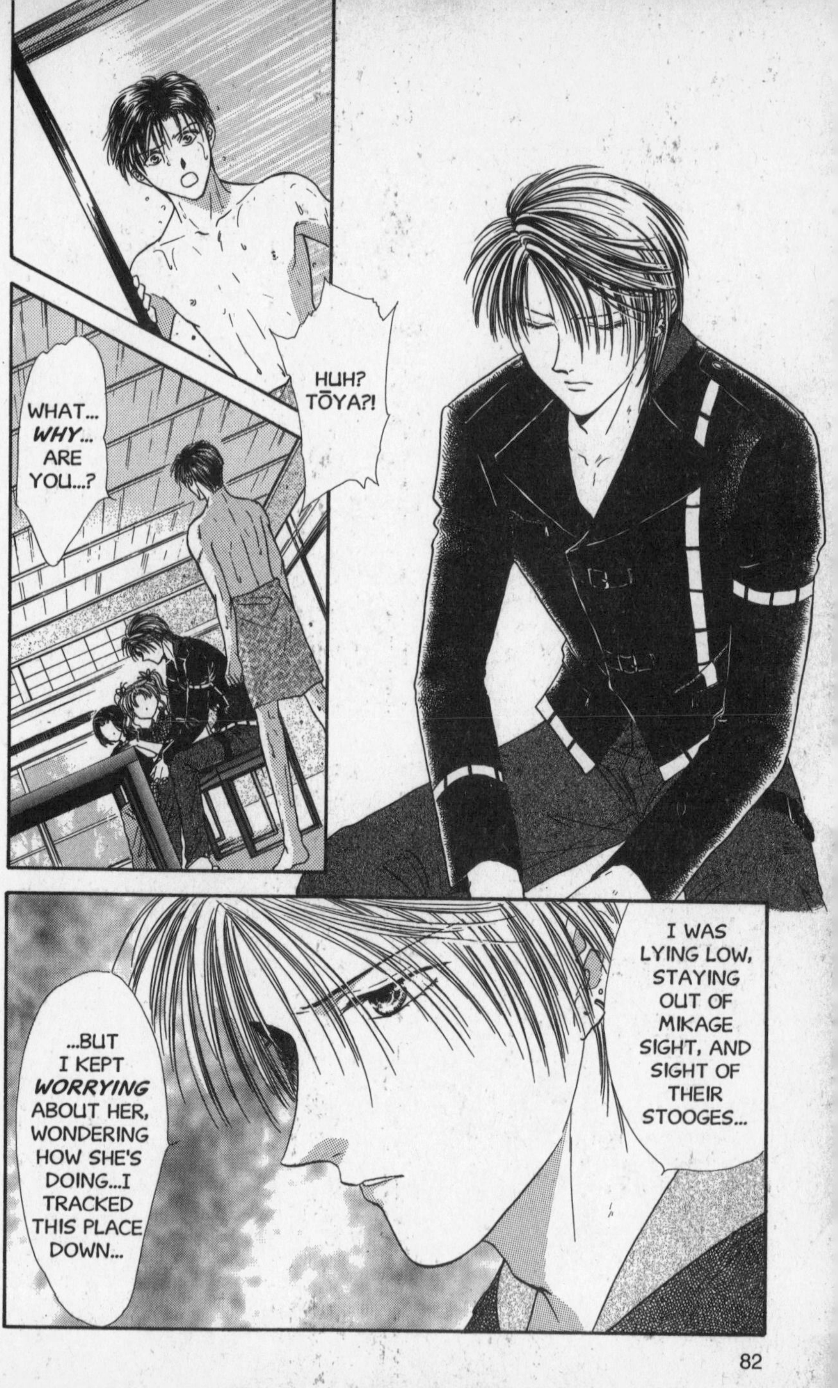
HUH? TŌYA?!
WHAT... *WHY*... ARE YOU...?
I WAS LYING LOW, STAYING OUT OF MIKAGE SIGHT, AND SIGHT OF THEIR STOOGES...
...BUT I KEPT *WORRYING* ABOUT HER, WONDERING HOW SHE'S DOING...I TRACKED THIS PLACE DOWN...

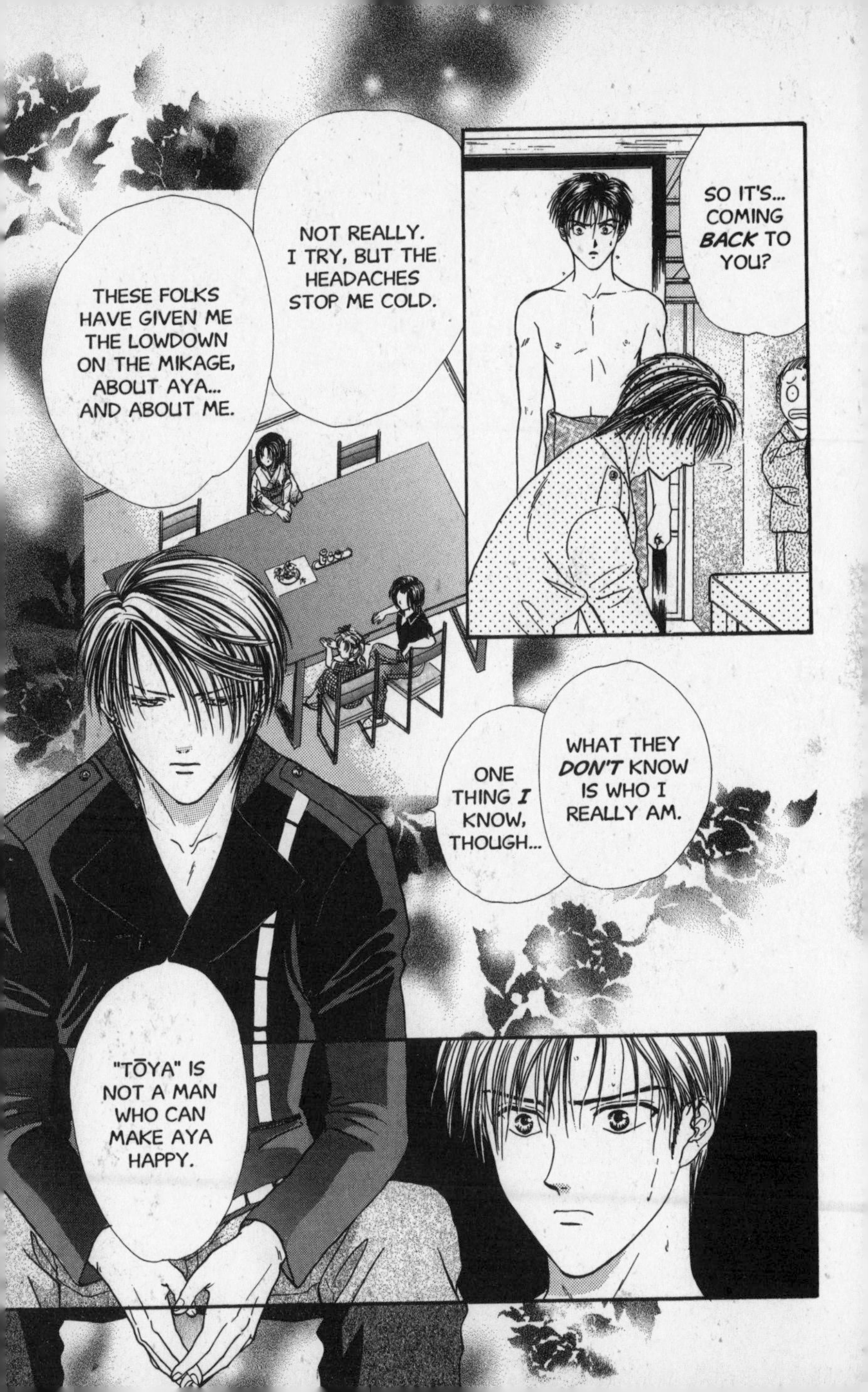
SO IT'S... COMING BACK TO YOU?
NOT REALLY. I TRY, BUT THE HEADACHES STOP ME COLD.
THESE FOLKS HAVE GIVEN ME THE LOWDOWN ON THE MIKAGE, ABOUT AYA... AND ABOUT ME.
WHAT THEY DON'T KNOW IS WHO I REALLY AM.
ONE THING I KNOW, THOUGH...
"TŌYA" IS NOT A MAN WHO CAN MAKE AYA HAPPY.

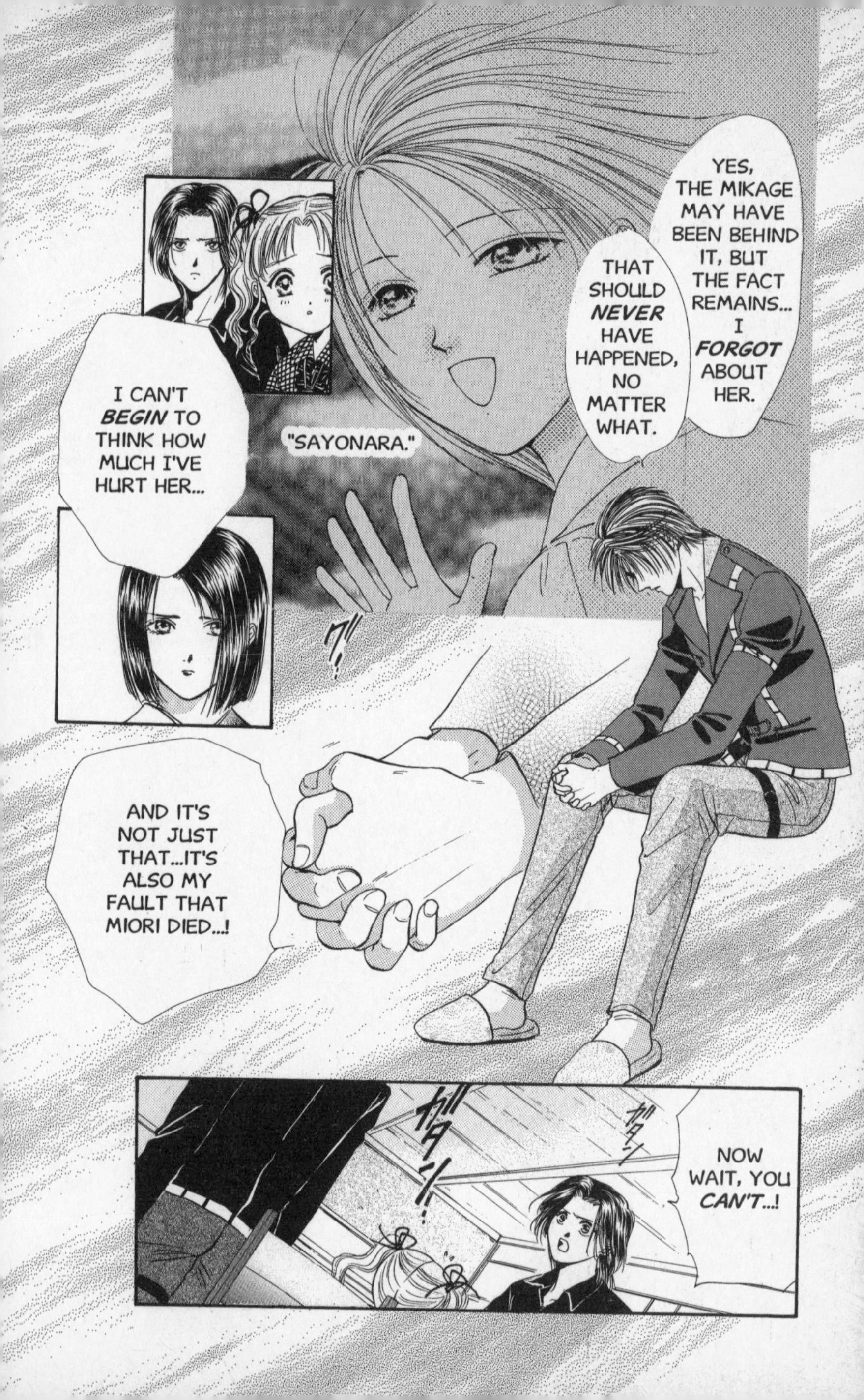
YES, THE MIKAGE MAY HAVE BEEN BEHIND IT, BUT THE FACT REMAINS... I *FORGOT* ABOUT HER.
THAT SHOULD *NEVER* HAVE HAPPENED, NO MATTER WHAT.
"SAYONARA."
I CAN'T *BEGIN* TO THINK HOW MUCH I'VE HURT HER...
AND IT'S NOT JUST THAT...IT'S ALSO MY FAULT THAT MIORI DIED...!
NOW WAIT, YOU *CAN'T*...!

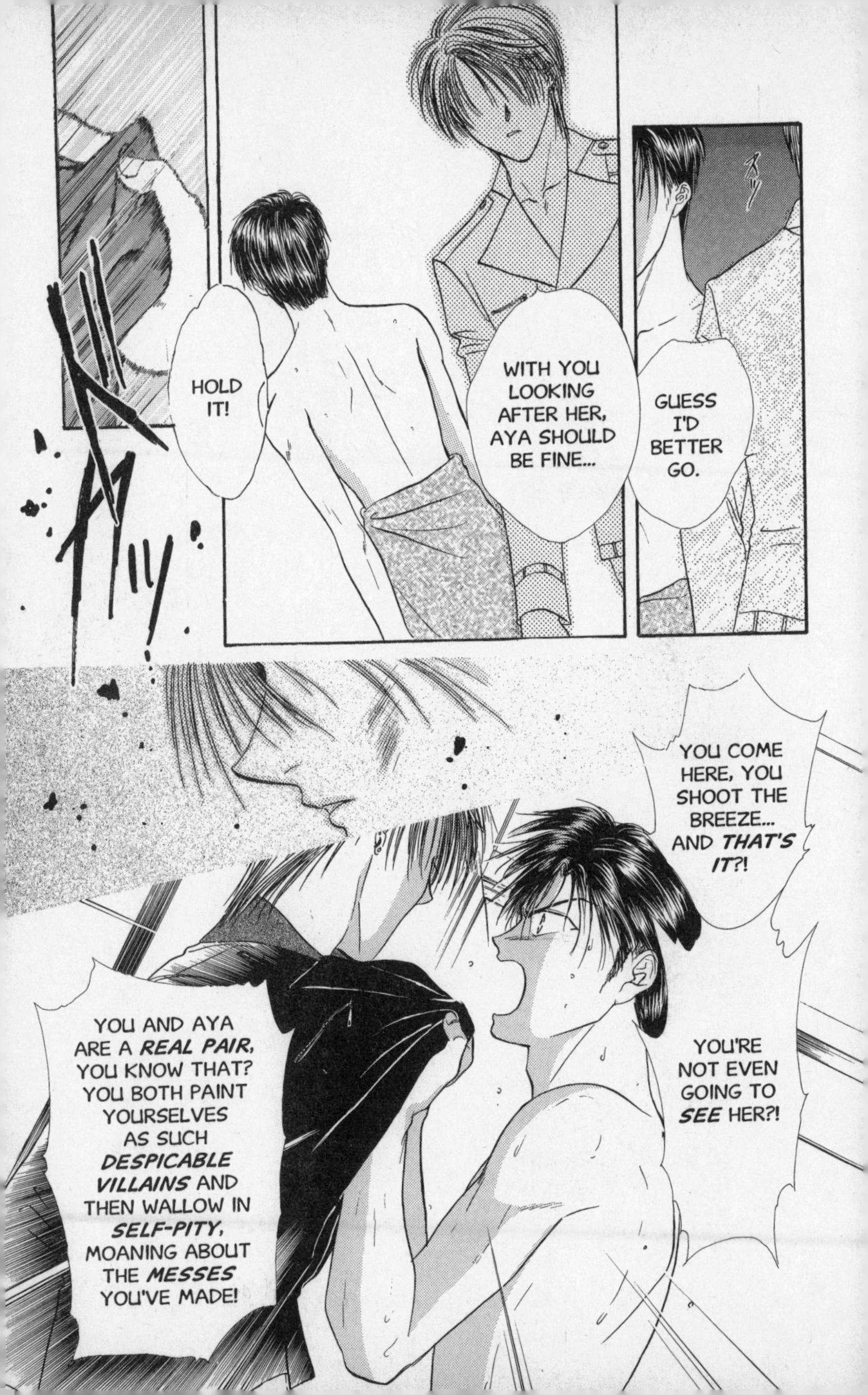
GUESS I'D BETTER GO.
WITH YOU LOOKING AFTER HER, AYA SHOULD BE FINE...
HOLD IT!
YOU COME HERE, YOU SHOOT THE BREEZE... AND *THAT'S IT*?!
YOU'RE NOT EVEN GOING TO *SEE* HER?!
YOU AND AYA ARE A *REAL PAIR*, YOU KNOW THAT? YOU BOTH PAINT YOURSELVES AS SUCH *DESPICABLE VILLAINS* AND THEN WALLOW IN *SELF-PITY*, MOANING ABOUT THE *MESSES* YOU'VE MADE!

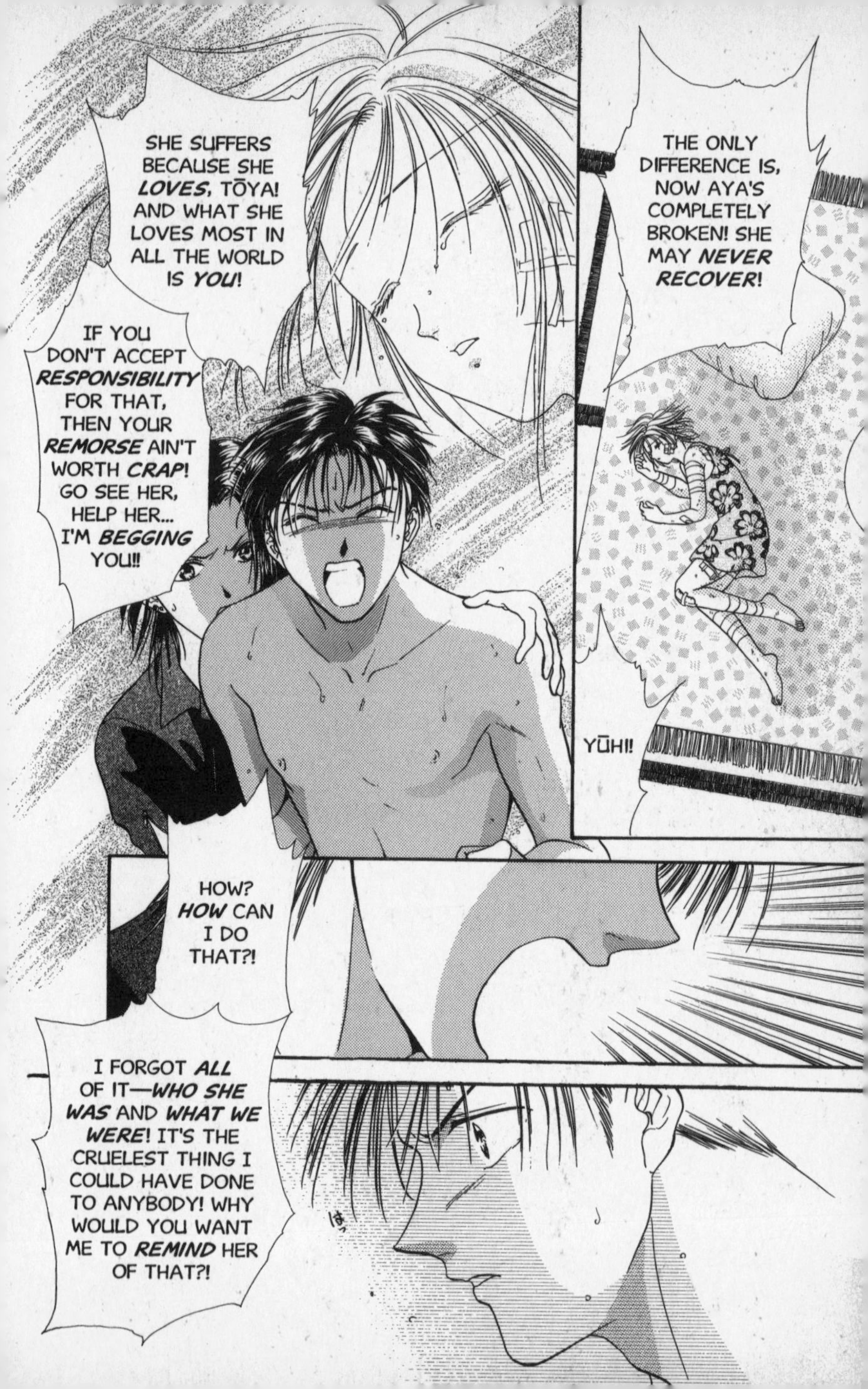
THE ONLY DIFFERENCE IS, NOW AYA'S COMPLETELY BROKEN! SHE MAY *NEVER RECOVER*!
YŪHI!
SHE SUFFERS BECAUSE SHE *LOVES*, TŌYA! AND WHAT SHE LOVES MOST IN ALL THE WORLD IS *YOU*!
IF YOU DON'T ACCEPT *RESPONSIBILITY* FOR THAT, THEN YOUR *REMORSE* AIN'T WORTH *CRAP*! GO SEE HER, HELP HER... I'M *BEGGING* YOU!!
HOW? *HOW* CAN I DO THAT?!
I FORGOT *ALL* OF IT—*WHO SHE WAS* AND *WHAT WE WERE*! IT'S THE CRUELEST THING I COULD HAVE DONE TO ANYBODY! WHY WOULD YOU WANT ME TO *REMIND* HER OF THAT?!
はっ

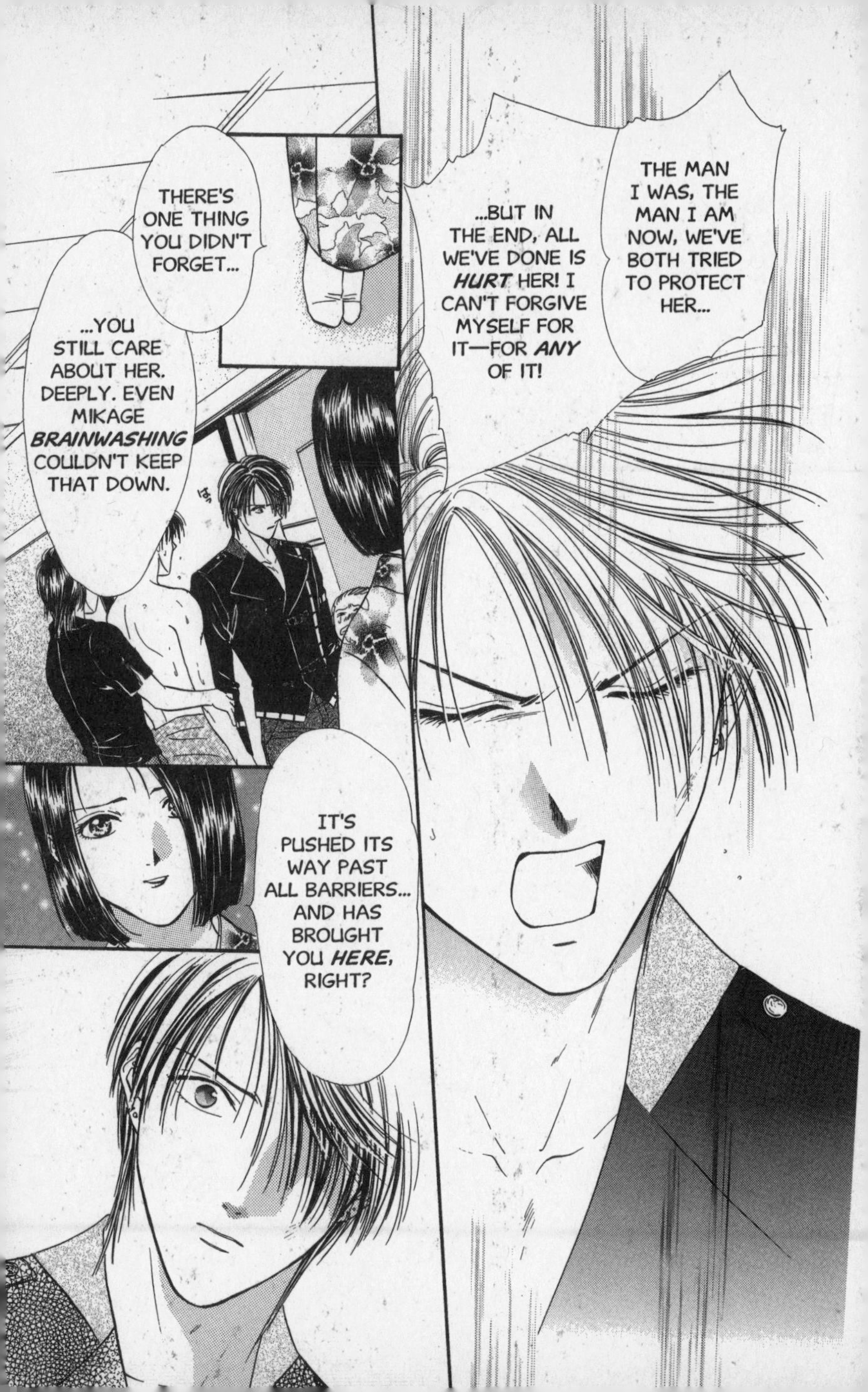
THE MAN I WAS, THE MAN I AM NOW, WE'VE BOTH TRIED TO PROTECT HER...
...BUT IN THE END, ALL WE'VE DONE IS *HURT* HER! I CAN'T FORGIVE MYSELF FOR IT—FOR *ANY* OF IT!
THERE'S ONE THING YOU DIDN'T FORGET...
...YOU STILL CARE ABOUT HER. DEEPLY. EVEN MIKAGE *BRAINWASHING* COULDN'T KEEP THAT DOWN.
IT'S PUSHED ITS WAY PAST ALL BARRIERS... AND HAS BROUGHT YOU *HERE*, RIGHT?

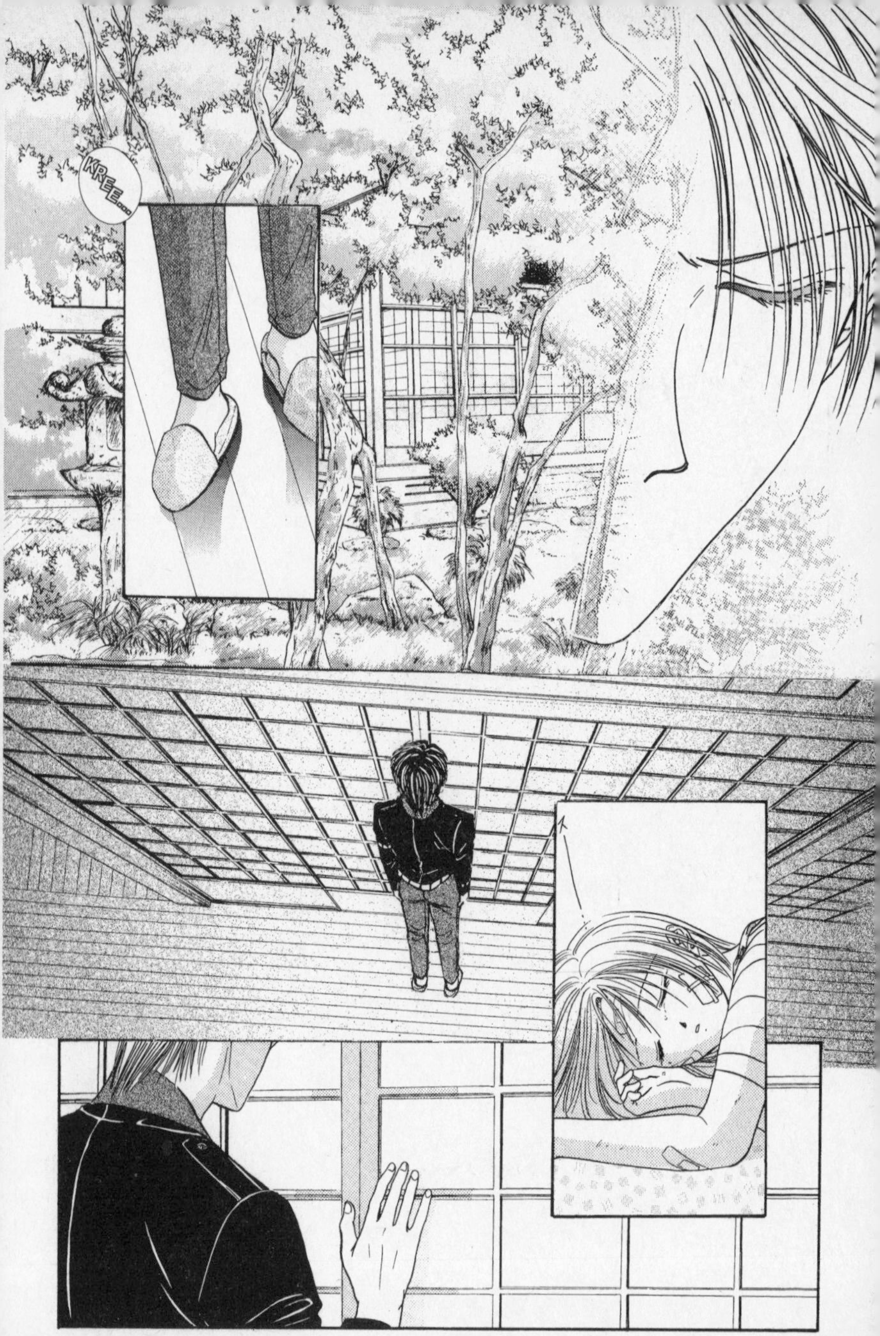
KREE...

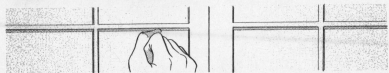

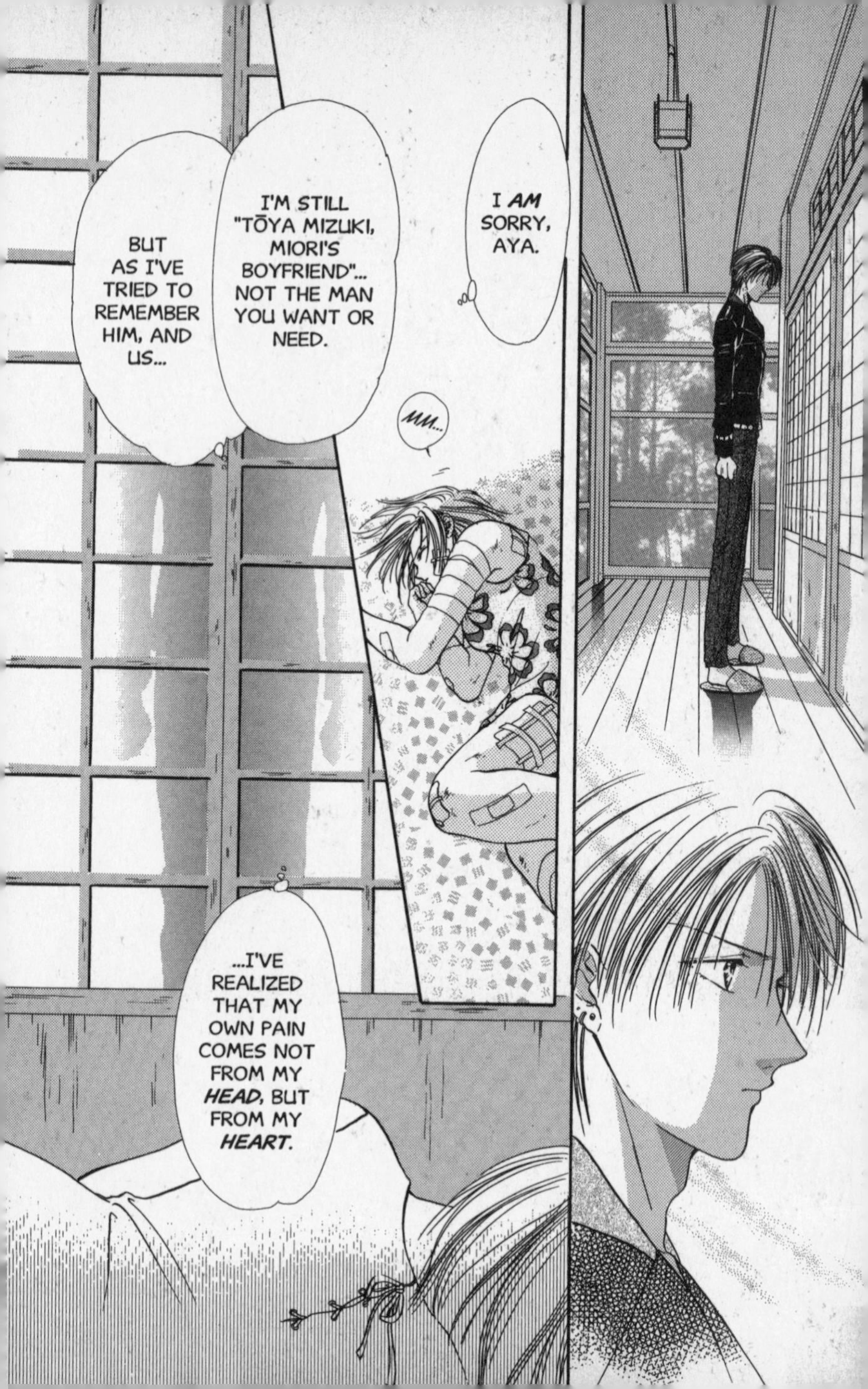
I *AM* SORRY, AYA.
I'M STILL "TŌYA MIZUKI, MIORI'S BOYFRIEND"... NOT THE MAN YOU WANT OR NEED.
BUT AS I'VE TRIED TO REMEMBER HIM, AND US...
MM...
...I'VE REALIZED THAT MY OWN PAIN COMES NOT FROM MY *HEAD*, BUT FROM MY *HEART*.

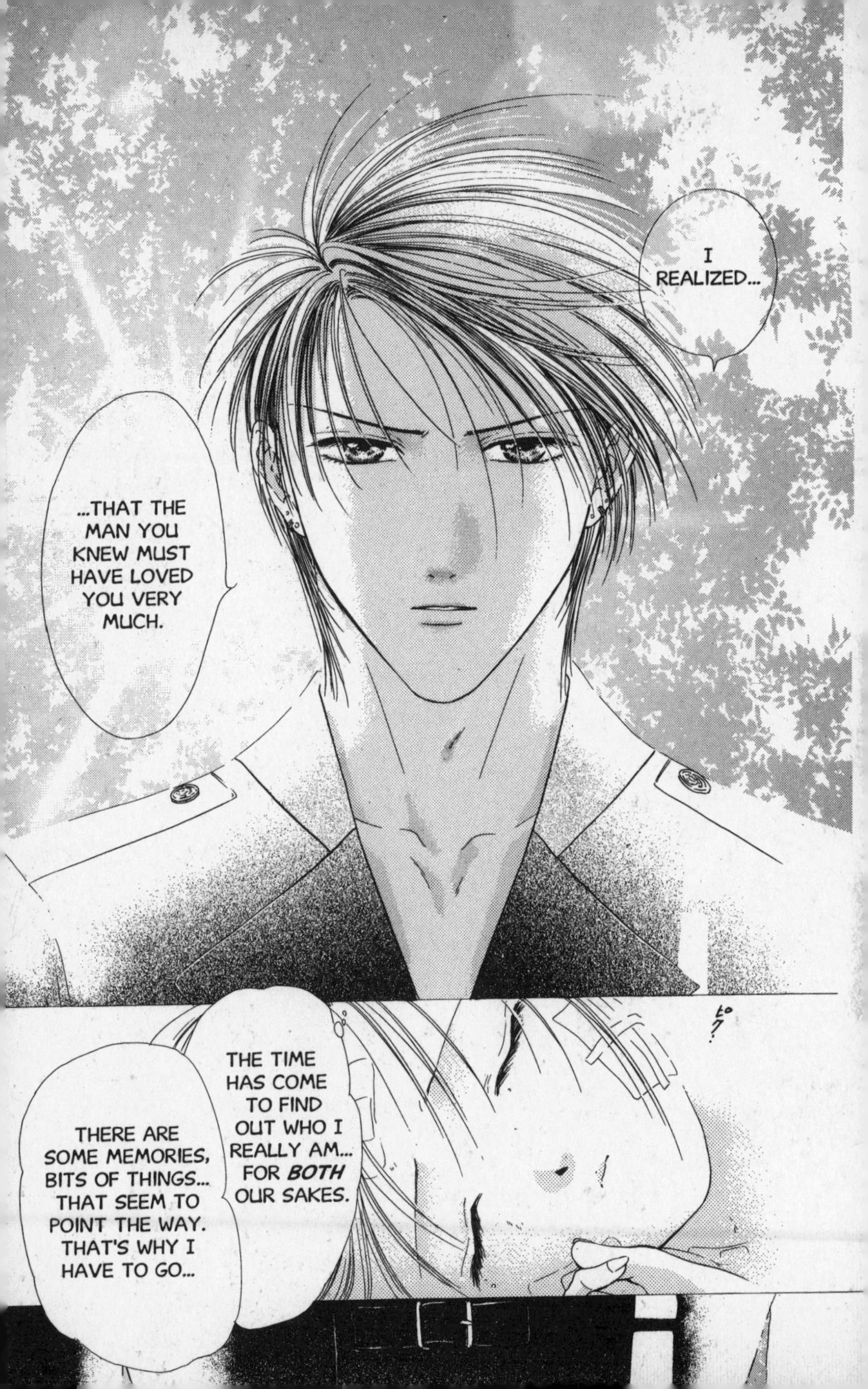
I REALIZED...
...THAT THE MAN YOU KNEW MUST HAVE LOVED YOU VERY MUCH.
THE TIME HAS COME TO FIND OUT WHO I REALLY AM... FOR *BOTH* OUR SAKES.
THERE ARE SOME MEMORIES, BITS OF THINGS... THAT SEEM TO POINT THE WAY. THAT'S WHY I HAVE TO GO...

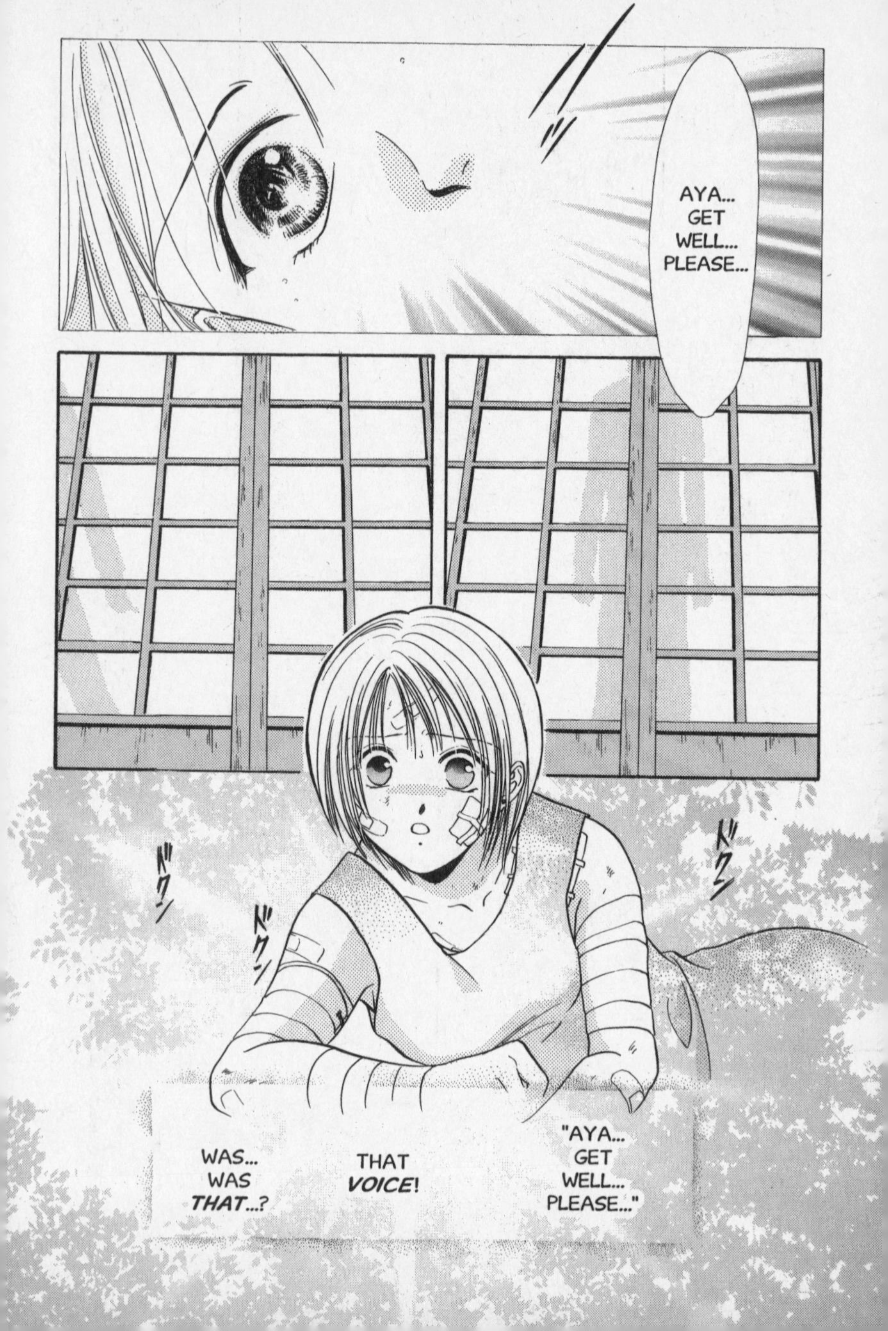
AYA... GET WELL... PLEASE...
ドクン
ドクン
ドクン
"AYA... GET WELL... PLEASE..."
THAT *VOICE*!
WAS... WAS *THAT*...?

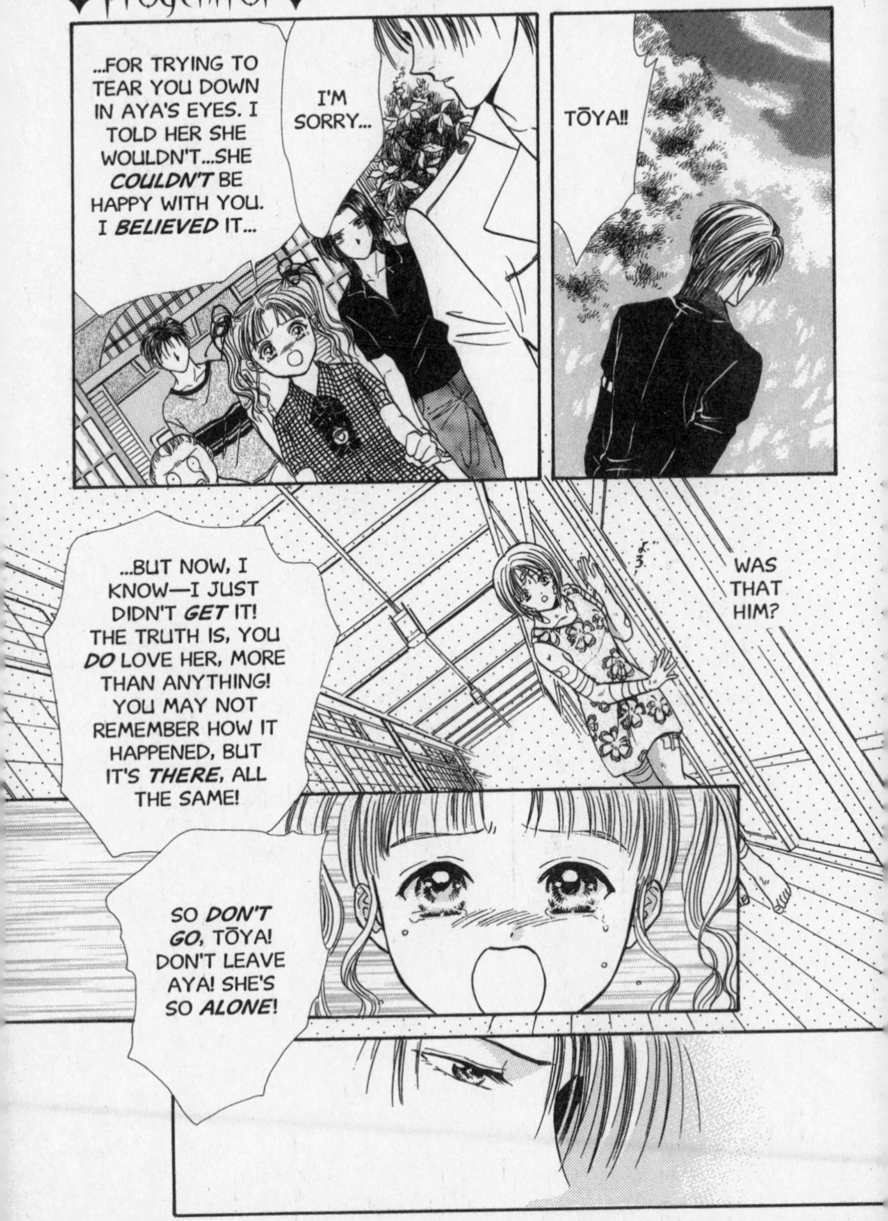
TŌYA!!
I'M SORRY...
...FOR TRYING TO TEAR YOU DOWN IN AYA'S EYES. I TOLD HER SHE WOULDN'T...SHE COULDN'T BE HAPPY WITH YOU. I BELIEVED IT...
WAS THAT HIM?
...BUT NOW, I KNOW—I JUST DIDN'T GET IT! THE TRUTH IS, YOU DO LOVE HER, MORE THAN ANYTHING! YOU MAY NOT REMEMBER HOW IT HAPPENED, BUT IT'S THERE, ALL THE SAME!
SO DON'T GO, TŌYA! DON'T LEAVE AYA! SHE'S SO ALONE!

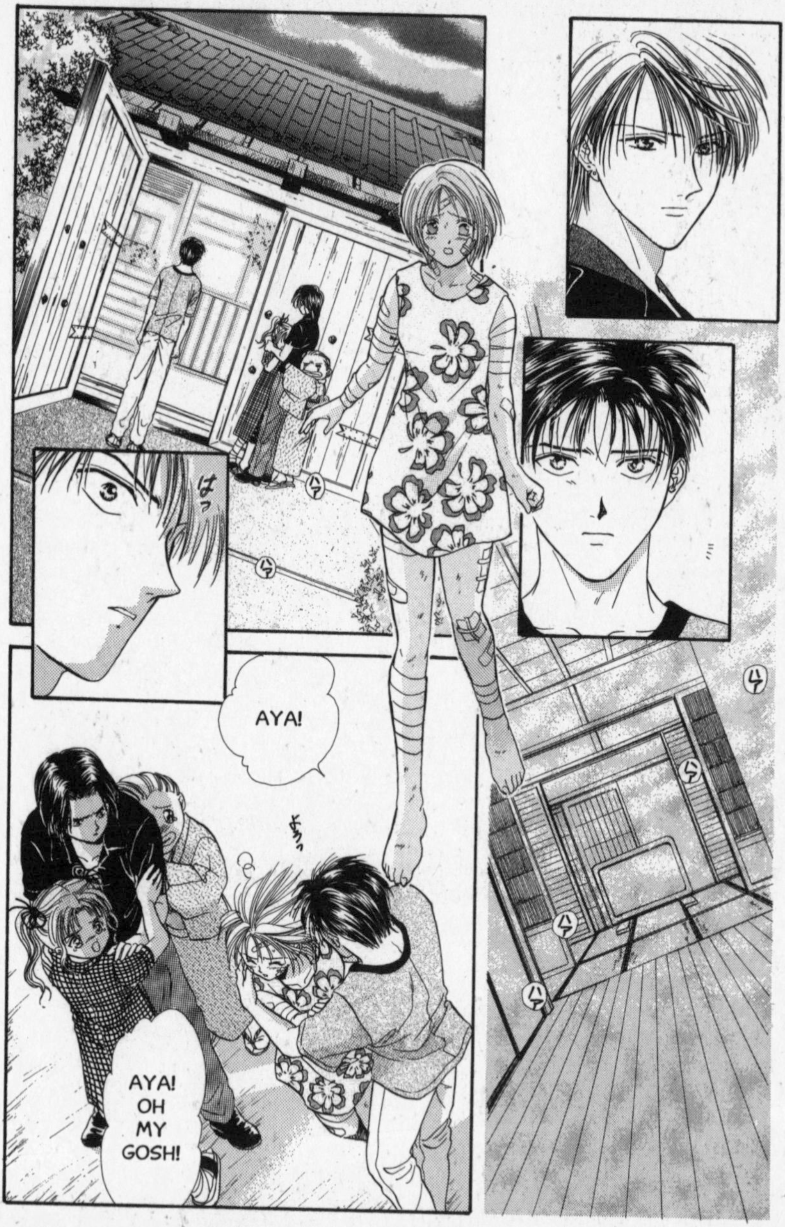
はっ
AYA!
よろっ
AYA! OH MY GOSH!

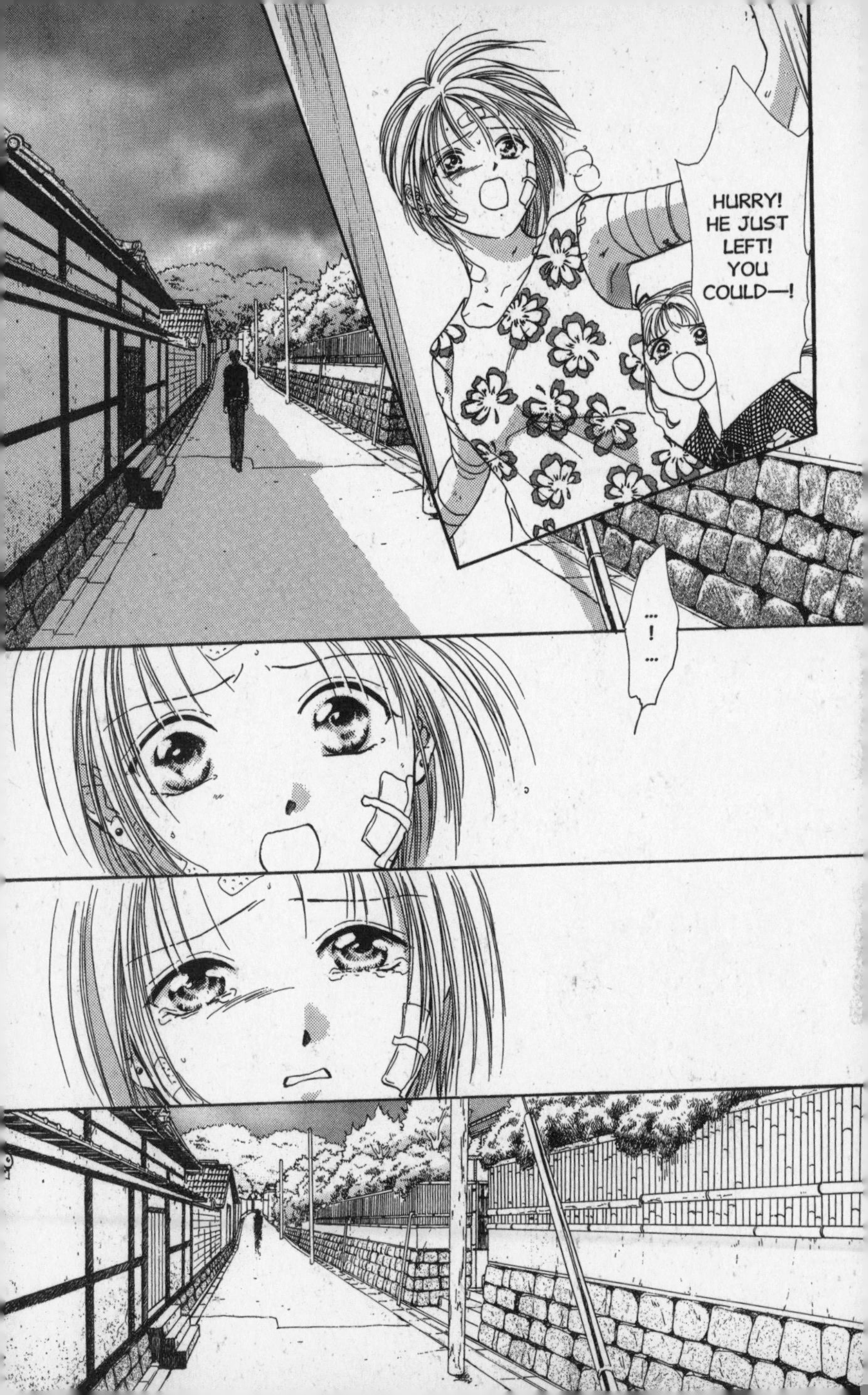
HURRY! HE JUST LEFT! YOU COULD—!
...!...

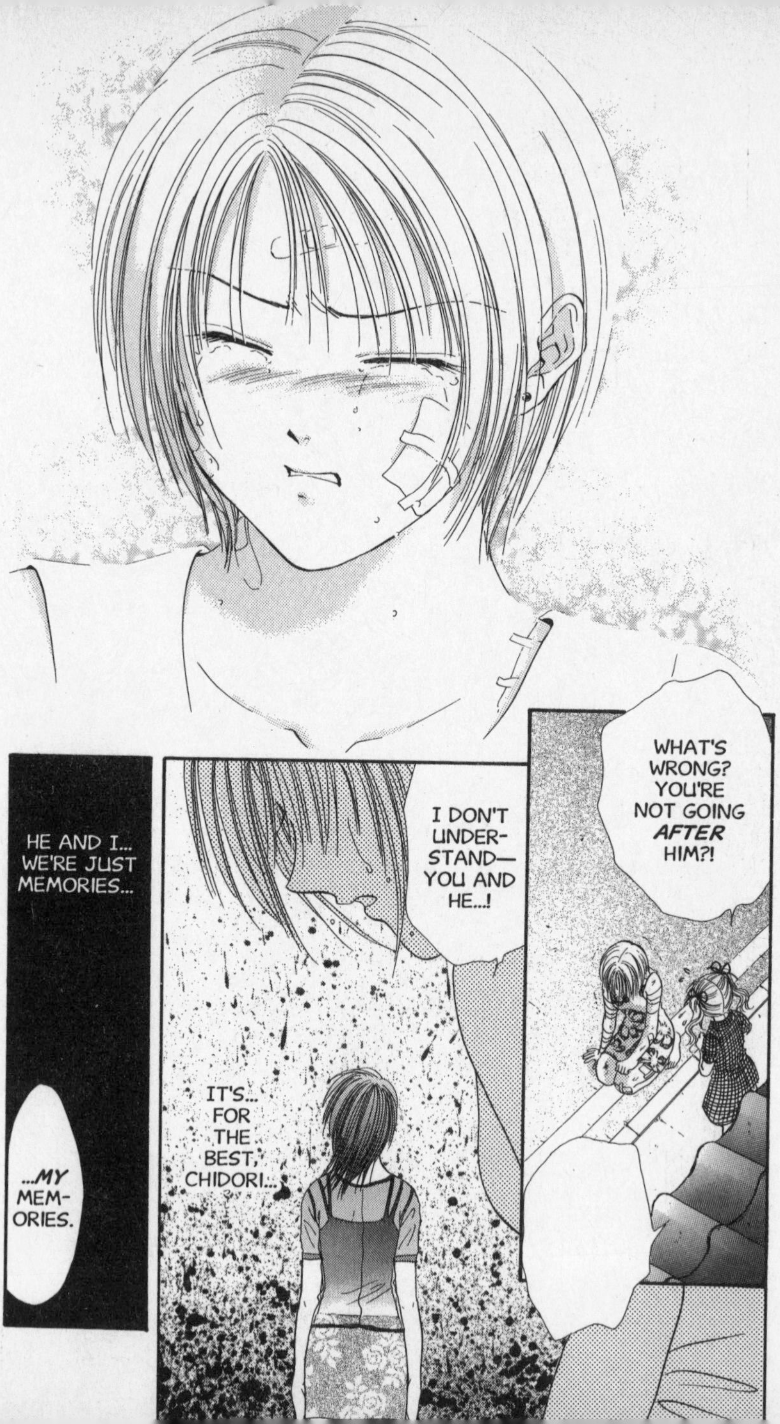
WHAT'S WRONG? YOU'RE NOT GOING *AFTER* HIM?!
I DON'T UNDER-STAND— YOU AND HE...!
IT'S... FOR THE BEST, CHIDORI...
HE AND I... WE'RE JUST MEMORIES...
...MY MEM-ORIES.

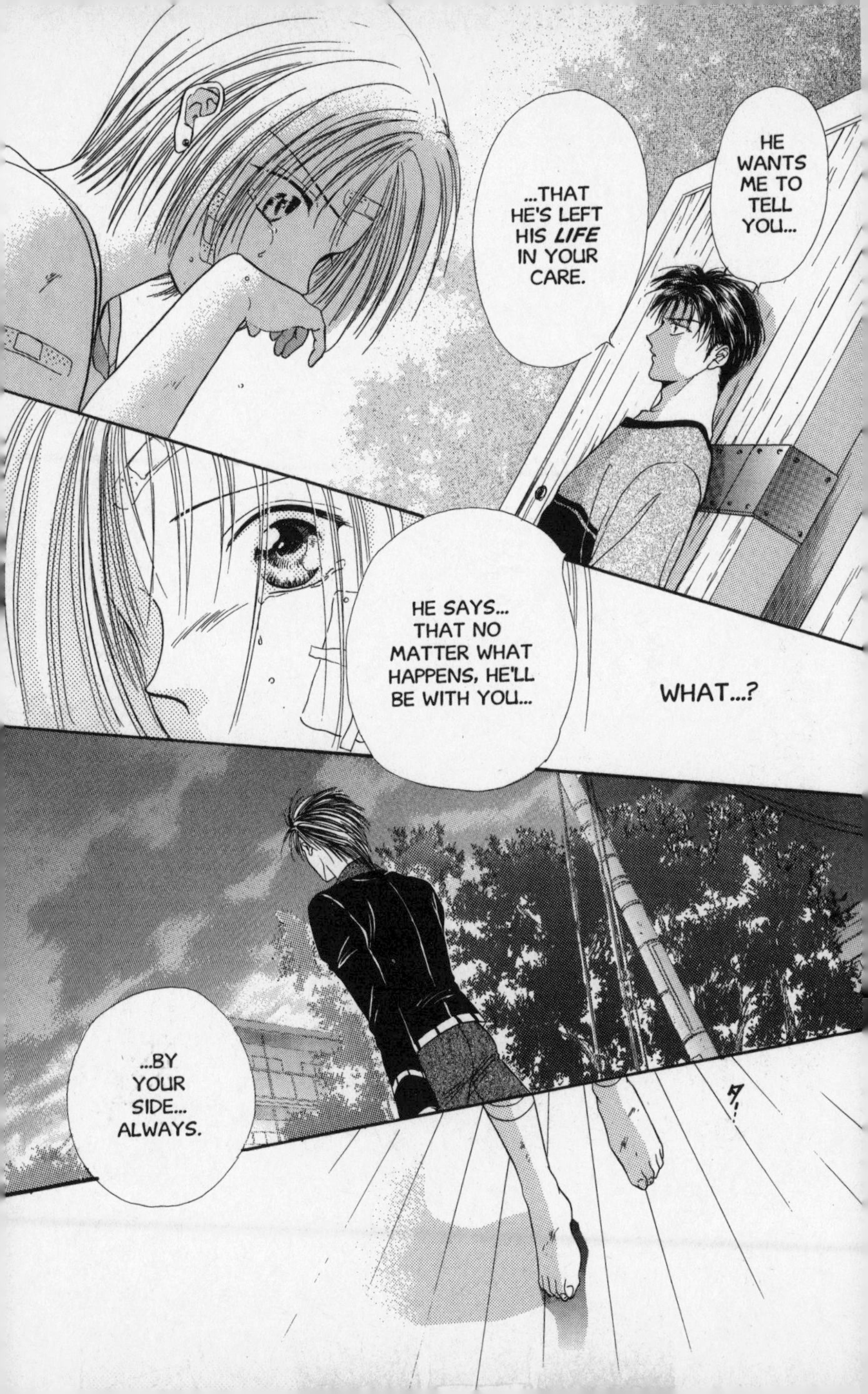
HE WANTS ME TO TELL YOU...
...THAT HE'S LEFT HIS *LIFE* IN YOUR CARE.
WHAT...?
HE SAYS... THAT NO MATTER WHAT HAPPENS, HE'LL BE WITH YOU...
...BY YOUR SIDE... ALWAYS.

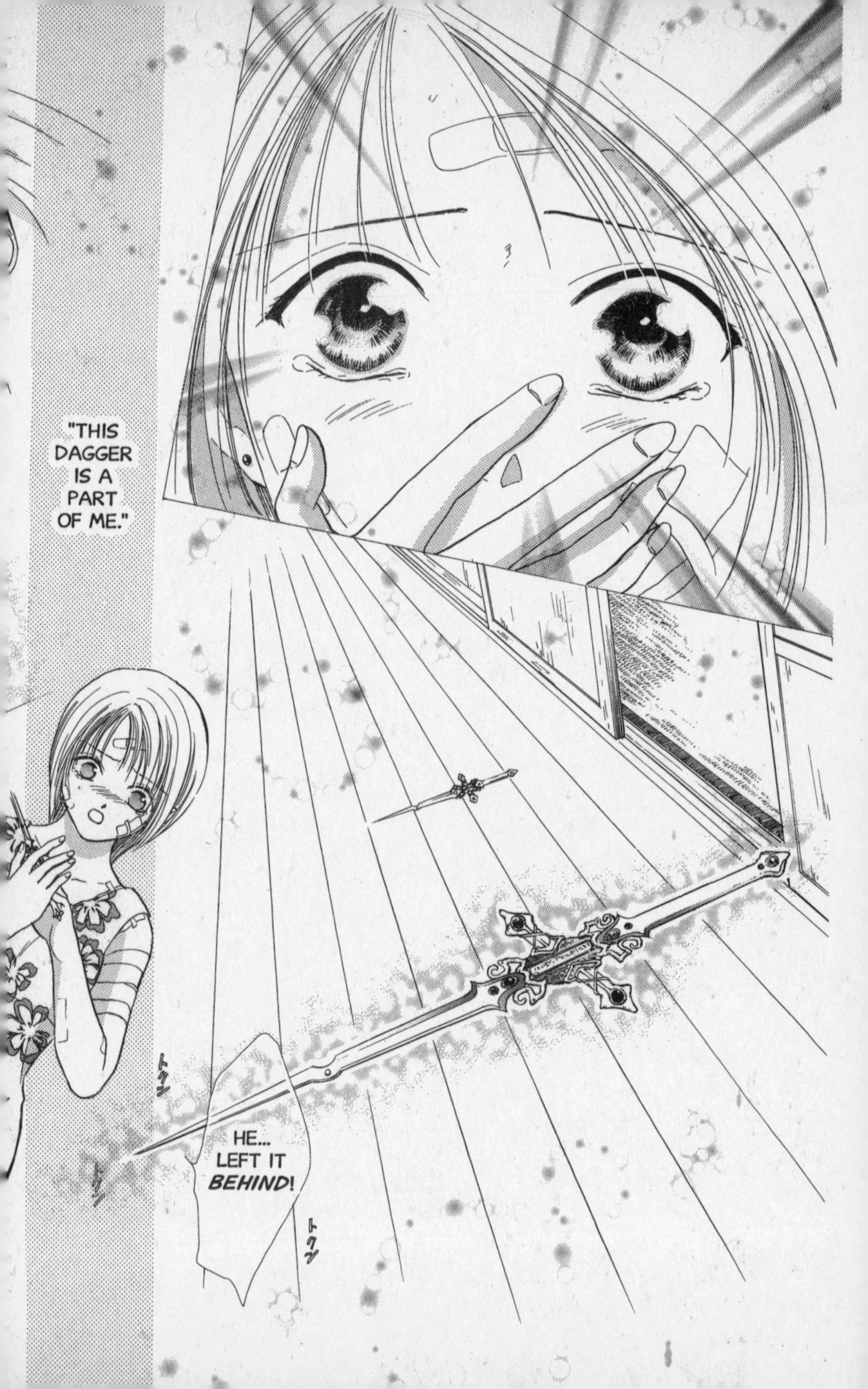
HE... LEFT IT BEHIND!
"THIS DAGGER IS A PART OF ME."

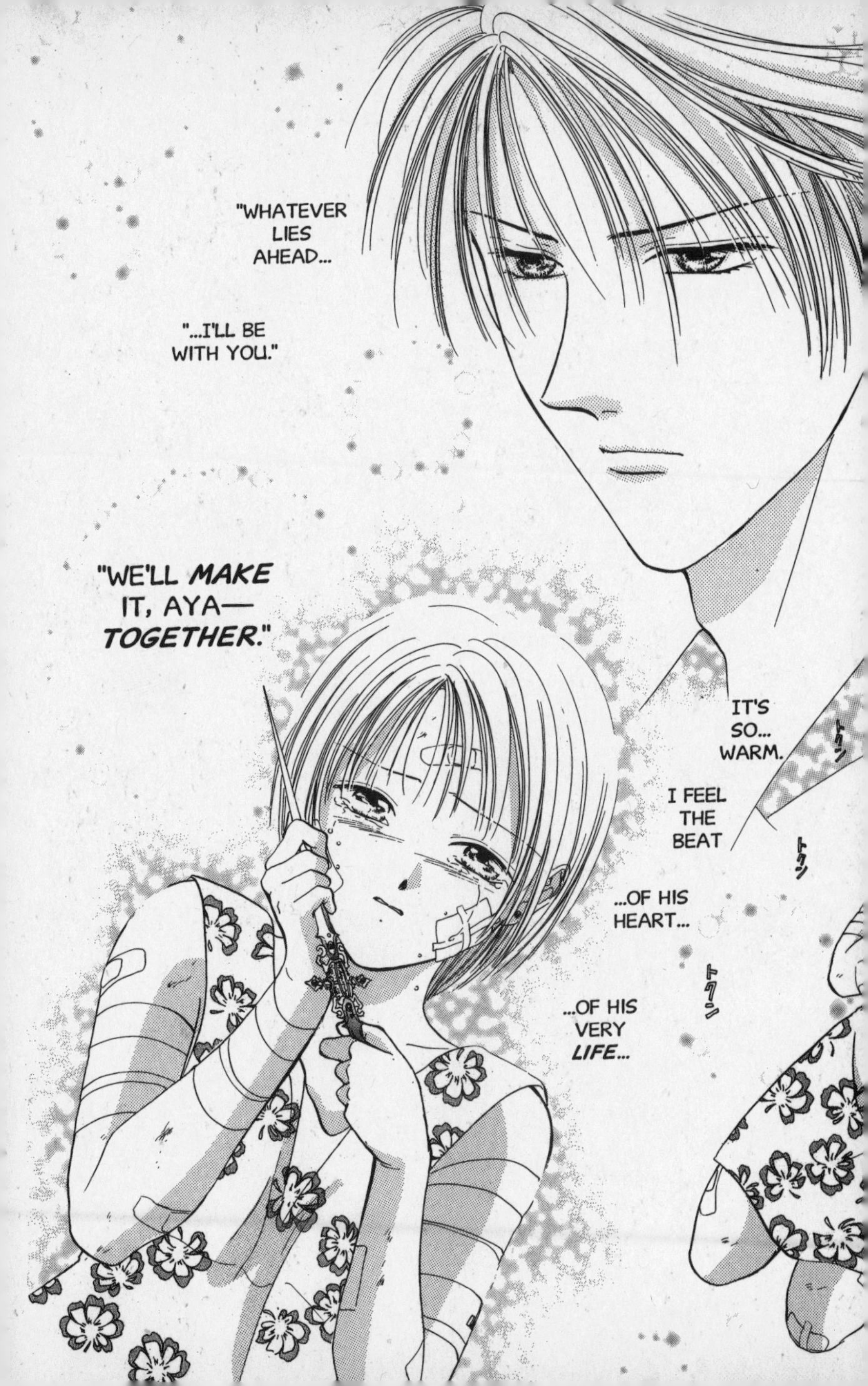
"WHATEVER LIES AHEAD...
"...I'LL BE WITH YOU."
"WE'LL *MAKE* IT, AYA—*TOGETHER.*"
IT'S SO... WARM.
I FEEL THE BEAT
...OF HIS HEART...
...OF HIS VERY *LIFE*...

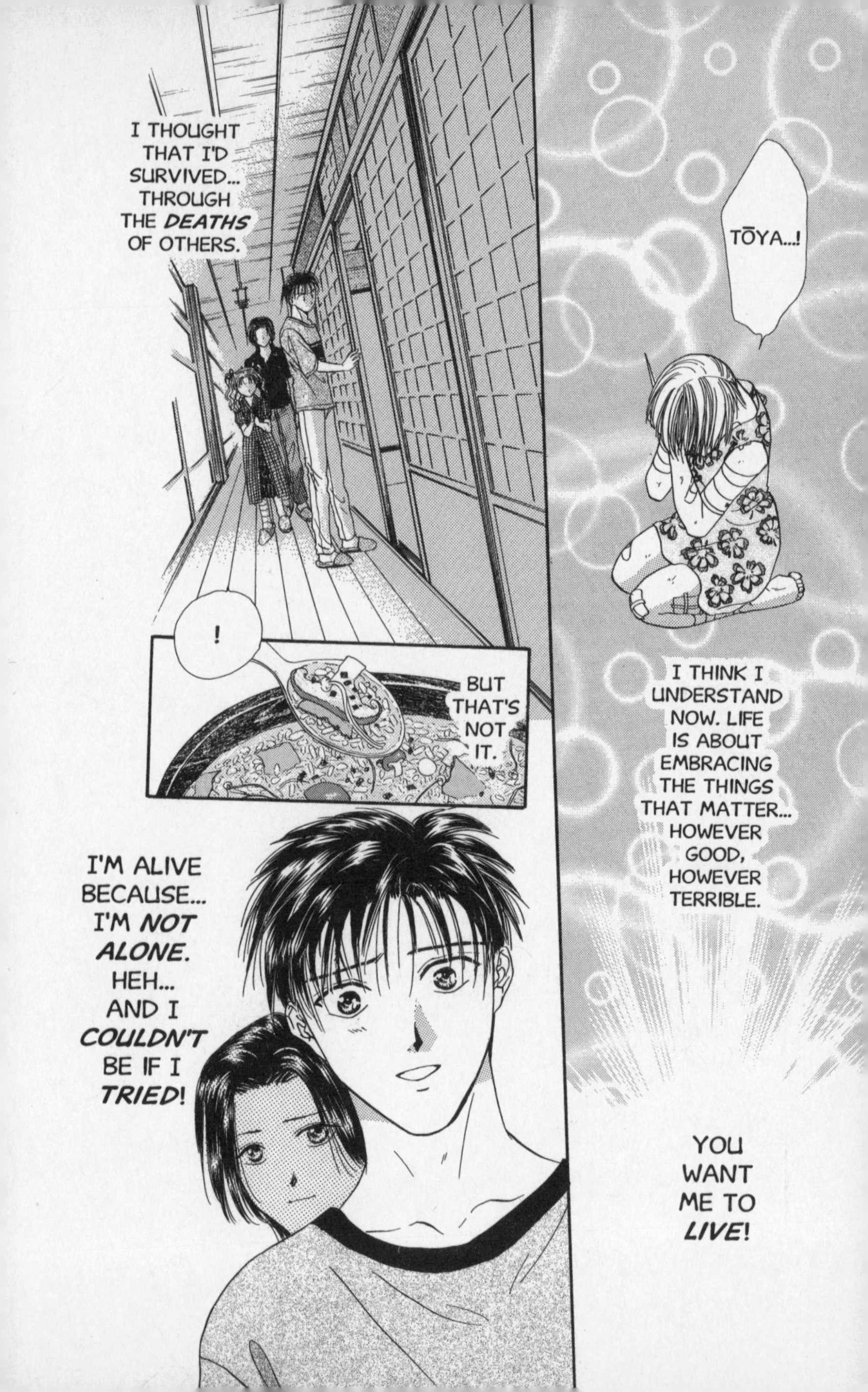

TŌYA...!
I THINK I UNDERSTAND NOW. LIFE IS ABOUT EMBRACING THE THINGS THAT MATTER... HOWEVER GOOD, HOWEVER TERRIBLE.
YOU WANT ME TO *LIVE*!
I THOUGHT THAT I'D SURVIVED... THROUGH THE *DEATHS* OF OTHERS.
!
BUT THAT'S NOT IT.
I'M ALIVE BECAUSE... I'M *NOT ALONE*. HEH... AND I *COULDN'T* BE IF I *TRIED*!

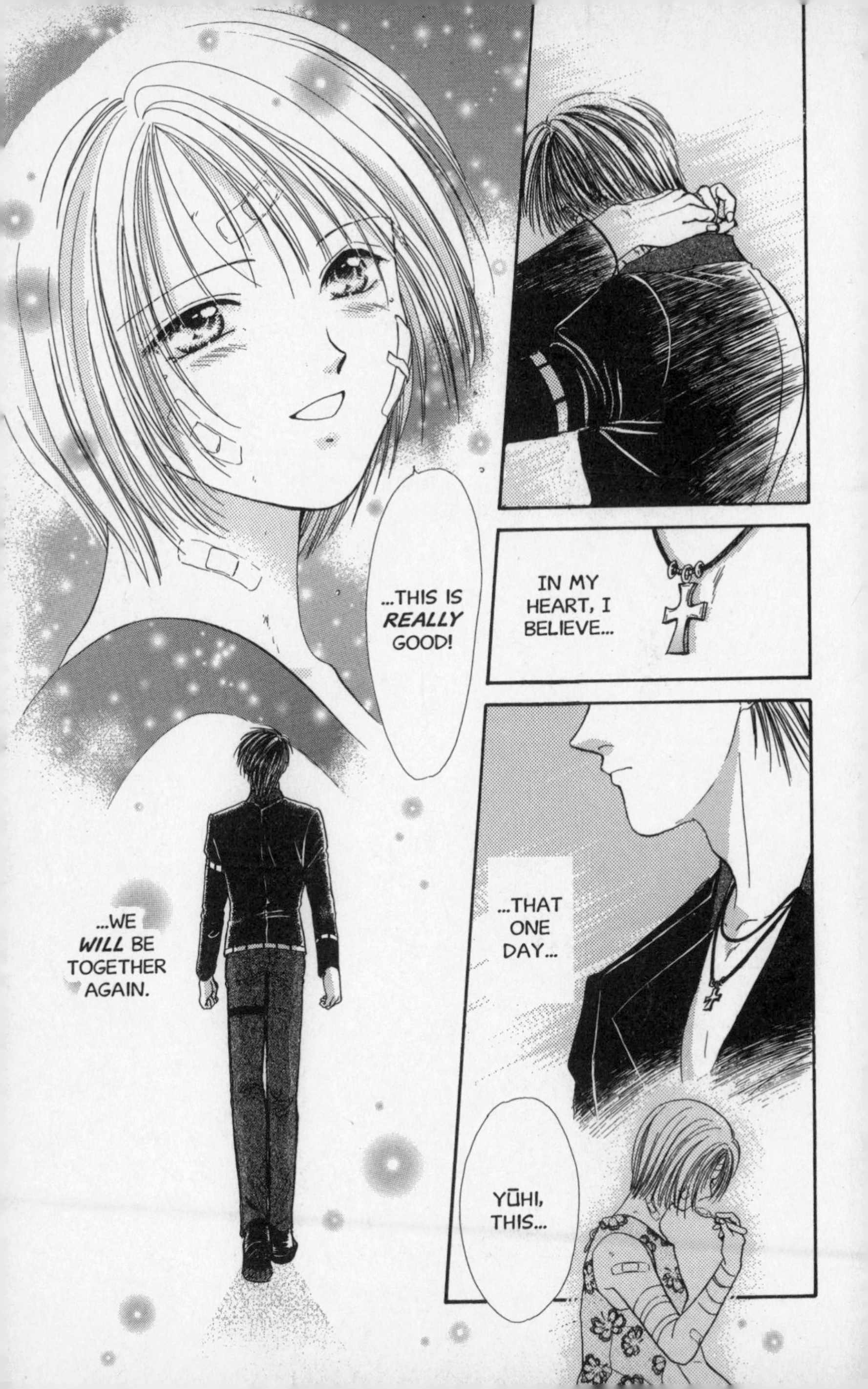
IN MY HEART, I BELIEVE...
...THAT ONE DAY...
YŪHI, THIS...
...THIS IS *REALLY* GOOD!
...WE *WILL* BE TOGETHER AGAIN.

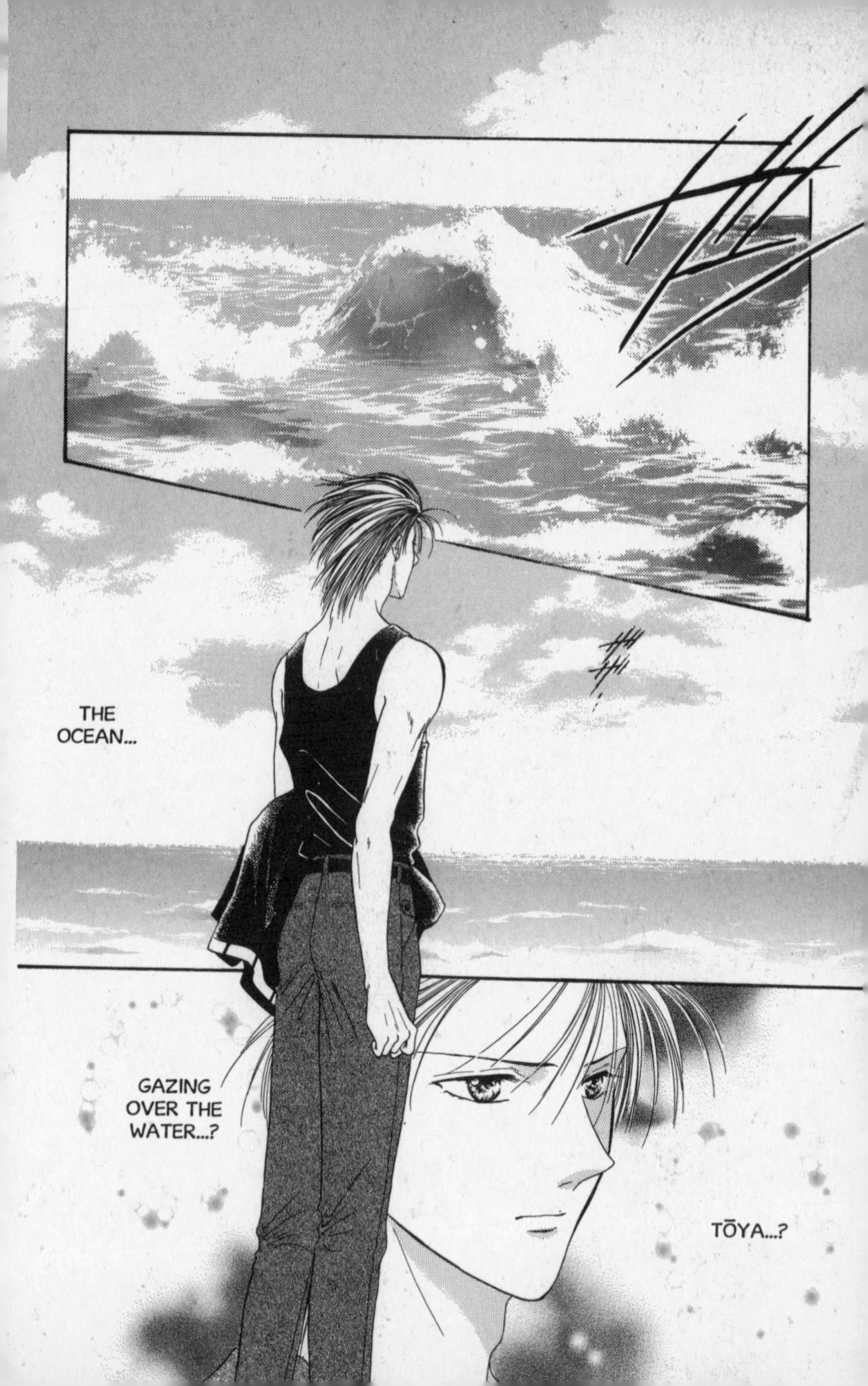
THE OCEAN...
TŌYA...?
GAZING OVER THE WATER...?

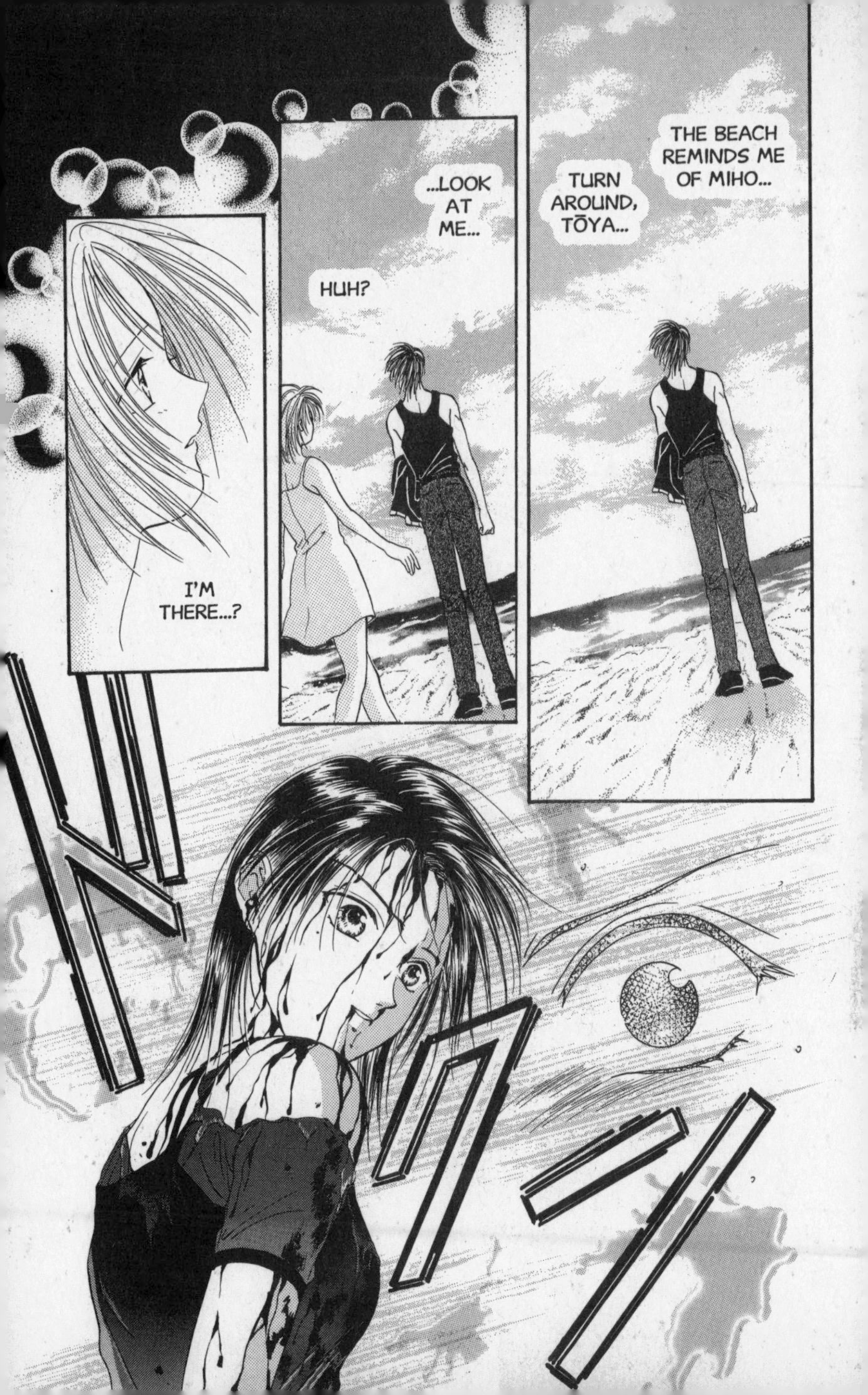
THE BEACH REMINDS ME OF MIHO...
TURN AROUND, TŌYA...
...LOOK AT ME...
HUH?
I'M THERE...?

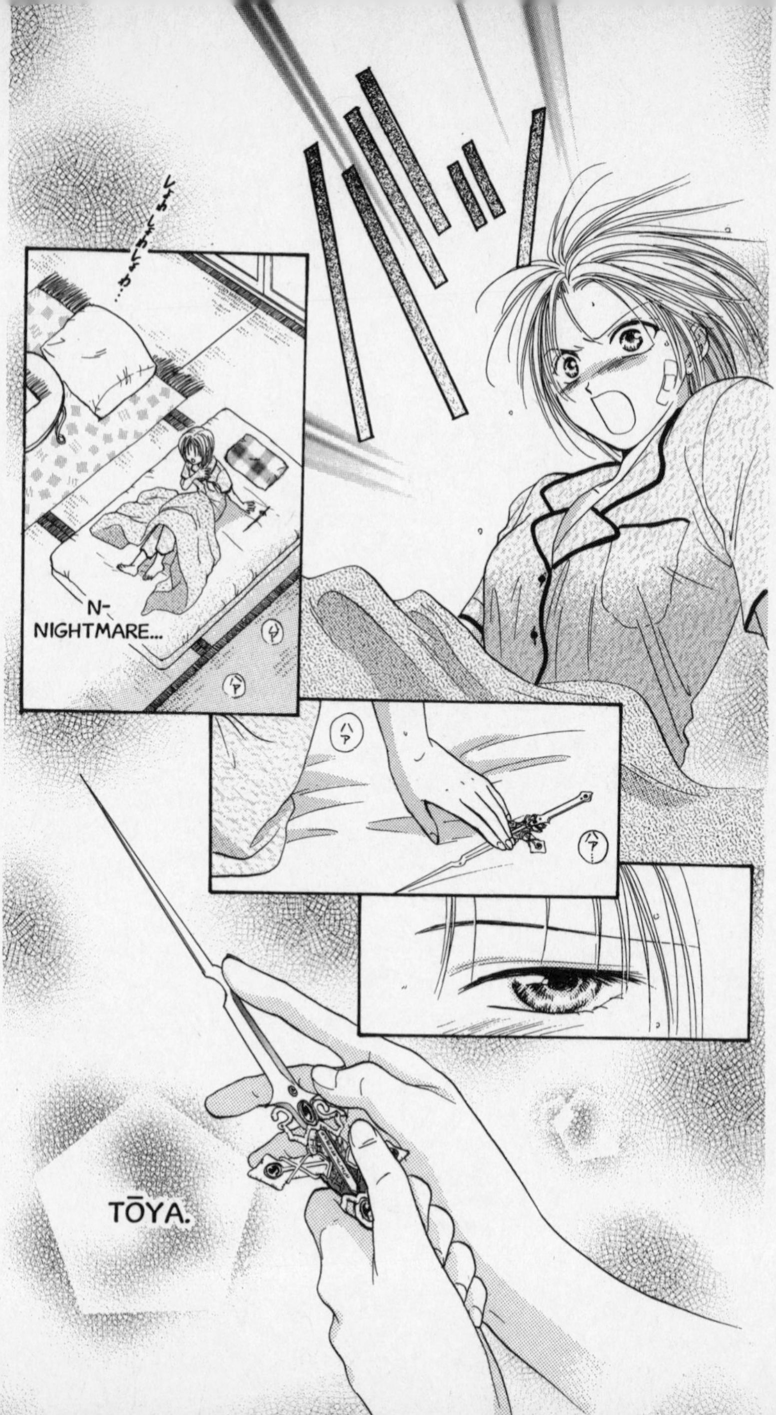
しょわしょわしょわ…
N-
NIGHTMARE...
ハァ
ハァ
ハァ
ハァ…
TŌYA.

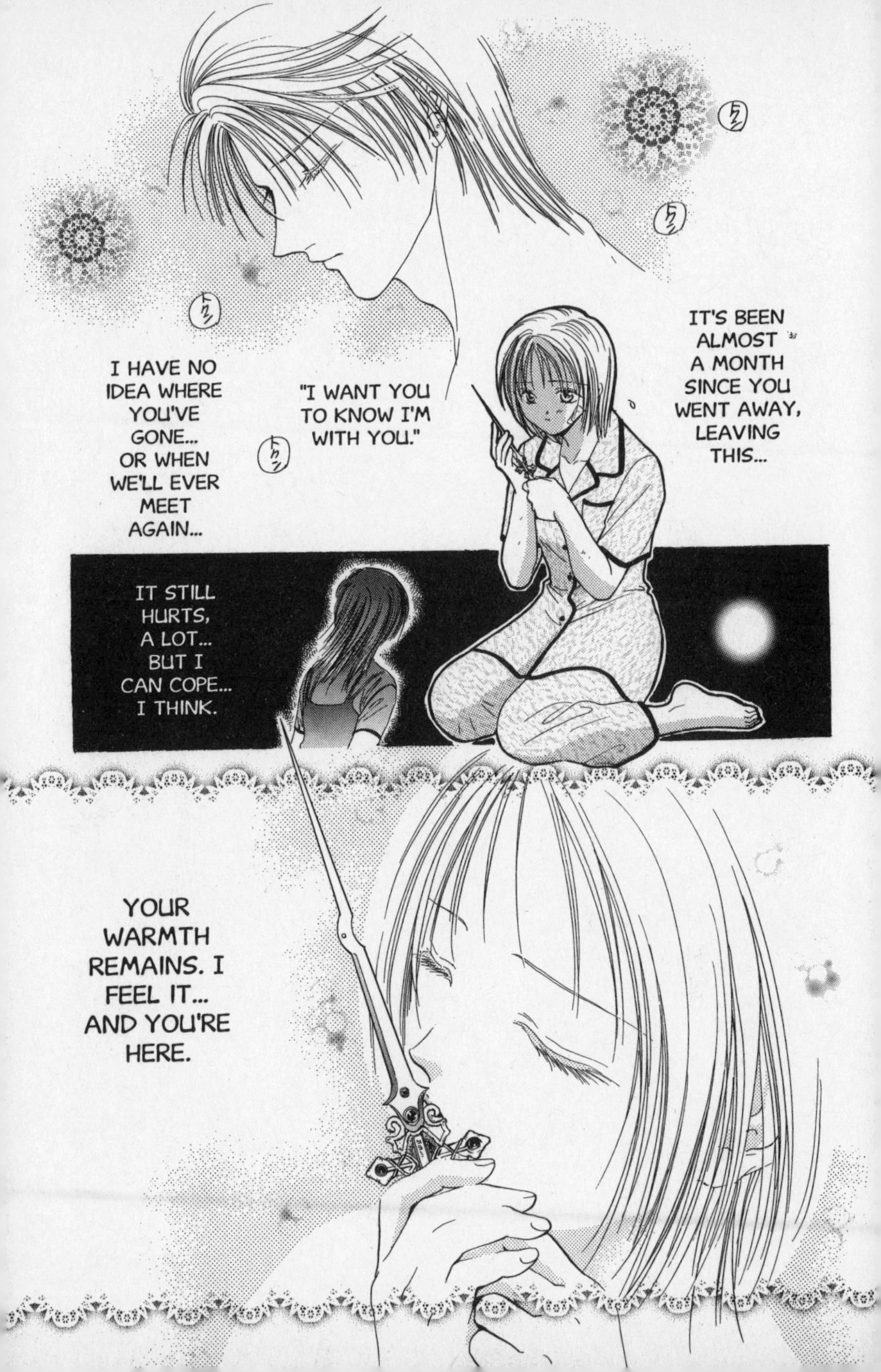
IT'S BEEN ALMOST A MONTH SINCE YOU WENT AWAY, LEAVING THIS...
"I WANT YOU TO KNOW I'M WITH YOU."
I HAVE NO IDEA WHERE YOU'VE GONE... OR WHEN WE'LL EVER MEET AGAIN...
IT STILL HURTS, A LOT... BUT I CAN COPE... I THINK.
YOUR WARMTH REMAINS. I FEEL IT... AND YOU'RE HERE.

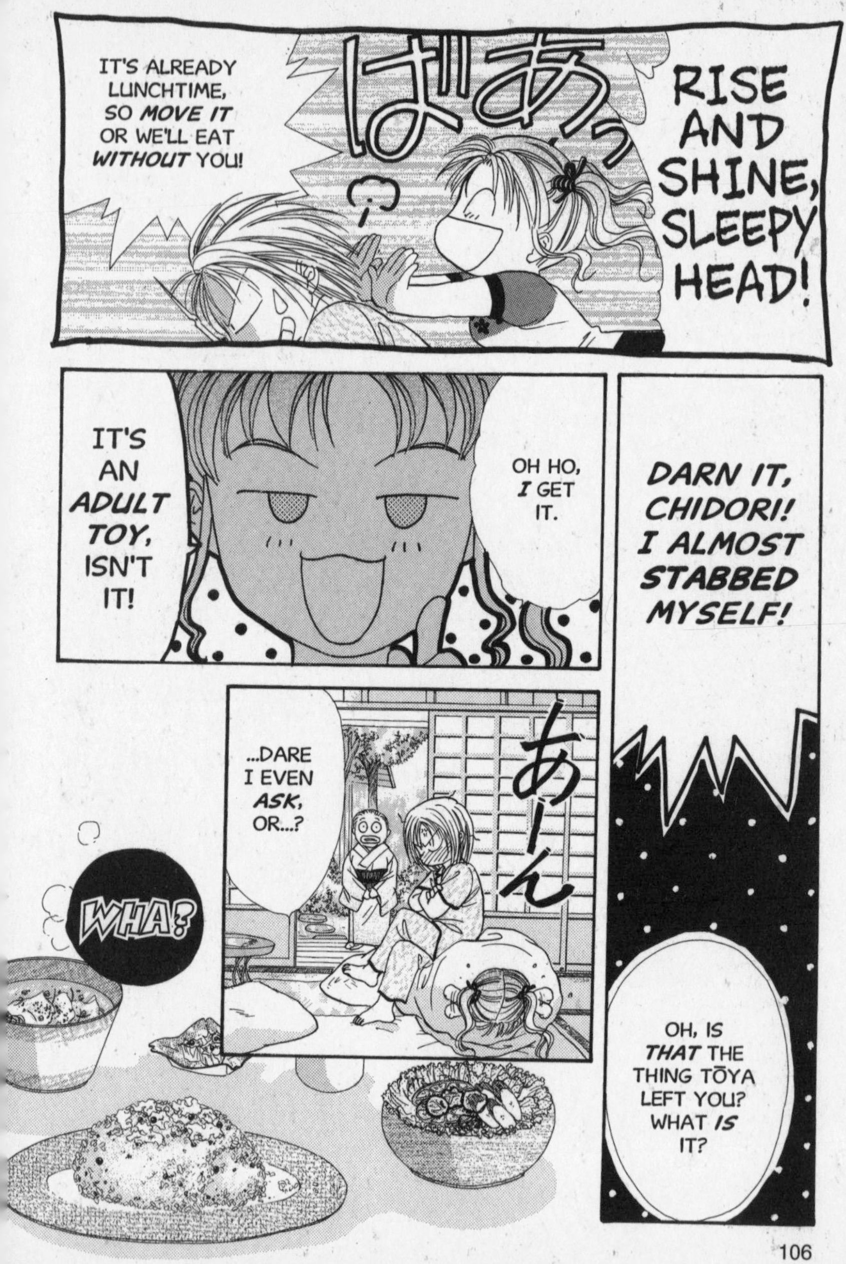
RISE AND SHINE, SLEEPY HEAD!
ばあっ
IT'S ALREADY LUNCHTIME, SO *MOVE IT* OR WE'LL EAT *WITHOUT* YOU!
DARN IT, CHIDORI! I ALMOST STABBED MYSELF!
OH, IS *THAT* THE THING TŌYA LEFT YOU? WHAT *IS* IT?
OH HO, *I* GET IT.
IT'S AN *ADULT TOY,* ISN'T IT!
あーん
...DARE I EVEN *ASK,* OR...?
WHA?

The "Shizuoka Arc" provoked tremendous reader response. Miori was quite a character—we quoted her a lot at my place. ◡̈

98% of the readers hated her! ...So, it turns out that Kagami tricked Tōya by implanting fake memories. I don't blame Tōya for insisting on finding his **real** memories now, after all that. But Miori...what a drama queen. ◡̈ People like her **do** exist in the real world, you know. Most readers protested, "Tōya should stay cool and mysterious, being nice **only** to Aya." I don't blame you **readers**, either. Tōya will be off-screen for a while—it'll be too confusing to be covering his storyline along with Aya's—but soon he'll be back again...with plenty of airtime for himself.

There's been a bit of business about Aya's hair, too—most readers were shocked! Some wrote, "It's cute, but long hair was better...." I hesitated, but I wanted **something** to trigger Aya into crying. It used to be a common thing, people cutting their hair after heartbreak, but no one—especially not Aya—would be likely to think of that these days. Still, it's different when it's by accident, as it was with Aya. It happened right after Tōya complimented her on her hair, too. I liked the idea of it because it was symbolic, but also had visual impact. A lot of readers say they cried at this scene. The assistants were weepy every week. I **like** the short hair on her, though—and it **is** slowly growing out. I'm giving Tōya and Yūhi evolving hairstyles, too. Change is good. Actually, I'd like everyone to think about what Miori did in the end. People were shocked, but I couldn't help thinking about all those teenage "ijime" or "bullying" suicides you hear about in the news. The assistants got depressed, too (and it was tough for me to have to draw it). We talked, among other things, about how her body would have been crushed....

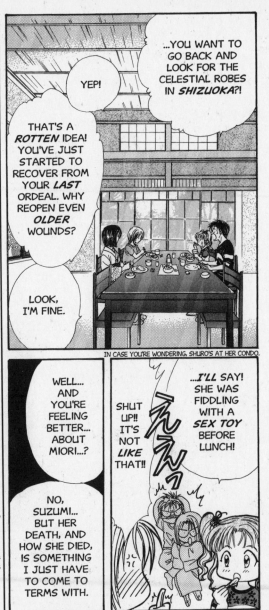

...YOU WANT TO GO BACK AND LOOK FOR THE CELESTIAL ROBES IN *SHIZUOKA*?!
YEP!
THAT'S A *ROTTEN* IDEA! YOU'VE JUST STARTED TO RECOVER FROM YOUR *LAST* ORDEAL. WHY REOPEN EVEN *OLDER* WOUNDS?
LOOK, I'M FINE.
IN CASE YOU'RE WONDERING, SHURO'S AT HER CONDO.
...*I'LL* SAY! SHE WAS FIDDLING WITH A *SEX TOY* BEFORE LUNCH!
SHUT UP!! IT'S NOT *LIKE* THAT!!
WELL... AND YOU'RE FEELING BETTER... ABOUT MIORI...?
NO, SUZUMI... BUT HER DEATH, AND HOW SHE DIED, IS SOMETHING I JUST HAVE TO COME TO TERMS WITH.

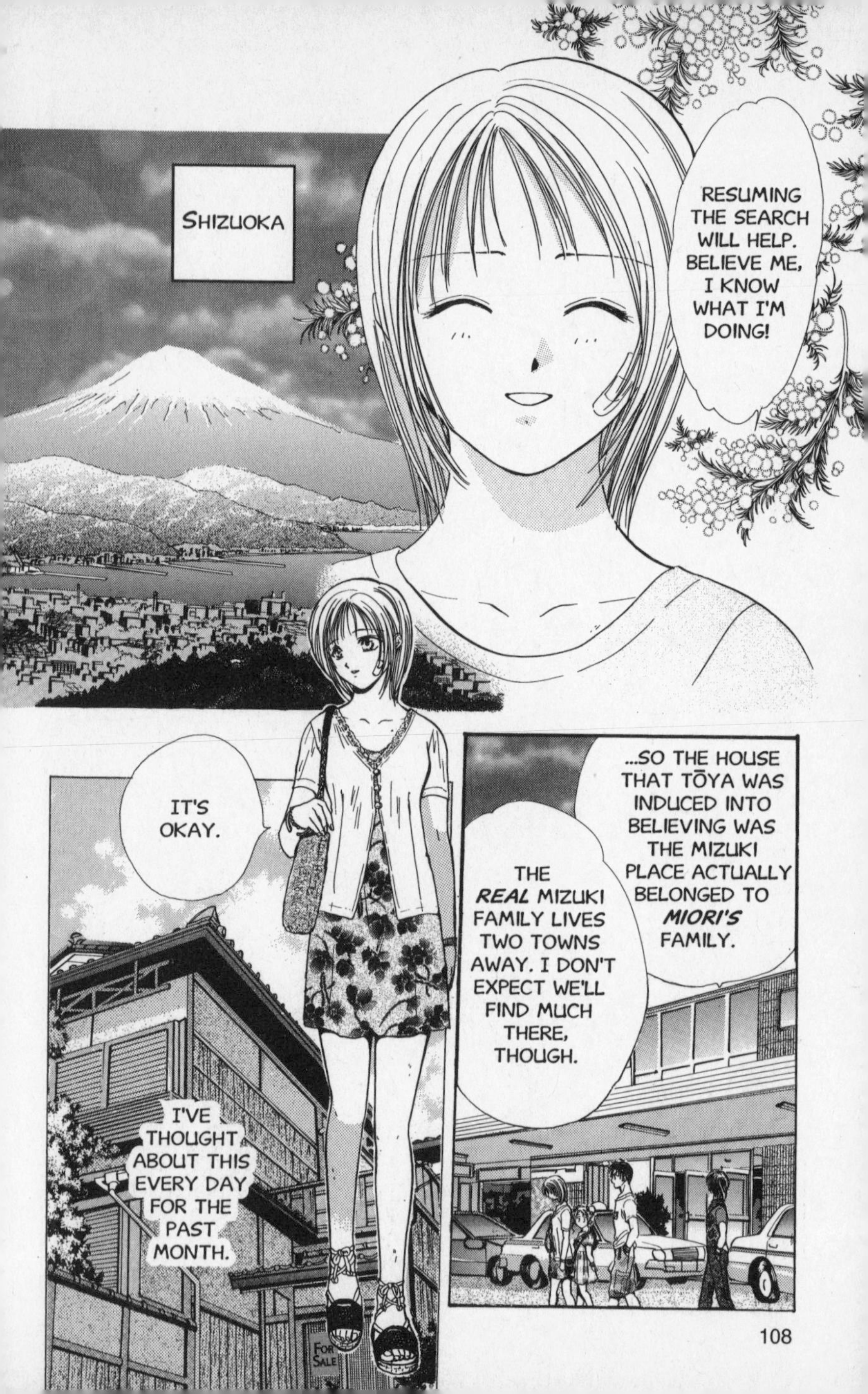
RESUMING THE SEARCH WILL HELP. BELIEVE ME, I KNOW WHAT I'M DOING!
SHIZUOKA
...SO THE HOUSE THAT TŌYA WAS INDUCED INTO BELIEVING WAS THE MIZUKI PLACE ACTUALLY BELONGED TO *MIORI'S* FAMILY.
THE *REAL* MIZUKI FAMILY LIVES TWO TOWNS AWAY. I DON'T EXPECT WE'LL FIND MUCH THERE, THOUGH.
IT'S OKAY.
I'VE THOUGHT ABOUT THIS EVERY DAY FOR THE PAST MONTH.
FOR SALE

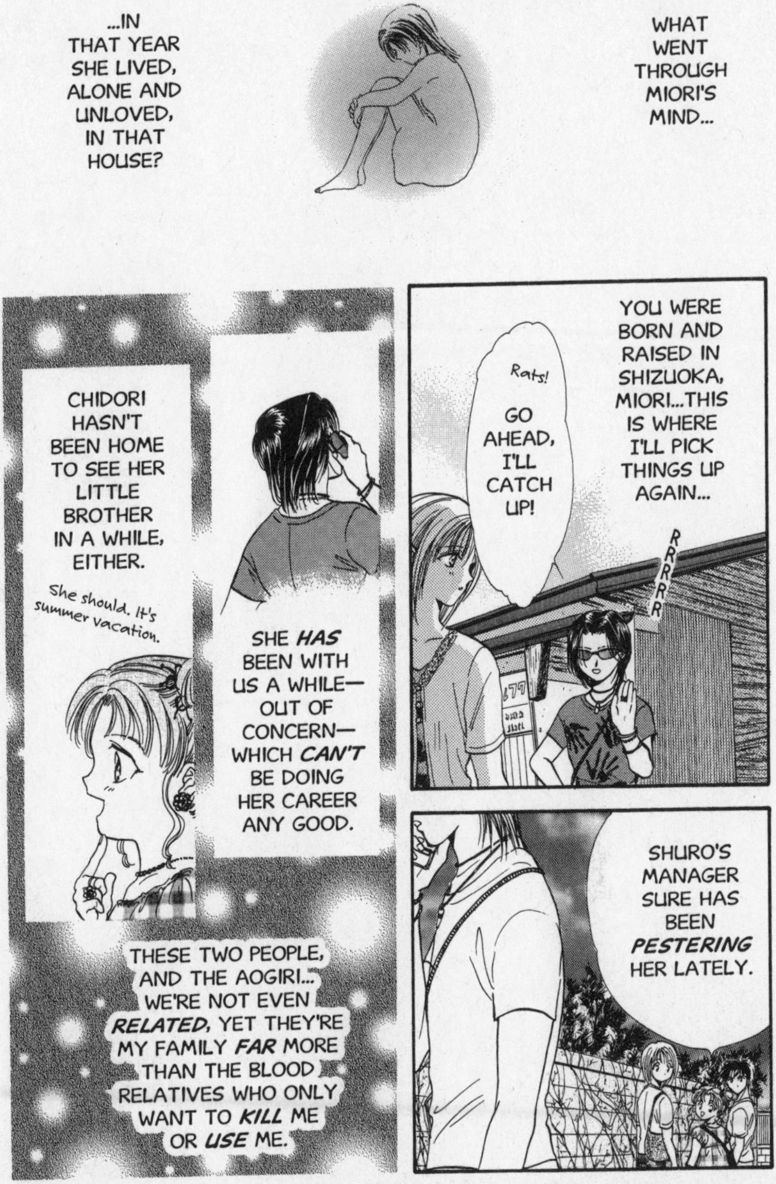
WHAT WENT THROUGH MIORI'S MIND...
...IN THAT YEAR SHE LIVED, ALONE AND UNLOVED, IN THAT HOUSE?
YOU WERE BORN AND RAISED IN SHIZUOKA, MIORI...THIS IS WHERE I'LL PICK THINGS UP AGAIN...
Rats!
GO AHEAD, I'LL CATCH UP!
RRRRR
SHURO'S MANAGER SURE HAS BEEN PESTERING HER LATELY.
SHE HAS BEEN WITH US A WHILE—OUT OF CONCERN—WHICH CAN'T BE DOING HER CAREER ANY GOOD.
CHIDORI HASN'T BEEN HOME TO SEE HER LITTLE BROTHER IN A WHILE, EITHER.
She should. It's summer vacation.
THESE TWO PEOPLE, AND THE AOGIRI... WE'RE NOT EVEN RELATED, YET THEY'RE MY FAMILY FAR MORE THAN THE BLOOD RELATIVES WHO ONLY WANT TO KILL ME OR USE ME.

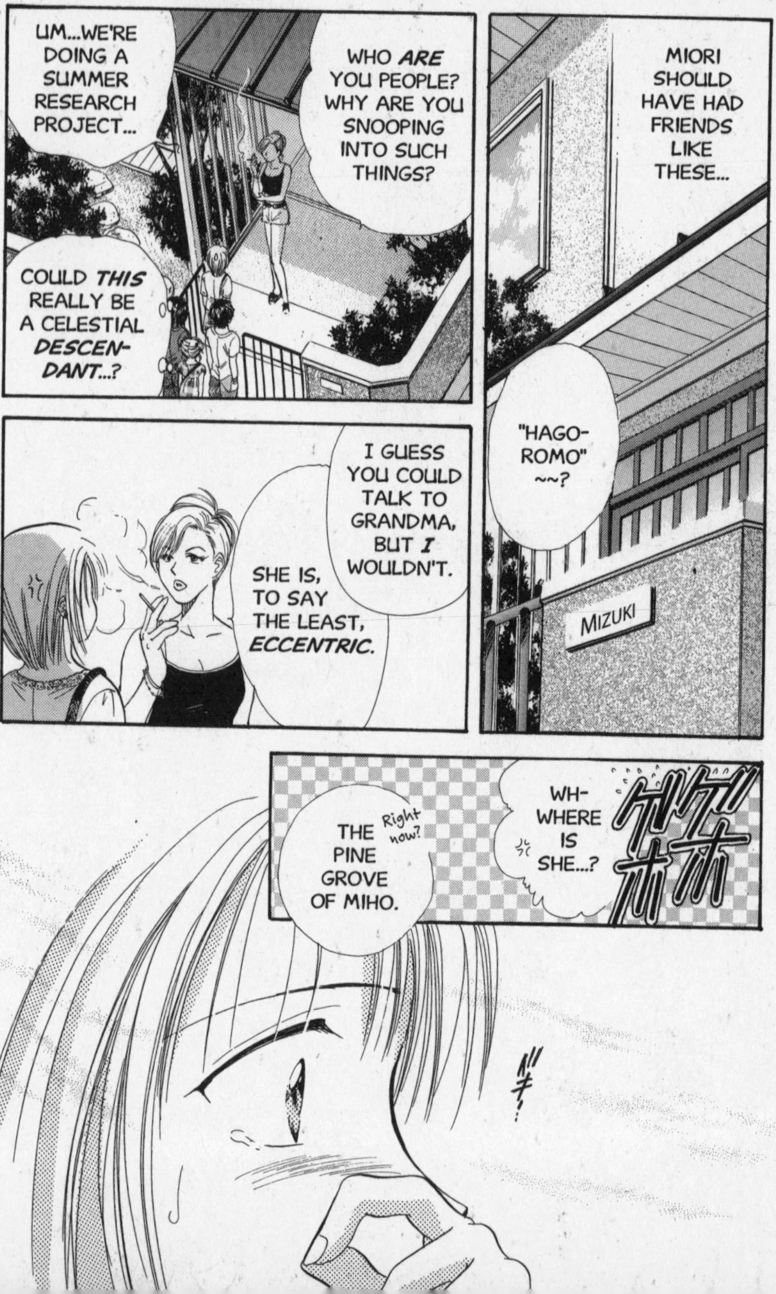
MIORI SHOULD HAVE HAD FRIENDS LIKE THESE...
"HAGO-ROMO" ~~?
MIZUKI
WHO *ARE* YOU PEOPLE? WHY ARE YOU SNOOPING INTO SUCH THINGS?
UM...WE'RE DOING A SUMMER RESEARCH PROJECT...
COULD *THIS* REALLY BE A CELESTIAL *DESCEN-DANT*...?
I GUESS YOU COULD TALK TO GRANDMA, BUT *I* WOULDN'T.
SHE IS, TO SAY THE LEAST, *ECCENTRIC*.
WH-WHERE IS SHE...?
THE PINE GROVE OF MIHO.
Right now?

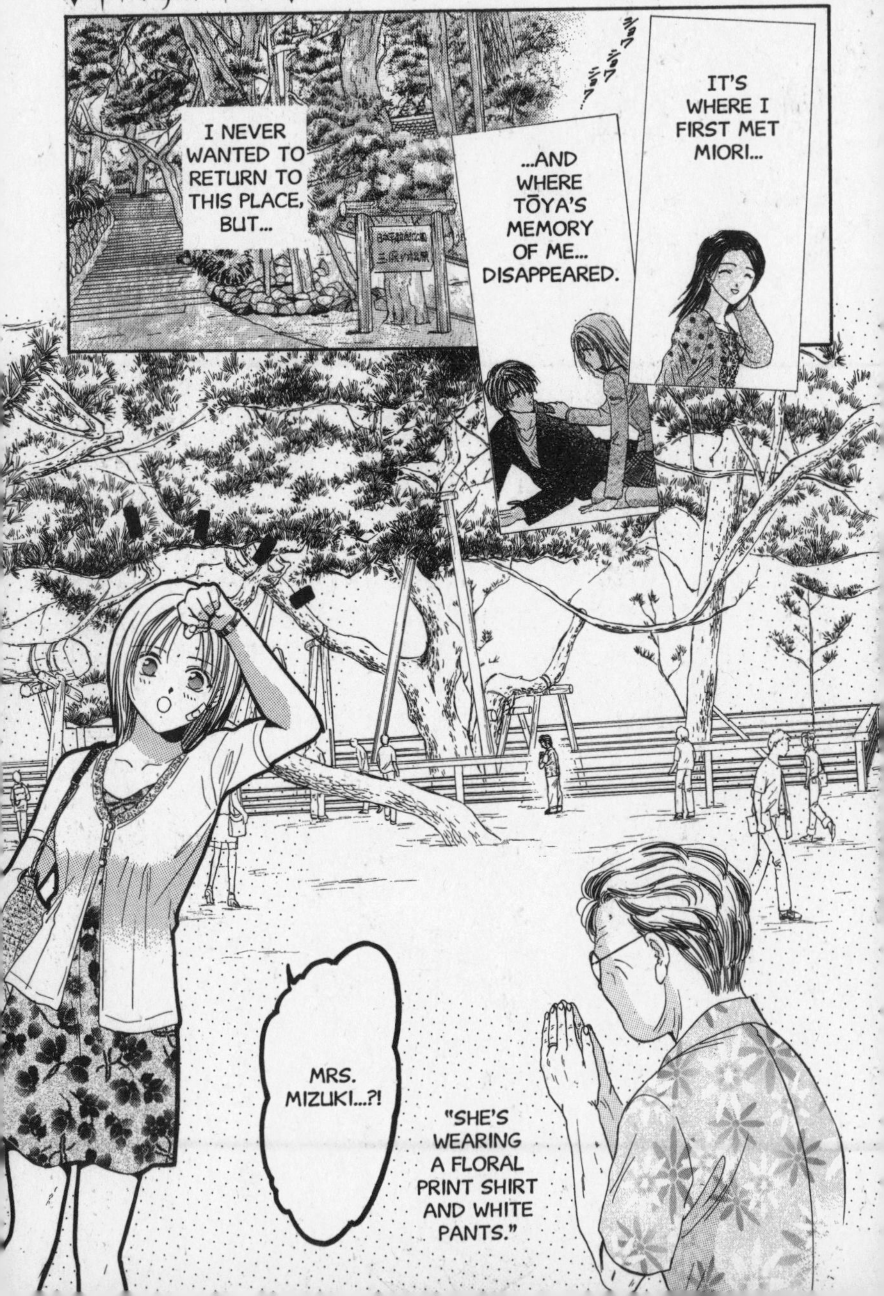
IT'S WHERE I FIRST MET MIORI...
...AND WHERE TŌYA'S MEMORY OF ME... DISAPPEARED.
I NEVER WANTED TO RETURN TO THIS PLACE, BUT...
"SHE'S WEARING A FLORAL PRINT SHIRT AND WHITE PANTS."
MRS. MIZUKI...?!

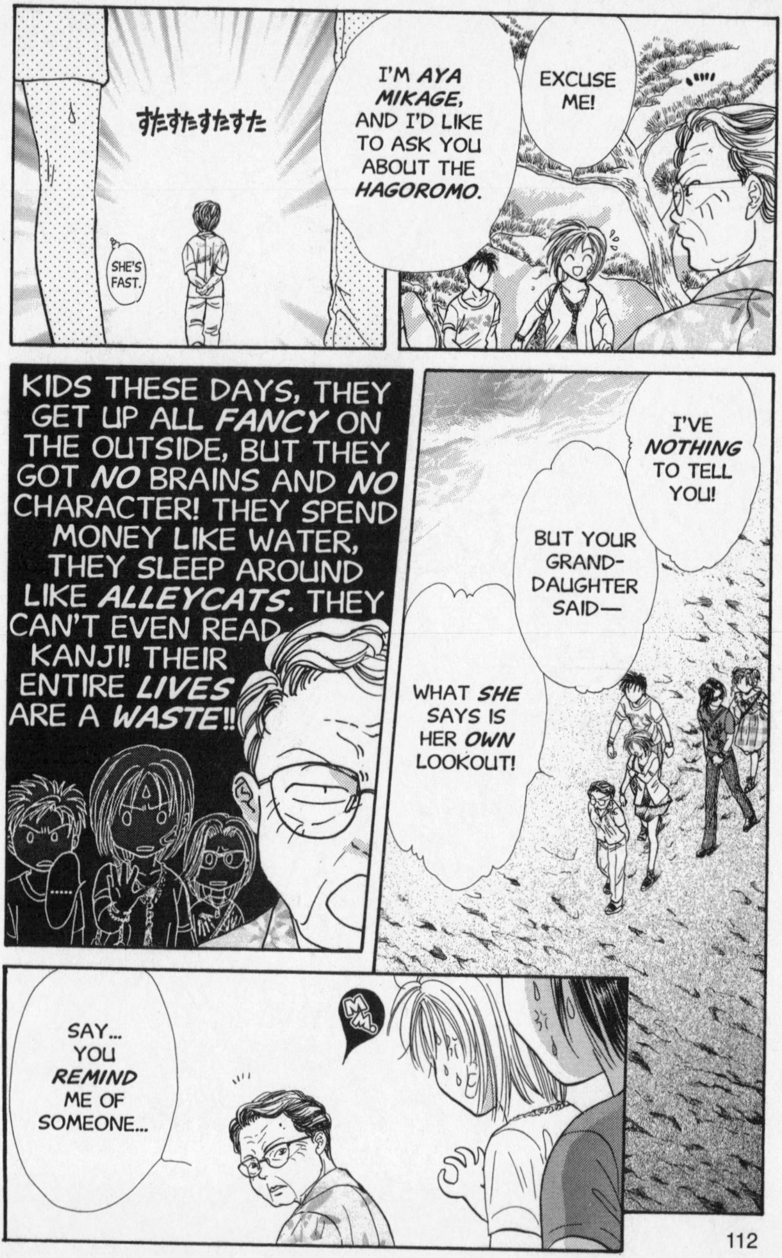
EXCUSE ME!
I'M AYA MIKAGE, AND I'D LIKE TO ASK YOU ABOUT THE HAGOROMO.
すたすたすたすた
SHE'S FAST.
I'VE NOTHING TO TELL YOU!
BUT YOUR GRAND-DAUGHTER SAID—
WHAT SHE SAYS IS HER OWN LOOKOUT!
KIDS THESE DAYS, THEY GET UP ALL FANCY ON THE OUTSIDE, BUT THEY GOT NO BRAINS AND NO CHARACTER! THEY SPEND MONEY LIKE WATER, THEY SLEEP AROUND LIKE ALLEYCATS. THEY CAN'T EVEN READ KANJI! THEIR ENTIRE LIVES ARE A WASTE!!
.....
SAY... YOU REMIND ME OF SOMEONE...

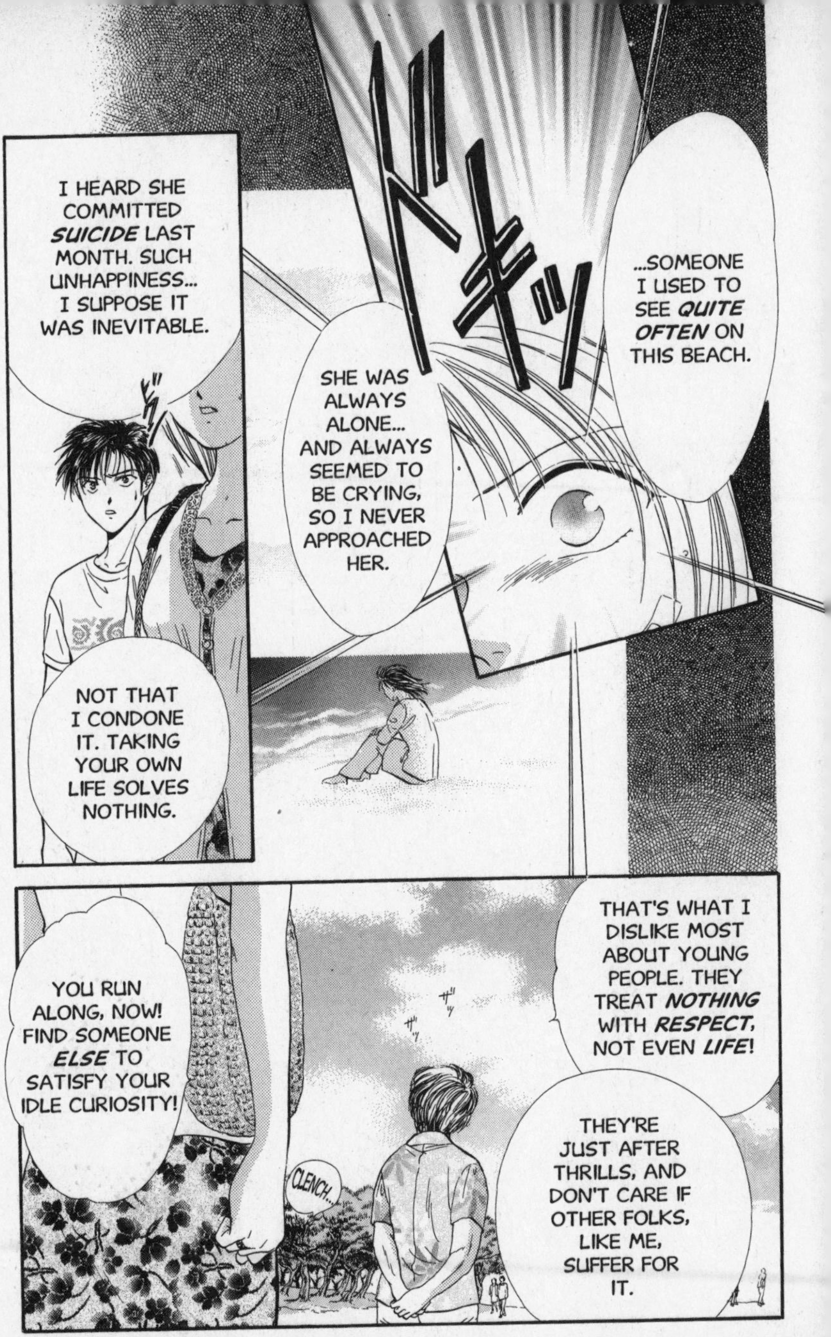
ドキッ
...SOMEONE I USED TO SEE *QUITE OFTEN* ON THIS BEACH.
SHE WAS ALWAYS ALONE... AND ALWAYS SEEMED TO BE CRYING, SO I NEVER APPROACHED HER.
I HEARD SHE COMMITTED *SUICIDE* LAST MONTH. SUCH UNHAPPINESS... I SUPPOSE IT WAS INEVITABLE.
NOT THAT I CONDONE IT. TAKING YOUR OWN LIFE SOLVES NOTHING.
THAT'S WHAT I DISLIKE MOST ABOUT YOUNG PEOPLE. THEY TREAT *NOTHING* WITH *RESPECT*, NOT EVEN *LIFE*!
THEY'RE JUST AFTER THRILLS, AND DON'T CARE IF OTHER FOLKS, LIKE ME, SUFFER FOR IT.
CLENCH...
YOU RUN ALONG, NOW! FIND SOMEONE *ELSE* TO SATISFY YOUR IDLE CURIOSITY!

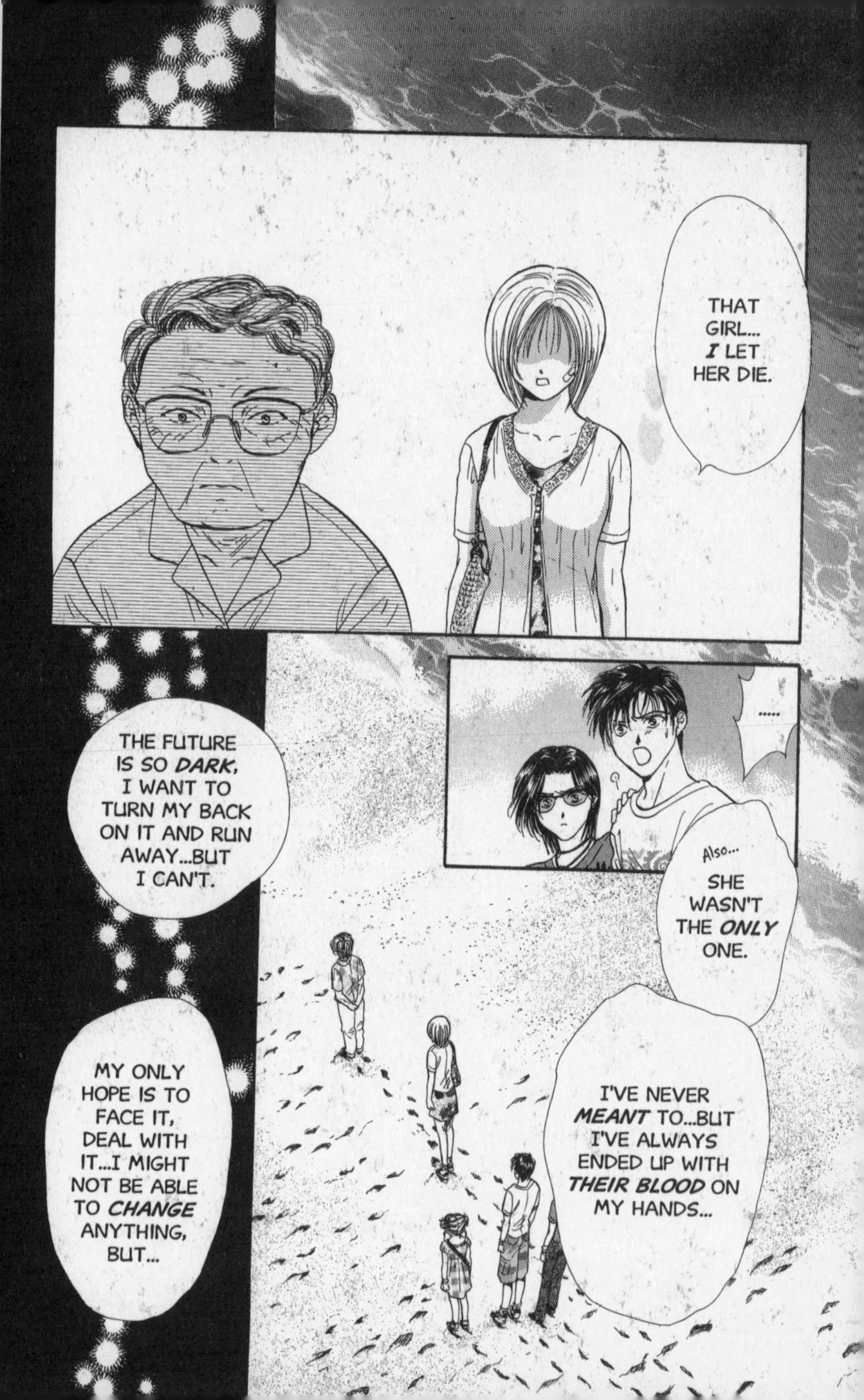
THAT GIRL... *I* LET HER DIE.
.....
Also...
SHE WASN'T THE *ONLY* ONE.
I'VE NEVER *MEANT* TO...BUT I'VE ALWAYS ENDED UP WITH *THEIR BLOOD* ON MY HANDS...
THE FUTURE IS SO *DARK,* I WANT TO TURN MY BACK ON IT AND RUN AWAY...BUT I CAN'T.
MY ONLY HOPE IS TO FACE IT, DEAL WITH IT...I MIGHT NOT BE ABLE TO *CHANGE* ANYTHING, BUT...

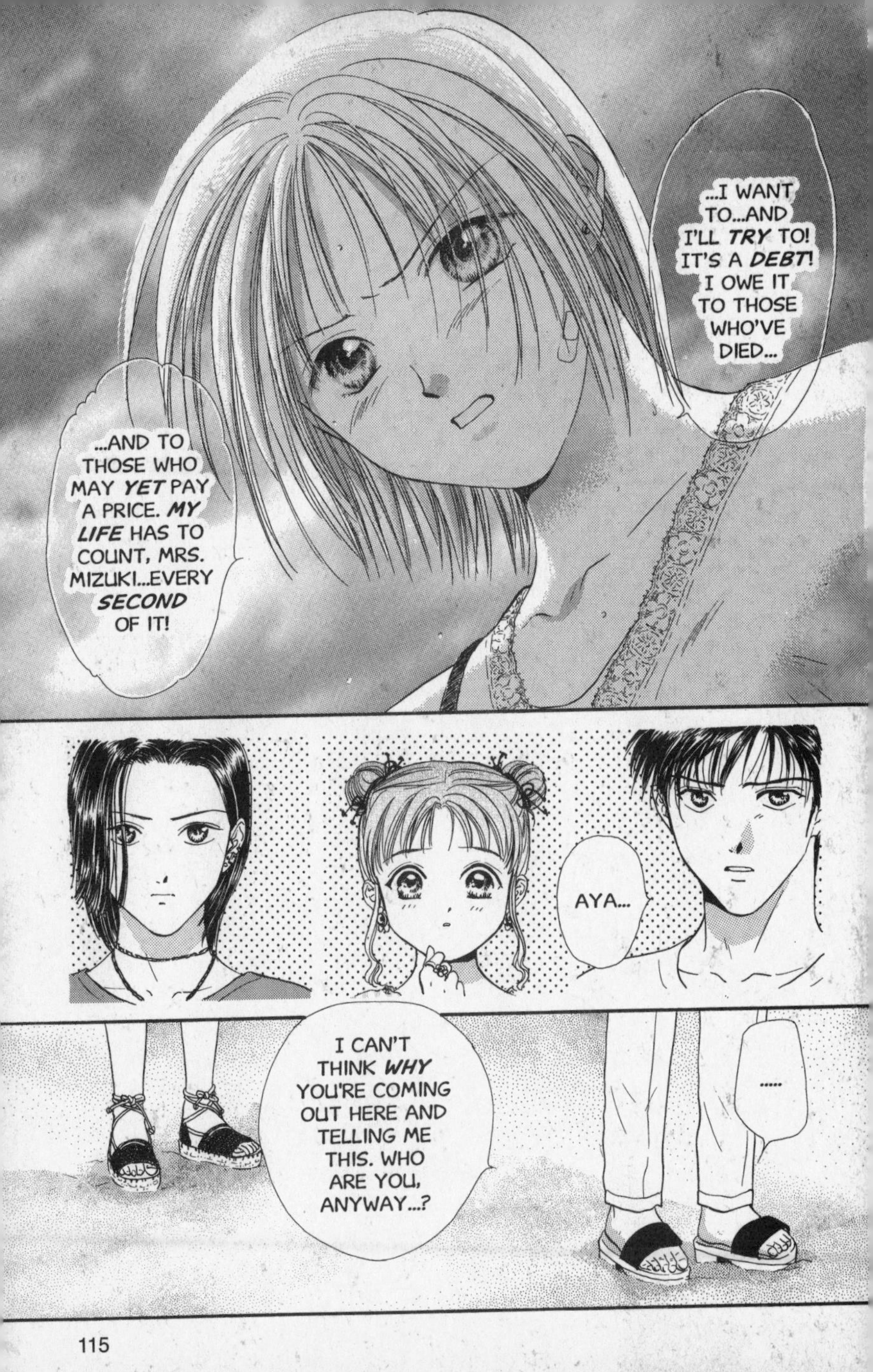
...I WANT TO...AND I'LL TRY TO! IT'S A DEBT! I OWE IT TO THOSE WHO'VE DIED...
...AND TO THOSE WHO MAY YET PAY A PRICE. MY LIFE HAS TO COUNT, MRS. MIZUKI...EVERY SECOND OF IT!
AYA...
.....
I CAN'T THINK WHY YOU'RE COMING OUT HERE AND TELLING ME THIS. WHO ARE YOU, ANYWAY...?

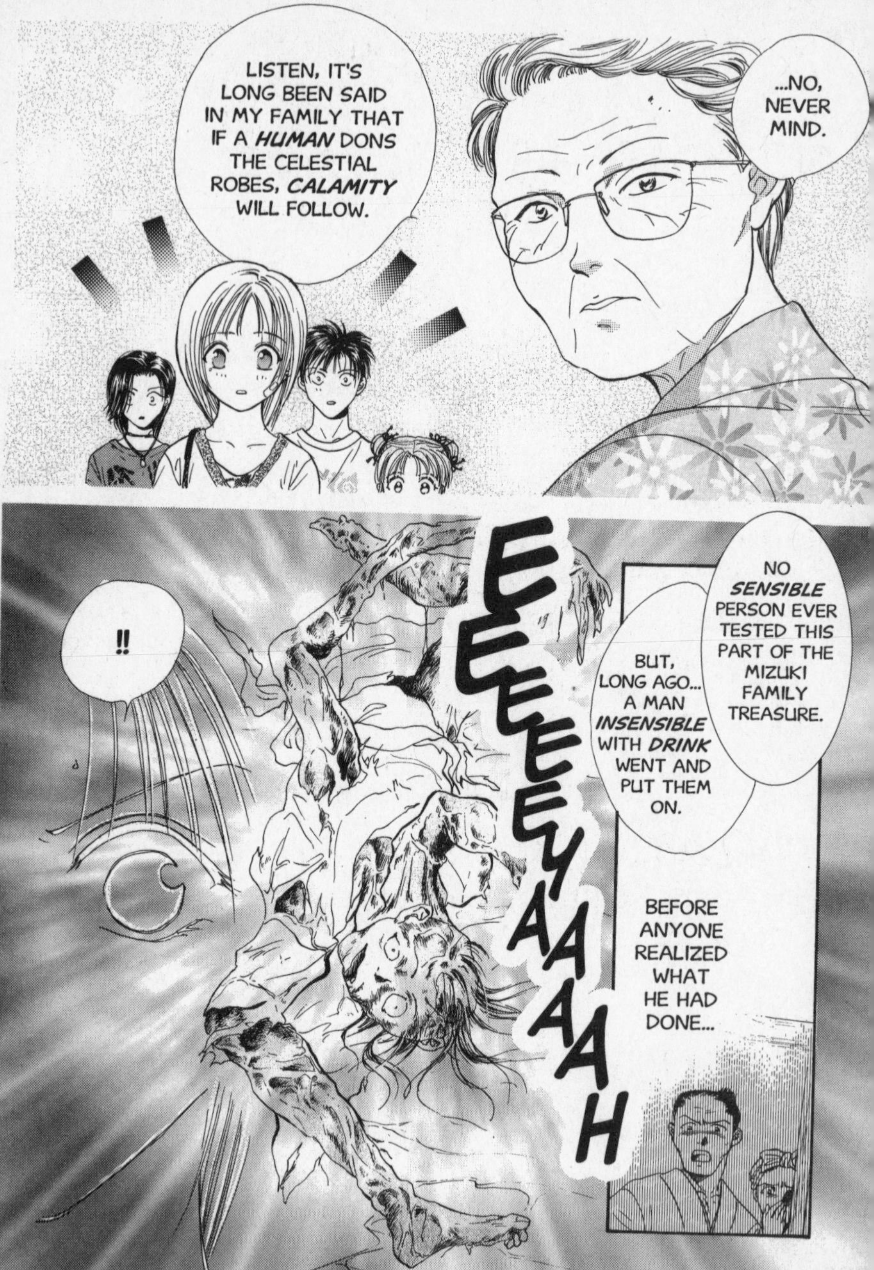
...NO, NEVER MIND.
LISTEN, IT'S LONG BEEN SAID IN MY FAMILY THAT IF A *HUMAN* DONS THE CELESTIAL ROBES, *CALAMITY* WILL FOLLOW.
NO *SENSIBLE* PERSON EVER TESTED THIS PART OF THE MIZUKI FAMILY TREASURE.
BUT, LONG AGO... A MAN *INSENSIBLE* WITH *DRINK* WENT AND PUT THEM ON.
BEFORE ANYONE REALIZED WHAT HE HAD DONE...
EEEEEEYAAAAH
!!

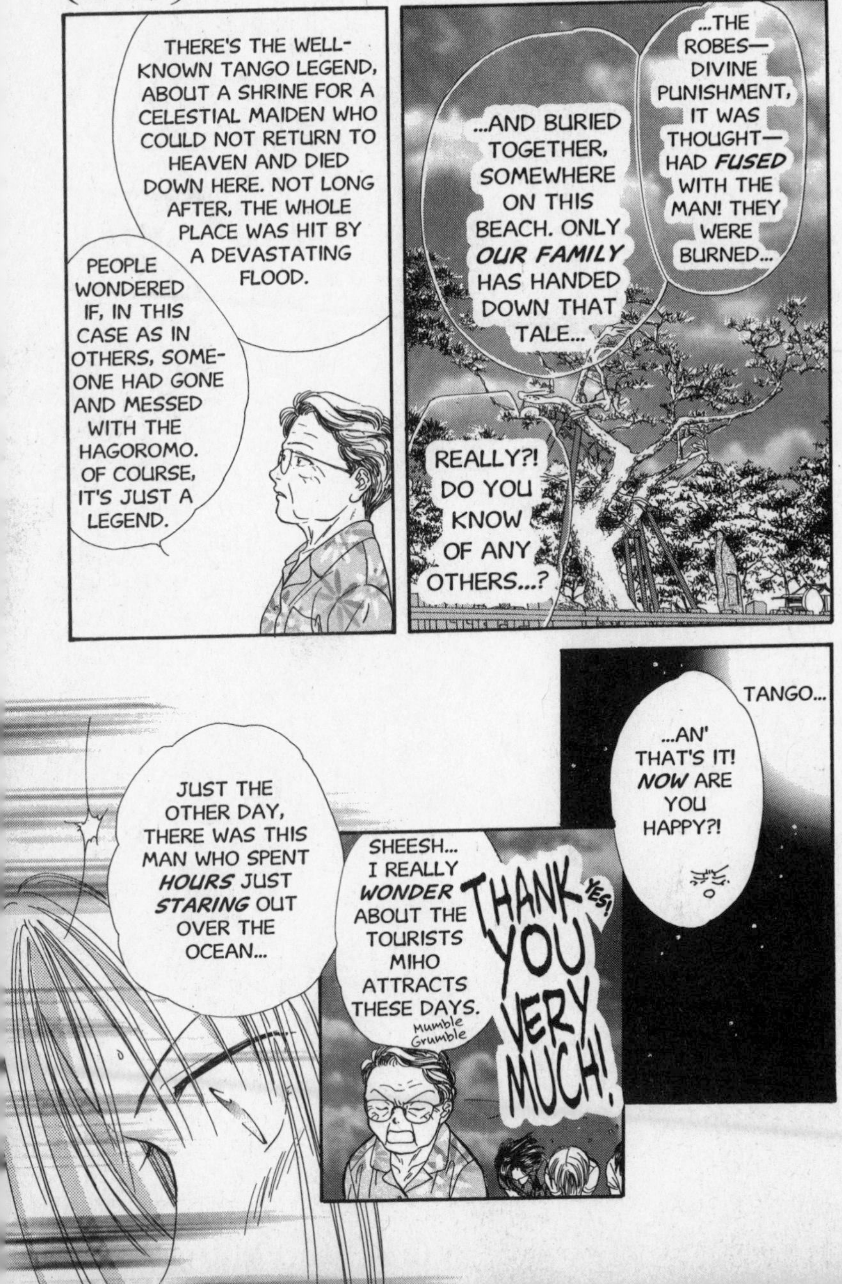
...THE ROBES—DIVINE PUNISHMENT, IT WAS THOUGHT—HAD FUSED WITH THE MAN! THEY WERE BURNED...
...AND BURIED TOGETHER, SOMEWHERE ON THIS BEACH. ONLY OUR FAMILY HAS HANDED DOWN THAT TALE...
REALLY?! DO YOU KNOW OF ANY OTHERS...?
THERE'S THE WELL-KNOWN TANGO LEGEND, ABOUT A SHRINE FOR A CELESTIAL MAIDEN WHO COULD NOT RETURN TO HEAVEN AND DIED DOWN HERE. NOT LONG AFTER, THE WHOLE PLACE WAS HIT BY A DEVASTATING FLOOD.
PEOPLE WONDERED IF, IN THIS CASE AS IN OTHERS, SOMEONE HAD GONE AND MESSED WITH THE HAGOROMO. OF COURSE, IT'S JUST A LEGEND.
TANGO...
...AN' THAT'S IT! NOW ARE YOU HAPPY?!
THANK YOU VERY MUCH!
YES!
SHEESH... I REALLY WONDER ABOUT THE TOURISTS MIHO ATTRACTS THESE DAYS.
Mumble Grumble
JUST THE OTHER DAY, THERE WAS THIS MAN WHO SPENT HOURS JUST STARING OUT OVER THE OCEAN...

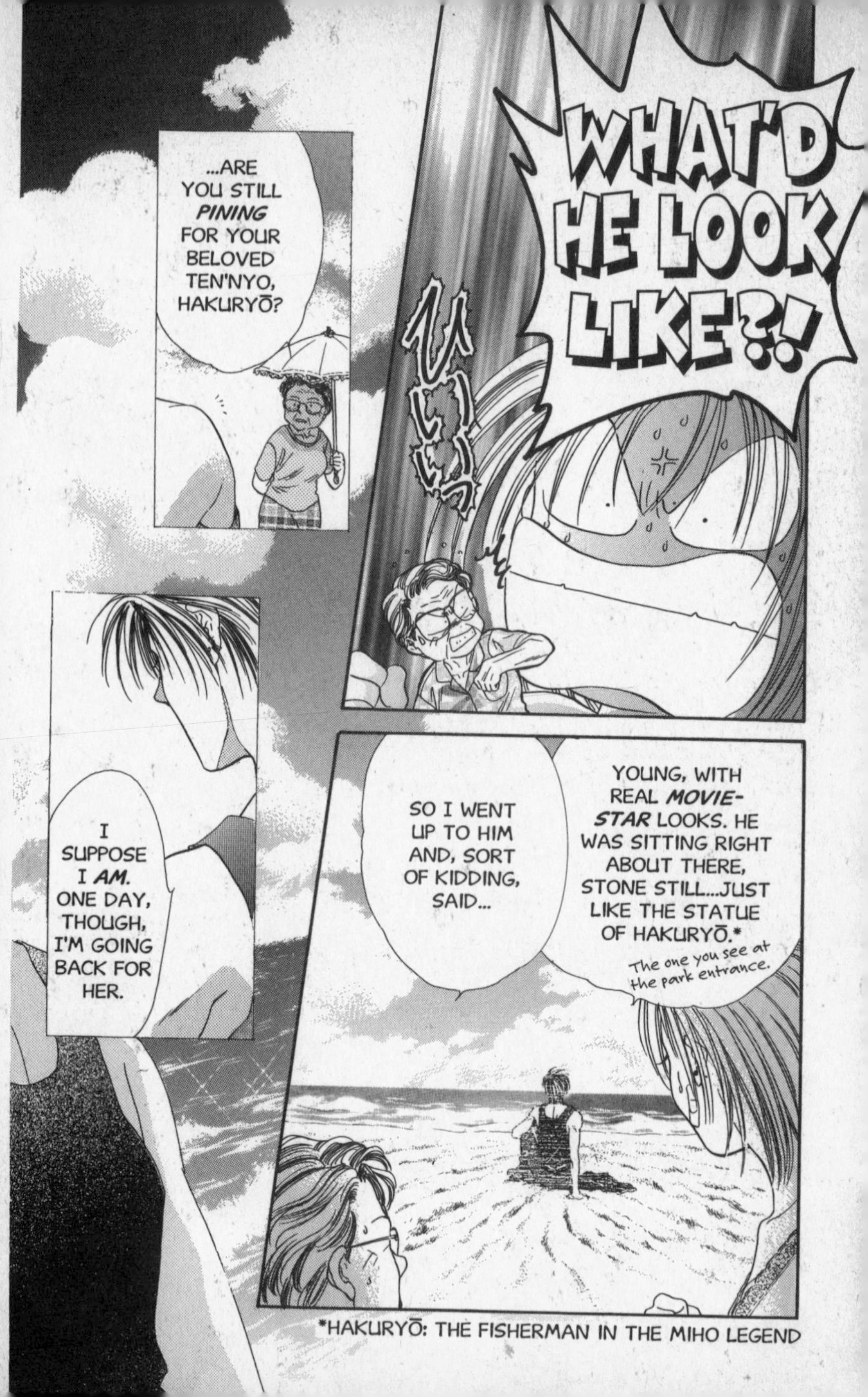
WHAT'D HE LOOK LIKE?!
YOUNG, WITH REAL MOVIE-STAR LOOKS. HE WAS SITTING RIGHT ABOUT THERE, STONE STILL...JUST LIKE THE STATUE OF HAKURYŌ.*
The one you see at the park entrance.
SO I WENT UP TO HIM AND, SORT OF KIDDING, SAID...
...ARE YOU STILL PINING FOR YOUR BELOVED TEN'NYO, HAKURYŌ?
I SUPPOSE I AM. ONE DAY, THOUGH, I'M GOING BACK FOR HER.

*HAKURYŌ: THE FISHERMAN IN THE MIHO LEGEND

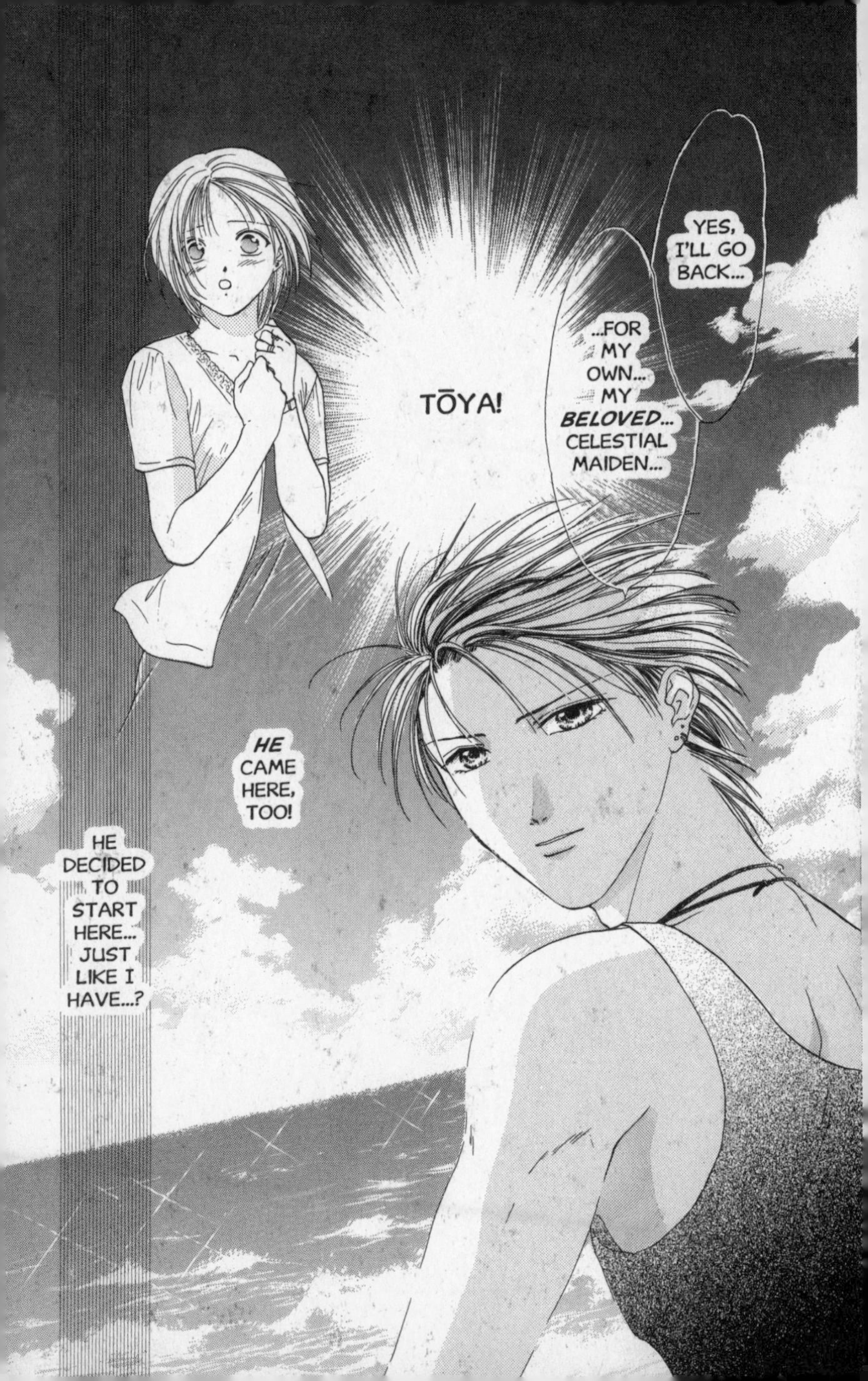
YES, I'LL GO BACK...
...FOR MY OWN... MY *BELOVED*... CELESTIAL MAIDEN...
TŌYA!
HE CAME HERE, TOO!
HE DECIDED TO START HERE... JUST LIKE I HAVE...?

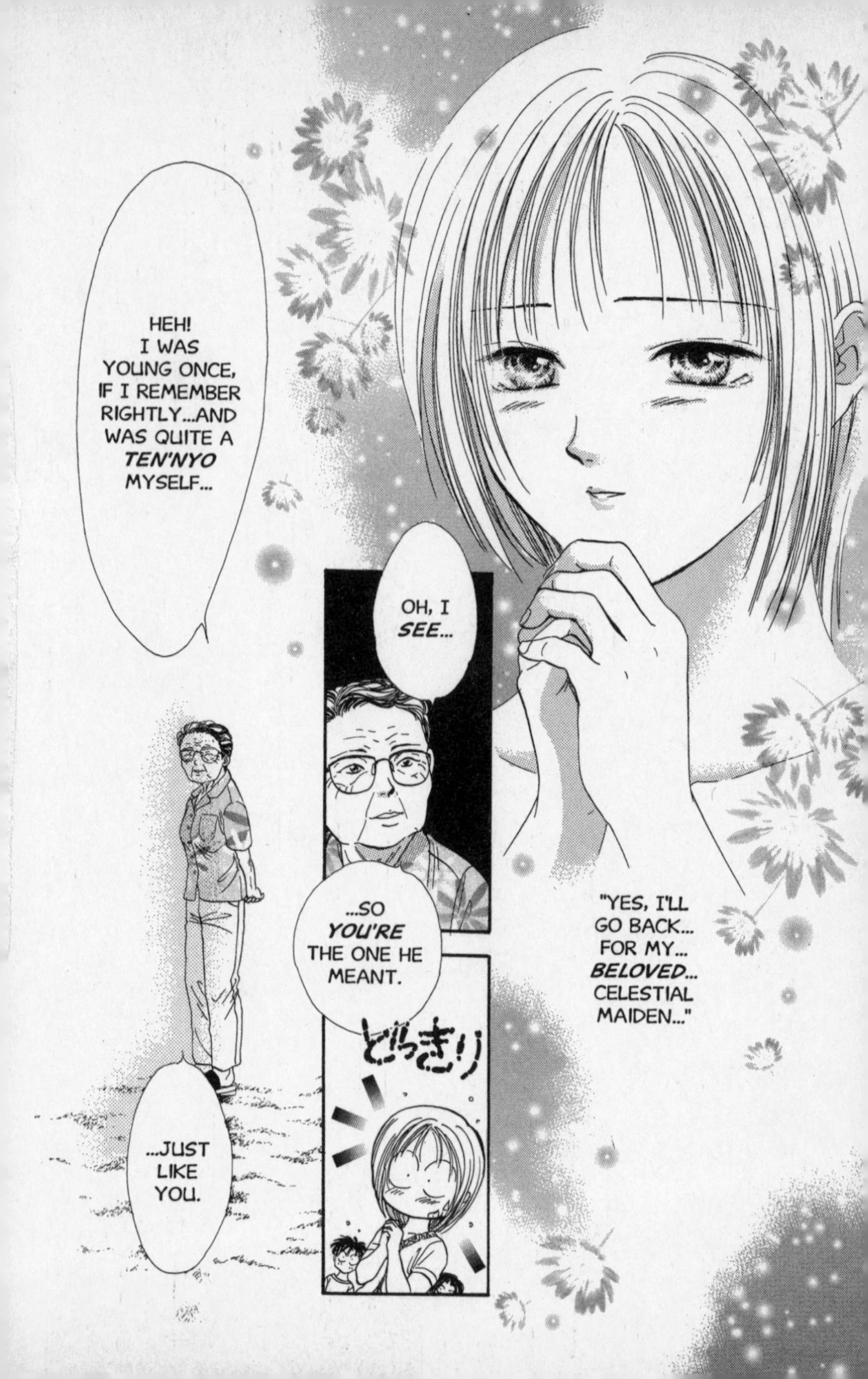
"YES, I'LL GO BACK... FOR MY... *BELOVED*... CELESTIAL MAIDEN..."
OH, I *SEE*...
...SO *YOU'RE* THE ONE HE MEANT.
どっきり
HEH! I WAS YOUNG ONCE, IF I REMEMBER RIGHTLY...AND WAS QUITE A *TEN'NYO* MYSELF...
...JUST LIKE YOU.

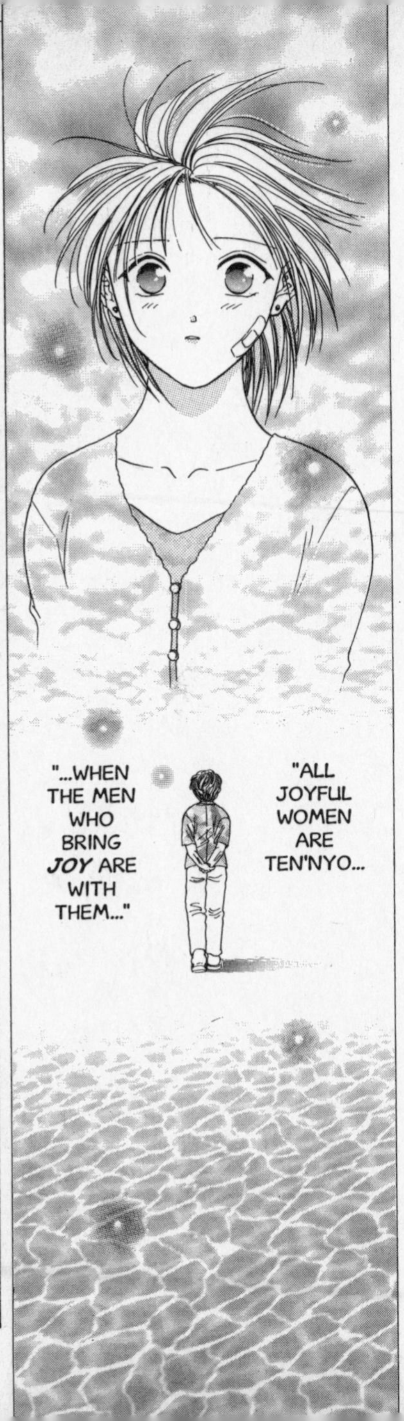
"ALL JOYFUL WOMEN ARE TEN'NYO...
"...WHEN THE MEN WHO BRING ***JOY*** ARE WITH THEM..."

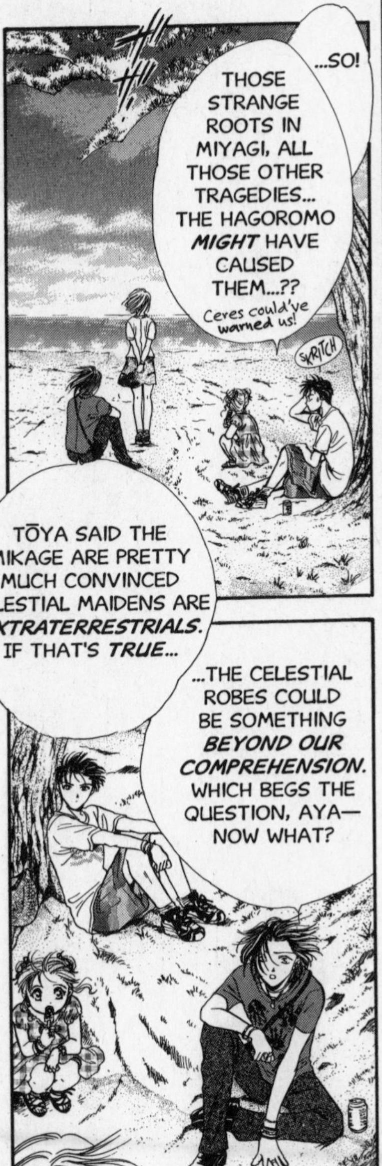
...SO!
THOSE STRANGE ROOTS IN MIYAGI, ALL THOSE OTHER TRAGEDIES... THE HAGOROMO ***MIGHT*** HAVE CAUSED THEM...??
Ceres could've warned us!
SKRITCH
TŌYA SAID THE MIKAGE ARE PRETTY MUCH CONVINCED CELESTIAL MAIDENS ARE ***EXTRATERRESTRIALS.*** IF THAT'S ***TRUE...***
...THE CELESTIAL ROBES COULD BE SOMETHING ***BEYOND OUR COMPREHENSION.*** WHICH BEGS THE QUESTION, AYA— NOW WHAT?

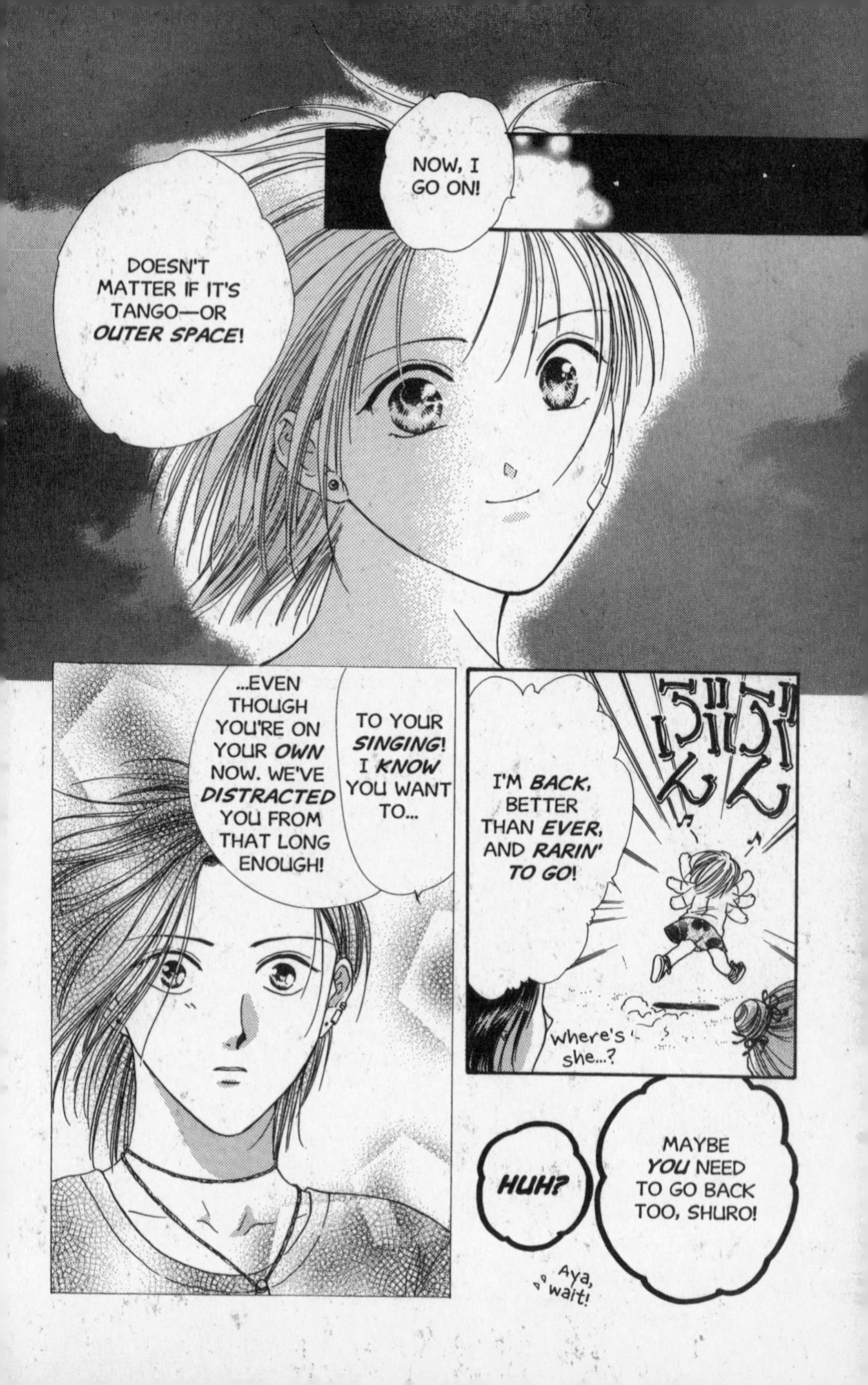
NOW, I GO ON!
DOESN'T MATTER IF IT'S TANGO—OR *OUTER SPACE*!
I'M *BACK*, BETTER THAN *EVER*, AND *RARIN' TO GO*!
where's she...?
MAYBE *YOU* NEED TO GO BACK TOO, SHURO!
HUH?
Aya, wait!
TO YOUR *SINGING*! I *KNOW* YOU WANT TO...
...EVEN THOUGH YOU'RE ON YOUR *OWN* NOW. WE'VE *DISTRACTED* YOU FROM THAT LONG ENOUGH!

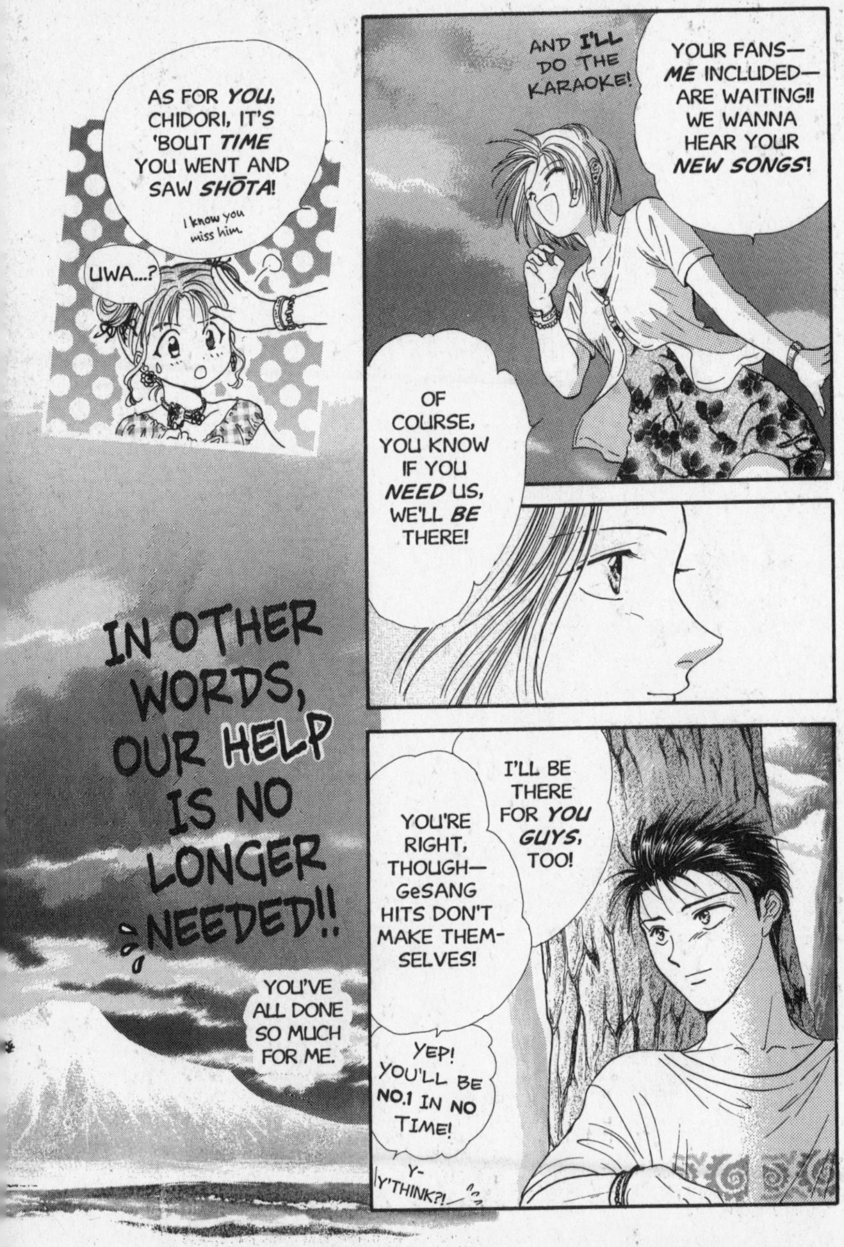
YOUR FANS—ME INCLUDED—ARE WAITING!! WE WANNA HEAR YOUR NEW SONGS!
AND I'LL DO THE KARAOKE!
AS FOR YOU, CHIDORI, IT'S 'BOUT TIME YOU WENT AND SAW SHŌTA!
I know you miss him.
UWA...?
OF COURSE, YOU KNOW IF YOU NEED US, WE'LL BE THERE!
YOU'VE ALL DONE SO MUCH FOR ME.
I'LL BE THERE FOR YOU GUYS, TOO!
YOU'RE RIGHT, THOUGH—GeSANG HITS DON'T MAKE THEMSELVES!
YEP! YOU'LL BE NO.1 IN NO TIME!
Y-Y'THINK?!
IN OTHER WORDS, OUR HELP IS NO LONGER NEEDED!!

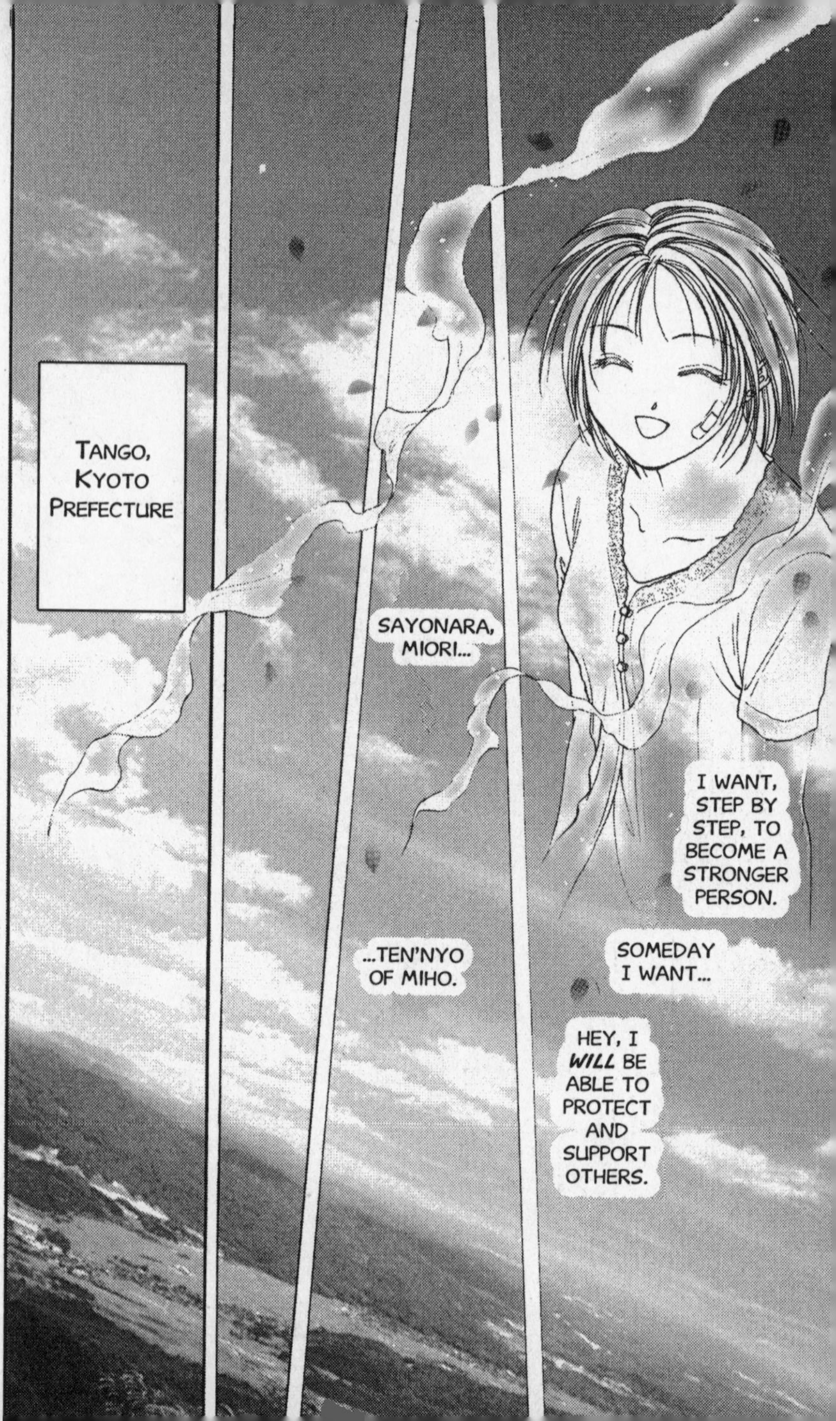

I WANT, STEP BY STEP, TO BECOME A STRONGER PERSON.
SOMEDAY I WANT...
HEY, I ***WILL*** BE ABLE TO PROTECT AND SUPPORT OTHERS.
SAYONARA, MIORI...
...TEN'NYO OF MIHO.
TANGO, KYOTO PREFECTURE

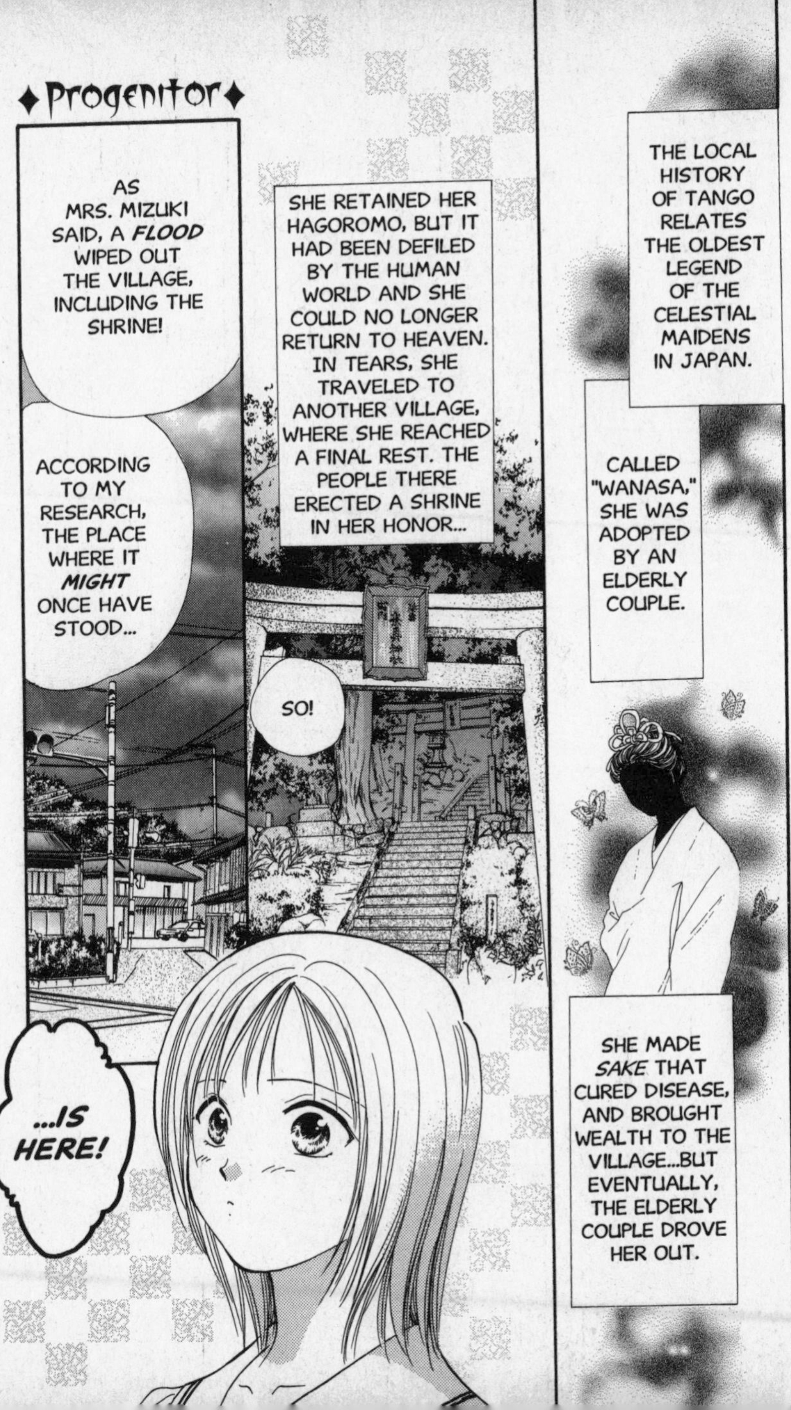
THE LOCAL HISTORY OF TANGO RELATES THE OLDEST LEGEND OF THE CELESTIAL MAIDENS IN JAPAN.
CALLED "WANASA," SHE WAS ADOPTED BY AN ELDERLY COUPLE.
SHE MADE *SAKE* THAT CURED DISEASE, AND BROUGHT WEALTH TO THE VILLAGE...BUT EVENTUALLY, THE ELDERLY COUPLE DROVE HER OUT.
♦Progenitor♦
SHE RETAINED HER HAGOROMO, BUT IT HAD BEEN DEFILED BY THE HUMAN WORLD AND SHE COULD NO LONGER RETURN TO HEAVEN. IN TEARS, SHE TRAVELED TO ANOTHER VILLAGE, WHERE SHE REACHED A FINAL REST. THE PEOPLE THERE ERECTED A SHRINE IN HER HONOR...
SO!
AS MRS. MIZUKI SAID, A *FLOOD* WIPED OUT THE VILLAGE, INCLUDING THE SHRINE!
ACCORDING TO MY RESEARCH, THE PLACE WHERE IT *MIGHT* ONCE HAVE STOOD...
...IS HERE!

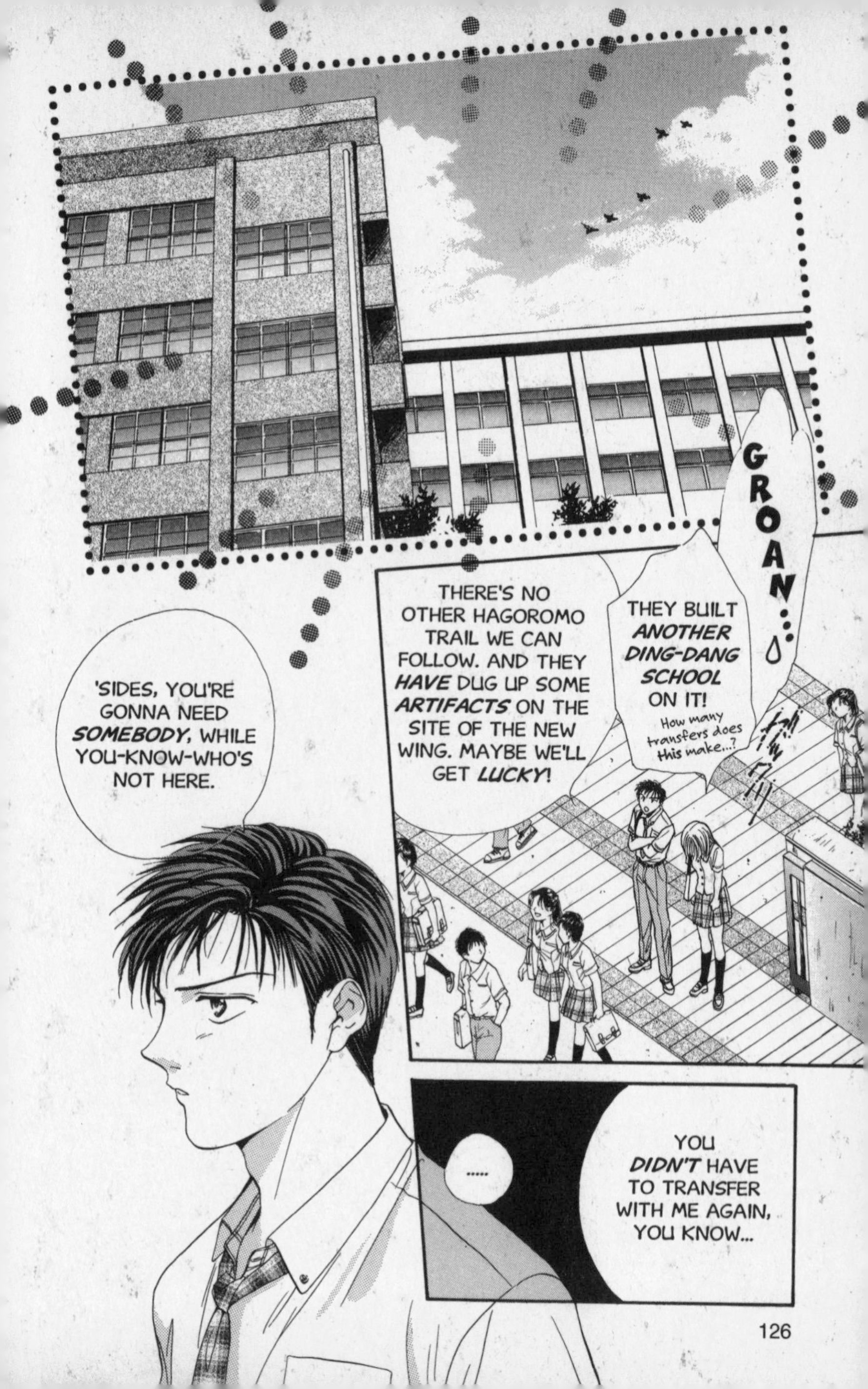
GROAN...
THEY BUILT ***ANOTHER DING-DANG SCHOOL*** ON IT!
How many transfers does this make...?
THERE'S NO OTHER HAGOROMO TRAIL WE CAN FOLLOW. AND THEY ***HAVE*** DUG UP SOME ***ARTIFACTS*** ON THE SITE OF THE NEW WING. MAYBE WE'LL GET ***LUCKY***!
YOU ***DIDN'T*** HAVE TO TRANSFER WITH ME AGAIN, YOU KNOW...
......
'SIDES, YOU'RE GONNA NEED ***SOMEBODY***, WHILE YOU-KNOW-WHO'S NOT HERE.

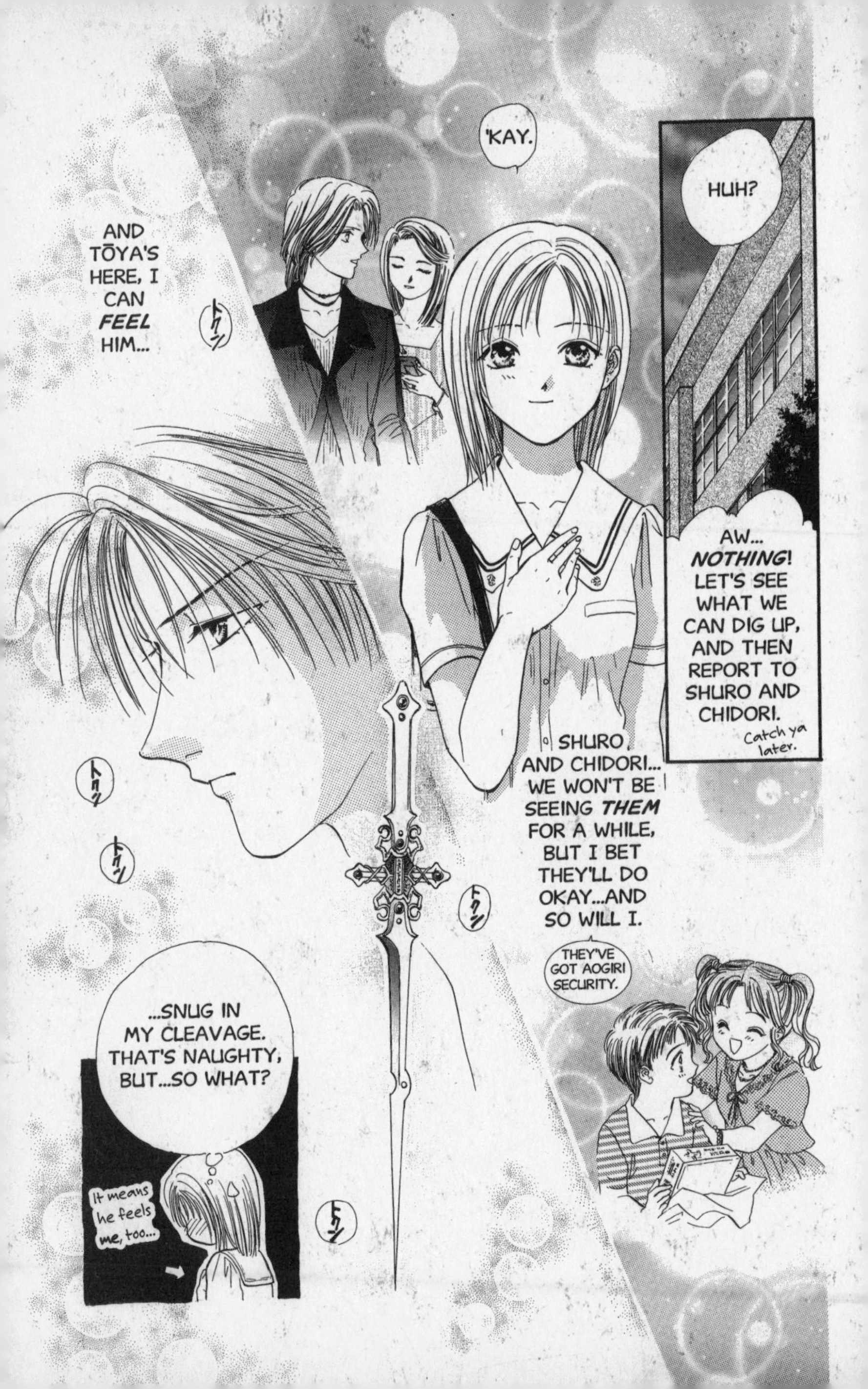
HUH?
AW... NOTHING! LET'S SEE WHAT WE CAN DIG UP, AND THEN REPORT TO SHURO AND CHIDORI.
Catch ya later.
'KAY.
AND TŌYA'S HERE, I CAN FEEL HIM...
SHURO AND CHIDORI... WE WON'T BE SEEING THEM FOR A WHILE, BUT I BET THEY'LL DO OKAY...AND SO WILL I.
THEY'VE GOT AOGIRI SECURITY.
...SNUG IN MY CLEAVAGE. THAT'S NAUGHTY, BUT...SO WHAT?
It means he feels me, too...

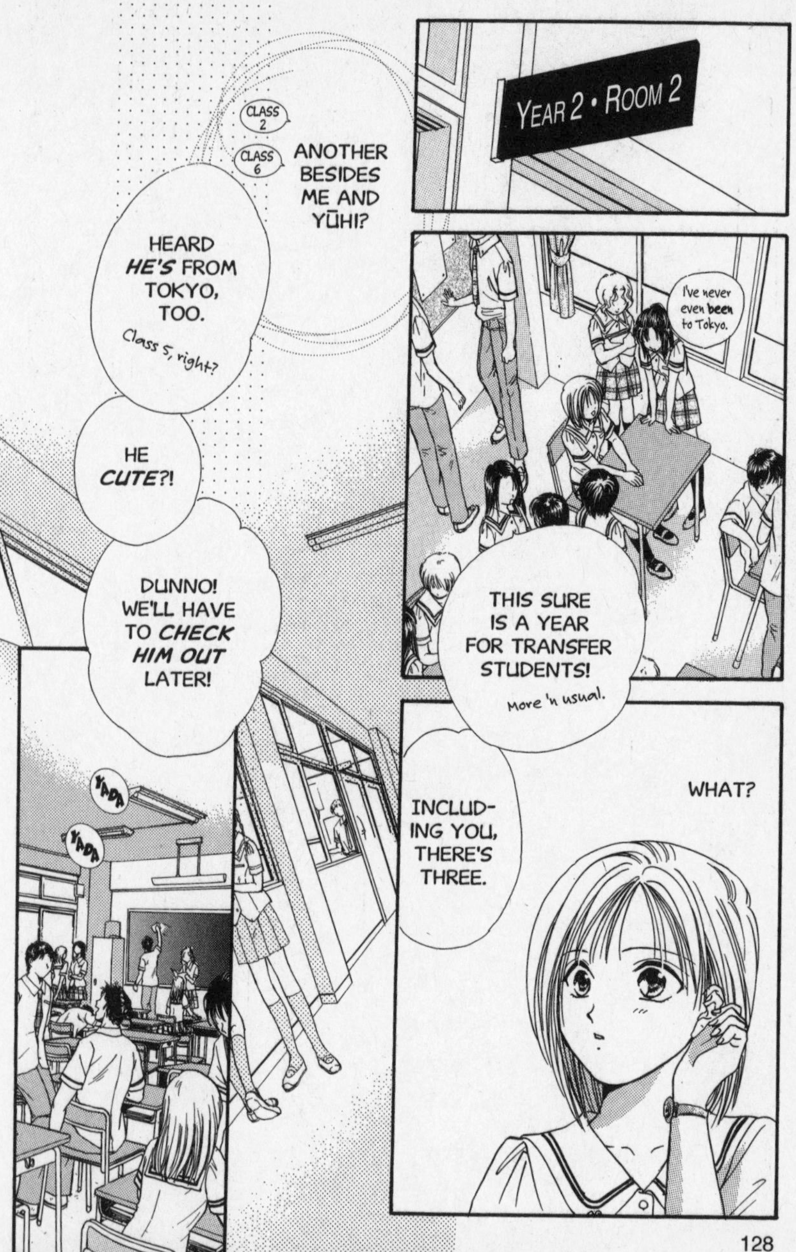
YEAR 2 • ROOM 2
CLASS 2
CLASS 6
ANOTHER BESIDES ME AND YŪHI?
HEARD *HE'S* FROM TOKYO, TOO.
Class 5, right?
HE *CUTE*?!
DUNNO! WE'LL HAVE TO *CHECK HIM OUT* LATER!
I've never even **been** to Tokyo.
THIS SURE IS A YEAR FOR TRANSFER STUDENTS!
More 'n usual.
WHAT?
INCLUD-ING YOU, THERE'S THREE.
YADA
YADA

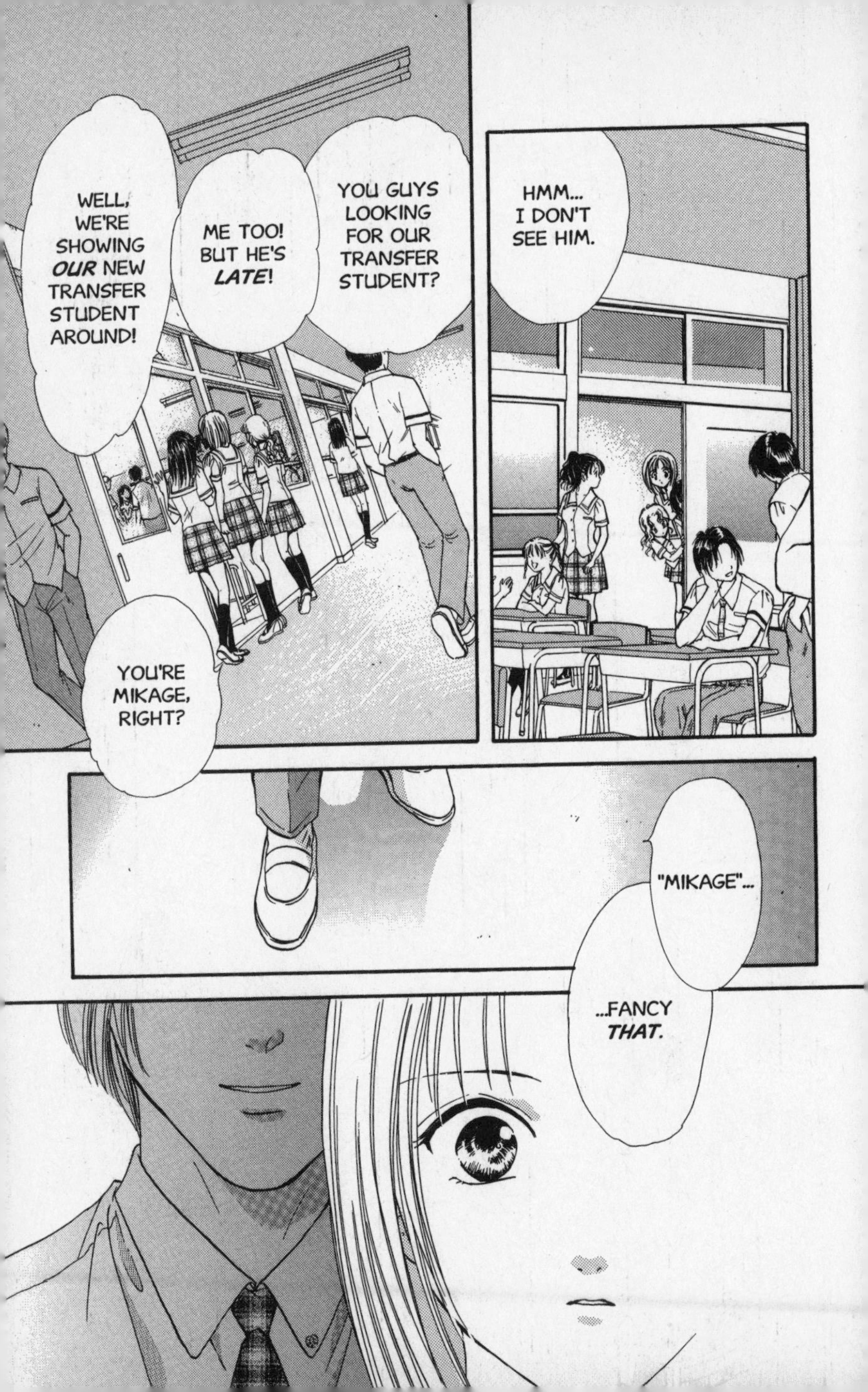
HMM... I DON'T SEE HIM.
YOU GUYS LOOKING FOR OUR TRANSFER STUDENT?
ME TOO! BUT HE'S *LATE*!
WELL, WE'RE SHOWING *OUR* NEW TRANSFER STUDENT AROUND!
YOU'RE MIKAGE, RIGHT?
"MIKAGE"...
...FANCY *THAT*.

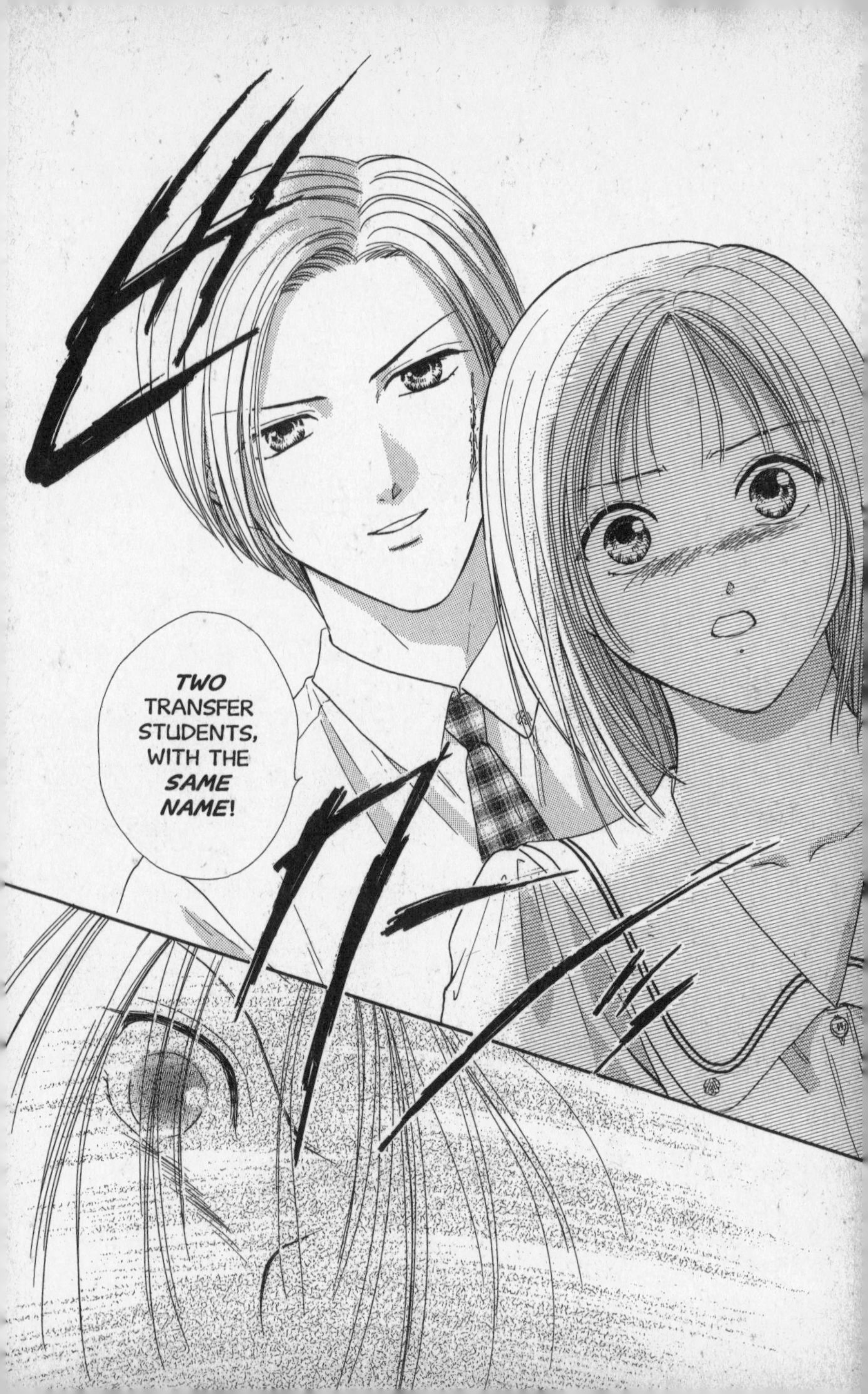
TWO TRANSFER STUDENTS, WITH THE SAME NAME!

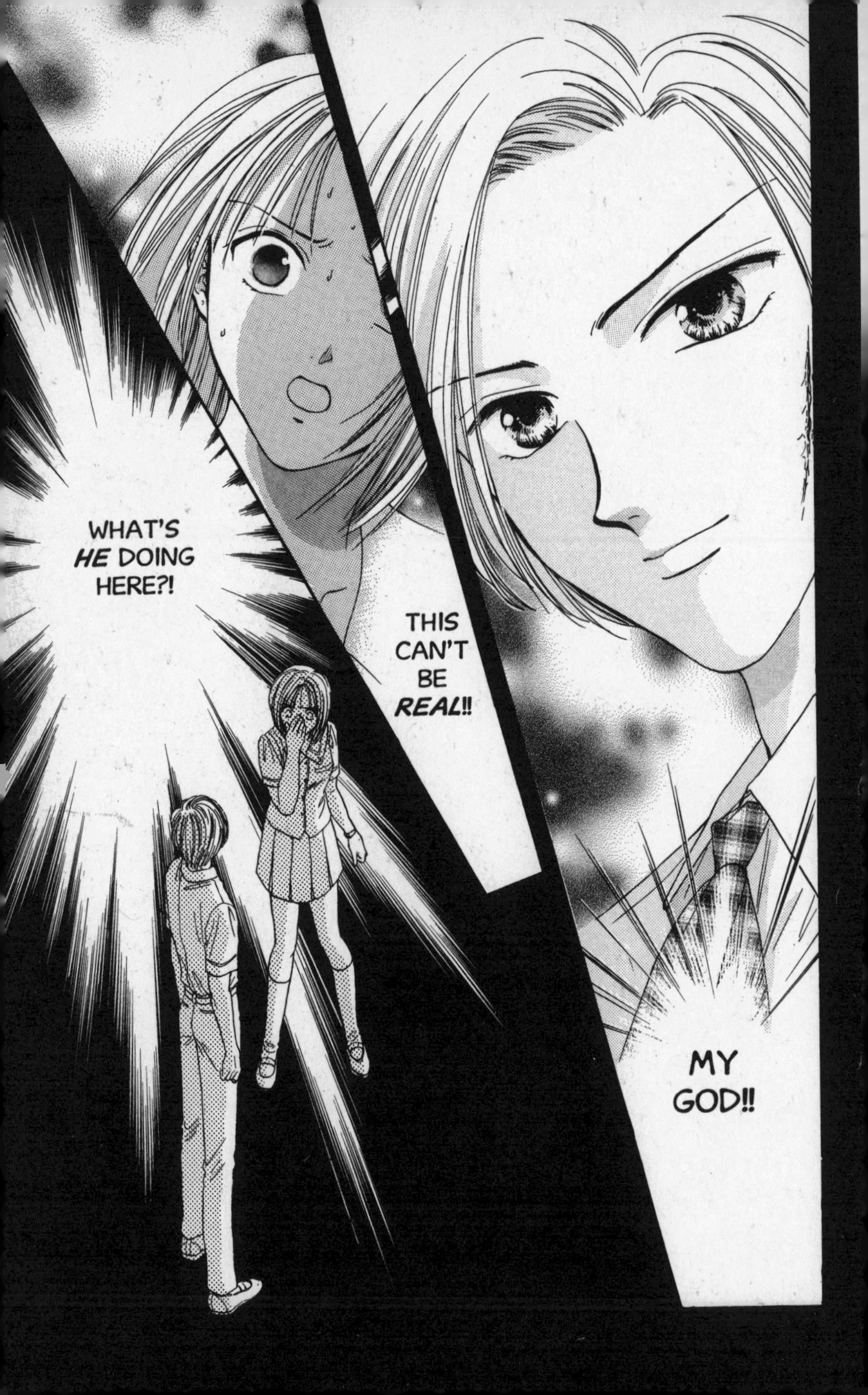
MY GOD!!
THIS CAN'T BE REAL!!
WHAT'S HE DOING HERE?!

CELESTIAL SPOOFS
–Part 2–

Ruins the **mood**, you say? Sorry, but it's **gots** t' be **done**!

·Another Great Escape·

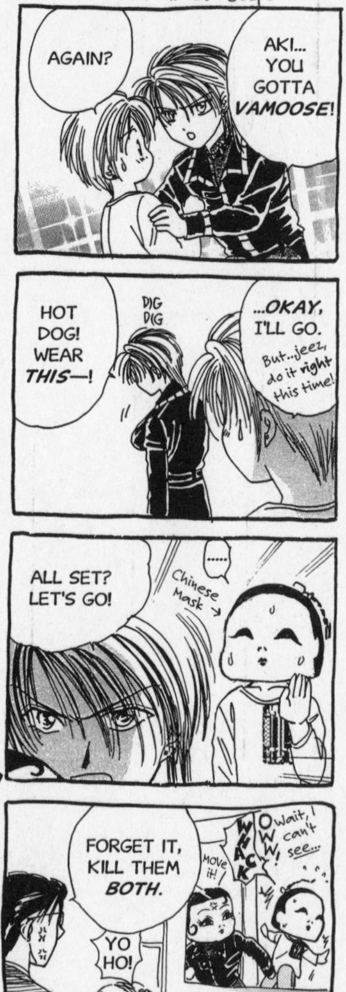
AKI... YOU GOTTA *VAMOOSE*!
AGAIN?
...OKAY, I'LL GO.
But...jeez, do it right this time!
DIG DIG
HOT DOG! WEAR *THIS*—!
Chinese Mask
......
ALL SET? LET'S GO!
OWW! wait, I can't see...
WHACK
Move it!
FORGET IT, KILL THEM *BOTH*.
YO HO!

"J"'s idea, after listening to Assistant "H."

·Mikage International·

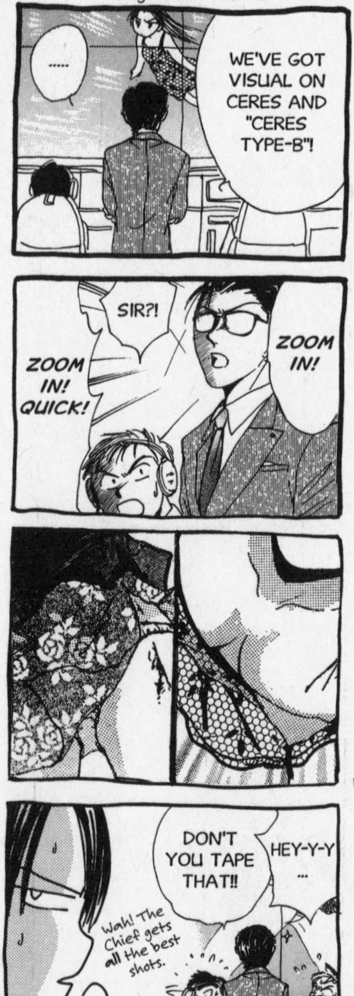
WE'VE GOT VISUAL ON CERES AND "CERES TYPE-B"!
......
ZOOM IN!
SIR?!
ZOOM IN! QUICK!
HEY-Y-Y ...
DON'T YOU TAPE THAT!!
Wah! The Chief gets all the best shots.
......

This one's mine (we clear?!)

Lots of Mikage in these gag strips. To Be Continued (?)

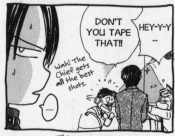

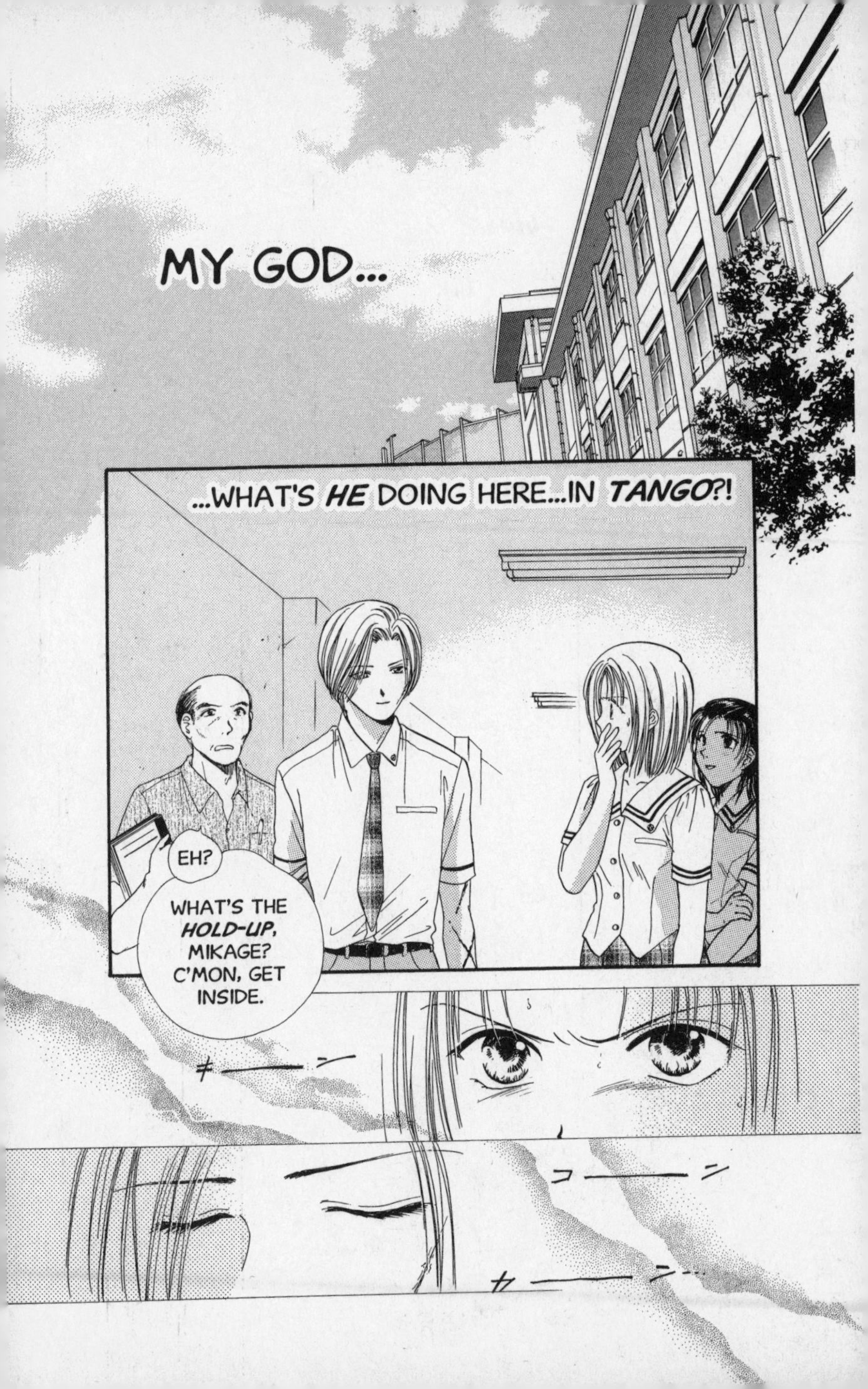
MY GOD...
...WHAT'S *HE* DOING HERE...IN *TANGO?!*
EH?
WHAT'S THE *HOLD-UP,* MIKAGE? C'MON, GET INSIDE.
キーーン
コーーン
カーーン

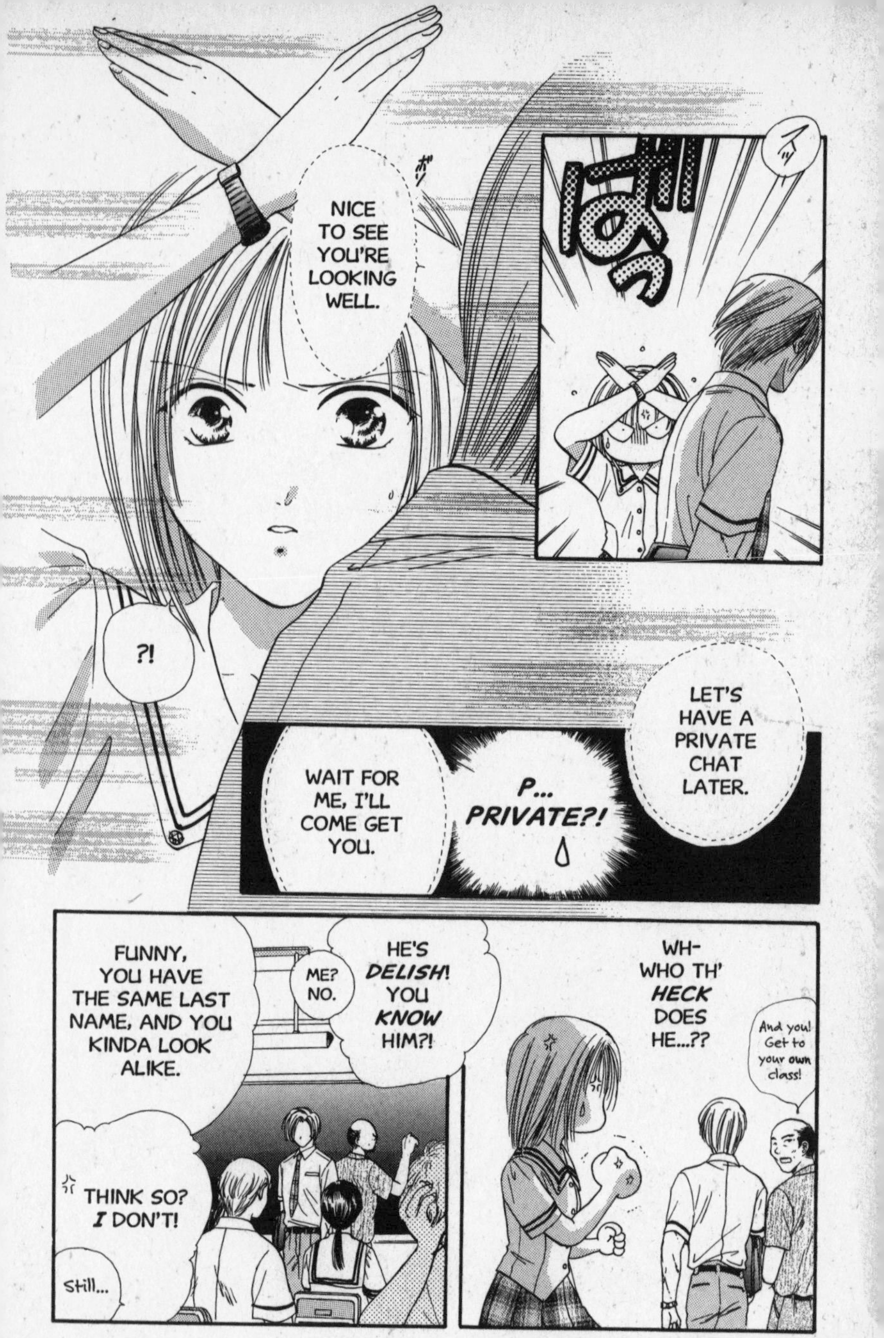
ばっ
NICE TO SEE YOU'RE LOOKING WELL.
?!
LET'S HAVE A PRIVATE CHAT LATER.
P... PRIVATE?!
WAIT FOR ME, I'LL COME GET YOU.
WH- WHO TH' *HECK* DOES HE...??
And you! Get to your own class!
HE'S *DELISH*! YOU *KNOW* HIM?!
ME? NO.
FUNNY, YOU HAVE THE SAME LAST NAME, AND YOU KINDA LOOK ALIKE.
THINK SO? *I* DON'T!
Still...

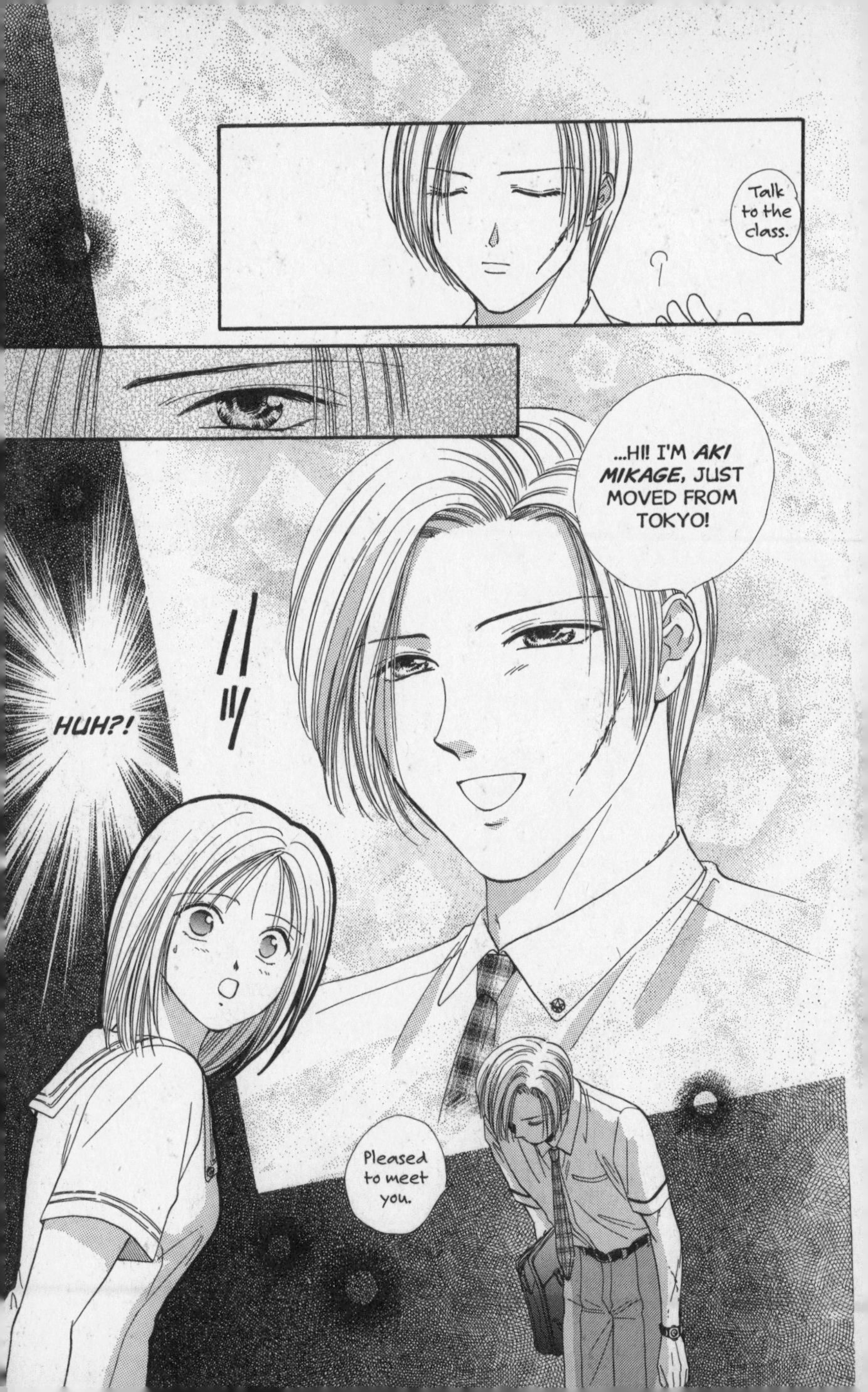
Talk to the class.
...HI! I'M AKI MIKAGE, JUST MOVED FROM TOKYO!
HUH?!
Pleased to meet you.

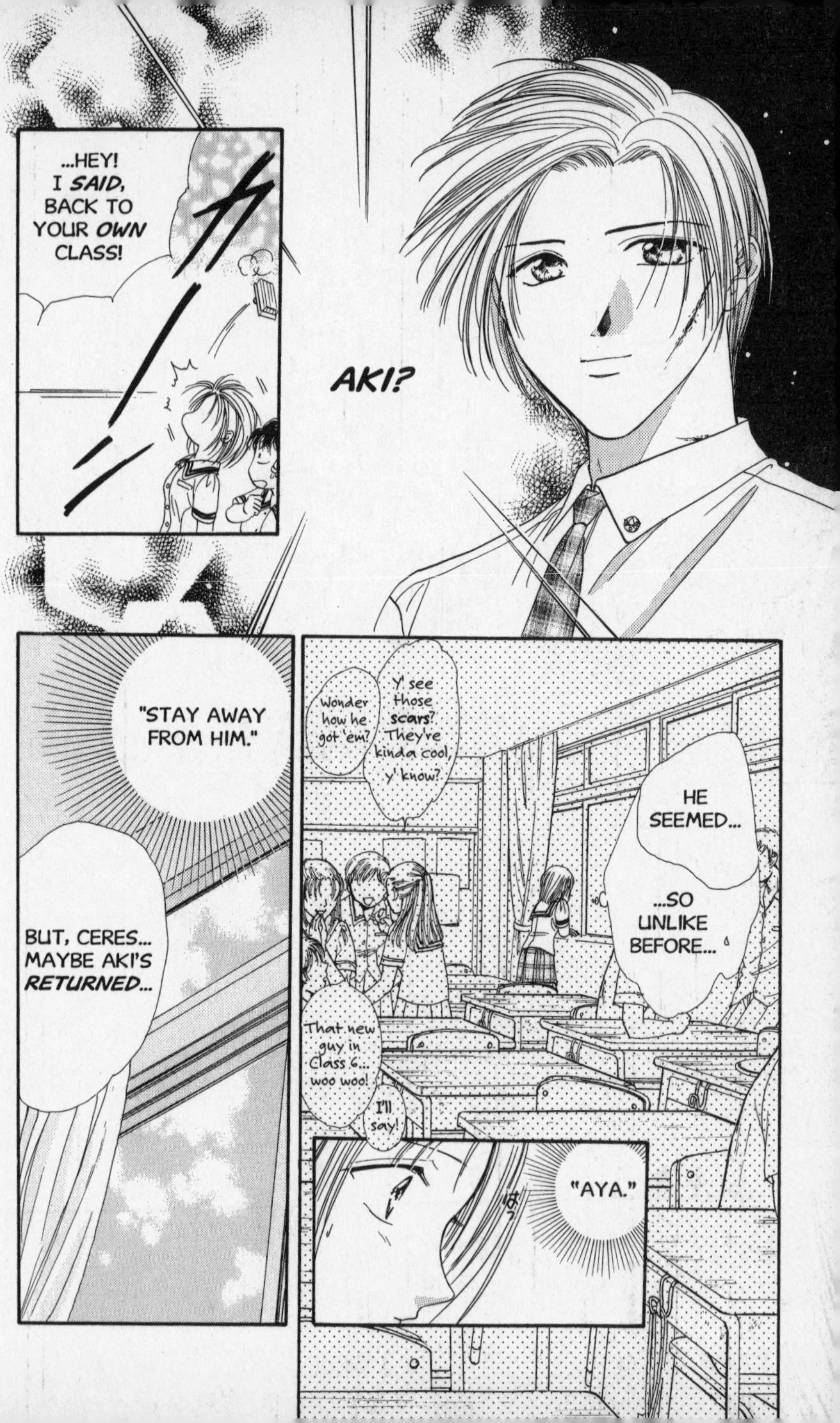
AKI?
...HEY! I SAID, BACK TO YOUR OWN CLASS!
HE SEEMED...
...SO UNLIKE BEFORE...
Y' see those scars? They're kinda cool, y'know?
Wonder how he got 'em?
That new guy in Class 6... woo woo!
I'll say!
"AYA."
"STAY AWAY FROM HIM."
BUT, CERES... MAYBE AKI'S RETURNED...

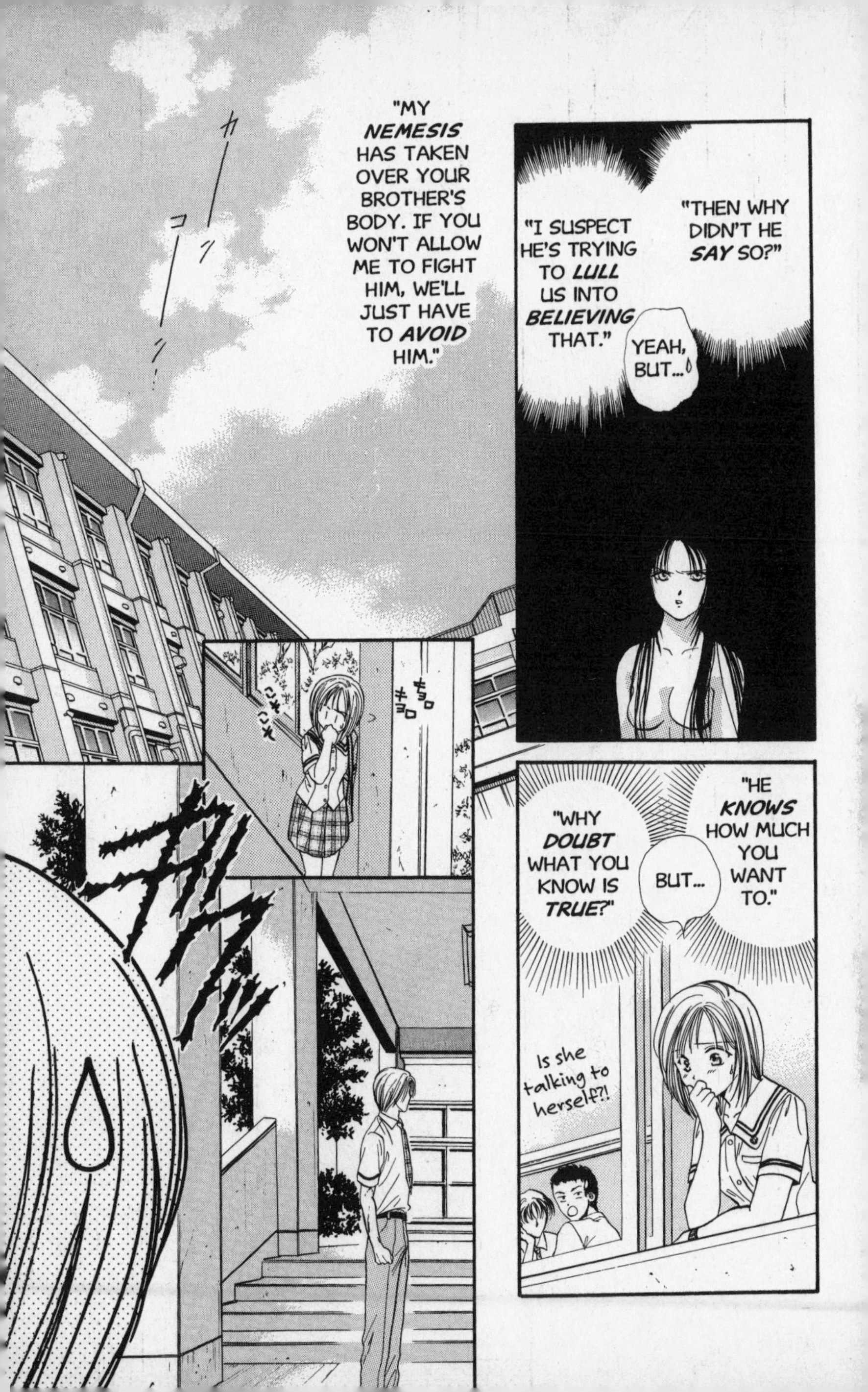
"THEN WHY DIDN'T HE SAY SO?"
"I SUSPECT HE'S TRYING TO LULL US INTO BELIEVING THAT."
YEAH, BUT...
"MY NEMESIS HAS TAKEN OVER YOUR BROTHER'S BODY. IF YOU WON'T ALLOW ME TO FIGHT HIM, WE'LL JUST HAVE TO AVOID HIM."
"HE KNOWS HOW MUCH YOU WANT TO."
BUT...
"WHY DOUBT WHAT YOU KNOW IS TRUE?"
Is she talking to herself?!

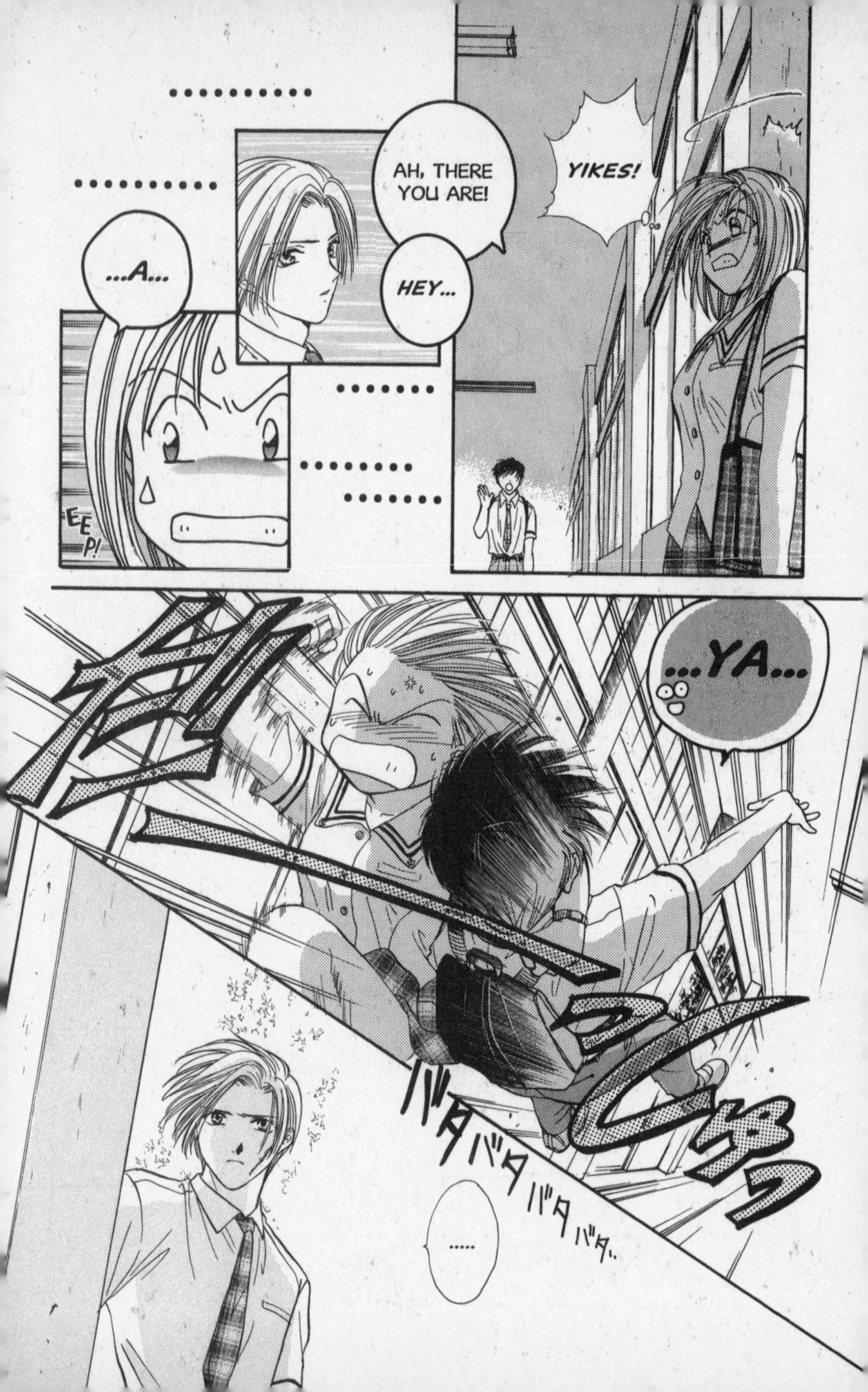
YIKES!
AH, THERE YOU ARE!
HEY...
....
....
...A...
....
....
....
EEP!
...YA...
バタバタ
バタバタ
.....

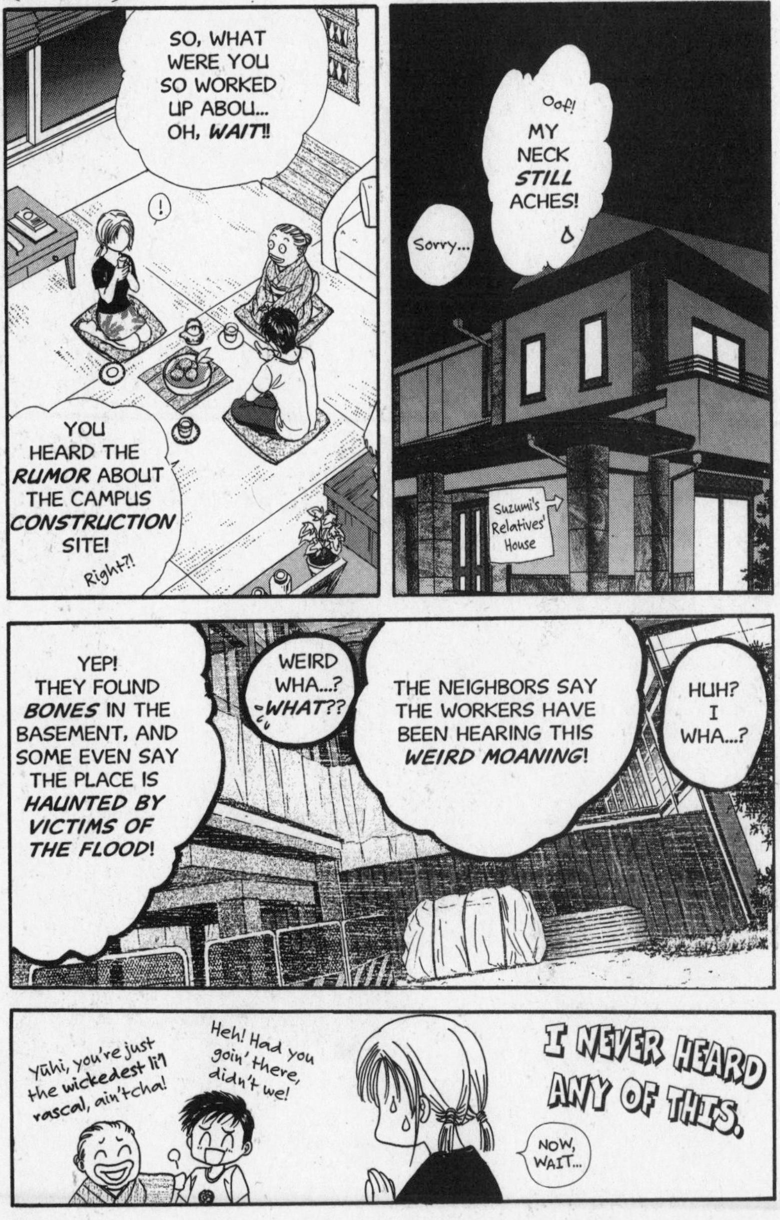
Oof!
MY NECK STILL ACHES!
Sorry...
Suzumi's Relatives' House
SO, WHAT WERE YOU SO WORKED UP ABOU... OH, WAIT!!
!
YOU HEARD THE RUMOR ABOUT THE CAMPUS CONSTRUCTION SITE!
Right?!
HUH? I WHA...?
THE NEIGHBORS SAY THE WORKERS HAVE BEEN HEARING THIS WEIRD MOANING!
WEIRD WHA...? WHAT??
YEP! THEY FOUND BONES IN THE BASEMENT, AND SOME EVEN SAY THE PLACE IS HAUNTED BY VICTIMS OF THE FLOOD!
I NEVER HEARD ANY OF THIS.
NOW, WAIT...
Heh! Had you goin' there, didn't we!
Yūhi, you're just the wickedest li'l rascal, ain'tcha!

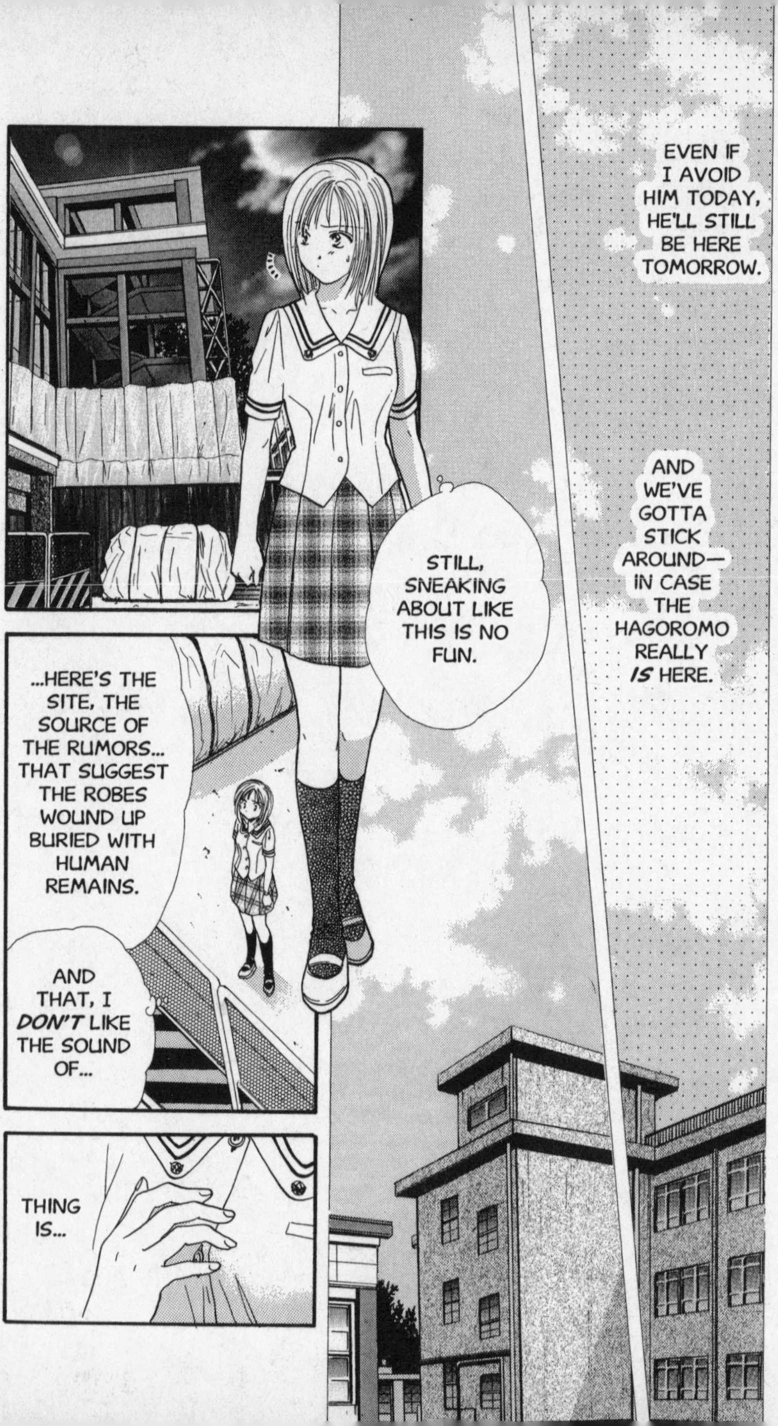
EVEN IF I AVOID HIM TODAY, HE'LL STILL BE HERE TOMORROW.
AND WE'VE GOTTA STICK AROUND— IN CASE THE HAGOROMO REALLY *IS* HERE.
STILL, SNEAKING ABOUT LIKE THIS IS NO FUN.
...HERE'S THE SITE, THE SOURCE OF THE RUMORS... THAT SUGGEST THE ROBES WOUND UP BURIED WITH HUMAN REMAINS.
AND THAT, I *DON'T* LIKE THE SOUND OF...
THING IS...

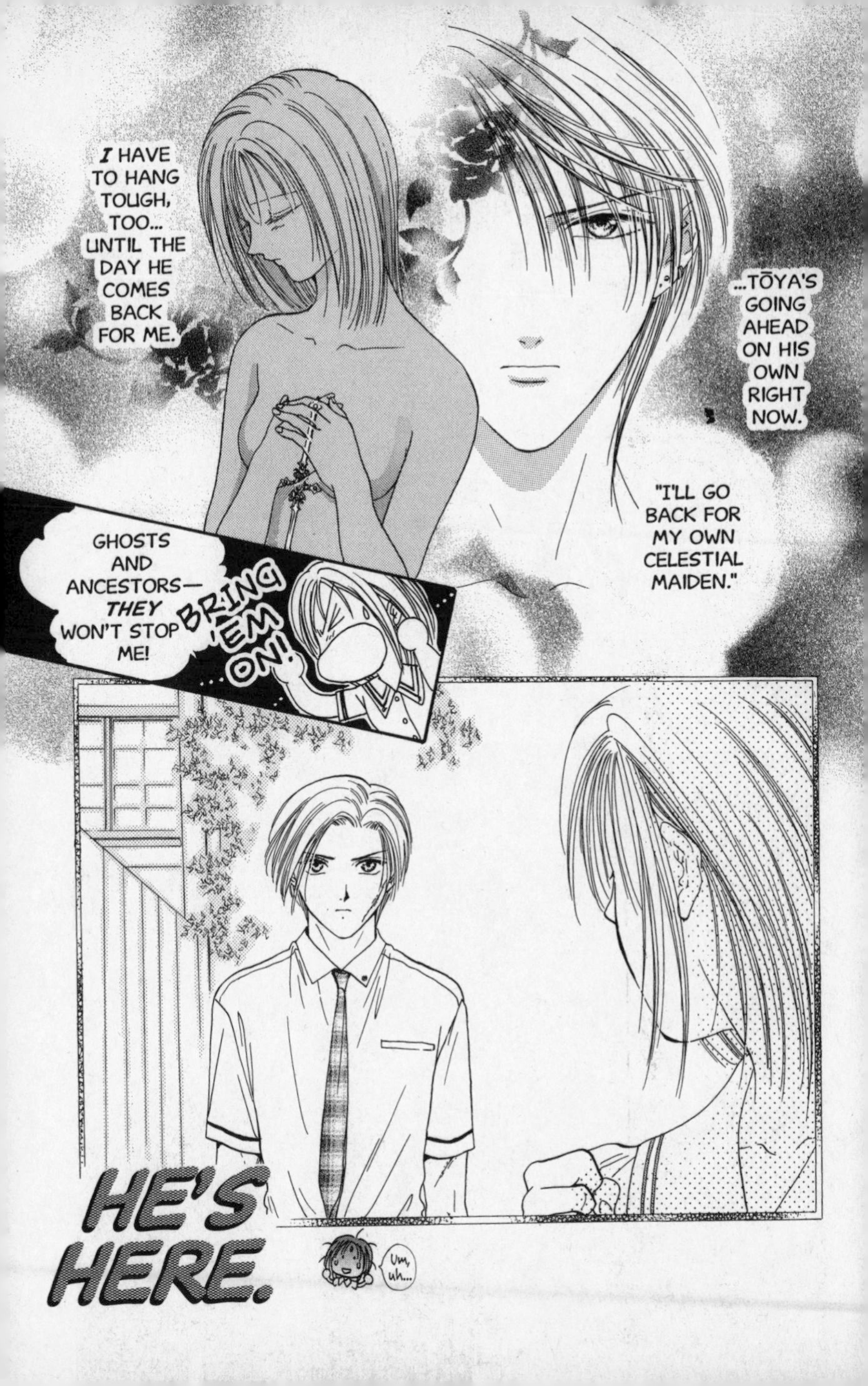
...TŌYA'S GOING AHEAD ON HIS OWN RIGHT NOW.
I HAVE TO HANG TOUGH, TOO... UNTIL THE DAY HE COMES BACK FOR ME.
"I'LL GO BACK FOR MY OWN CELESTIAL MAIDEN."
BRING 'EM ON!
GHOSTS AND ANCESTORS—THEY WON'T STOP ME!
HE'S HERE.
Um, uh...

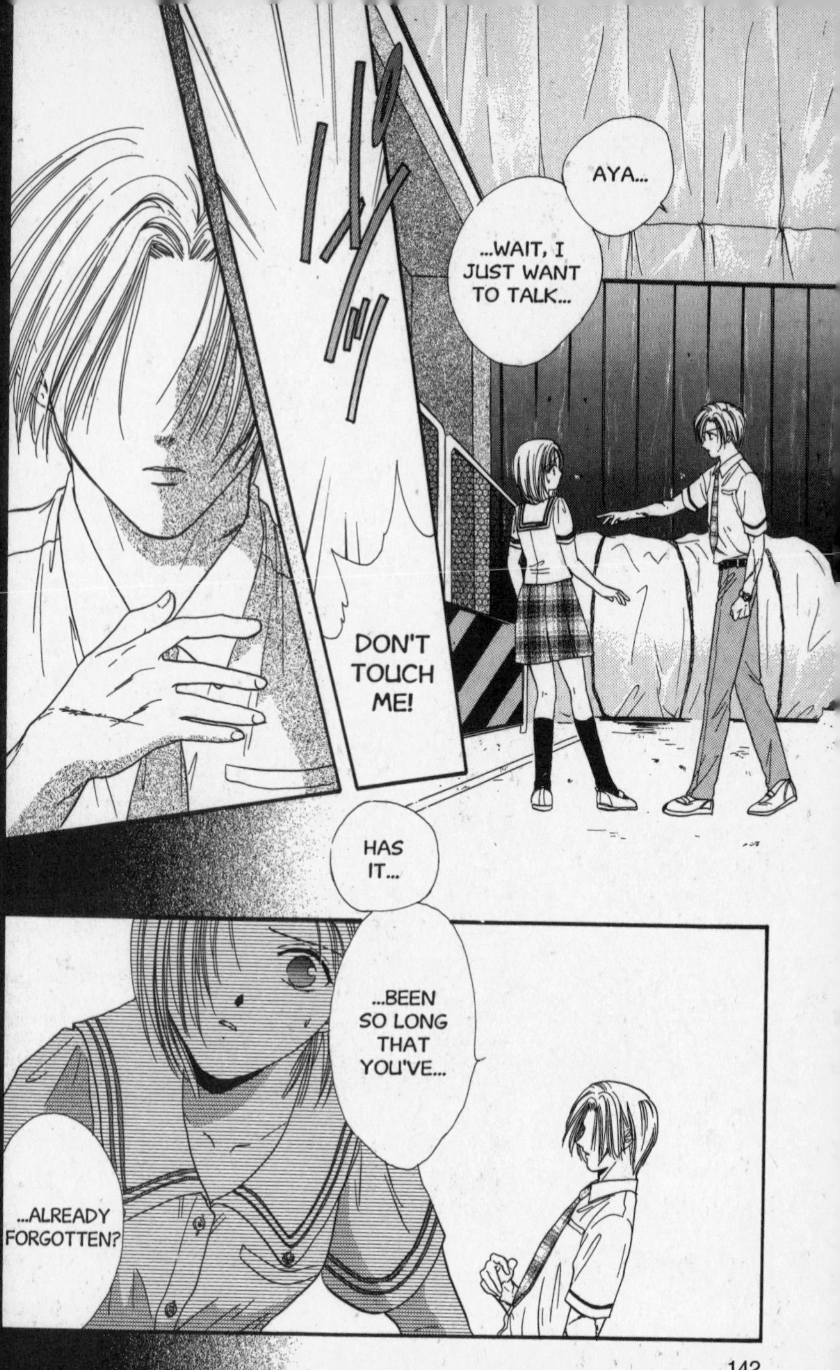
AYA...
...WAIT, I JUST WANT TO TALK...
DON'T TOUCH ME!
HAS IT...
...BEEN SO LONG THAT YOU'VE...
...ALREADY FORGOTTEN?

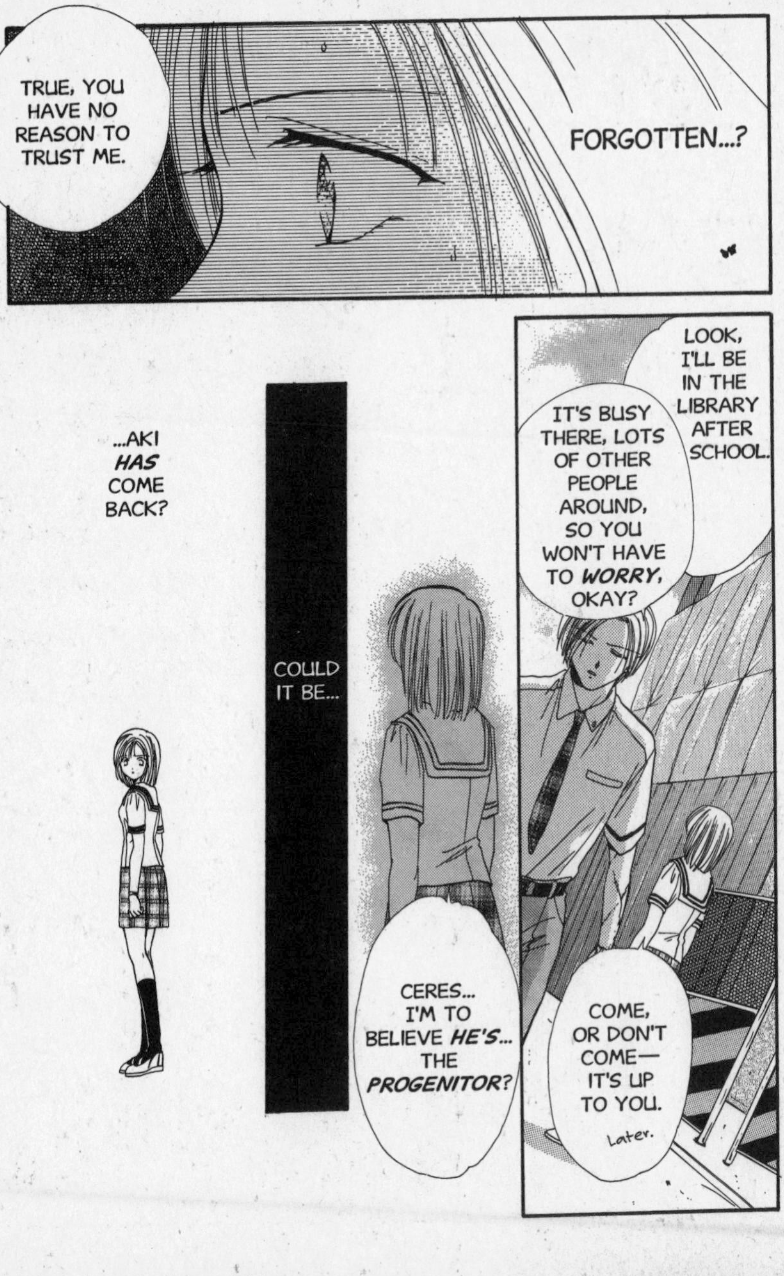
FORGOTTEN...?
TRUE, YOU HAVE NO REASON TO TRUST ME.
LOOK, I'LL BE IN THE LIBRARY AFTER SCHOOL.
IT'S BUSY THERE, LOTS OF OTHER PEOPLE AROUND, SO YOU WON'T HAVE TO WORRY, OKAY?
COME, OR DON'T COME— IT'S UP TO YOU.
Later.
COULD IT BE...
CERES... I'M TO BELIEVE HE'S... THE PROGENITOR?
...AKI HAS COME BACK?

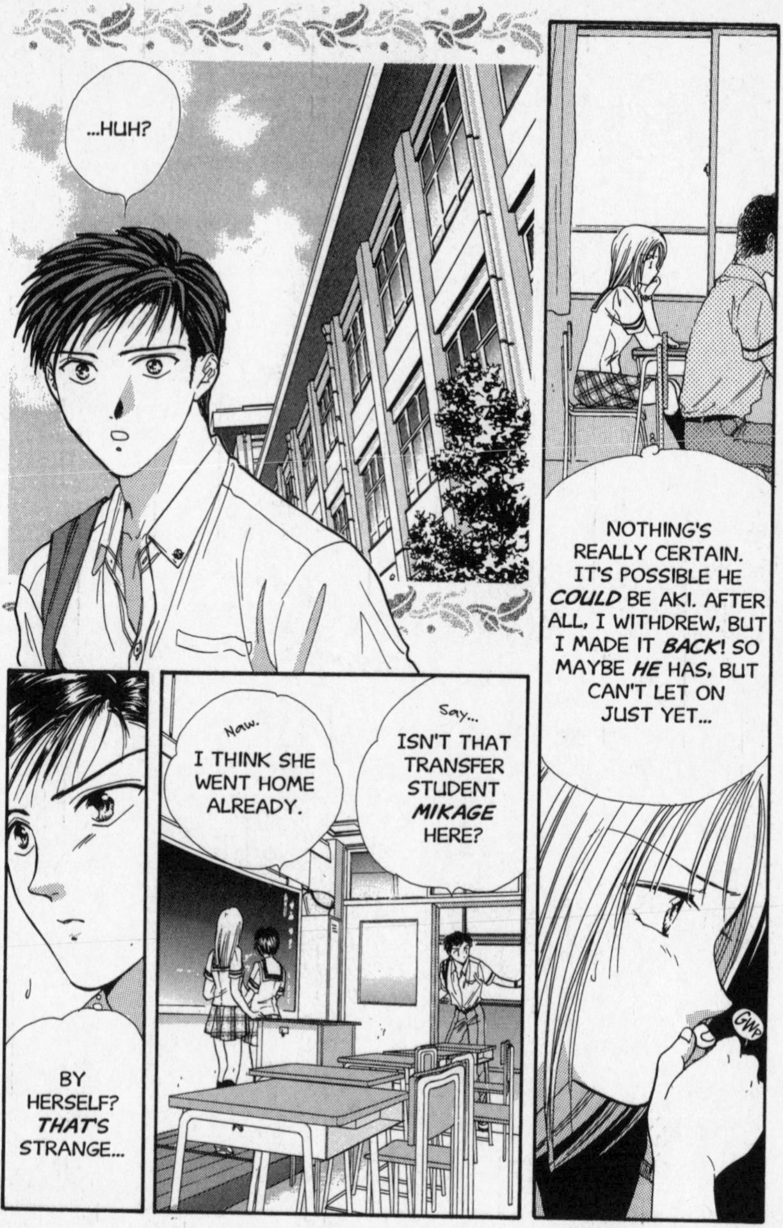
NOTHING'S REALLY CERTAIN. IT'S POSSIBLE HE *COULD* BE AKI. AFTER ALL, I WITHDREW, BUT I MADE IT *BACK*! SO MAYBE *HE* HAS, BUT CAN'T LET ON JUST YET...
GWP
...HUH?
Say...
ISN'T THAT TRANSFER STUDENT *MIKAGE* HERE?
Naw.
I THINK SHE WENT HOME ALREADY.
BY HERSELF? *THAT'S* STRANGE...

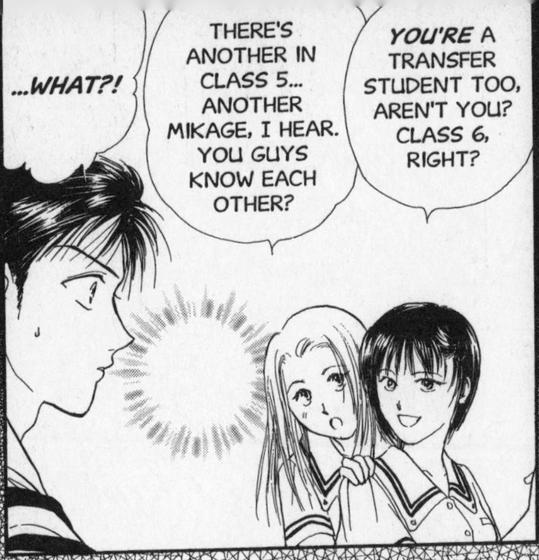
YOU'RE A TRANSFER STUDENT TOO, AREN'T YOU? CLASS 6, RIGHT?
THERE'S ANOTHER IN CLASS 5... ANOTHER MIKAGE, I HEAR. YOU GUYS KNOW EACH OTHER?
...WHAT?!

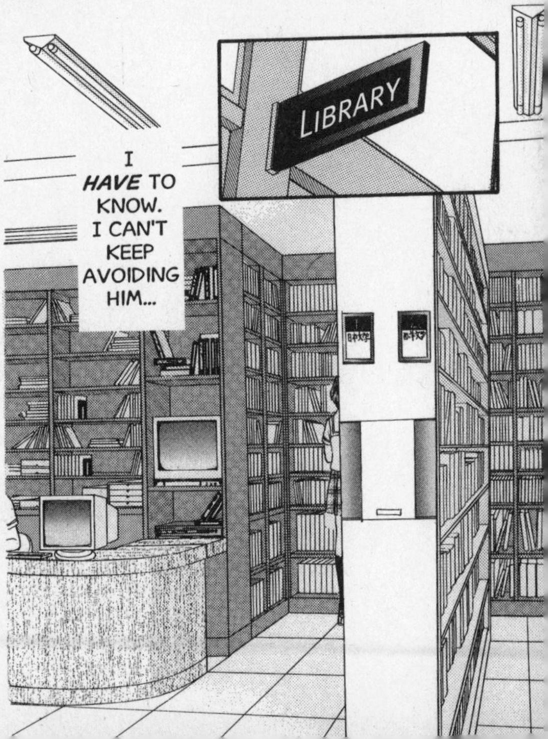
LIBRARY
I *HAVE* TO KNOW. I CAN'T KEEP AVOIDING HIM...

Well!! I hear all the time that people argue about Aya being with Tōya, with Yūhi, or even Aki ◡̈ but, these days, more seem to be staying neutral. "I'm a Tōya fan, but Yūhi's a nice guy, so I want him to be happy, too." Or, "I'm a Yūhi fan, but Aya should be with Tōya, and Yūhi should go out with me." ◡̈ Or, "Aya should be with Aki..." Oh, I so don't think so...! They're **brother** and **sister**, for crying out loud. Sometimes people "trash talk" the characters who aren't their favorites—I don't think that's a good thing. I know you're just being passionate, but to me it's kinda sad. Having likes and dislikes is only natural, but you don't have to run down other people for characters **they** like. Let's get together on this, huh? The world doesn't revolve around your personal opinions. To each his own. You can't force your own opinion on others. I'm asked all the time, "Who do you like better in **FFVII**, Tifa or Aeris?" I liked Aeris, but I thought Tifa had her points, too. To be fair, though, I **am** pretty particular. It's also true for human interaction in **real** life. You can't fly off the handle every time things don't go the way you want. You may not like something, but try to consider that there **can** be different perspectives.

Get this: There's an actual Aya among you readers—with the same kanji, even! She herself was surprised about it. Why **did** your parents pick that name...? Someone else had a son named Yūhi. No Tōya, though, I guess. ...Oh! That's right. One more day until "Shishunki Miman O-Kotowari: Kanketsu-Hen (No Interest in Prepubescence: The Conclusion)" is out in graphic novel format. (Demand was high....) I'll have to write two more short stories to fill out a full book... This isn't the first you've heard of it, is it? Please be patient....

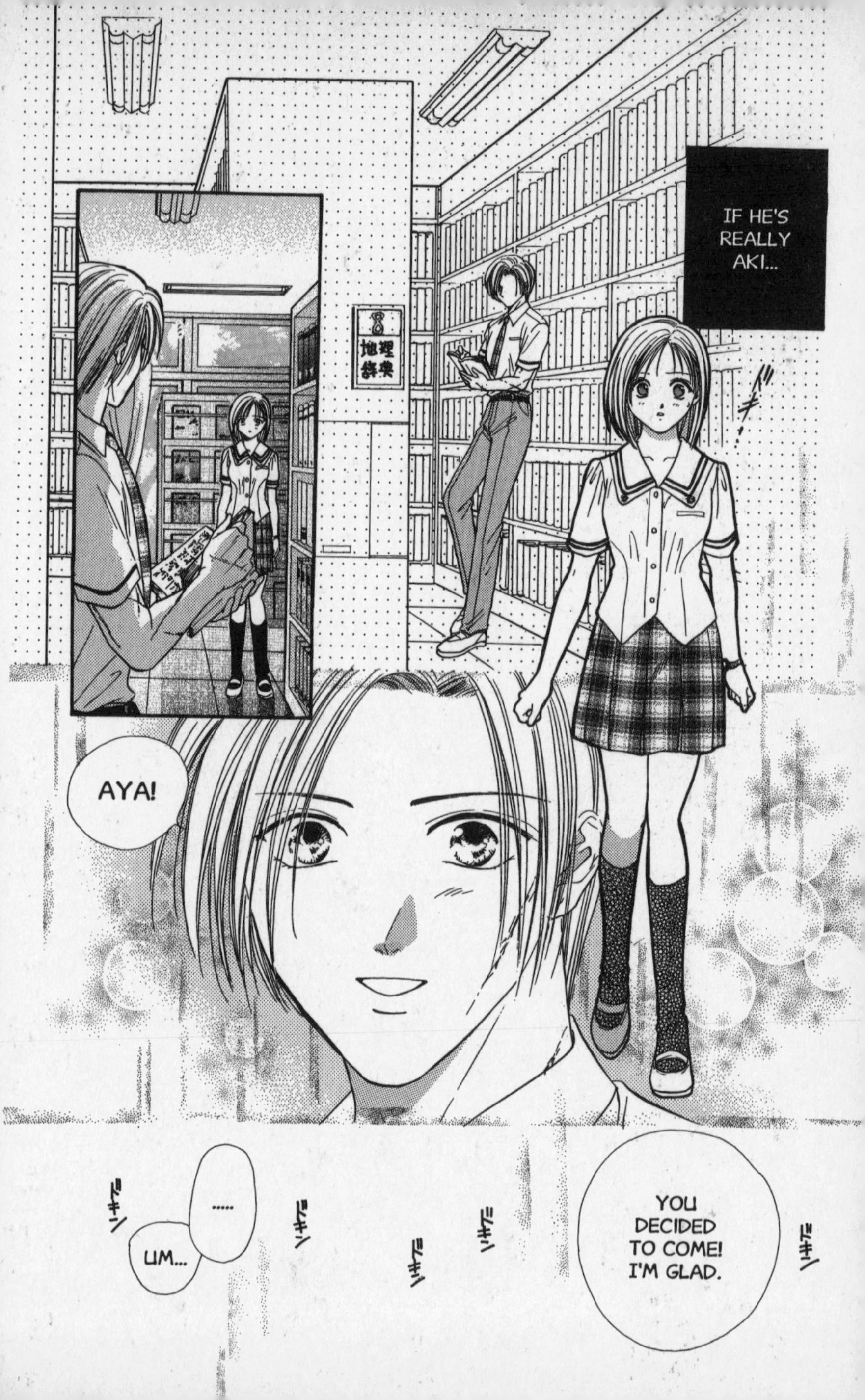
IF HE'S REALLY AKI...
AYA!
YOU DECIDED TO COME! I'M GLAD.
......
UM...

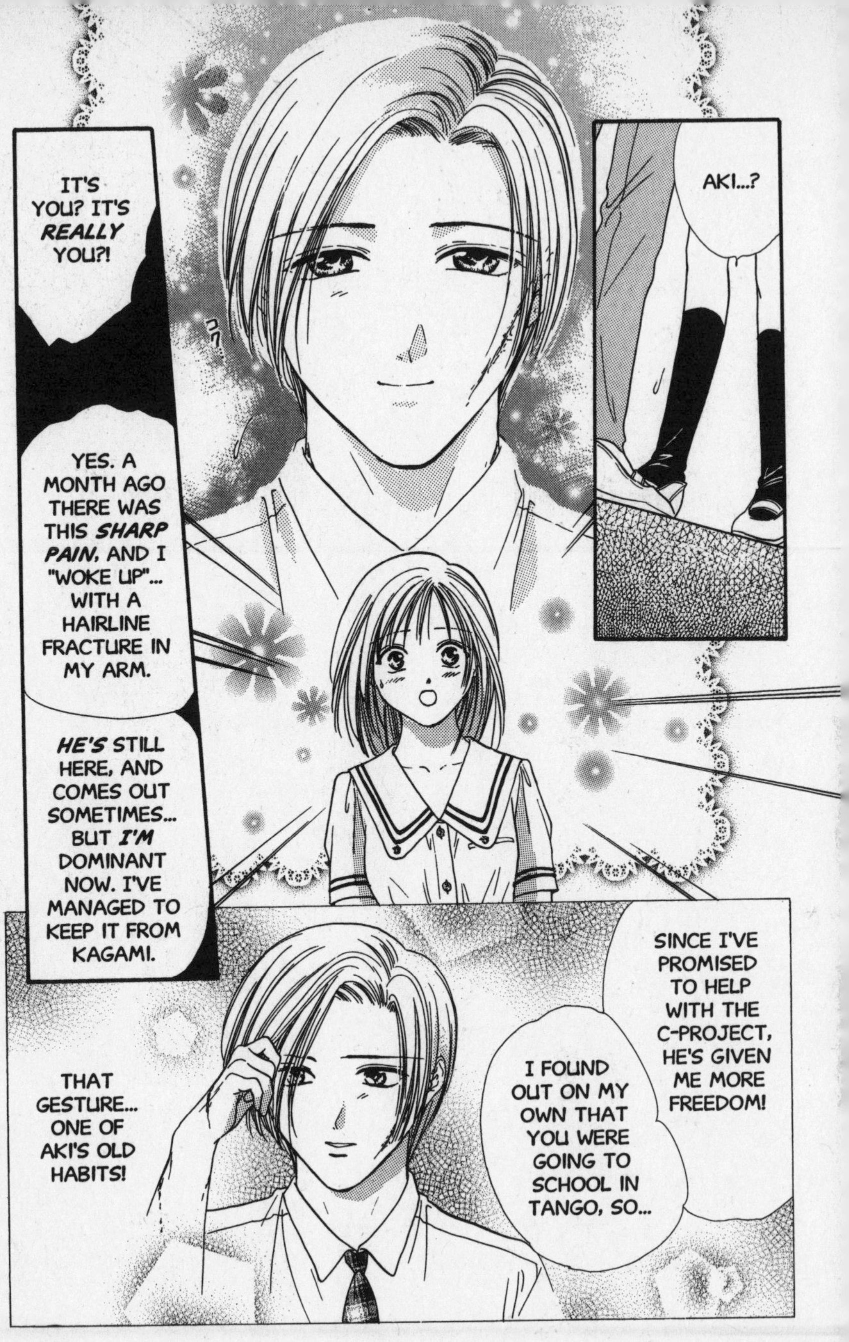
AKI...?
IT'S YOU? IT'S *REALLY* YOU?!
YES. A MONTH AGO THERE WAS THIS *SHARP PAIN,* AND I "WOKE UP"... WITH A HAIRLINE FRACTURE IN MY ARM.
HE'S STILL HERE, AND COMES OUT SOMETIMES... BUT *I'M* DOMINANT NOW. I'VE MANAGED TO KEEP IT FROM KAGAMI.
SINCE I'VE PROMISED TO HELP WITH THE C-PROJECT, HE'S GIVEN ME MORE FREEDOM!
I FOUND OUT ON MY OWN THAT YOU WERE GOING TO SCHOOL IN TANGO, SO...
THAT GESTURE... ONE OF AKI'S OLD HABITS!

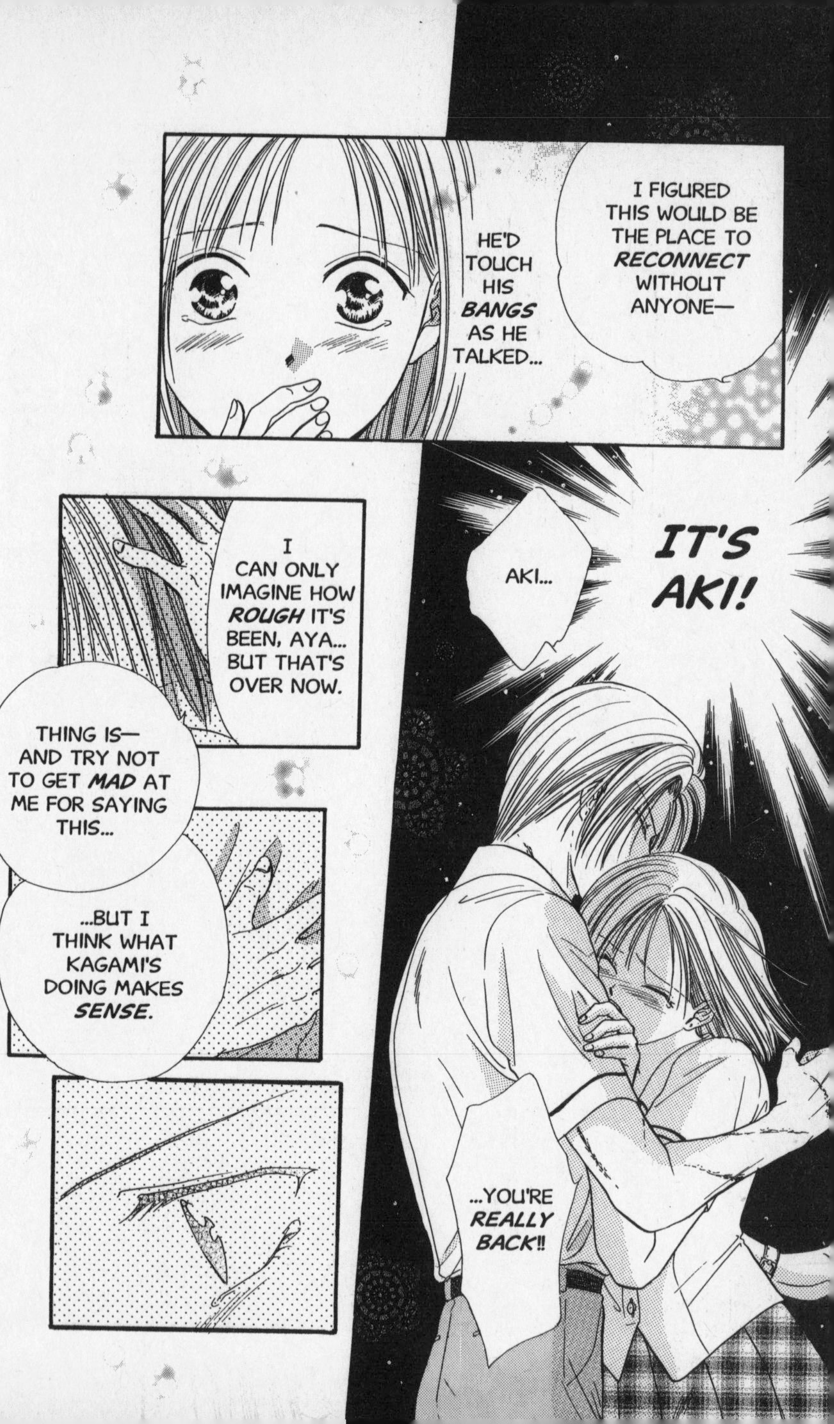
I FIGURED THIS WOULD BE THE PLACE TO *RECONNECT* WITHOUT ANYONE—
HE'D TOUCH HIS *BANGS* AS HE TALKED...
IT'S AKI!
AKI...
...YOU'RE *REALLY BACK*!!
I CAN ONLY IMAGINE HOW *ROUGH* IT'S BEEN, AYA... BUT THAT'S OVER NOW.
THING IS— AND TRY NOT TO GET *MAD* AT ME FOR SAYING THIS...
...BUT I THINK WHAT KAGAMI'S DOING MAKES *SENSE*.

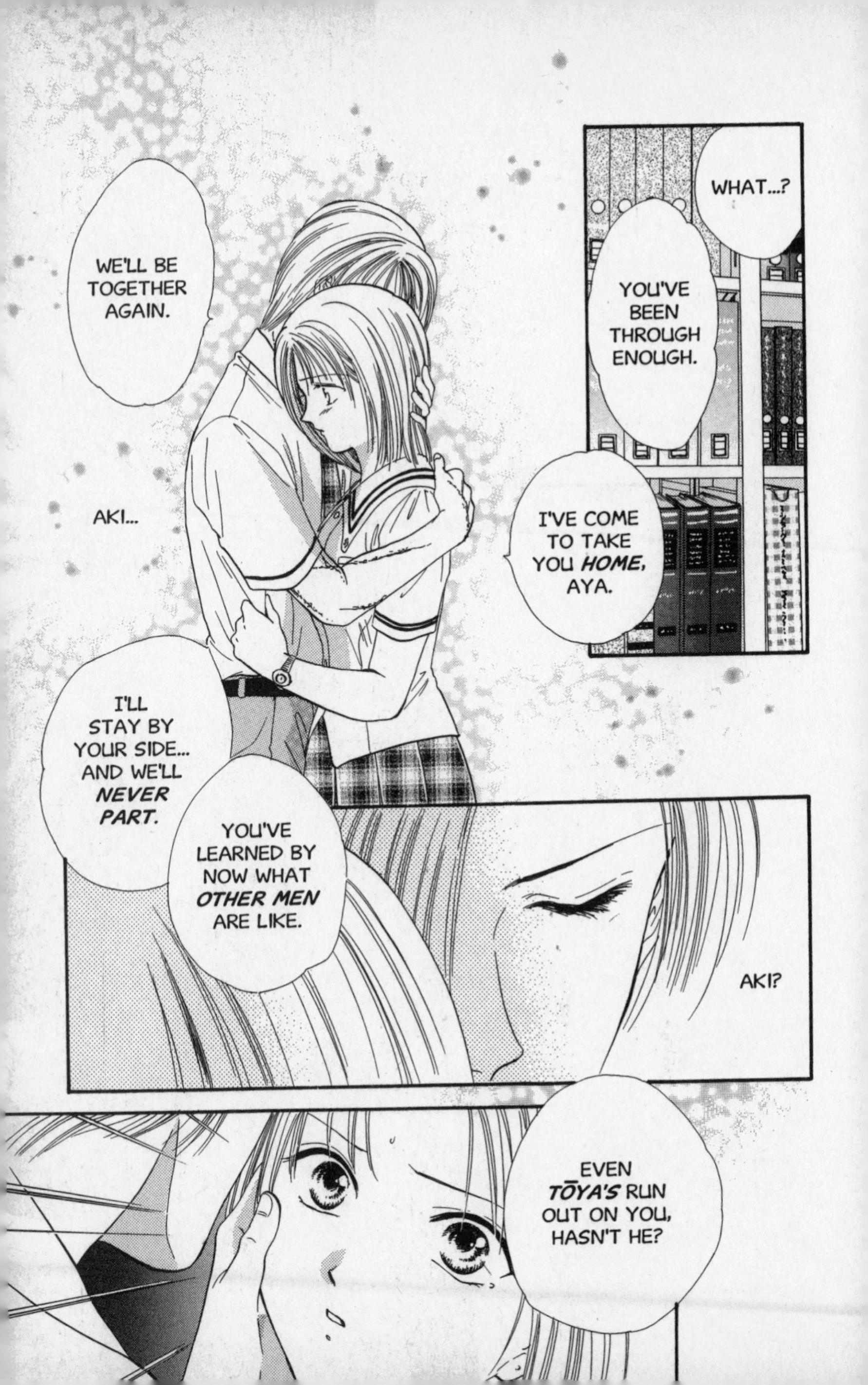
WHAT...?
YOU'VE BEEN THROUGH ENOUGH.
I'VE COME TO TAKE YOU *HOME*, AYA.
WE'LL BE TOGETHER AGAIN.
AKI...
I'LL STAY BY YOUR SIDE... AND WE'LL *NEVER PART*.
YOU'VE LEARNED BY NOW WHAT *OTHER MEN* ARE LIKE.
AKI?
EVEN *TŌYA'S* RUN OUT ON YOU, HASN'T HE?

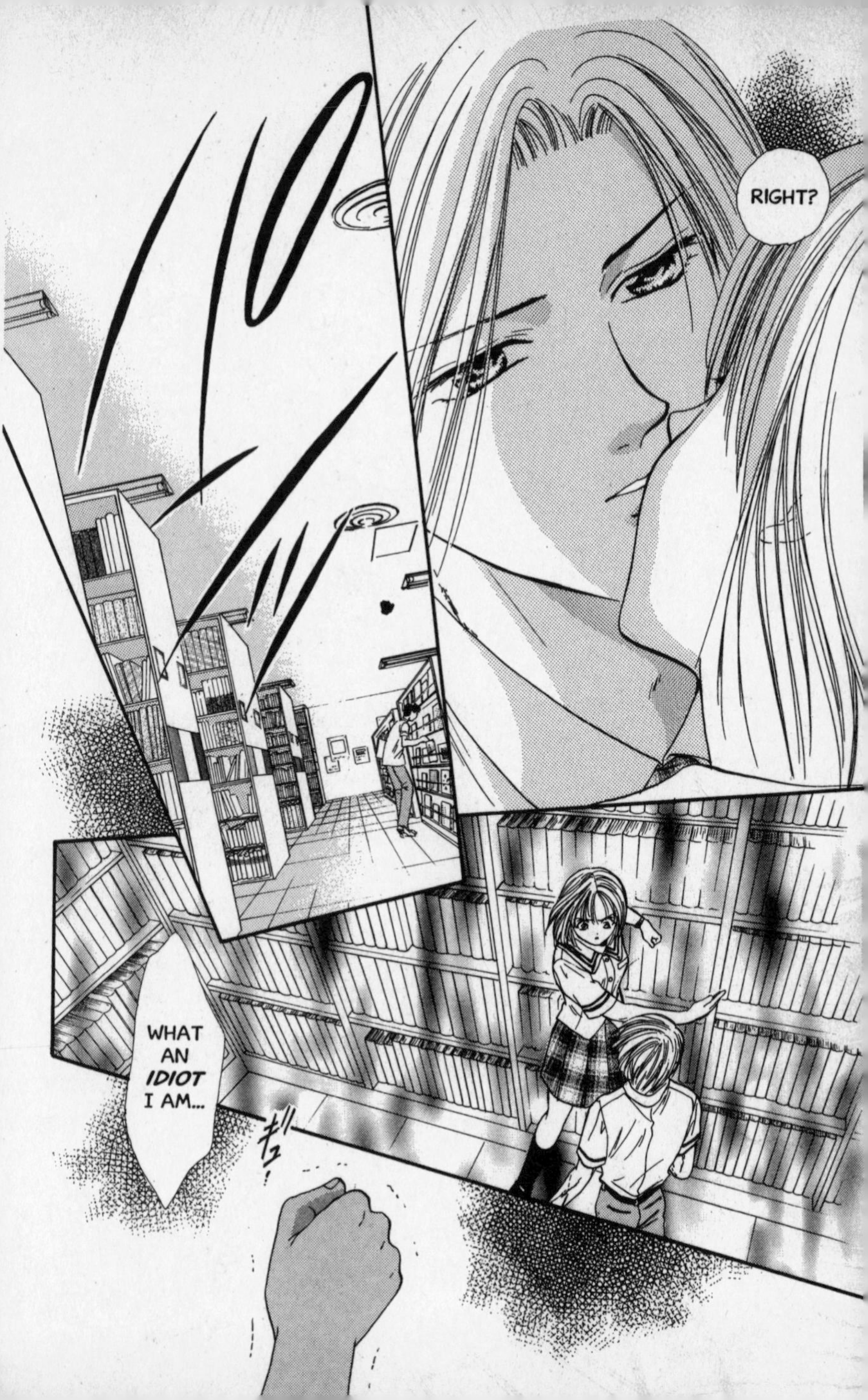
RIGHT?
WHAT AN *IDIOT* I AM...

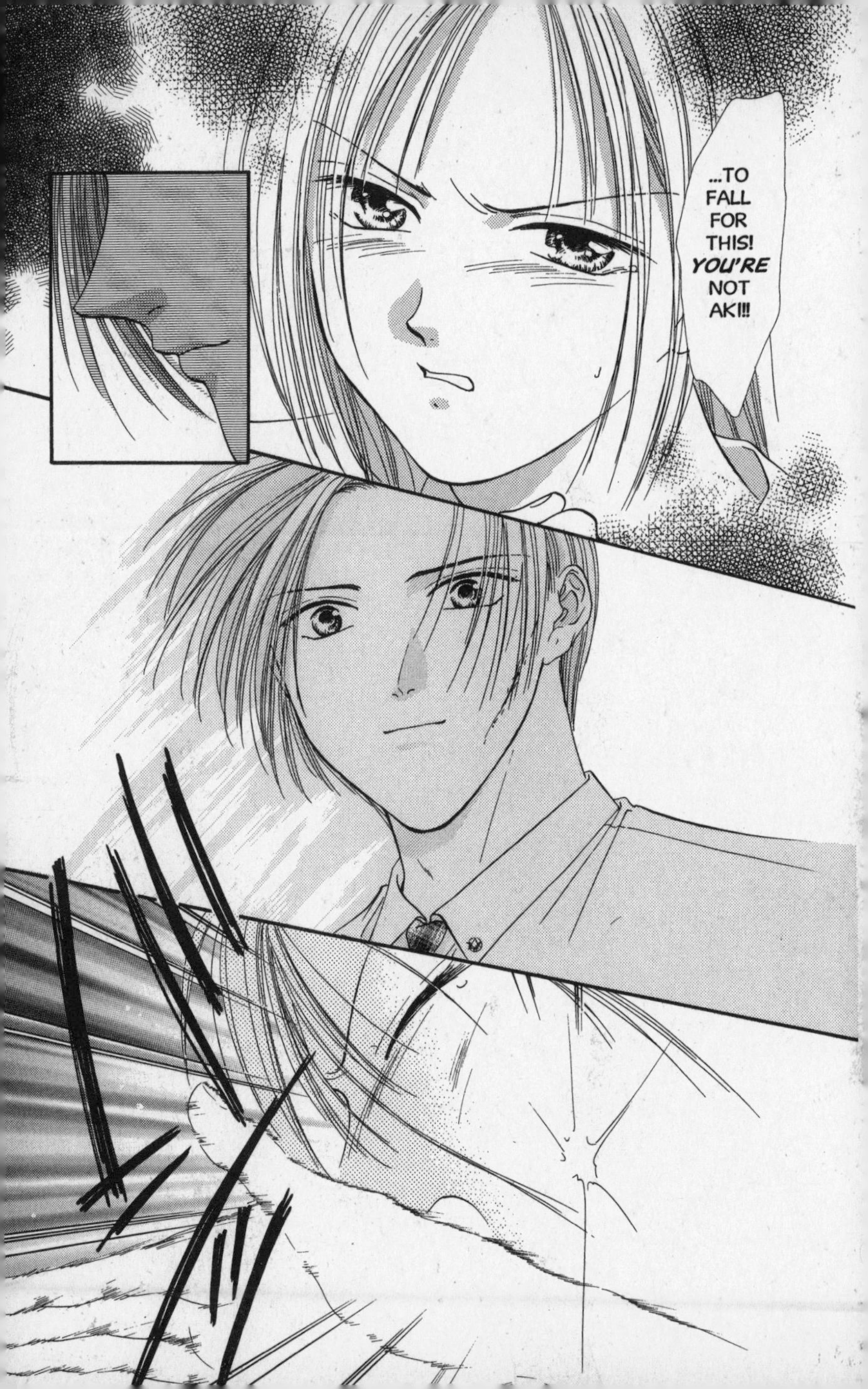
...TO FALL FOR THIS! *YOU'RE* NOT AKI!!

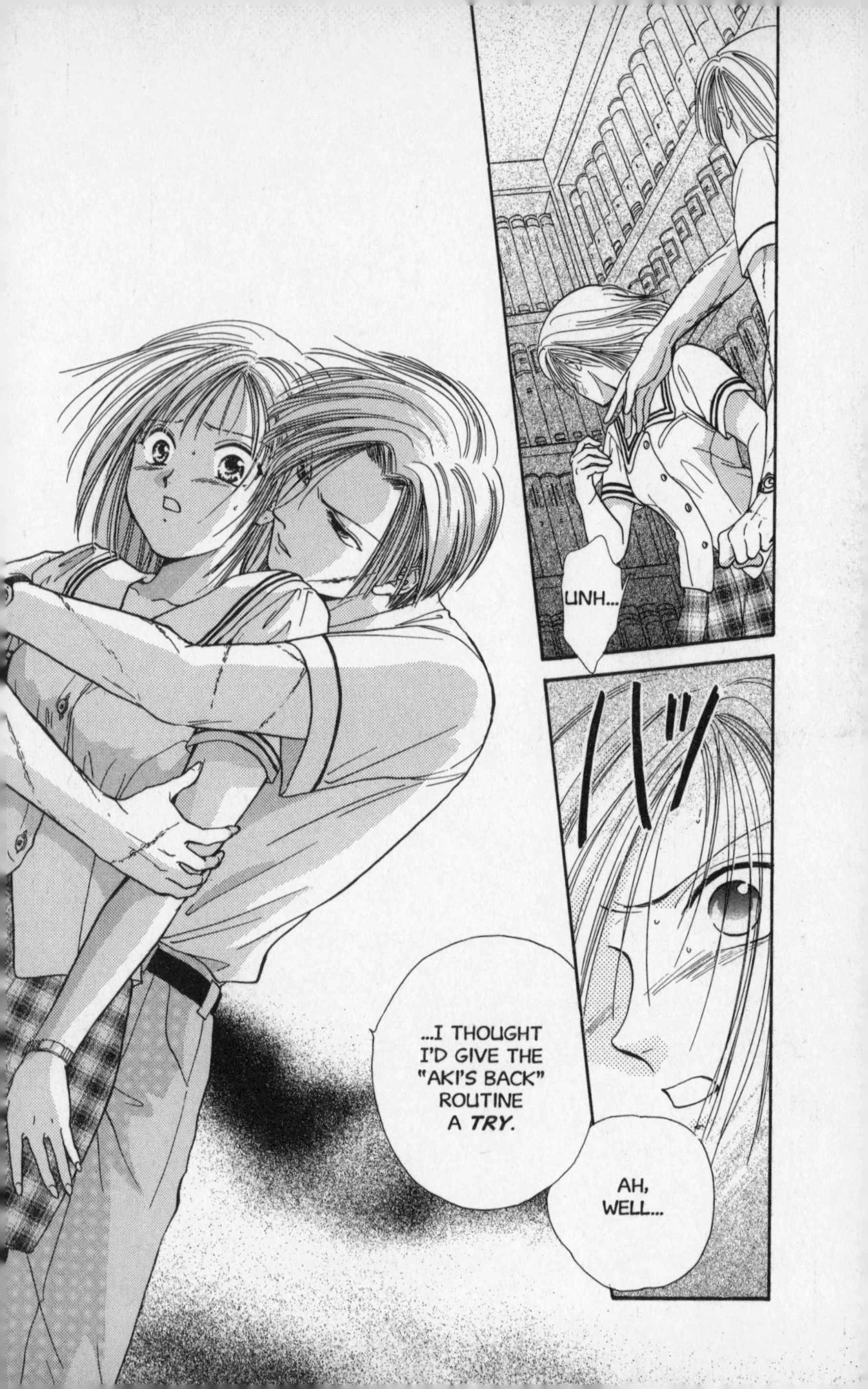
UNH...
ハッ
AH, WELL...
...I THOUGHT I'D GIVE THE "AKI'S BACK" ROUTINE A *TRY*.

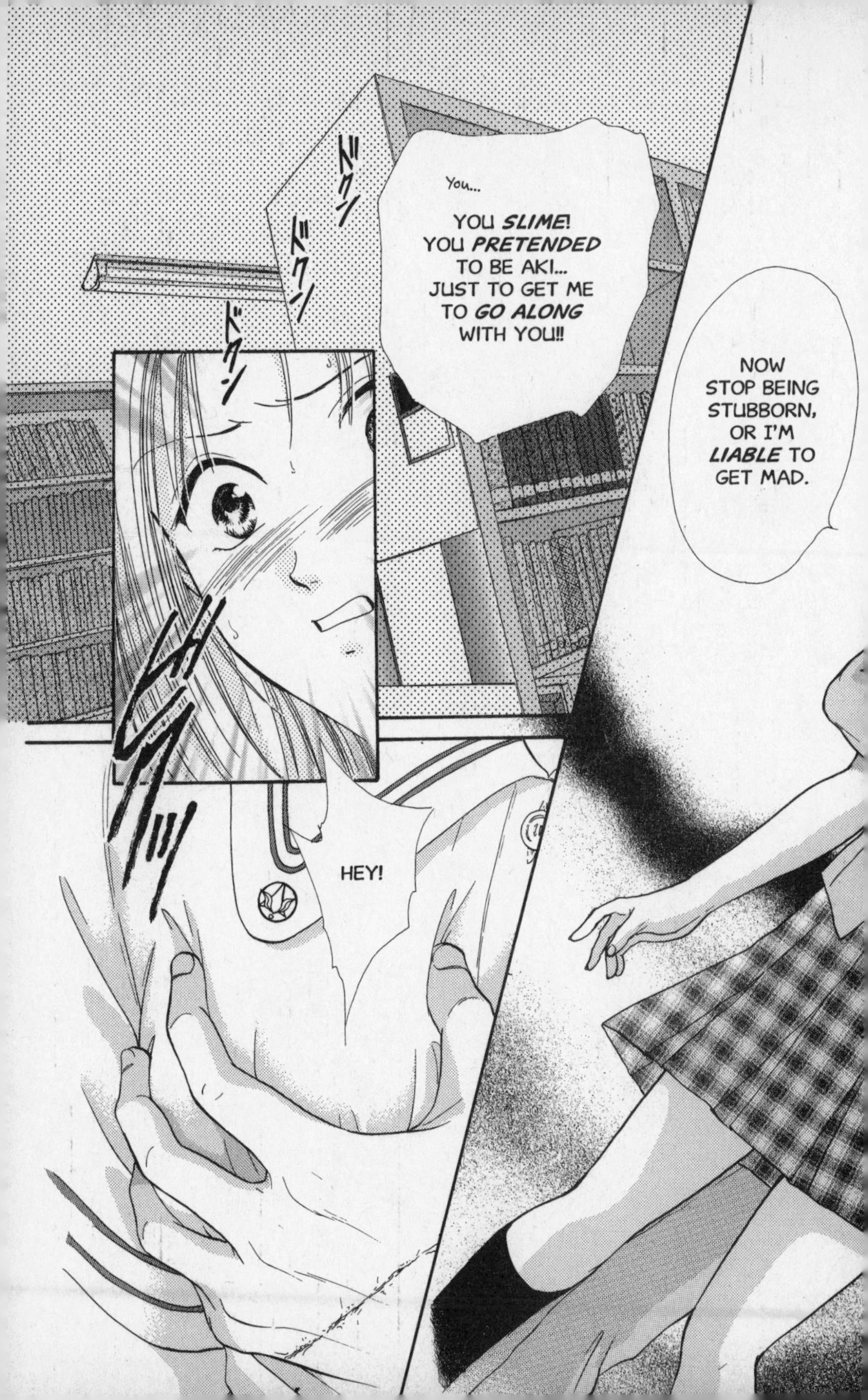
NOW STOP BEING STUBBORN, OR I'M LIABLE TO GET MAD.
You...
YOU SLIME! YOU PRETENDED TO BE AKI... JUST TO GET ME TO GO ALONG WITH YOU!!
HEY!

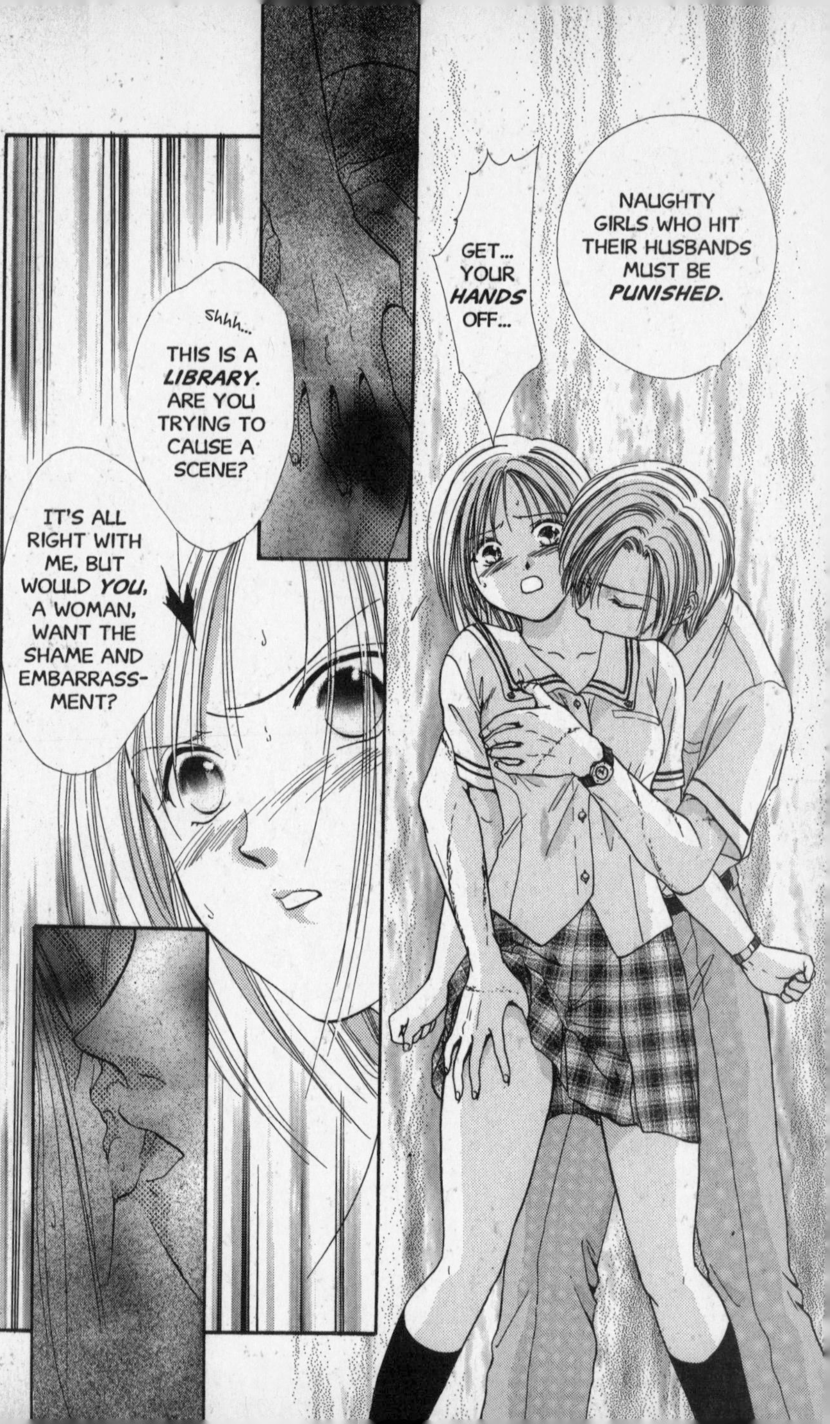

NAUGHTY GIRLS WHO HIT THEIR HUSBANDS MUST BE *PUNISHED*.
GET... YOUR *HANDS* OFF...
shhh... THIS IS A *LIBRARY*. ARE YOU TRYING TO CAUSE A SCENE?
IT'S ALL RIGHT WITH ME, BUT WOULD *YOU*, A WOMAN, WANT THE SHAME AND EMBARRASS-MENT?

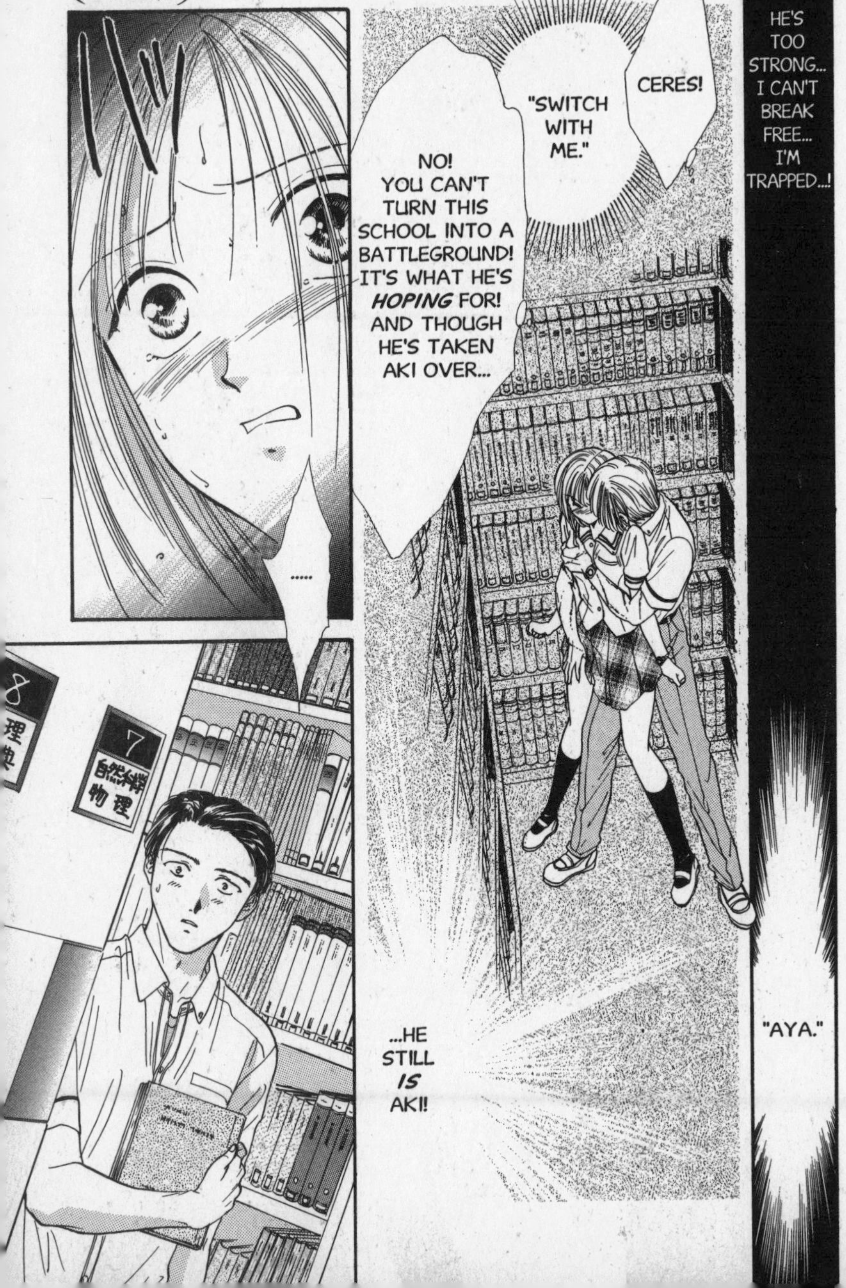
HE'S TOO STRONG... I CAN'T BREAK FREE... I'M TRAPPED...!
CERES!
"SWITCH WITH ME."
NO! YOU CAN'T TURN THIS SCHOOL INTO A BATTLEGROUND! IT'S WHAT HE'S *HOPING* FOR! AND THOUGH HE'S TAKEN AKI OVER...
...HE STILL *IS* AKI!
.....
"AYA."

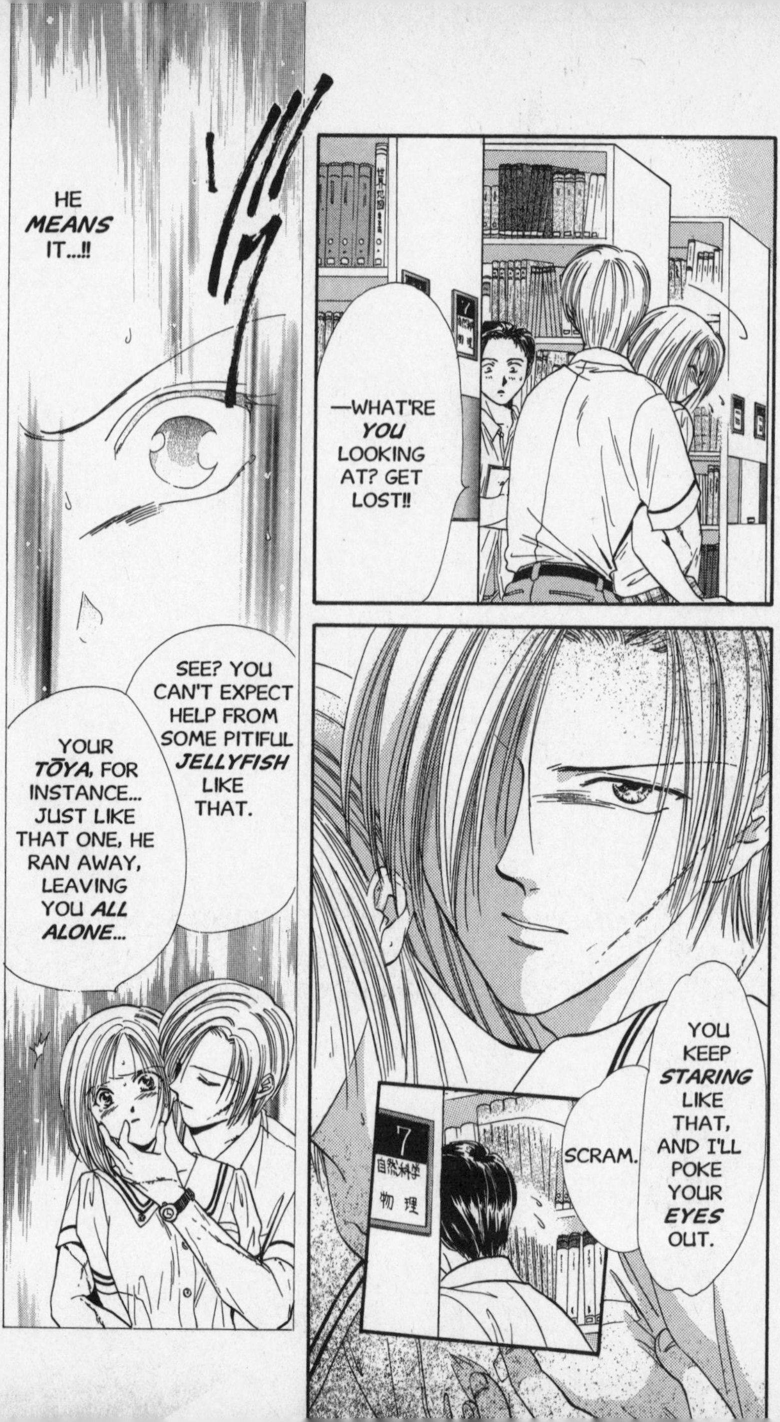
—WHAT'RE YOU LOOKING AT? GET LOST!!
YOU KEEP STARING LIKE THAT, AND I'LL POKE YOUR EYES OUT.
SCRAM.
7
自然科学
物理
HE MEANS IT...!!
SEE? YOU CAN'T EXPECT HELP FROM SOME PITIFUL JELLYFISH LIKE THAT.
YOUR TŌYA, FOR INSTANCE... JUST LIKE THAT ONE, HE RAN AWAY, LEAVING YOU ALL ALONE...

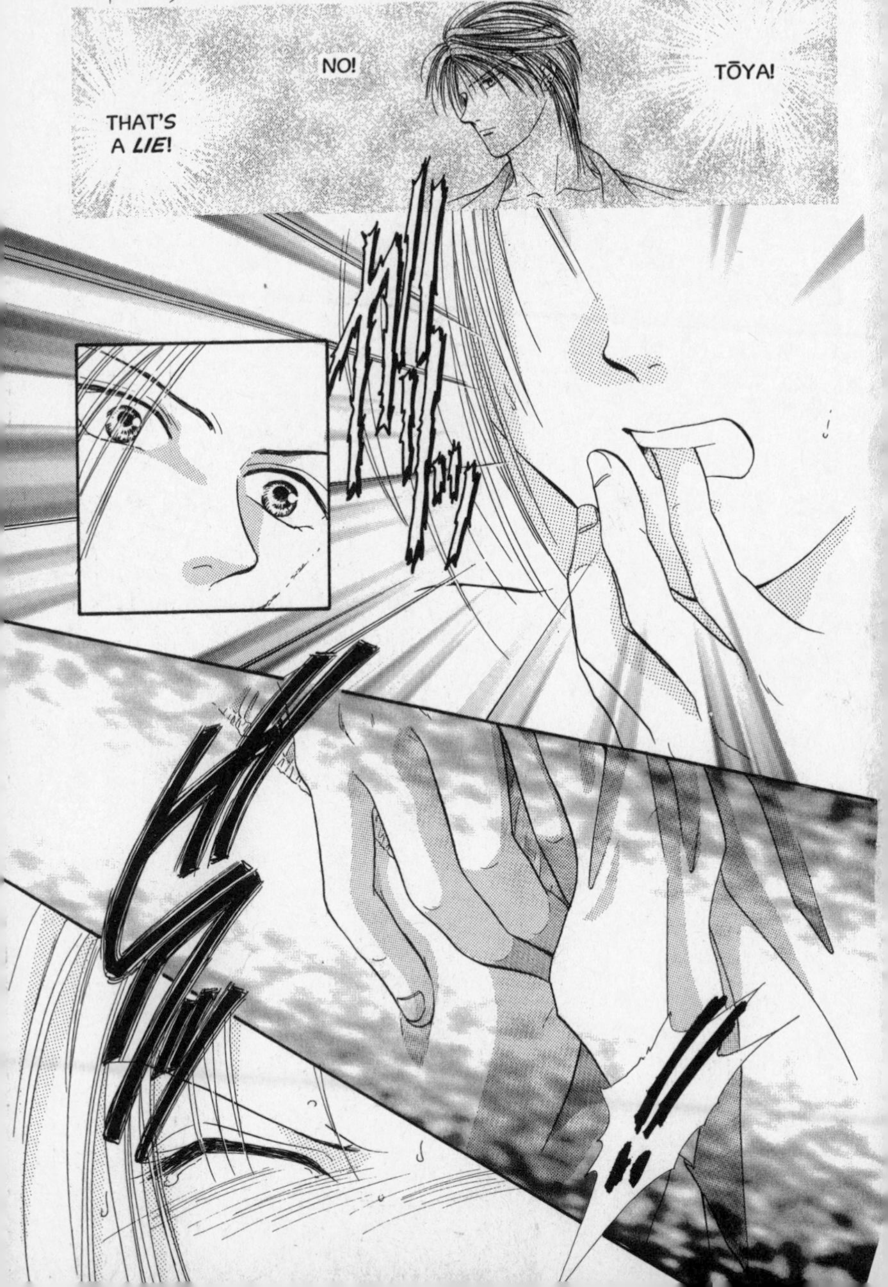
TŌYA!
NO!
THAT'S A *LIE*!

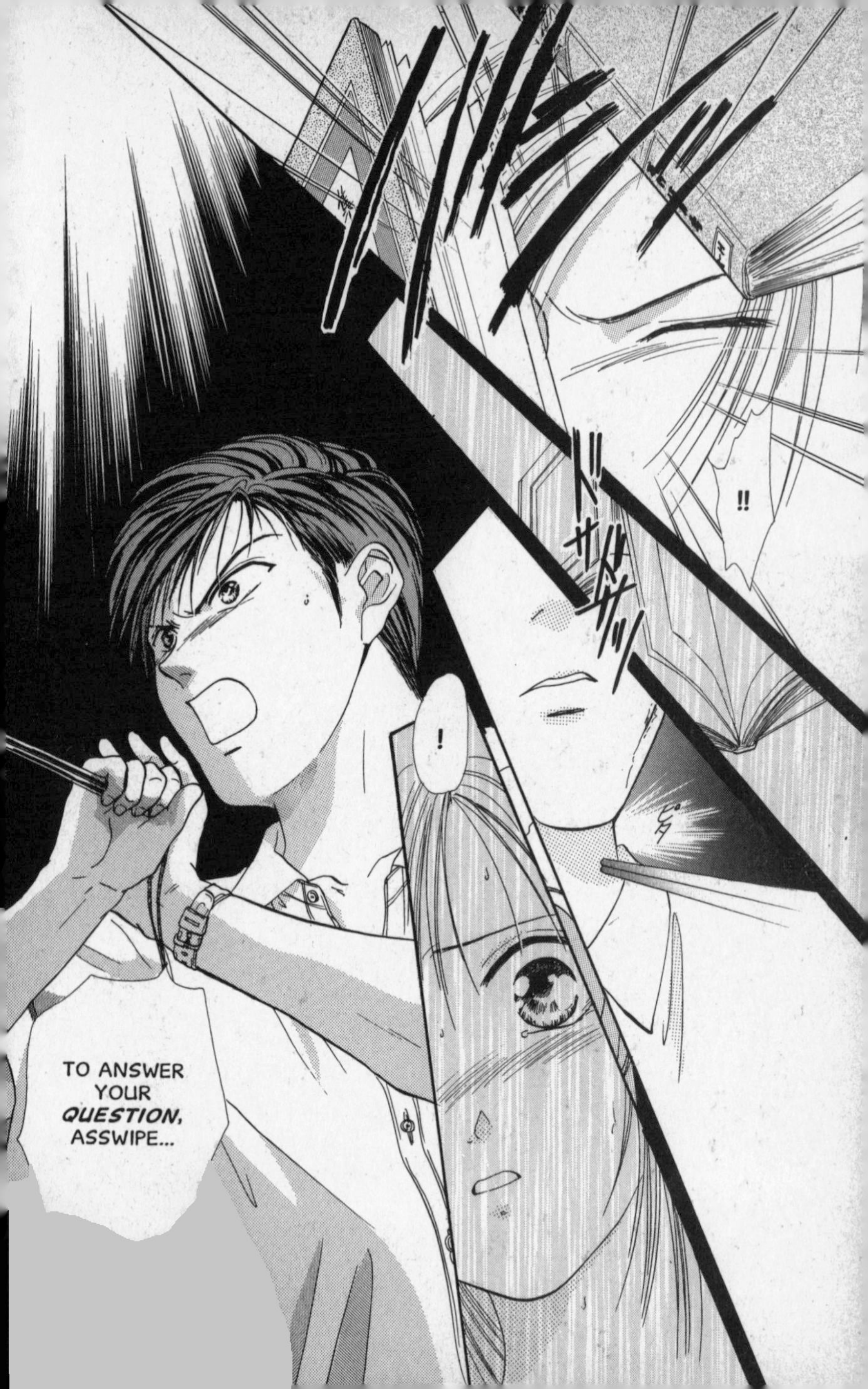
!!
!
TO ANSWER YOUR *QUESTION,* ASSWIPE...

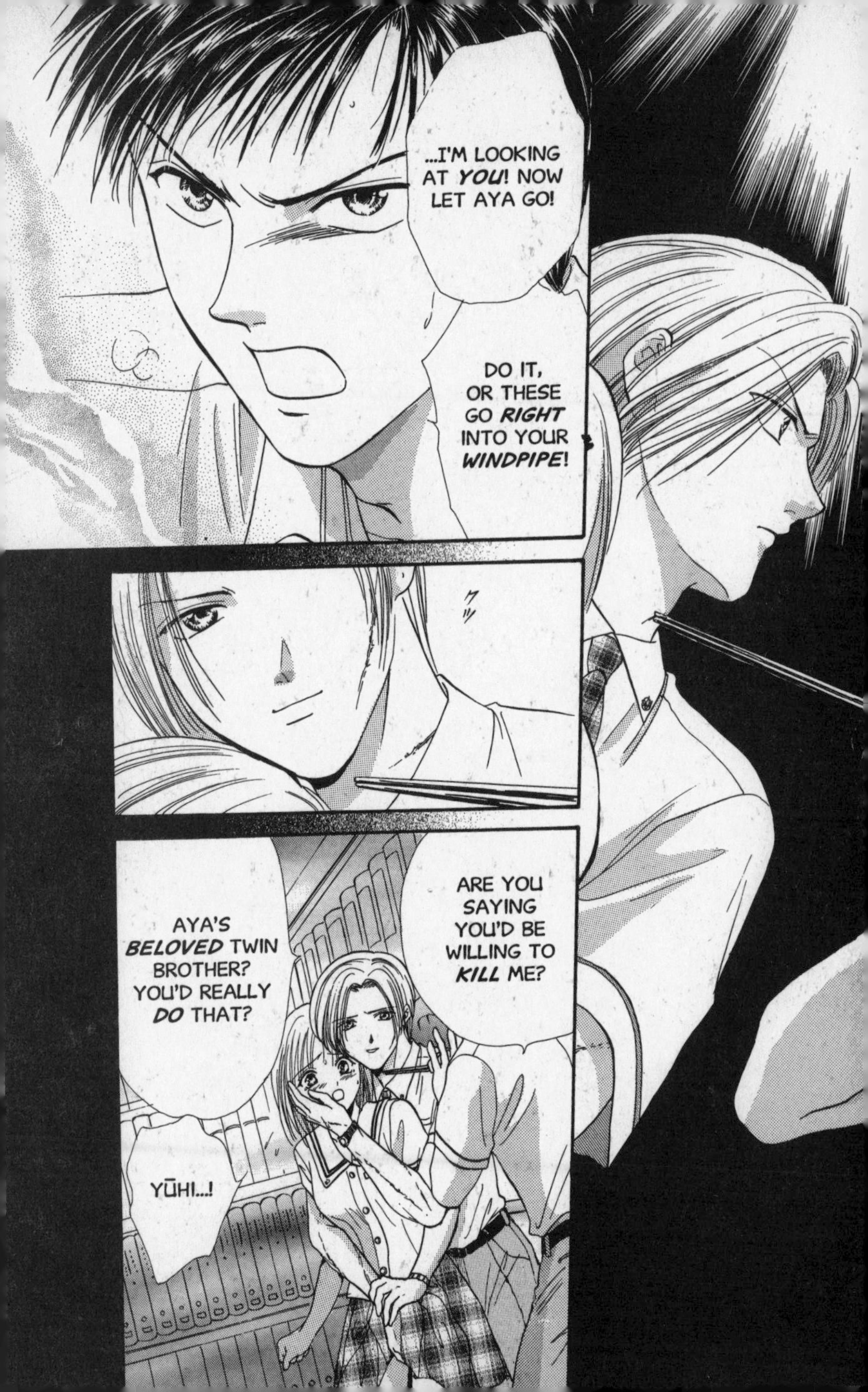
...I'M LOOKING AT YOU! NOW LET AYA GO!
DO IT, OR THESE GO RIGHT INTO YOUR WINDPIPE!
ARE YOU SAYING YOU'D BE WILLING TO KILL ME?
AYA'S BELOVED TWIN BROTHER? YOU'D REALLY DO THAT?
YŪHI...!

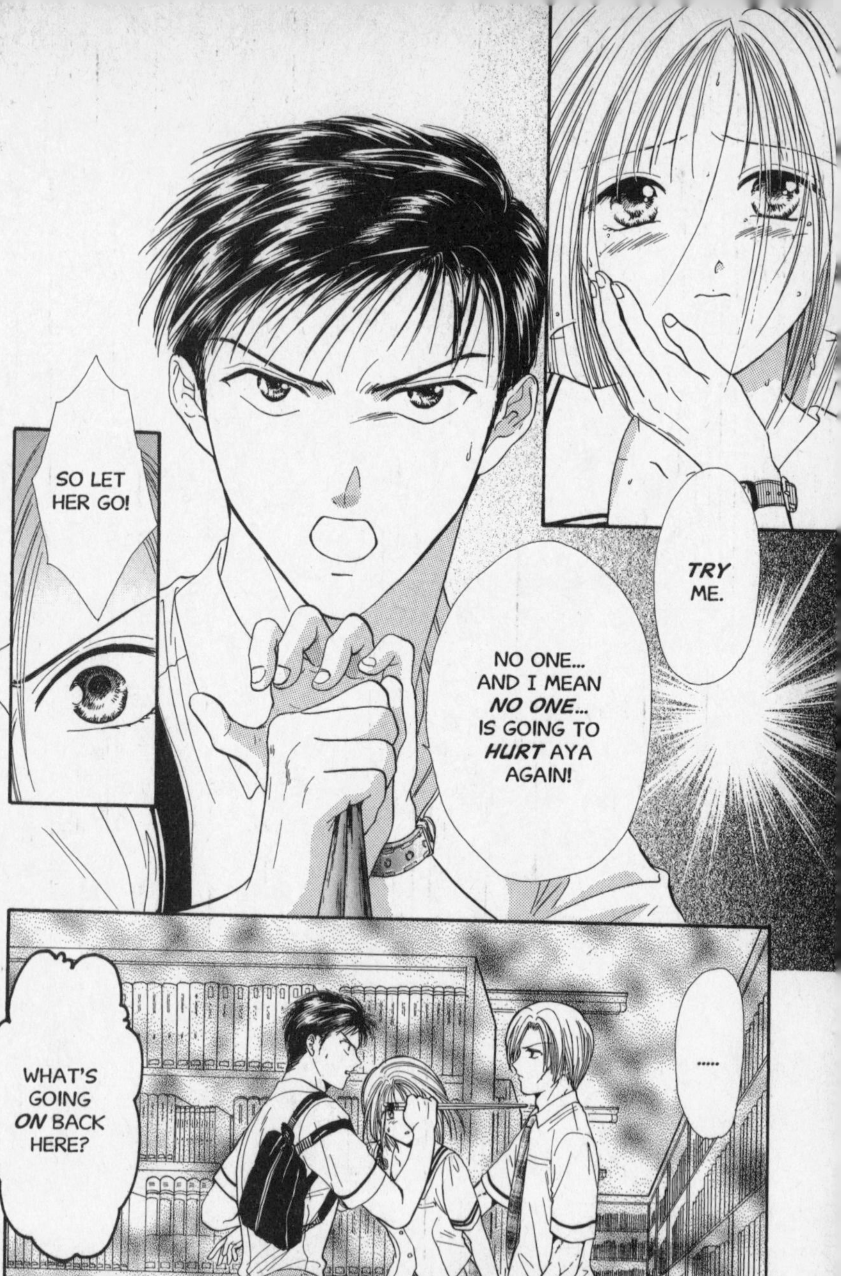
TRY ME.
NO ONE... AND I MEAN NO ONE... IS GOING TO HURT AYA AGAIN!
SO LET HER GO!
.....
WHAT'S GOING ON BACK HERE?

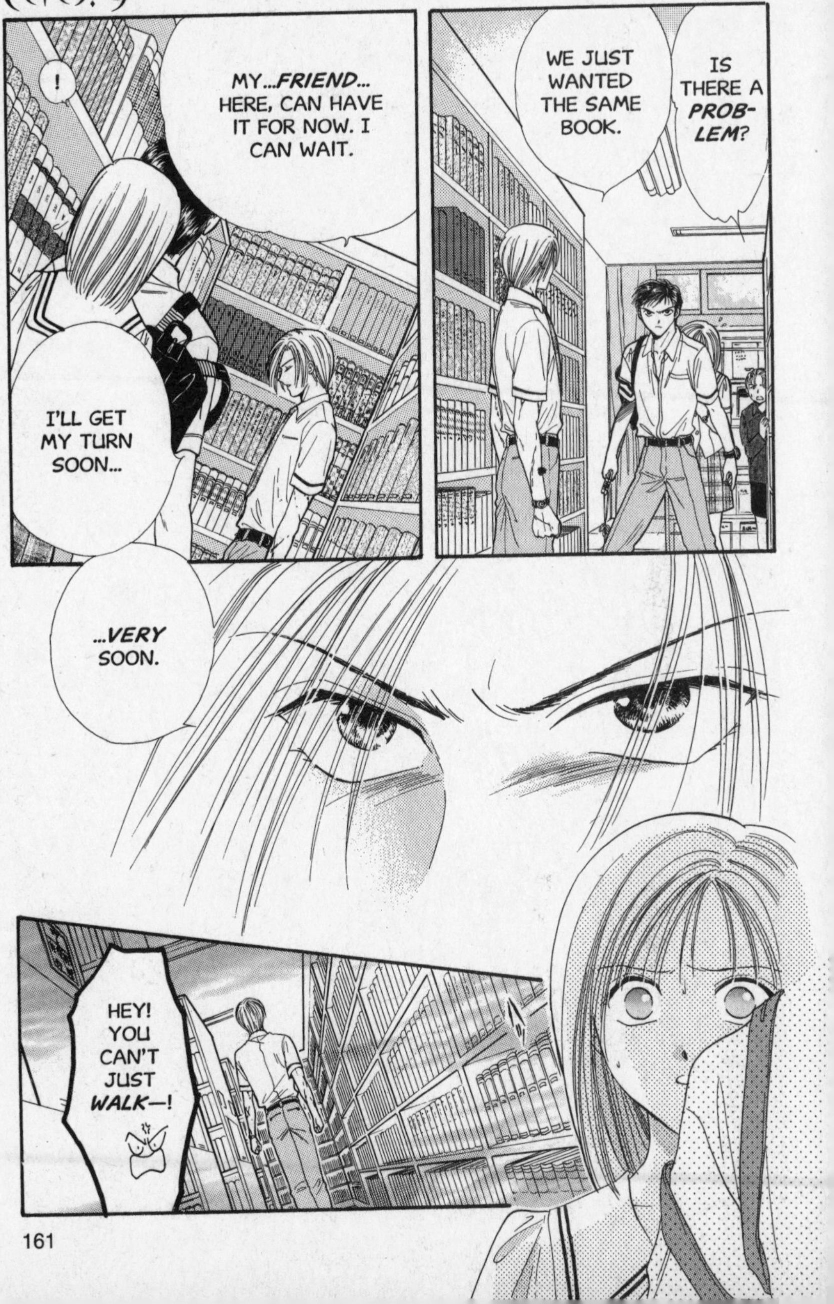
IS THERE A *PROBLEM*?
WE JUST WANTED THE SAME BOOK.
MY...*FRIEND*... HERE, CAN HAVE IT FOR NOW. I CAN WAIT.
!
I'LL GET MY TURN SOON...
...*VERY* SOON.
HEY! YOU CAN'T JUST *WALK*—!

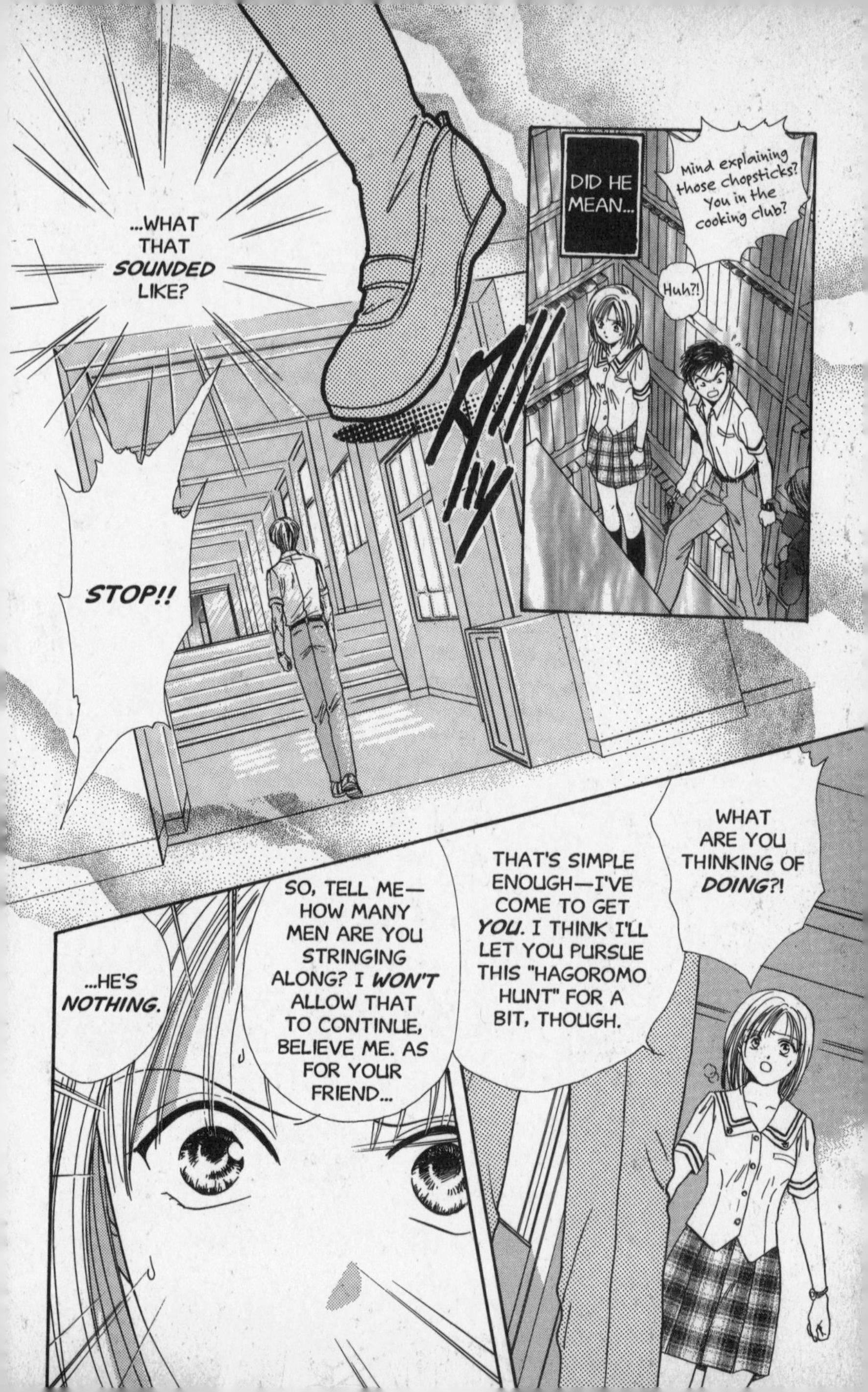
Mind explaining those chopsticks? You in the cooking club?
Huh?!
DID HE MEAN...
...WHAT THAT *SOUNDED* LIKE?
STOP!!
WHAT ARE YOU THINKING OF *DOING*?!
THAT'S SIMPLE ENOUGH—I'VE COME TO GET *YOU*. I THINK I'LL LET YOU PURSUE THIS "HAGOROMO HUNT" FOR A BIT, THOUGH.
SO, TELL ME—HOW MANY MEN ARE YOU STRINGING ALONG? I *WON'T* ALLOW THAT TO CONTINUE, BELIEVE ME. AS FOR YOUR FRIEND...
...HE'S *NOTHING*.

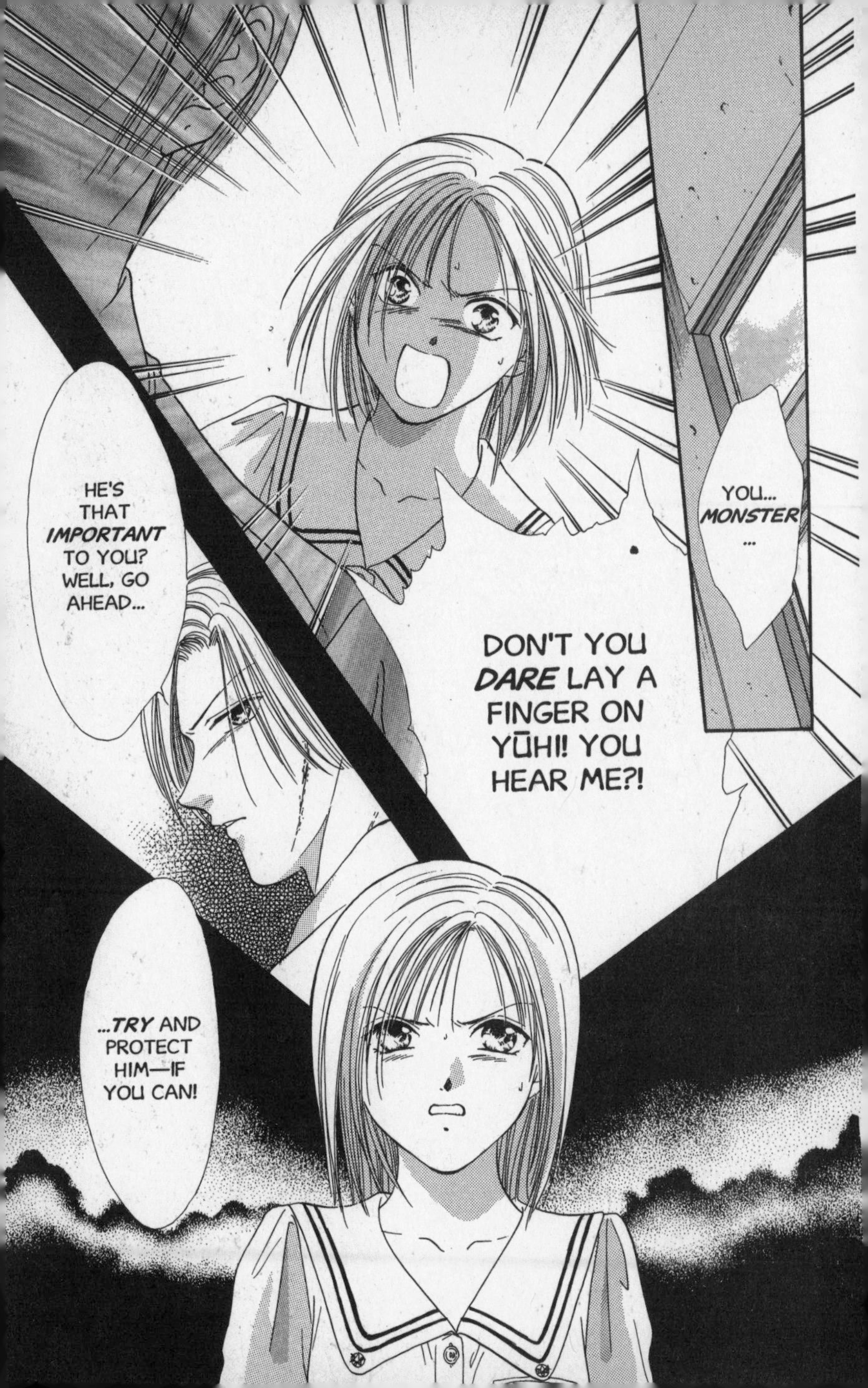
YOU... MONSTER ...
DON'T YOU DARE LAY A FINGER ON YŪHI! YOU HEAR ME?!
HE'S THAT IMPORTANT TO YOU? WELL, GO AHEAD...
...TRY AND PROTECT HIM—IF YOU CAN!

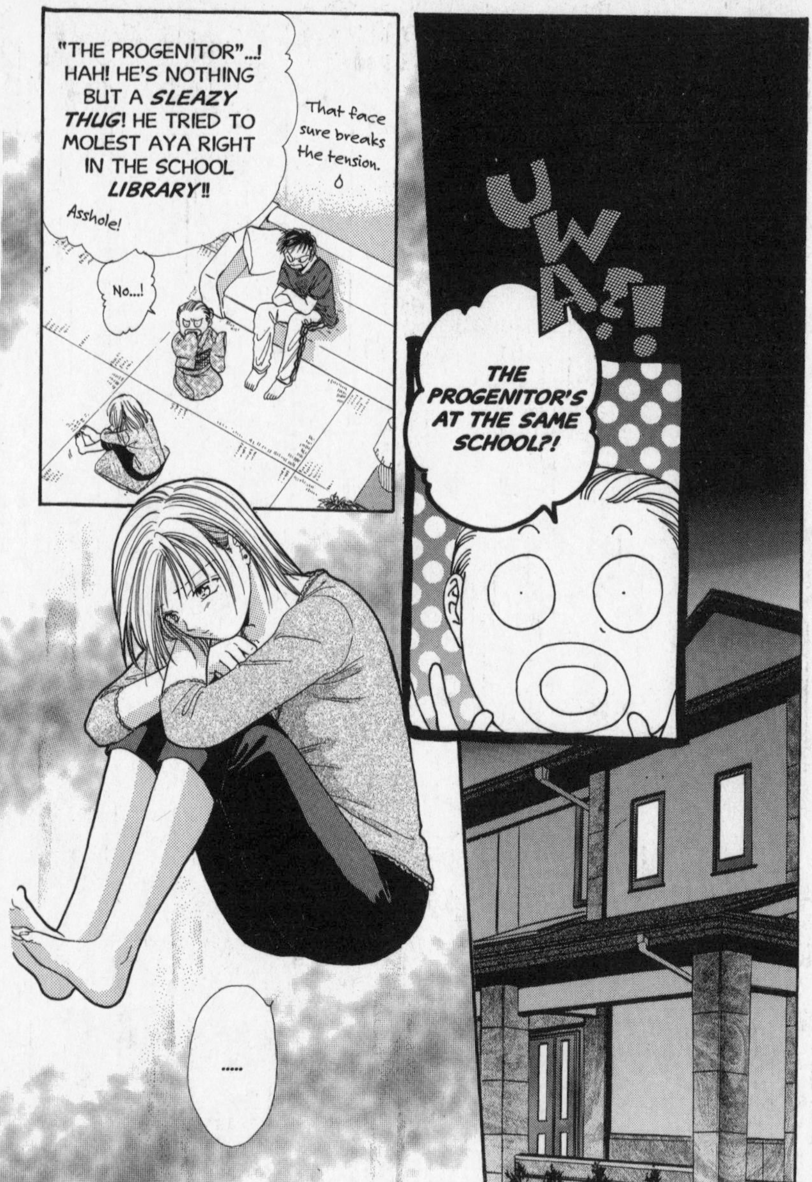
UWA?!
THE PROGENITOR'S AT THE SAME SCHOOL?!
"THE PROGENITOR"...! HAH! HE'S NOTHING BUT A SLEAZY THUG! HE TRIED TO MOLEST AYA RIGHT IN THE SCHOOL LIBRARY!!
Asshole!
That face sure breaks the tension.
No...!
......

♦ Progenitor ♦

People have recently pointed out that my art style's changed. Actually, this is how I **used** to draw to begin with. It was when I turned pro that I changed my style. This current style is easiest to keep up. Speaking of change, comments have been coming in as of Volume 4 or 5 saying, "Aya's gotten cuter," or "Tōya looks nicer." Most recently, it's been "Aya's grown beautiful since becoming a woman." Wow! ◡̈ I didn't do it on purpose. I guess the characters are reflecting their **own** inner changes.

Tōya's facial expressions are softening up, too. As for Yūhi, the assistants say that he's gotten "manlier." ◡̈ I guess he's growing up! Another reader says, "Aya looks more mature with the new haircut, but it's when she's with Tōya that she's prettiest." I loved this comment. ☺

"Serious" stuff is easier and more fun for me to draw, so my art and stories tend to get graphic. **Ceres** really is geared for an audience of high-school age and above. (I welcome younger readers too, of course.) There may be some tricky scenes now and again, but they all (?) have their raison d'être. Please stick with me, all the way to the end.

I also get questions about how to draw better, but there are no shortcuts. You just have to keep practicing. Everyone gets better after drawing pages and pages of art, and by studying form. It takes effort. (My art's finally stabilized...and I've been doing this for nine years! I still have room to improve, too.) You see, your **artwork** may get better with practice...but you can't be a good **manga artist** with only good **art**. It helps, sure, but the most important thing is content, and putting your **heart** into it. People talk about how everything in Japan these days is superficial, that there's no substance. Stories are like that, too. I almost feel as though I'm drawing manga solely to send the messages I want to get across.... Life has hardly even **begun** for you, if you're still a teenager. Don't give up—try hard. Keep it up! *PANT PANT* ...There, you see? I've gone and riled myself up again.... ...Oh, and thank you to everyone who bought my calendars! '98/11

See you next time!

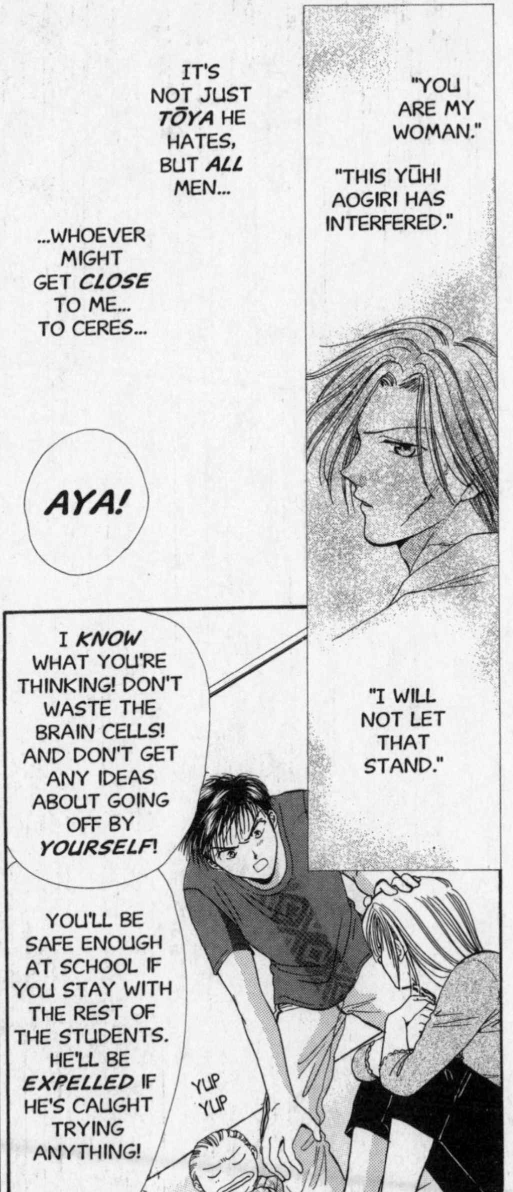
"YOU ARE MY WOMAN."
"THIS YŪHI AOGIRI HAS INTERFERED."
"I WILL NOT LET THAT STAND."
IT'S NOT JUST *TŌYA* HE HATES, BUT *ALL* MEN...
...WHOEVER MIGHT GET *CLOSE* TO ME... TO CERES...
AYA!
I *KNOW* WHAT YOU'RE THINKING! DON'T WASTE THE BRAIN CELLS! AND DON'T GET ANY IDEAS ABOUT GOING OFF BY *YOURSELF*!
YOU'LL BE SAFE ENOUGH AT SCHOOL IF YOU STAY WITH THE REST OF THE STUDENTS. HE'LL BE *EXPELLED* IF HE'S CAUGHT TRYING ANYTHING!
YUP YUP

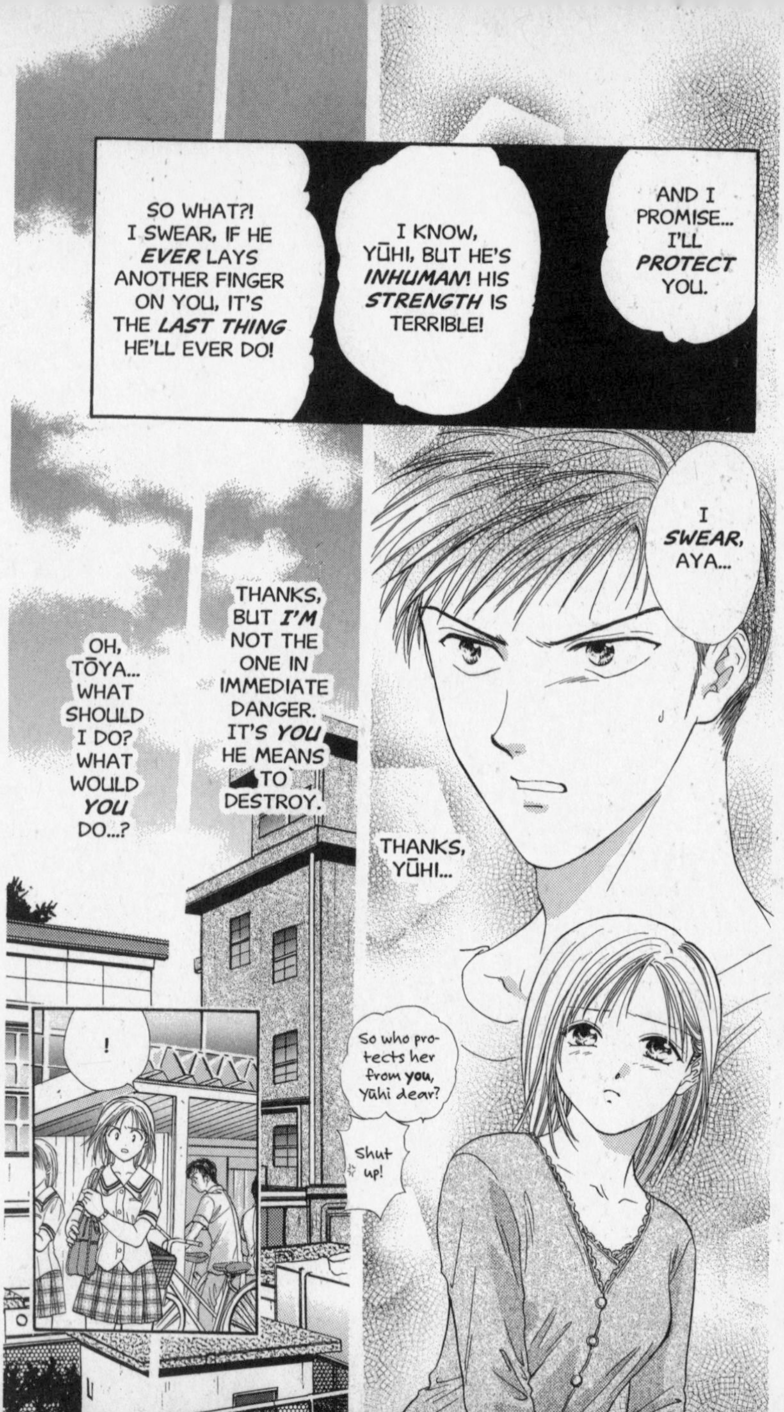

AND I PROMISE... I'LL PROTECT YOU.
I KNOW, YŪHI, BUT HE'S INHUMAN! HIS STRENGTH IS TERRIBLE!
SO WHAT?! I SWEAR, IF HE EVER LAYS ANOTHER FINGER ON YOU, IT'S THE LAST THING HE'LL EVER DO!
I SWEAR, AYA...
THANKS, YŪHI...
So who protects her from you, Yūhi dear?
Shut up!
THANKS, BUT I'M NOT THE ONE IN IMMEDIATE DANGER. IT'S YOU HE MEANS TO DESTROY.
OH, TŌYA... WHAT SHOULD I DO? WHAT WOULD YOU DO...?
!

Ceres: 9

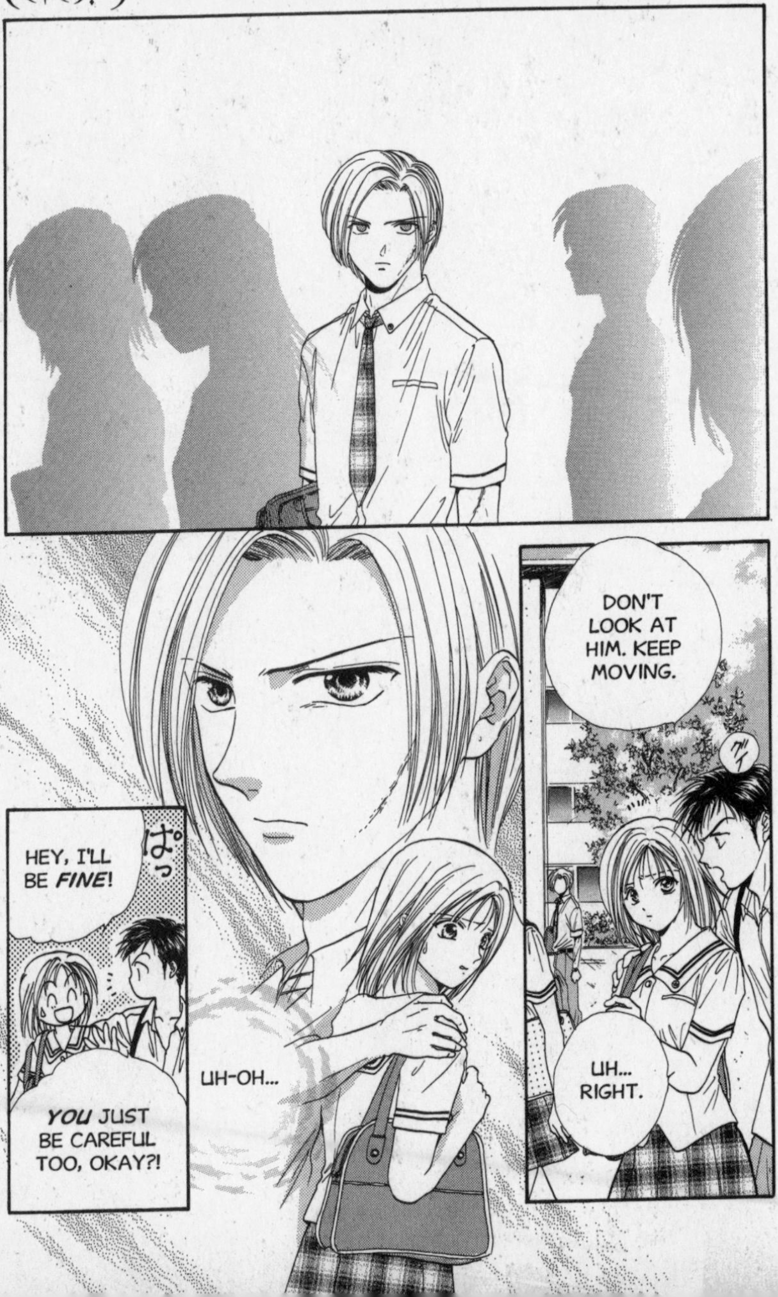
DON'T LOOK AT HIM. KEEP MOVING.
UH... RIGHT.
UH-OH...
HEY, I'LL BE *FINE*!
ぱっ
YOU JUST BE CAREFUL TOO, OKAY?!

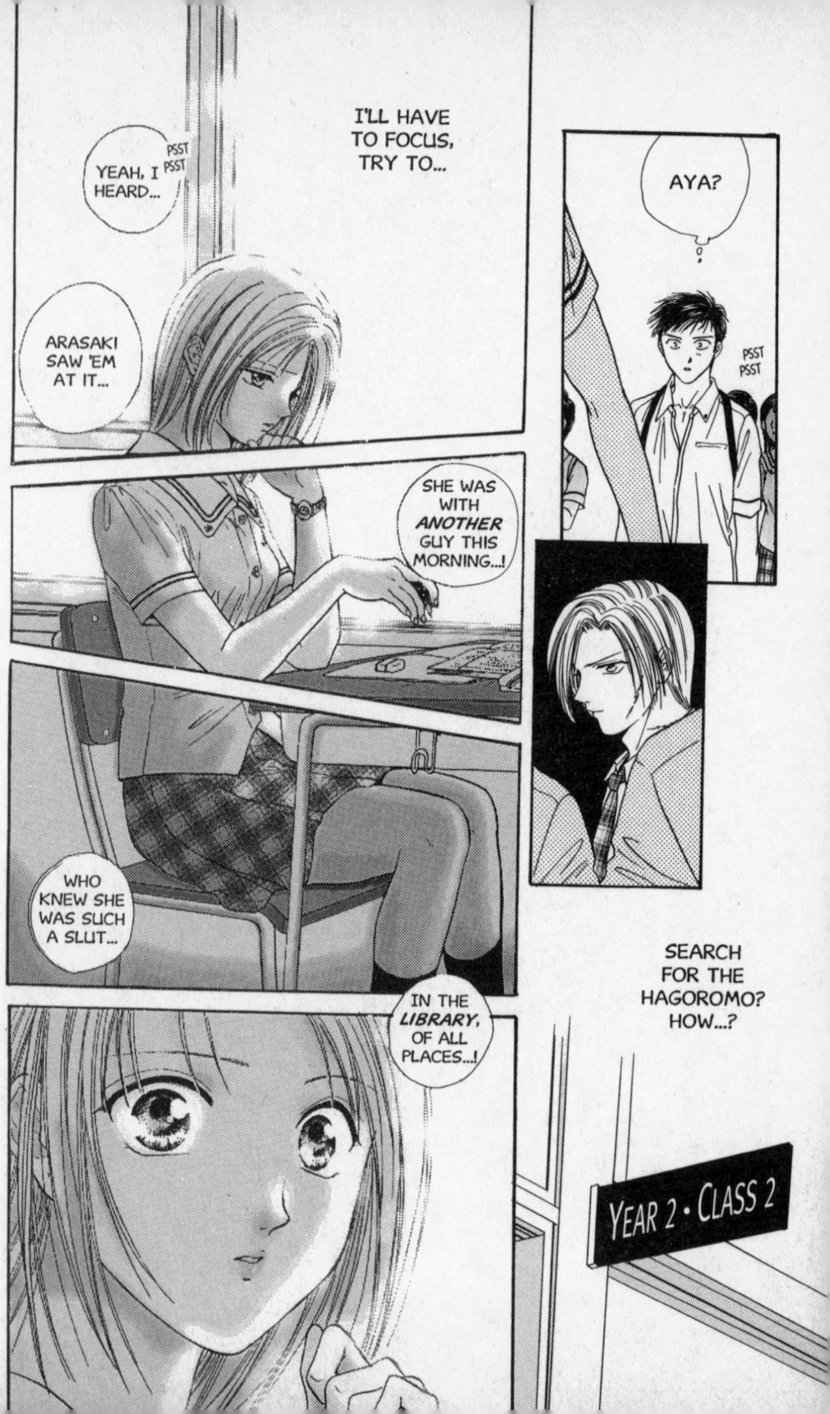

AYA?
PSST PSST
I'LL HAVE TO FOCUS, TRY TO...
PSST PSST
YEAH, I HEARD...
ARASAKI SAW 'EM AT IT...
SHE WAS WITH ***ANOTHER*** GUY THIS MORNING...!
WHO KNEW SHE WAS SUCH A SLUT...
SEARCH FOR THE HAGOROMO? HOW...?
YEAR 2 • CLASS 2
IN THE ***LIBRARY***, OF ALL PLACES...!

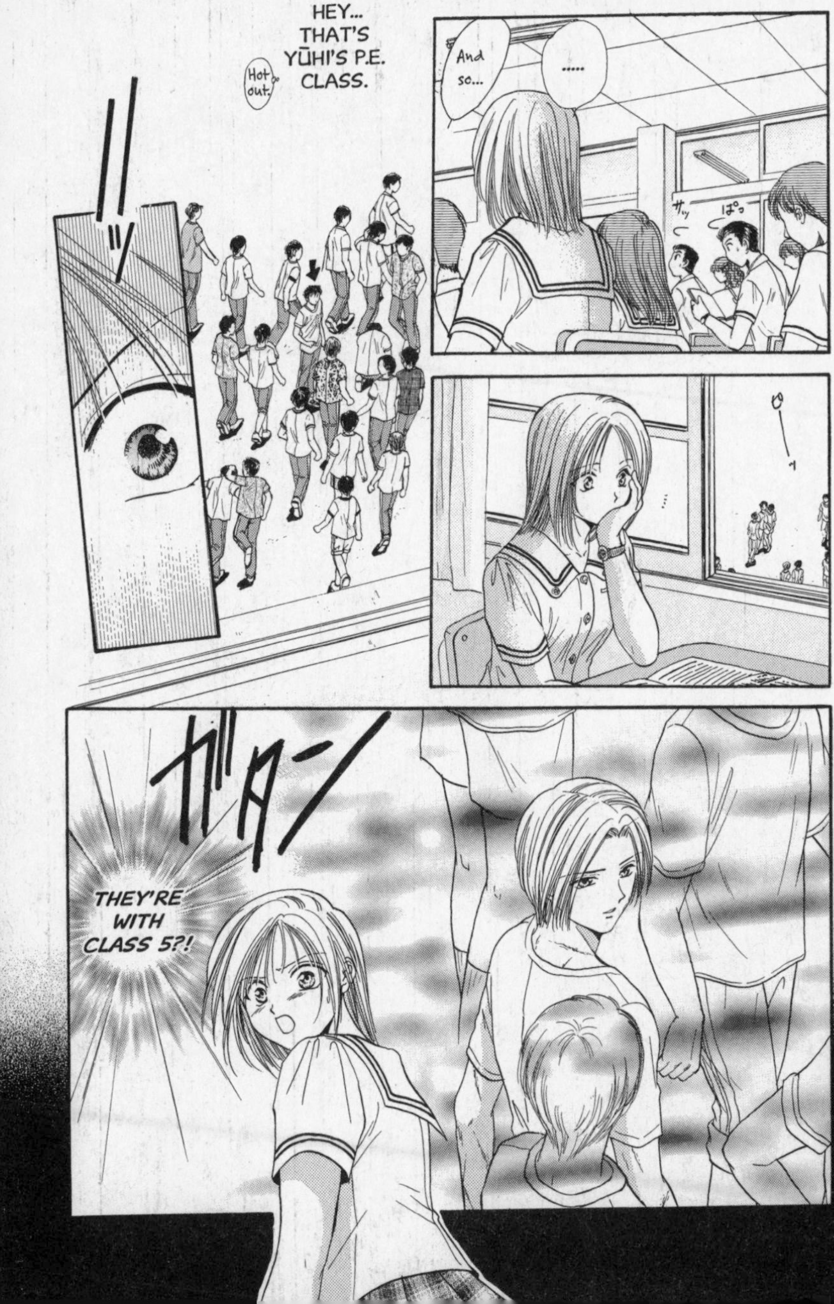

And so...
......
サッ
ぱっ
ぴーッ
HEY... THAT'S YŪHI'S P.E. CLASS.
Hot out.
ガタン
THEY'RE WITH CLASS 5?!

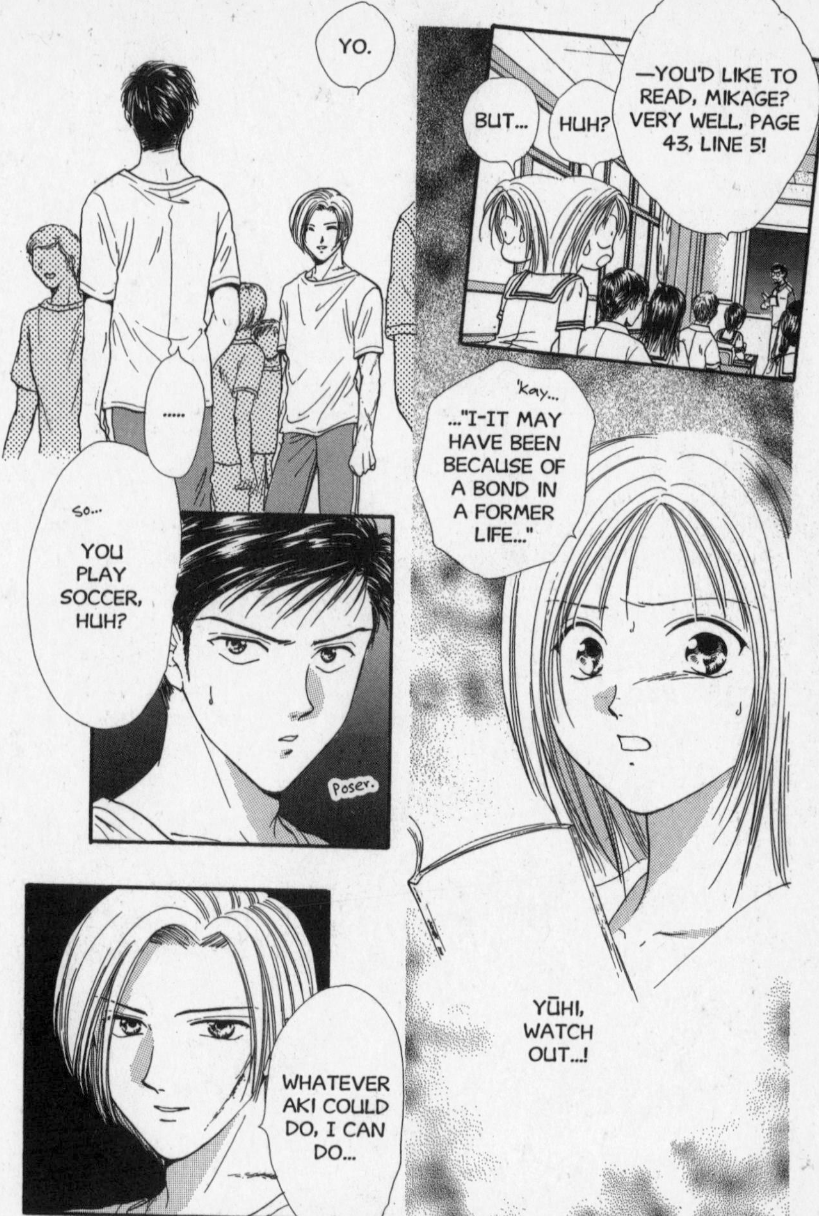
—YOU'D LIKE TO READ, MIKAGE? VERY WELL, PAGE 43, LINE 5!
HUH?
BUT...
'kay...
..."I-IT MAY HAVE BEEN BECAUSE OF A BOND IN A FORMER LIFE..."
YŪHI, WATCH OUT...!
YO.
.....
So...
YOU PLAY SOCCER, HUH?
Poser.
WHATEVER AKI COULD DO, I CAN DO...

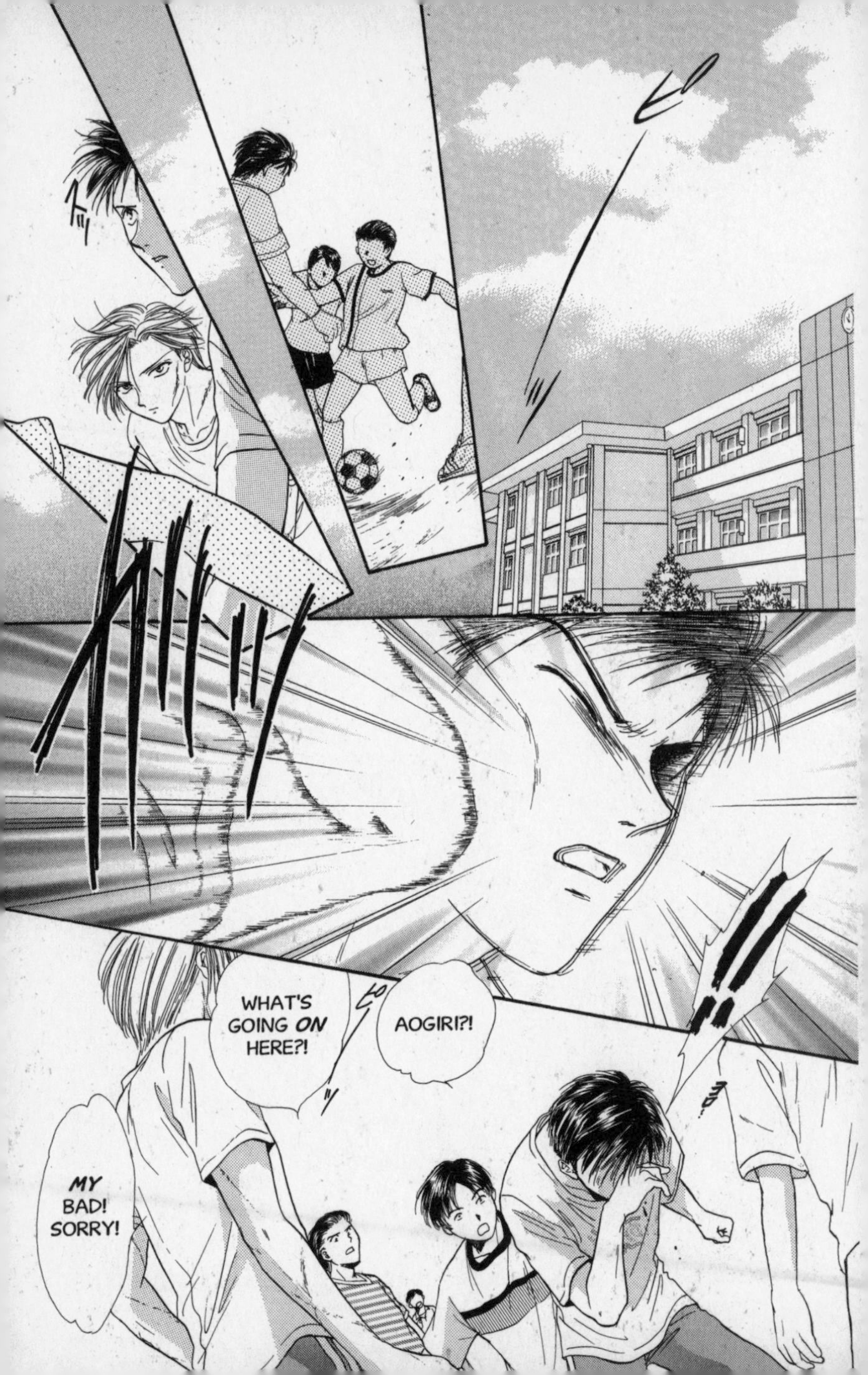
AOGIRI?!
WHAT'S GOING ON HERE?!
MY BAD! SORRY!

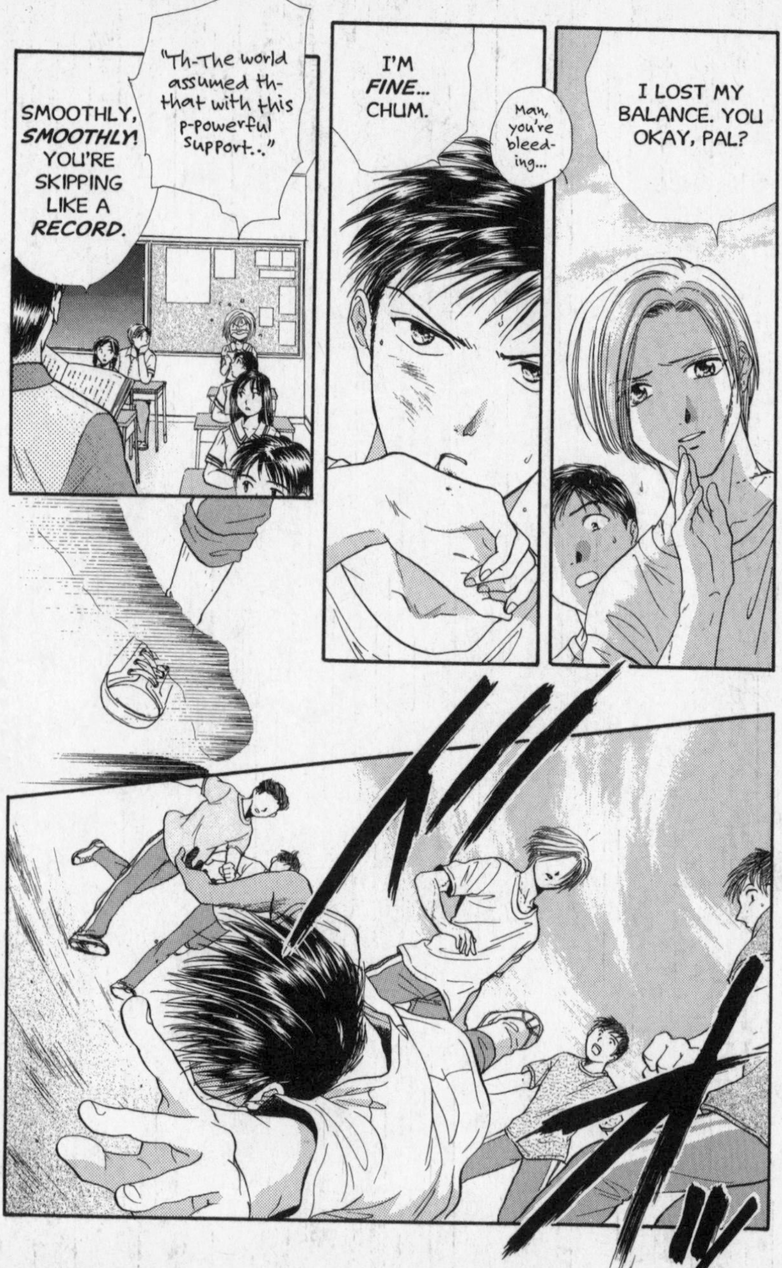
I LOST MY BALANCE. YOU OKAY, PAL?
Man, you're bleed-ing...
I'M *FINE*... CHUM.
"Th-The world assumed th-that with this p-powerful support..."
SMOOTHLY, *SMOOTHLY*! YOU'RE SKIPPING LIKE A *RECORD*.

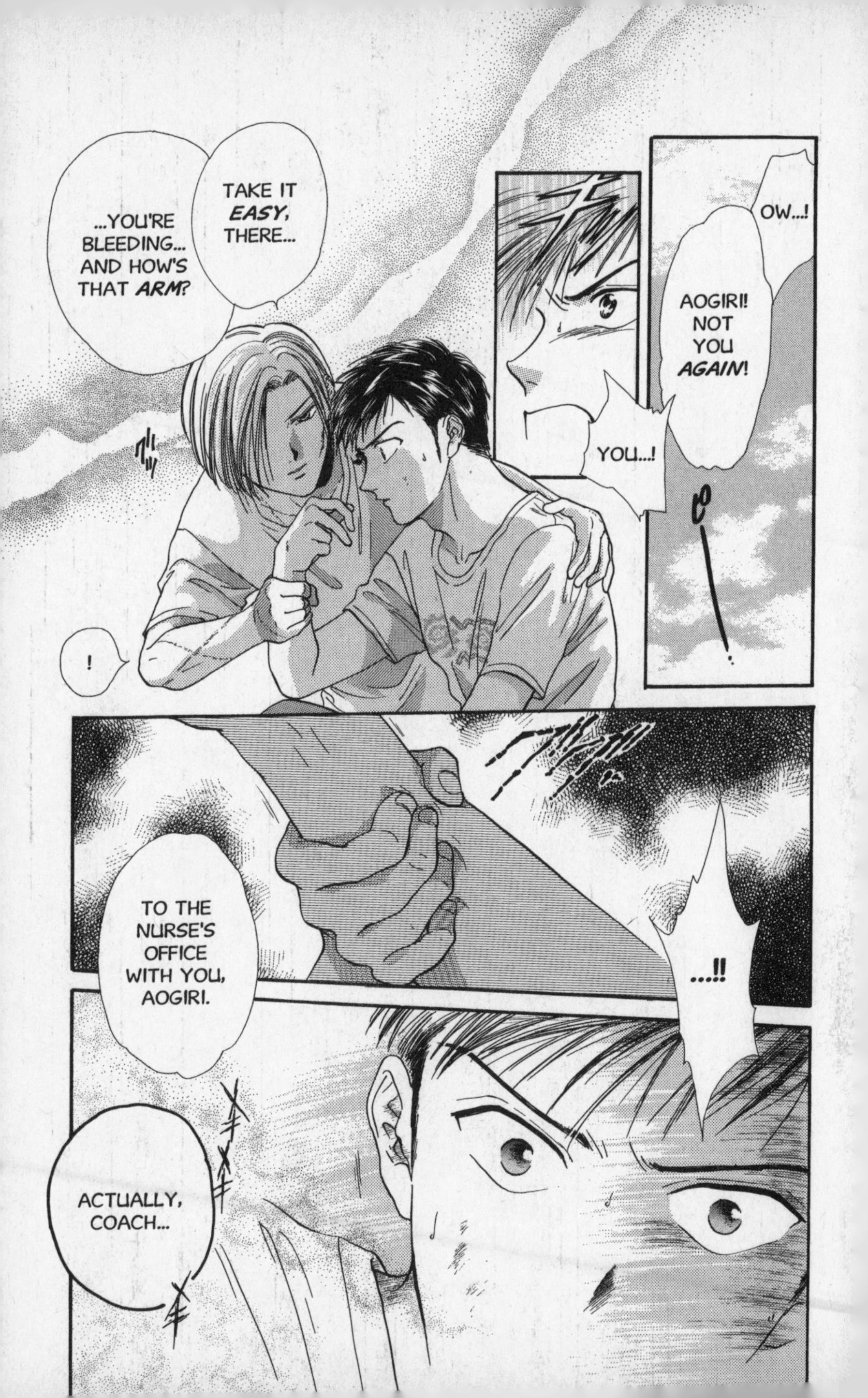
OW...!
AOGIRI! NOT YOU AGAIN!
YOU...!
TAKE IT EASY, THERE...
...YOU'RE BLEEDING... AND HOW'S THAT ARM?
!
...!!
TO THE NURSE'S OFFICE WITH YOU, AOGIRI.
ACTUALLY, COACH...

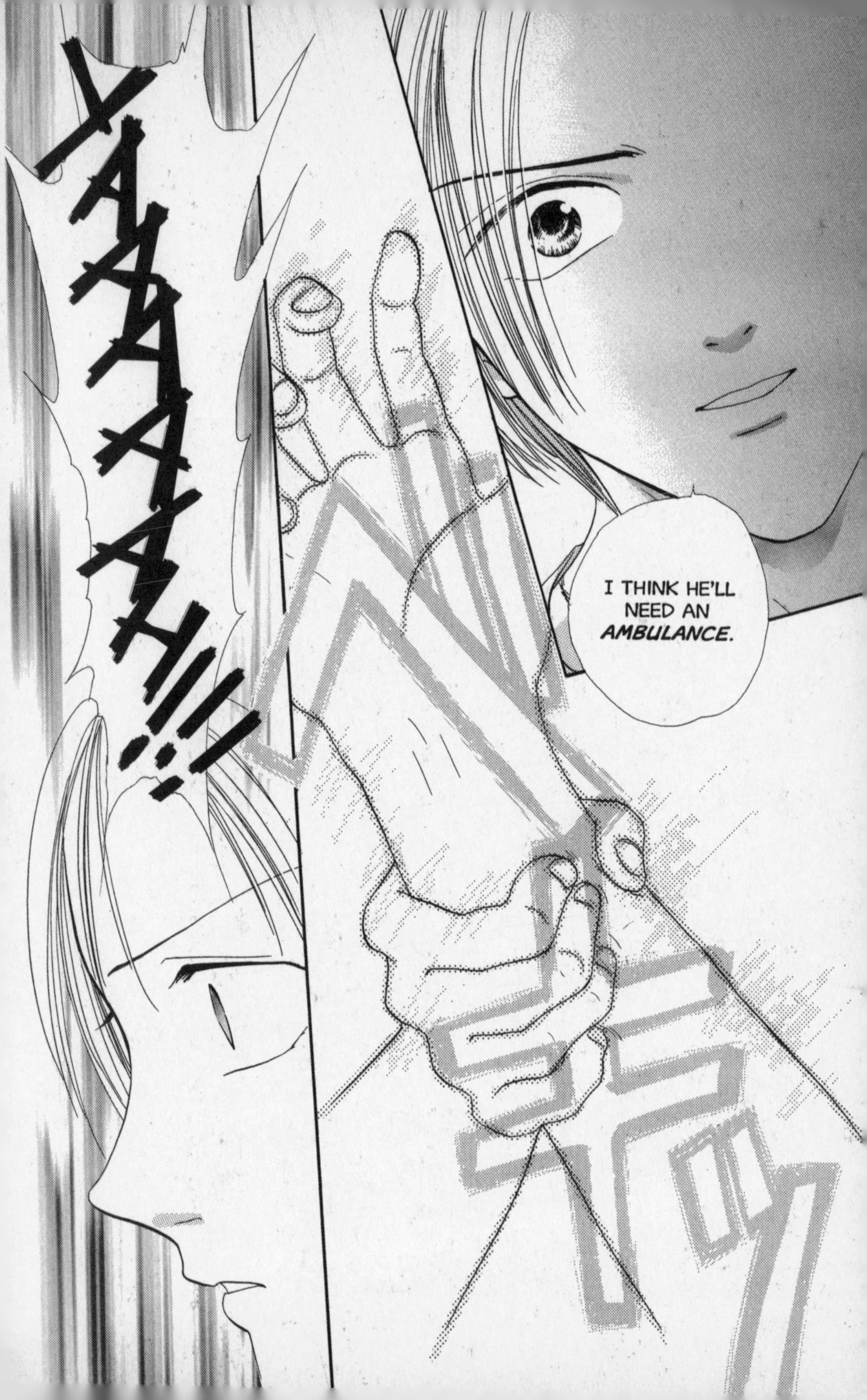
I THINK HE'LL NEED AN *AMBULANCE.*
YAAAAAH!!!!

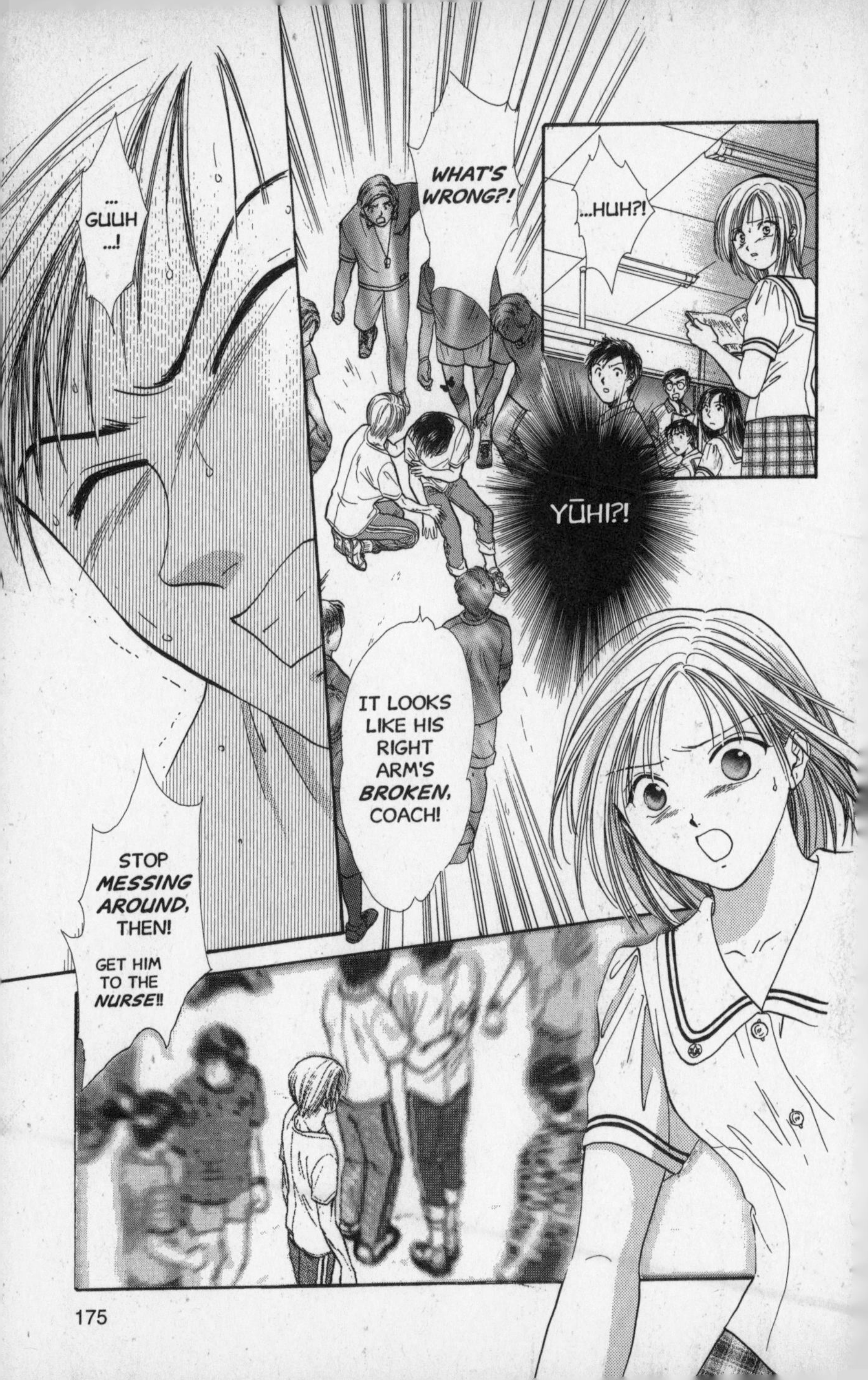
...HUH?!
YŪHI?!
WHAT'S WRONG?!
... GUUH ...!
IT LOOKS LIKE HIS RIGHT ARM'S BROKEN, COACH!
STOP MESSING AROUND, THEN!
GET HIM TO THE NURSE!!

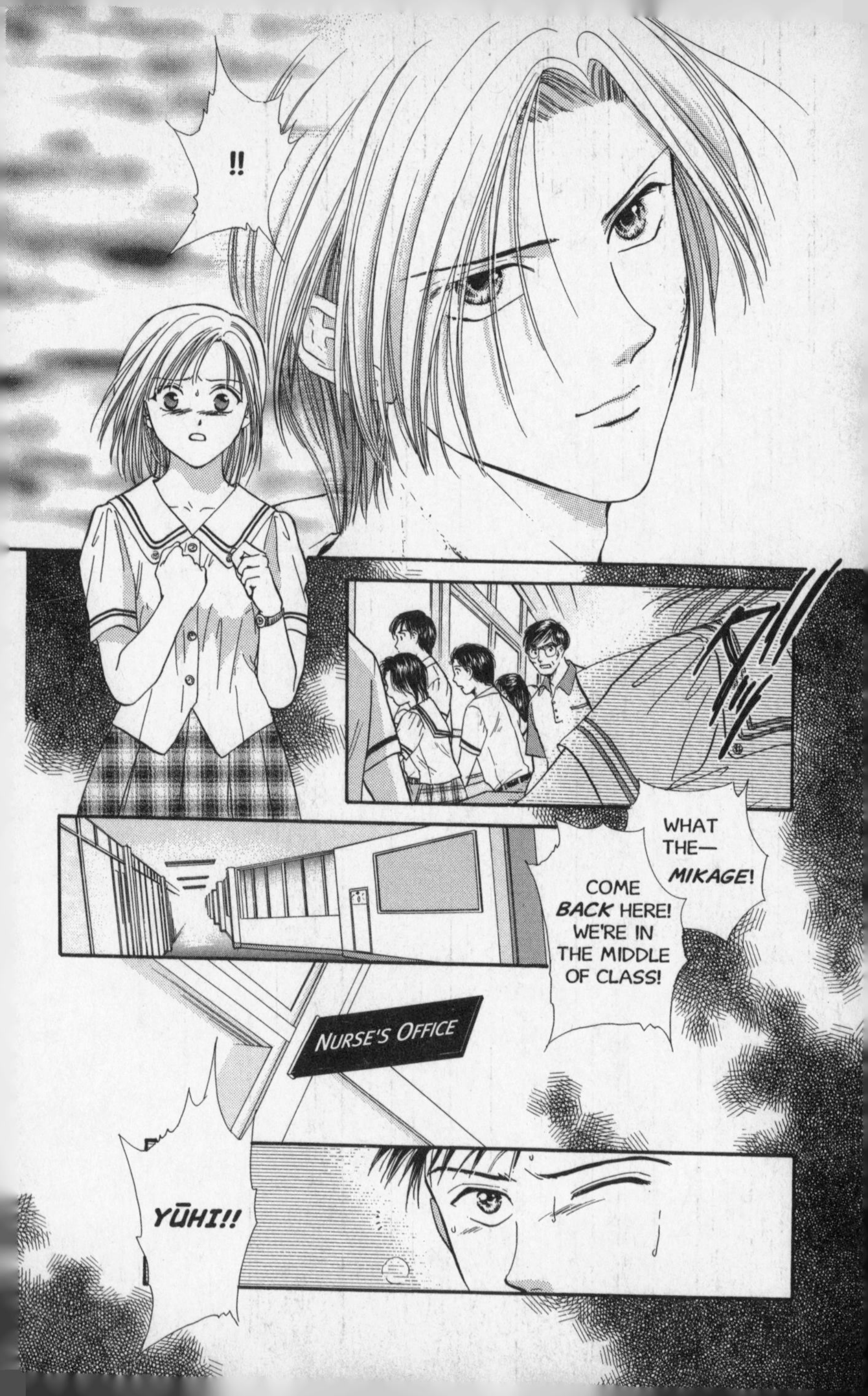
!!
WHAT THE— MIKAGE!
COME BACK HERE! WE'RE IN THE MIDDLE OF CLASS!
NURSE'S OFFICE
YŪHI!!

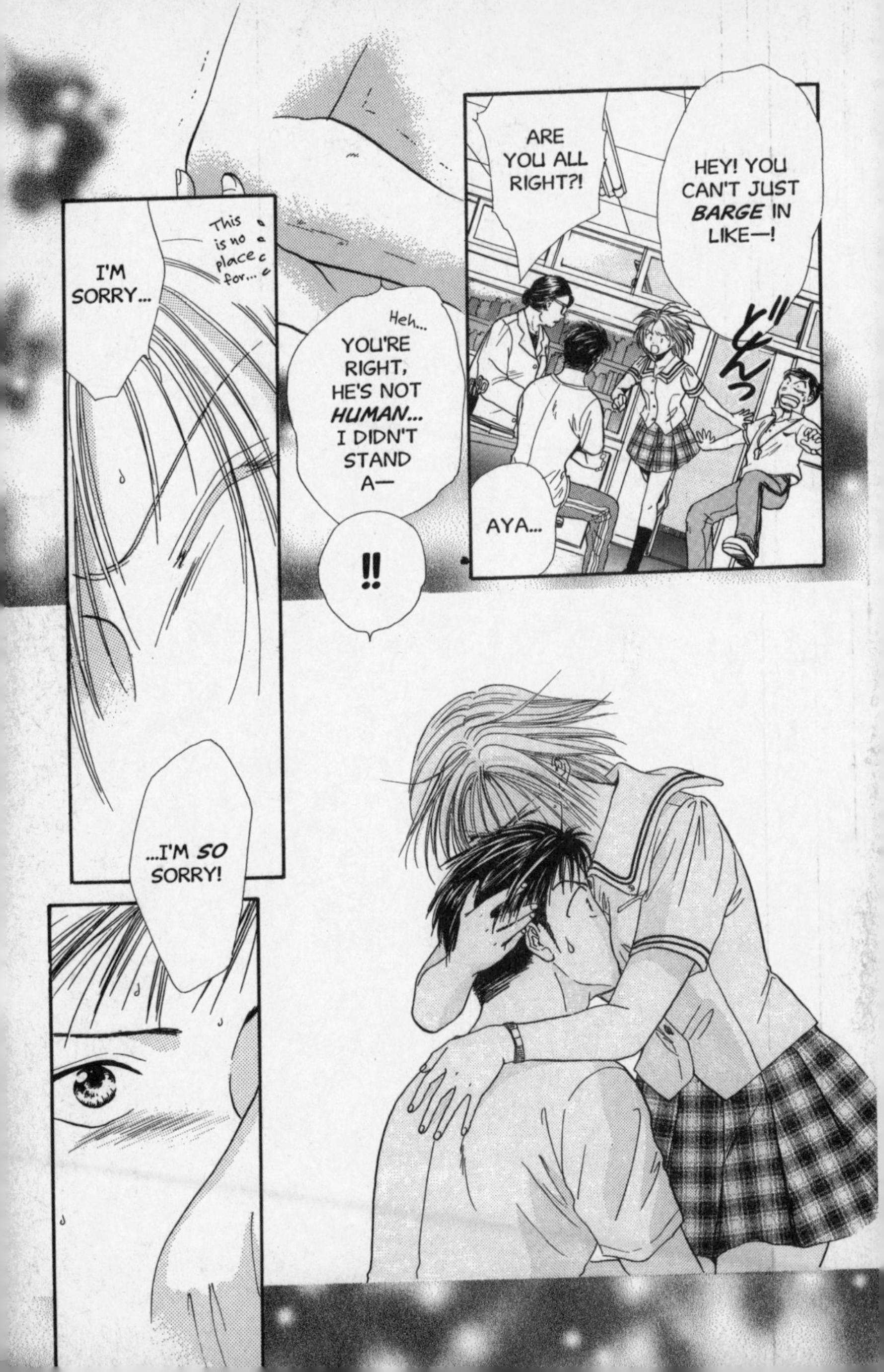
HEY! YOU CAN'T JUST *BARGE* IN LIKE—!
ARE YOU ALL RIGHT?!
AYA...
Heh...
YOU'RE RIGHT, HE'S NOT *HUMAN*... I DIDN'T STAND A—
!!
This is no place for...
I'M SORRY...
...I'M *SO* SORRY!

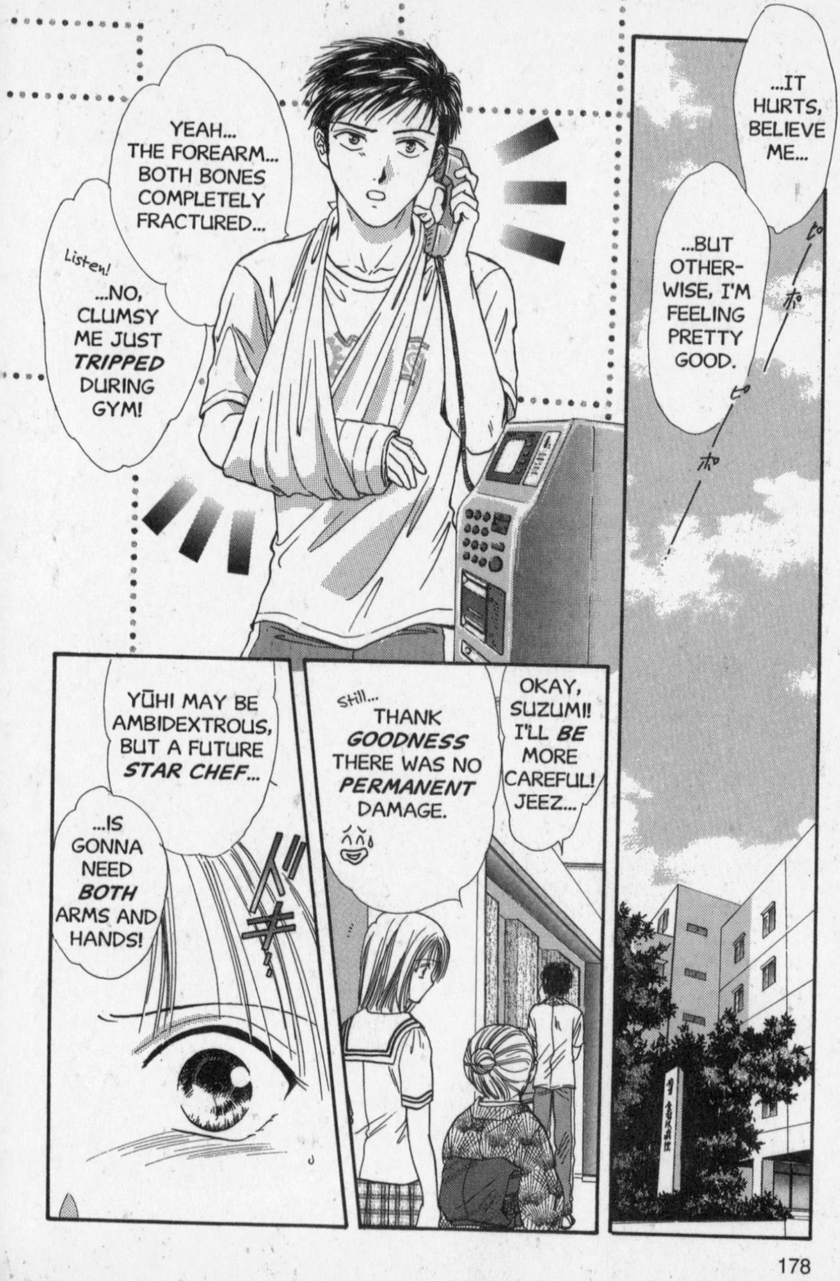
...IT HURTS, BELIEVE ME...
...BUT OTHERWISE, I'M FEELING PRETTY GOOD.
ピーポー ピーポー
YEAH... THE FOREARM... BOTH BONES COMPLETELY FRACTURED...
Listen!
...NO, CLUMSY ME JUST *TRIPPED* DURING GYM!
OKAY, SUZUMI! I'LL *BE* MORE CAREFUL! JEEZ...
Still...
THANK *GOODNESS* THERE WAS NO *PERMANENT* DAMAGE.
YŪHI MAY BE AMBIDEXTROUS, BUT A FUTURE *STAR CHEF*...
...IS GONNA NEED *BOTH* ARMS AND HANDS!

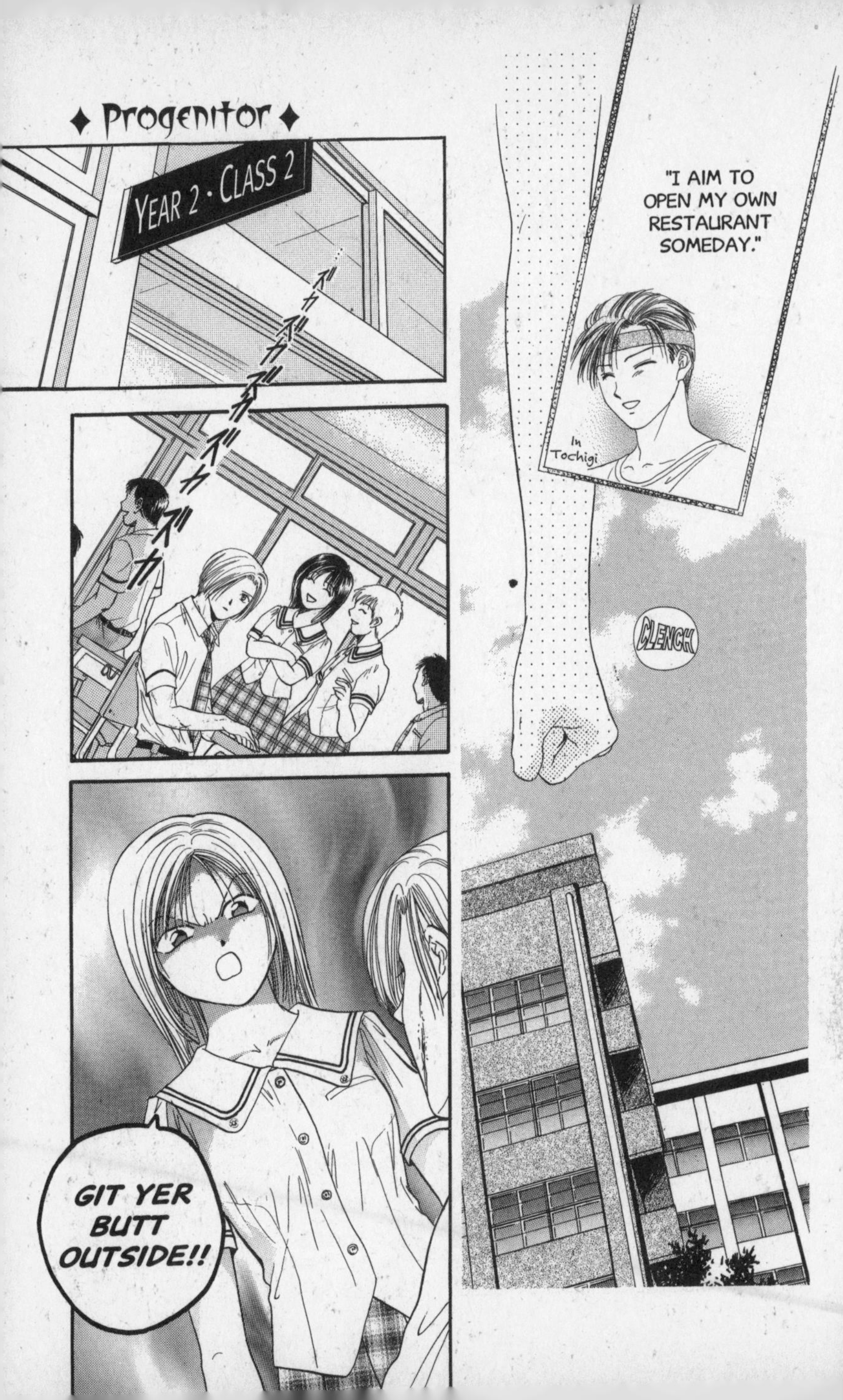
"I AIM TO OPEN MY OWN RESTAURANT SOMEDAY."
In Tochigi
CLENCH
YEAR 2 · CLASS 2
ズカズカズカズカズカ
GIT YER BUTT OUTSIDE!!

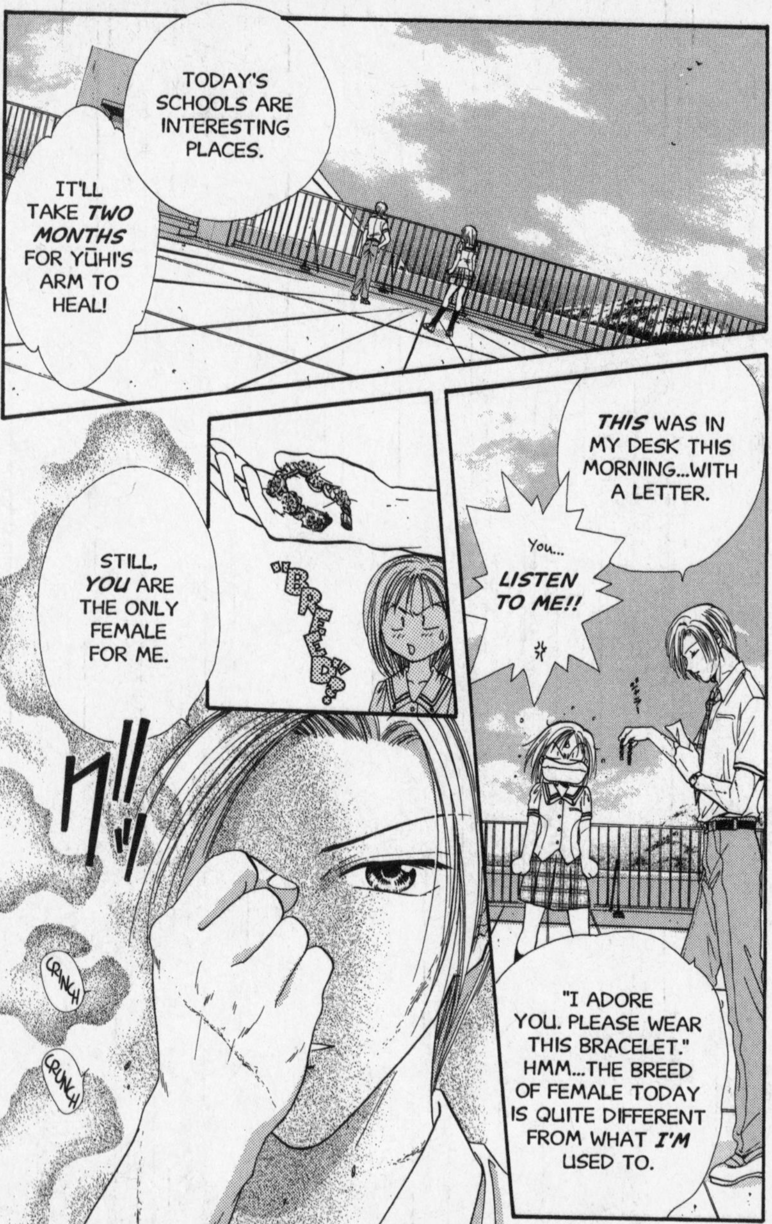
TODAY'S SCHOOLS ARE INTERESTING PLACES.
IT'LL TAKE *TWO MONTHS* FOR YŪHI'S ARM TO HEAL!
THIS WAS IN MY DESK THIS MORNING...WITH A LETTER.
You... *LISTEN TO ME!!*
"I ADORE YOU. PLEASE WEAR THIS BRACELET." HMM...THE BREED OF FEMALE TODAY IS QUITE DIFFERENT FROM WHAT *I'M* USED TO.
STILL, *YOU* ARE THE ONLY FEMALE FOR ME.
CRUNCH
CRUNCH

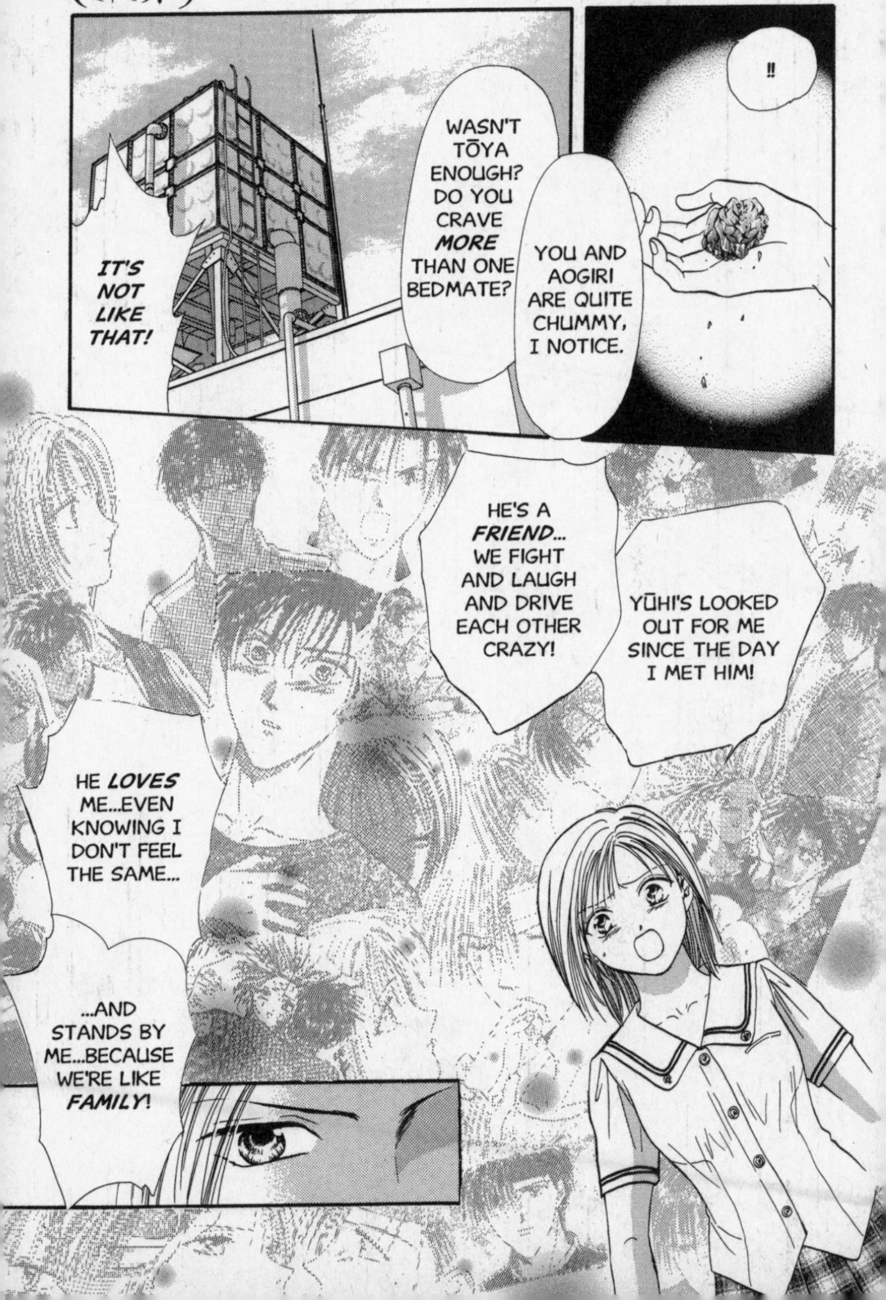
!!
YOU AND AOGIRI ARE QUITE CHUMMY, I NOTICE.
WASN'T TŌYA ENOUGH? DO YOU CRAVE *MORE* THAN ONE BEDMATE?
IT'S NOT LIKE THAT!
YŪHI'S LOOKED OUT FOR ME SINCE THE DAY I MET HIM!
HE'S A *FRIEND*... WE FIGHT AND LAUGH AND DRIVE EACH OTHER CRAZY!
HE *LOVES* ME...EVEN KNOWING I DON'T FEEL THE SAME...
...AND STANDS BY ME...BECAUSE WE'RE LIKE *FAMILY*!

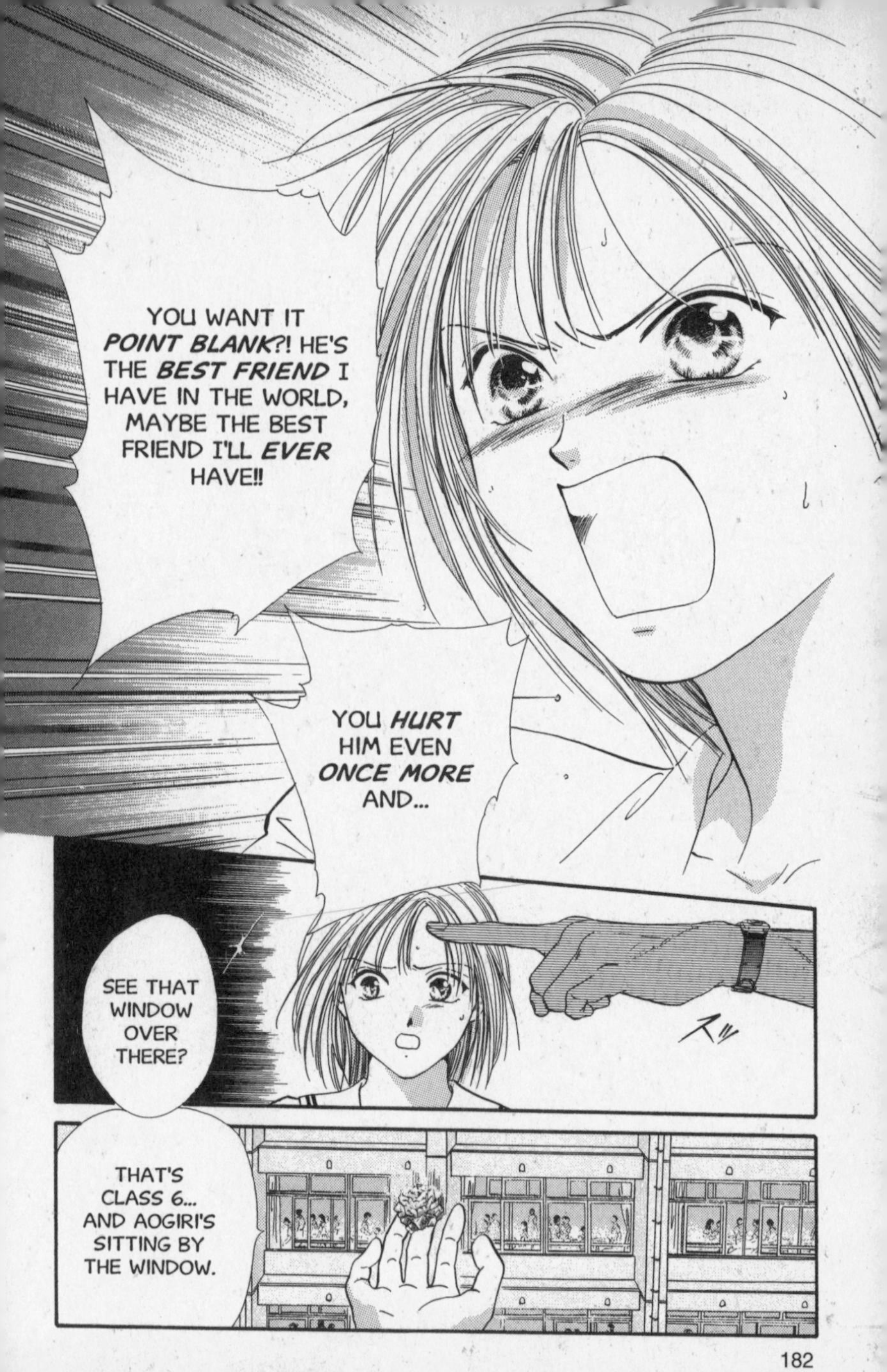
YOU WANT IT *POINT BLANK*?! HE'S THE *BEST FRIEND* I HAVE IN THE WORLD, MAYBE THE BEST FRIEND I'LL *EVER* HAVE!!
YOU *HURT* HIM EVEN *ONCE MORE* AND...
SEE THAT WINDOW OVER THERE?
スッ
THAT'S CLASS 6... AND AOGIRI'S SITTING BY THE WINDOW.

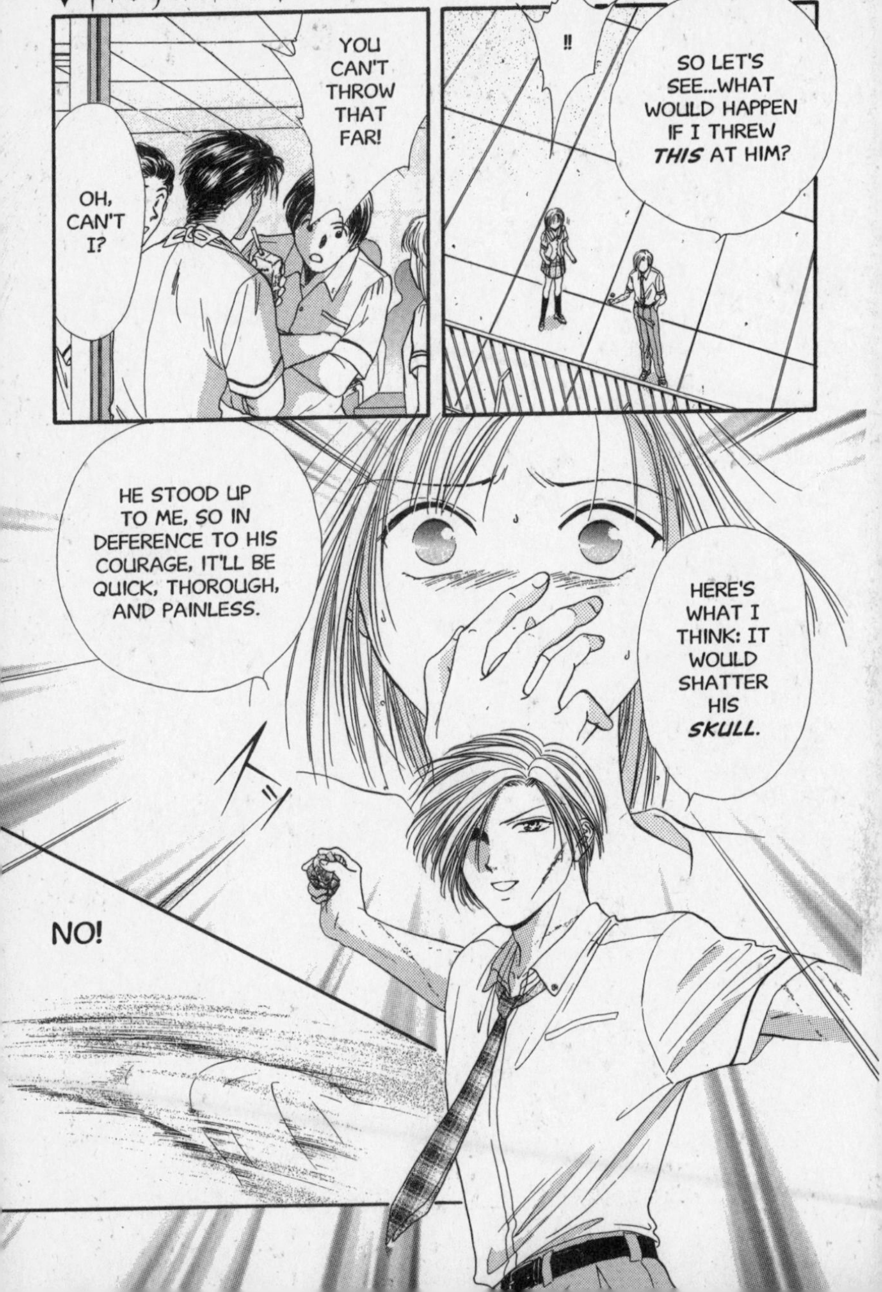
!!
SO LET'S SEE...WHAT WOULD HAPPEN IF I THREW *THIS* AT HIM?
YOU CAN'T THROW THAT FAR!
OH, CAN'T I?
HERE'S WHAT I THINK: IT WOULD SHATTER HIS *SKULL*.
HE STOOD UP TO ME, SO IN DEFERENCE TO HIS COURAGE, IT'LL BE QUICK, THOROUGH, AND PAINLESS.
NO!

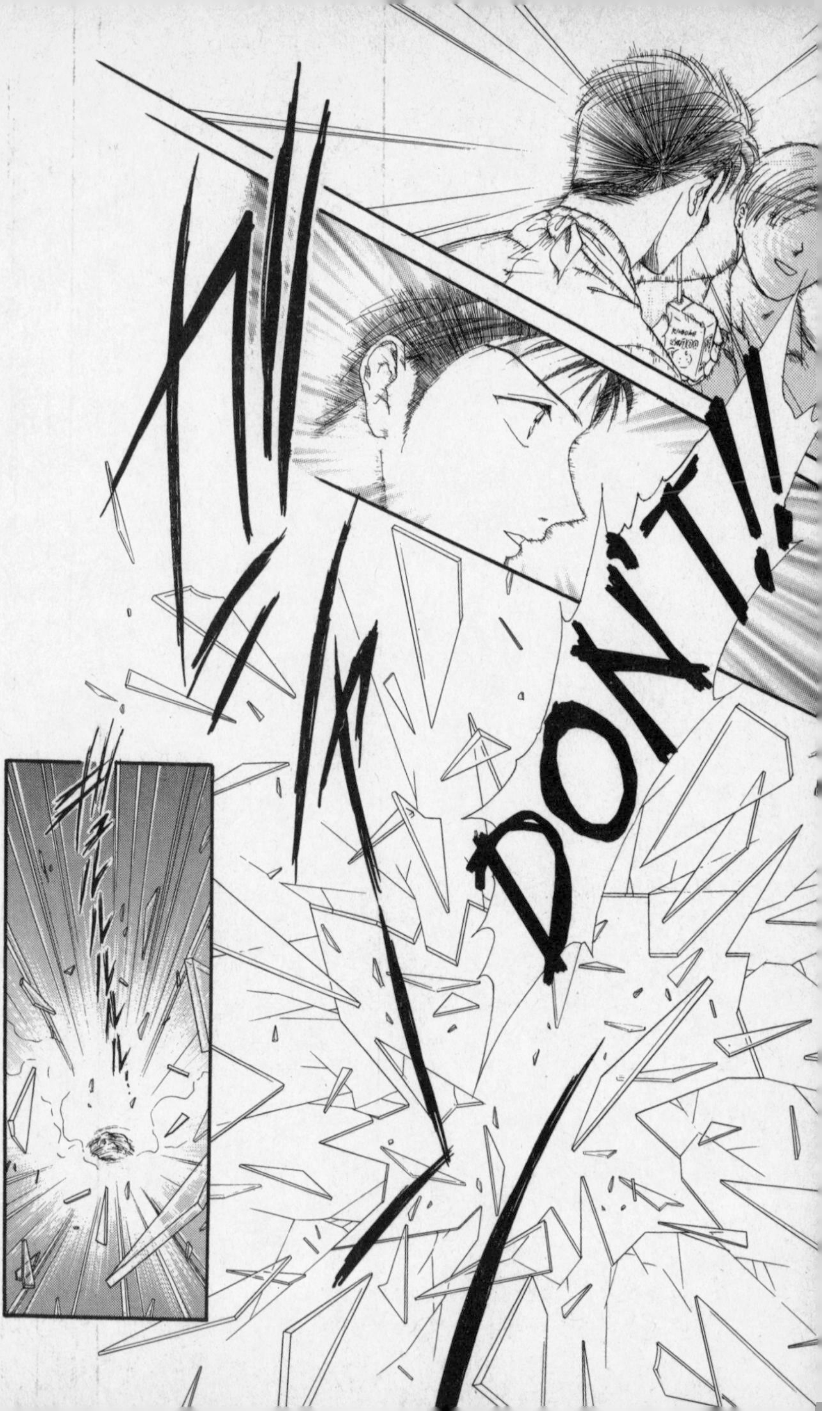
DON'T!!

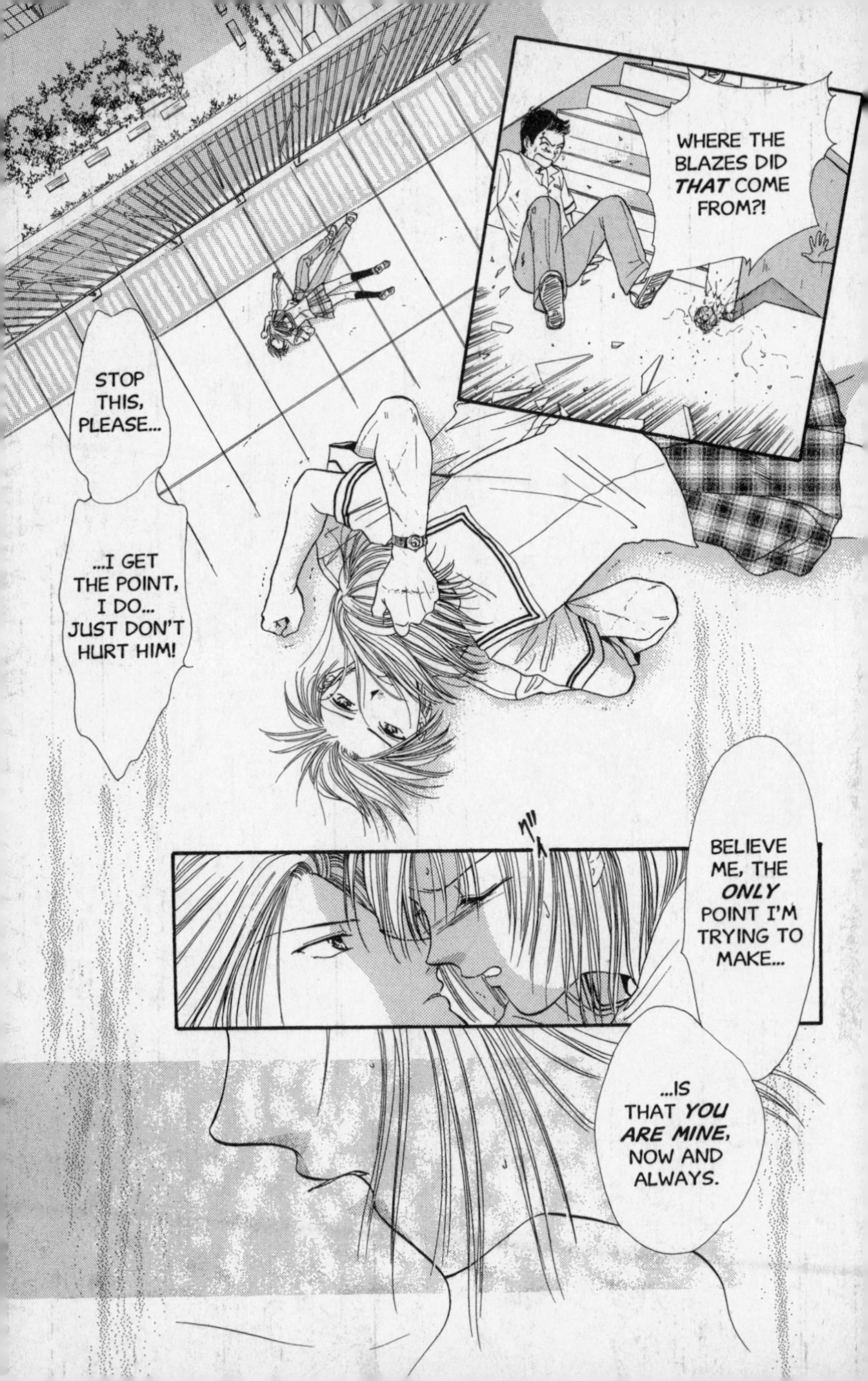
WHERE THE BLAZES DID *THAT* COME FROM?!
STOP THIS, PLEASE...
...I GET THE POINT, I DO... JUST DON'T HURT HIM!
BELIEVE ME, THE *ONLY* POINT I'M TRYING TO MAKE...
...IS THAT *YOU ARE MINE*, NOW AND ALWAYS.

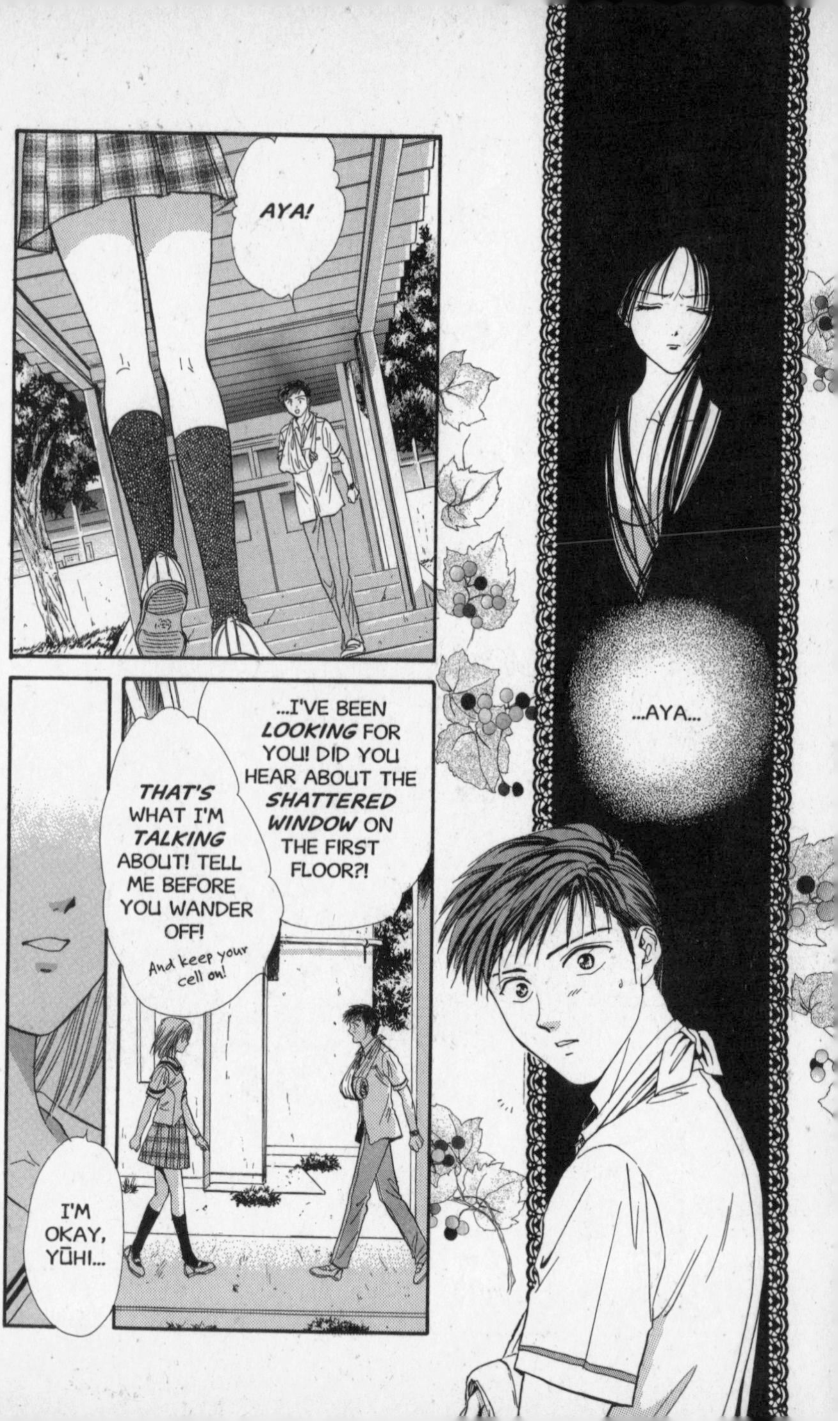
...AYA...
AYA!
...I'VE BEEN LOOKING FOR YOU! DID YOU HEAR ABOUT THE SHATTERED WINDOW ON THE FIRST FLOOR?!
THAT'S WHAT I'M TALKING ABOUT! TELL ME BEFORE YOU WANDER OFF!
And keep your cell on!
I'M OKAY, YŪHI...

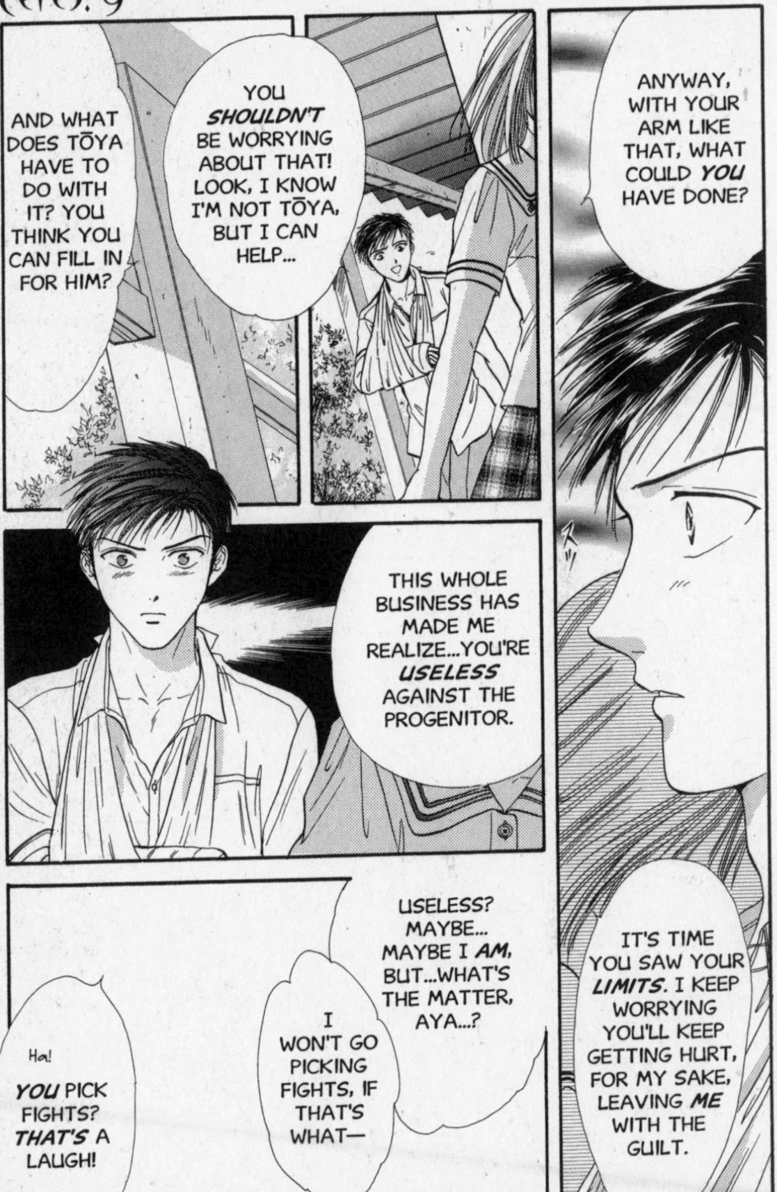
ANYWAY, WITH YOUR ARM LIKE THAT, WHAT COULD YOU HAVE DONE?
IT'S TIME YOU SAW YOUR LIMITS. I KEEP WORRYING YOU'LL KEEP GETTING HURT, FOR MY SAKE, LEAVING ME WITH THE GUILT.
YOU SHOULDN'T BE WORRYING ABOUT THAT! LOOK, I KNOW I'M NOT TŌYA, BUT I CAN HELP...
AND WHAT DOES TŌYA HAVE TO DO WITH IT? YOU THINK YOU CAN FILL IN FOR HIM?
THIS WHOLE BUSINESS HAS MADE ME REALIZE...YOU'RE USELESS AGAINST THE PROGENITOR.
USELESS? MAYBE... MAYBE I AM, BUT...WHAT'S THE MATTER, AYA...?
I WON'T GO PICKING FIGHTS, IF THAT'S WHAT—
Ha!
YOU PICK FIGHTS? THAT'S A LAUGH!

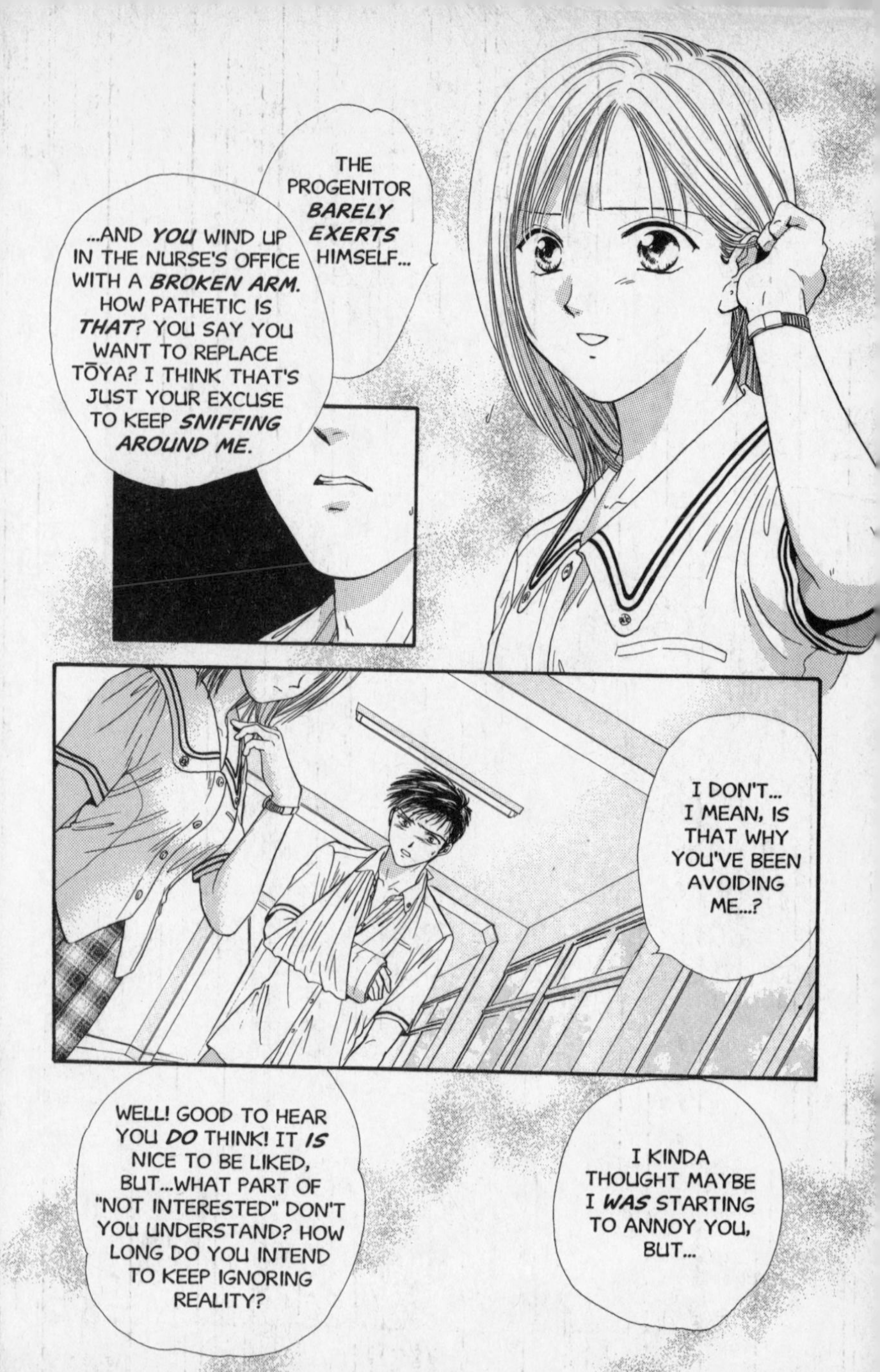
THE PROGENITOR *BARELY EXERTS* HIMSELF...
...AND *YOU* WIND UP IN THE NURSE'S OFFICE WITH A *BROKEN ARM.* HOW PATHETIC IS *THAT*? YOU SAY YOU WANT TO REPLACE TŌYA? I THINK THAT'S JUST YOUR EXCUSE TO KEEP *SNIFFING AROUND ME.*
I DON'T... I MEAN, IS THAT WHY YOU'VE BEEN AVOIDING ME...?
I KINDA THOUGHT MAYBE I *WAS* STARTING TO ANNOY YOU, BUT...
WELL! GOOD TO HEAR YOU *DO* THINK! IT *IS* NICE TO BE LIKED, BUT...WHAT PART OF "NOT INTERESTED" DON'T YOU UNDERSTAND? HOW LONG DO YOU INTEND TO KEEP IGNORING REALITY?

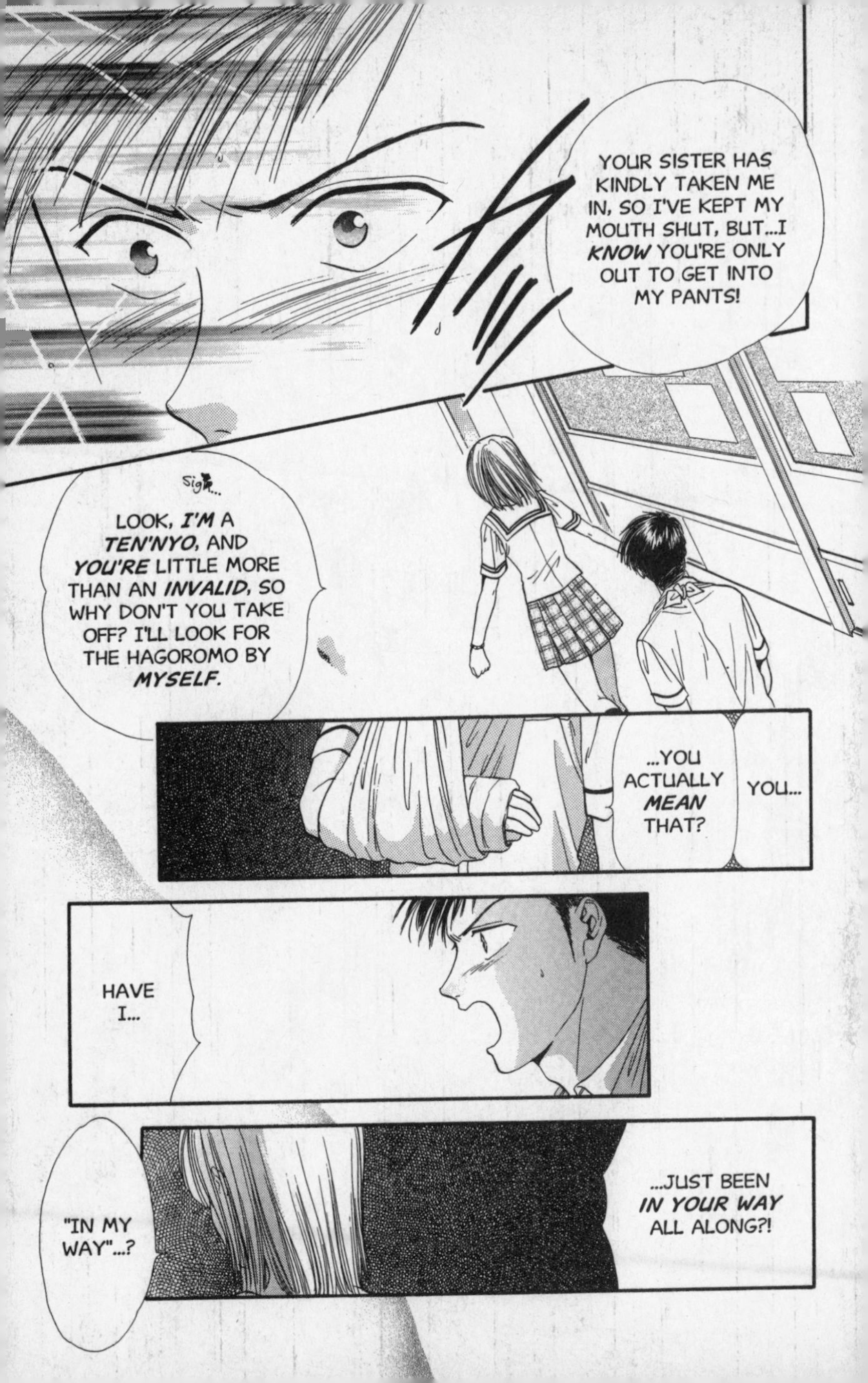
YOUR SISTER HAS KINDLY TAKEN ME IN, SO I'VE KEPT MY MOUTH SHUT, BUT...I *KNOW* YOU'RE ONLY OUT TO GET INTO MY PANTS!
Sigh...
LOOK, *I'M* A *TEN'NYO*, AND *YOU'RE* LITTLE MORE THAN AN *INVALID*, SO WHY DON'T YOU TAKE OFF? I'LL LOOK FOR THE HAGOROMO BY *MYSELF*.
YOU...
...YOU ACTUALLY *MEAN* THAT?
HAVE I...
...JUST BEEN *IN YOUR WAY* ALL ALONG?!
"IN MY WAY"...?

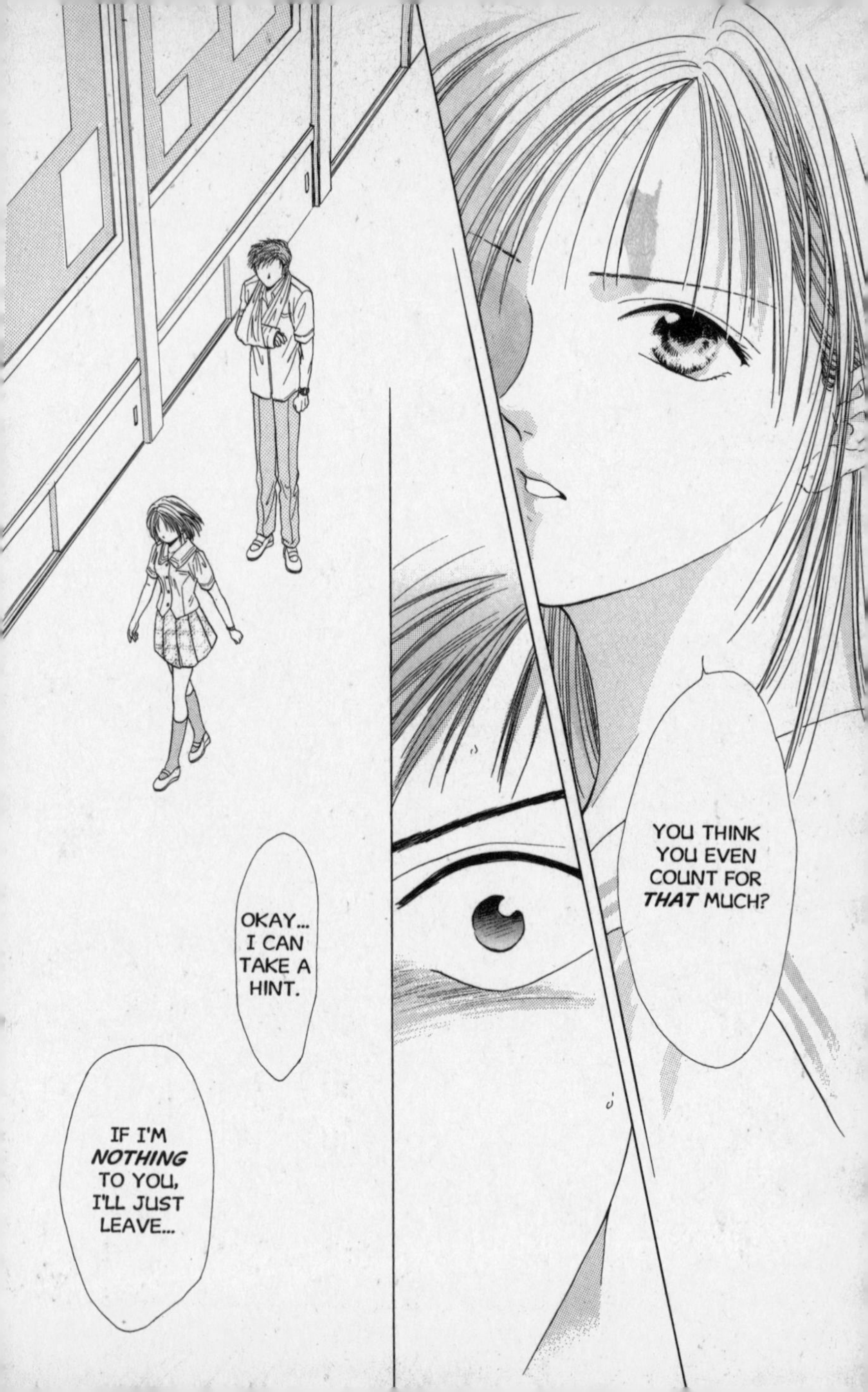
YOU THINK YOU EVEN COUNT FOR *THAT* MUCH?
OKAY... I CAN TAKE A HINT.
IF I'M *NOTHING* TO YOU, I'LL JUST LEAVE...

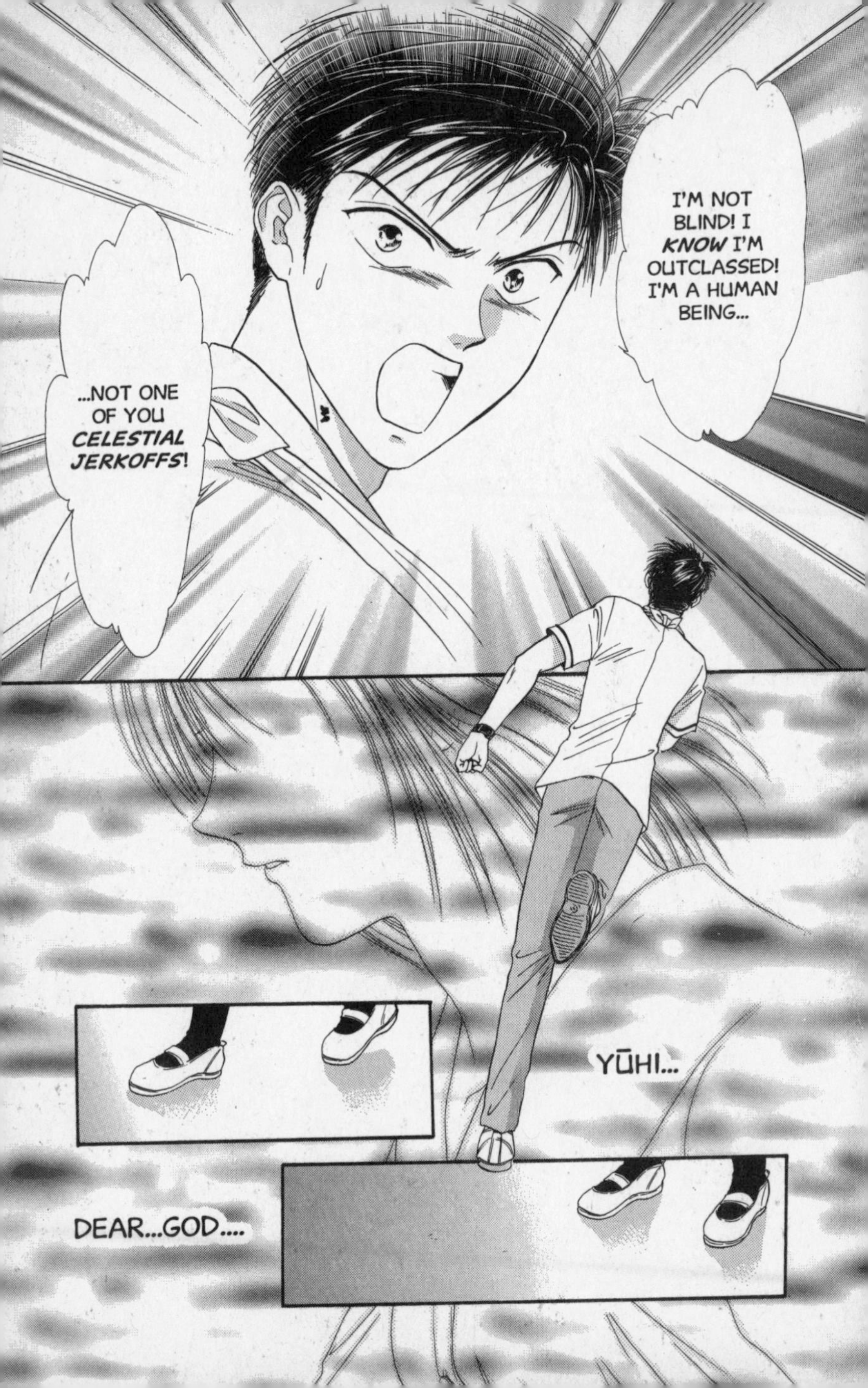
I'M NOT BLIND! I KNOW I'M OUTCLASSED! I'M A HUMAN BEING...
...NOT ONE OF YOU CELESTIAL JERKOFFS!
YŪHI...
DEAR...GOD....

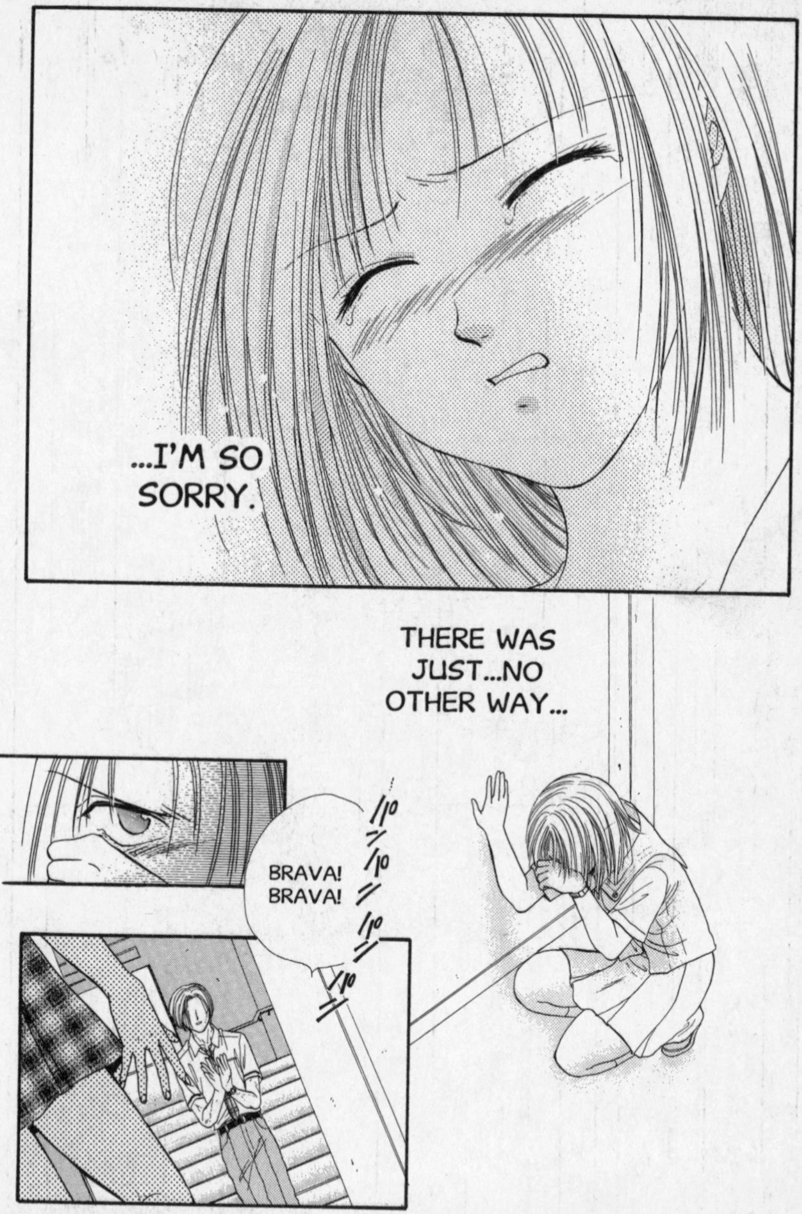
...I'M SO SORRY.
THERE WAS JUST...NO OTHER WAY...
BRAVA! BRAVA!

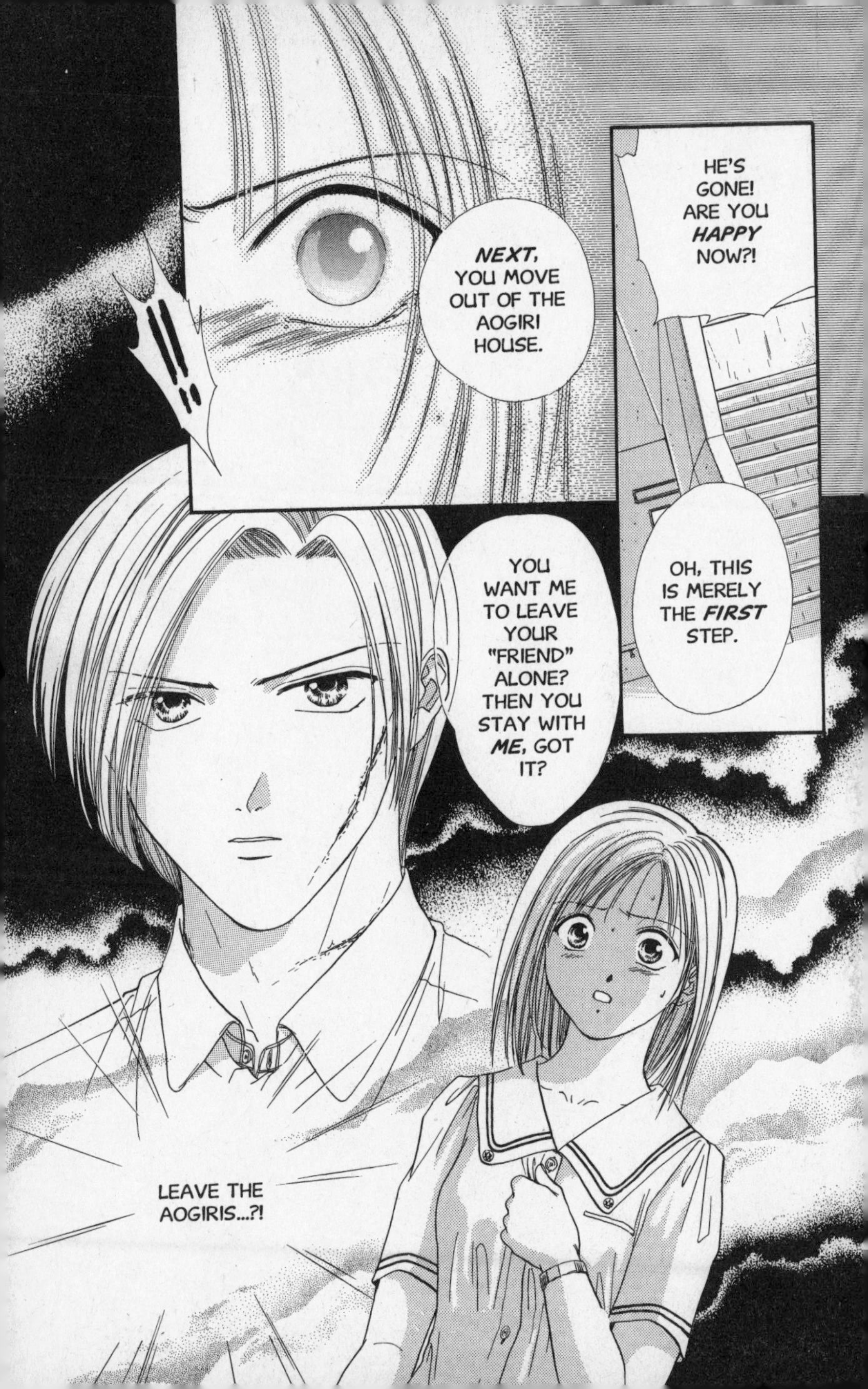
HE'S GONE! ARE YOU *HAPPY* NOW?!
OH, THIS IS MERELY THE *FIRST* STEP.
NEXT, YOU MOVE OUT OF THE AOGIRI HOUSE.
!!
YOU WANT ME TO LEAVE YOUR "FRIEND" ALONE? THEN YOU STAY WITH *ME*, GOT IT?
LEAVE THE AOGIRIS...?!

The CERES Guide to Sound Effects

We've left most of the sound effects in CERES as Yû Watase originally created them–in Japanese. VIZ has created this glossary to help you decipher, page-by-page and panel-by-panel, what all those foreign words and background noises mean. Use this guide to impress your friends with your new Japanese vocabulary. The glossary lists the page number then panel. For example, 3.1 indicates page 3, panel 1.

006.2 FX: Fu (a sudden "void," or "burst")
007.3 FX: Ha ("gasp!")
009.1 FX: Ka (startlement)
012.1 FX: Da ("dash")
016.3 FX: Don ("boom!")
020.1 FX: Ki ki ki ki (screeching of car brakes)
020.1 FX: Doga ("crash!")
020.4 FX: Ha ("gasp!")
022.2 FX: Ban ("slam")
023.1 FX: Kotsu kotsu (hollow, "ringing" footsteps)
024.1 FX: Zun ("smash")
024.2 FX: Ha ("gasp!")
024.3 FX: Dan ("thud")
026.4 FX: Zâ ("sloosh" of waves)
027.1 FX: Za za (rhythmic waves)
027.2 FX: Za ("sloosh")
027.3 FX: Piku ("twitch," as in sudden alertness)
028.3 FX: Ha ("gasp!")
030.1 FX: Gu gu (choking anger)
033.1 FX: Ba (leap; sudden, "big" movement)
035.4 FX: Bita (sudden press against window)
040.1 FX: Gura (feeling of "faintness")
040.2 FX: Gaku gaku (trembling)
041.3 FX: Ban ("crash")
042.4 FX: Ba (leap; sudden, "big" movement)
042.5 FX: Kashan ("clink," as in metal hitting floor)
043.1 FX: Dan ("thud")
043.4 FX: Da ("dash")
044.4 FX: Do do do do (explosive force)
045.5 FX: Doka ("slam")
047.3 FX: Ha ("gasp!")
047.4 FX: Pappâ (laying on of car horn)
048.4 FX: Buru buru buru (quivering)
053.4 FX: Biku (sudden "alertness" – less "sharp" than "piku," above)
054.1 FX: Ban ("crash")

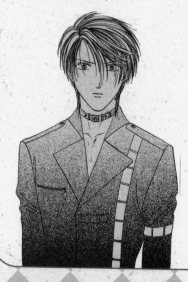

057.1 FX: Ba (leap; sudden, "big" movement)

061.4 FX: Zuru (slipping)

062.2 FX: Keho keho ("koff, koff")

063.3 FX: Fan fan fan u— (police siren)

065.2 FX: Zawa zawa (buzz, murmur of crowd)

066.2 FX: Pii ("tweet" of police whistle)

067.1 FX: Piku ("twitch")

068.1 FX: Do do do do do do (heartbeats, increasing in loudness)

069.1 FX: Ha ("gasp!")

070.1 FX: Jiiwa jiwa jii (cry of cicadas—signifying summer heat)

071.1 FX: Kû (sniffling sob)

071.2 FX: Chi—n (blowing nose)

071.4 FX: Dan ("bam")

072.4 FX: Gara ("rattle")

073.1 FX: Cha ("chk")

076.4 FX: Jiiwa jiwa jii (cicadas)

078.4 FX: Ka (footstep)

079.2 FX: Ban ("slam")

079.3 FX: Kya—! ("eeek!")

082.4 FX: Gu ("clench")

082.5 FX: Gatan gatan ("clunk, clunk")

083.1 FX: Su (something lightly brushing against something else)

083.3 FX: Doka ("thwack!")

084.4 FX: Ha ("gasp!")

085.3 FX: Ha ("gasp!")

086.4 FX: Su— (light breathing of sleep)

089.2 FX: Piku ("twitch")

090.1 FX: Ha ("gasp!")

090.4 FX: Dokun dokun dokun (heartbeats)

091.3 FX: Yoro ("wobble," "stagger")

092.3 FX: Hâ hâ hâ hâ ("huff, huff, huff, huff")

092.4 FX: Hâ hâ ("huff, huff")

092.5 FX: Ha ("gasp!")

092.6 FX: Yoro ("wobble," "stagger")

095.4 FX: Ta (light "running")

096.2 FX: Tokun tokun tokun (heartbeats, as heard through Tôya's dagger)

097.1 FX: Tokun tokun tokun (heartbeats)

100.1 FX: Zan (waves)

100.2 FX: Za za ("sloosh" of waves)

101.4 FX: Dokun ("heavy" heartbeat)

102.1 FX: Ba (sudden movement)

102.2 FX: Showa showa showa (more cicadas)

102.2 FX: Hâ hâ ("huff, huff")

102.3 FX: Hâ hâ ("huff, huff")

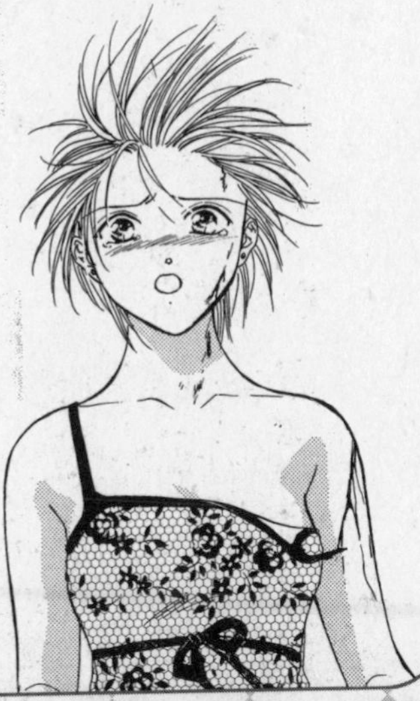

103.1 FX: Tokun tokun...
(dagger heartbeats)
104.1 FX: Ba— (sudden, violent shove)
104.4 FX: A—n (distressed wail)
105.2 FX: E—?!
(rising astonishment, dismay)
108.5 FX: Doki (sudden elevation in
blood pressure)
109.3 FX: Showa showa showa
(cicadas)
110.2 FX: Suta suta suta suta
("tromping" off)
111.1 FX: Doki (sudden quickening
of breath)
111.3 FX: Bikun ("twitch")
111.4 FX: Za za (waves)
116.1 FX: Hi—! (cringing cry)
118.3 FX: Dokkiri ("gurking" surprise)
119.2 FX: Za Za (waves)
120.3 FX: Bun Bun (flailing arms)
124.2 FX: Gakkuri
("sigh" of disappointment)
125.3 FX: Tokun tokun...
(dagger heartbeats)
128.1 FX: Bikun ("sharp" gasp,
startlement)
131.3 FX: Ki—n (school bell)
131.4 FX: Ko—n ka—n (school bell)
132.1 FX: Su
(something lightly brushing
against something else)
132.1 FX: Ba (sudden recoil)
132.2 FX: Boso ("psst!")
133.3 FX: Ha ("gasp!")
134.2 FX: Ka—n ("whack!")
134.4 FX: Ha ("gasp!")
135.3 FX: Ka—n ko—n (school bell)
135.4 FX: Kyoro kyoro koso koso
(furtive glancing)
135.5 FX: Giku ("urk!")
136.4 FX: Dâshu ("dash")
136.5 FX: Bata bata bata bata
("vrooming" away into
distance)
140.2 FX: Pan ("slap")
144.1 FX: Doki ("ba-bump")
144.4 FX: Dokin dokin...
(escalating heartbeats)
145.2 FX: Koku ("nod")
148.2 FX: Pan ("slap")
148.4 FX: Gyu ("clench")
149.4 FX: Bashi ("whap")
150.2 FX: Ha ("gasp!")
151.3 FX: Dokun dokun dokun
("heavy" heartbeats)
151.4 FX: Biku (startled reaction)

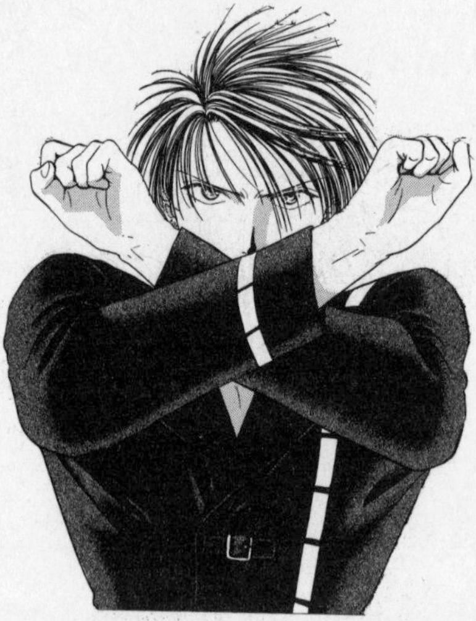

153.3 FX: Ha ("gasp!")
154.4 FX: Zoku ("brr!")
155.2 FX: Gari ("chomp")
155.4 FX: Biku (startled reaction)
156.1 FX: Bashi ("whap")
156.2 FX: Dosa dosa ("thump" of falling books)
156.3 FX: Pita (tip of blade against throat)
157.3 FX: Ku (sound of amusement)
159.4 FX: Ha ("gasp!")
160.2 FX: Da ("dash")
165.2 FX: Gui ("tug")
165.4 FX: Pa ("vip")
167.1 FX: Pa, sa ("vip," "voop")
167.2 FX: Pi'i ("tweet" of whistle)
167.4 FX: Ha ("gasp!")
167.5 FX: Gatan ("clunk")
169.1 FX: Pi'i ("tweet" of whistle)
169.3 FX: Su ("slippage" of air)
169.4 FX: Ga ("bash")
169.5 FX: Yoro ("stagger," "stumble")
169.5 FX: Pi'i ("tweet" of whistle)
170.5 FX: Dô ("thud")
171.1 FX: Pi'i ("tweet" of whistle)
171.2 FX: Ki ("glare")
171.3 FX: Gu ("grip")
171.4 FX: Gu Gu (increasing grip, "squeeze")
171.5 FX: Meki meki... ("krak krak")
172.2 FX: Beki (big "krak")
174.2 FX: Da ("dash")
175.1 FX: Don ("shove")
176.1 FX: Pi—po— Pi—po— (wailing of ambulance)
176.4 FX: Doki (startled heartbeat)
177.3 FX: Zuka zuka... ("stomp, stomp," coming closer)
178.2 FX: Jara ("jangle" of bracelet)
178.4 FX: Gu ("clench")
180.2 FX: Su (something brushing lightly against something else)
181.3 FX: Su ("slippage" of air as arm draws back)
182.3 FX: Gasha—n ("smash")
182.4 FX: Gyururururururu (spinning, whirling)
183.3 FX: Gui ("tug")
185.1 FX: Su (something brushing lightly against something else)
187.1 FX: Ka (sudden flush of embarrassment)
190.4 FX: Pan pan... ("clap, clap")

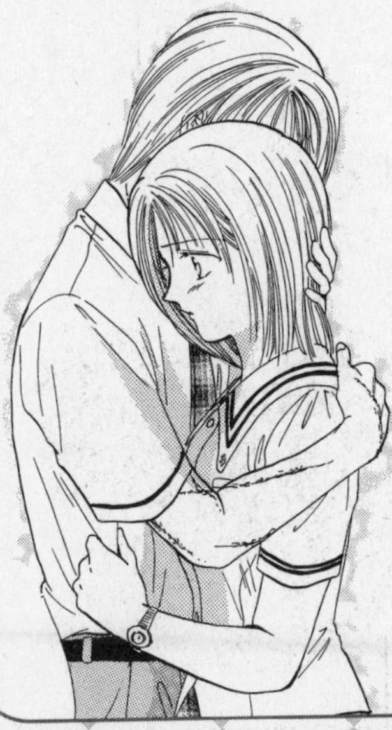

Yû Watase was born on March 5 in a town near Osaka, Japan, and she was raised there before moving to Tokyo to follow her dream of creating manga. In the decade since her debut short story, *PAJAMA DE OJAMA* ("An Intrusion in Pajamas"), she has produced more than 50 compiled volumes of short stories and continuing series. Her latest series, *ZETTAI KARESHI* ("He'll Be My Boyfriend"), is currently running in the anthology magazine *SHÔJO COMIC*. Watase's long-running historical romance story *FUSHIGI YÛGI* (THE MYSTERIOUS PLAY) and her most recent completed series, *ALICE 19TH*, are now available in North America, published by VIZ. She loves science fiction, fantasy and comedy.

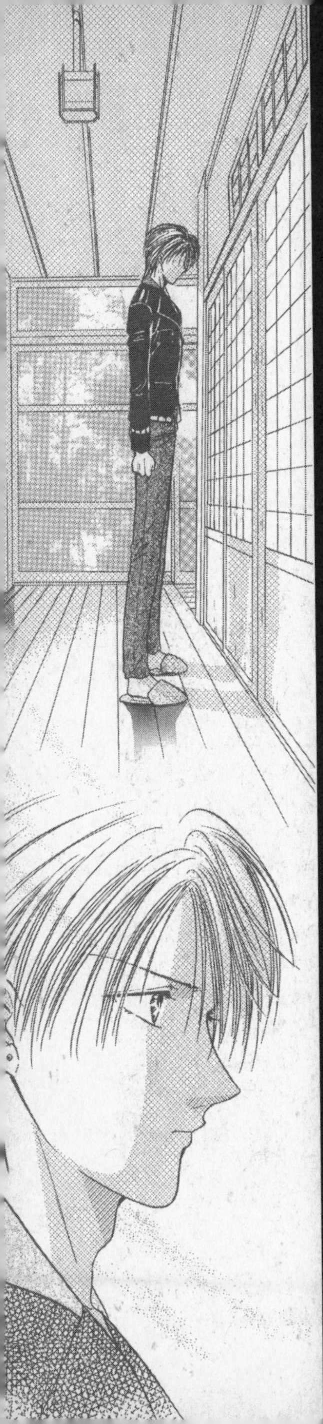

If you enjoyed *CERES: CELESTIAL LEGEND*, here are some other titles VIZ recommends you read:

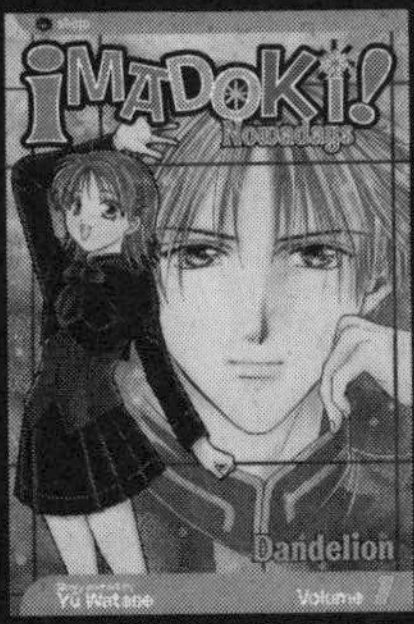
iMADOKi!
Nowadays
Dandelion
Yû Watase

© 2000 Yuu Watase / Shogakukan, Inc.

IMADOKI! (NOWADAYS)

The newest series from Yû Watase available in America, *Imadoki!* follows the trials and tribulations of Tanpopo Yamazaki, a budding young horticulturist, as she makes her way down the winding road to friendship. Snubbed by the rich kids at her new school, the elite Meio Academy, Tanpopo starts up a gardening club. But will this help her survive in an environment where superficiality and nepotism reign supreme?

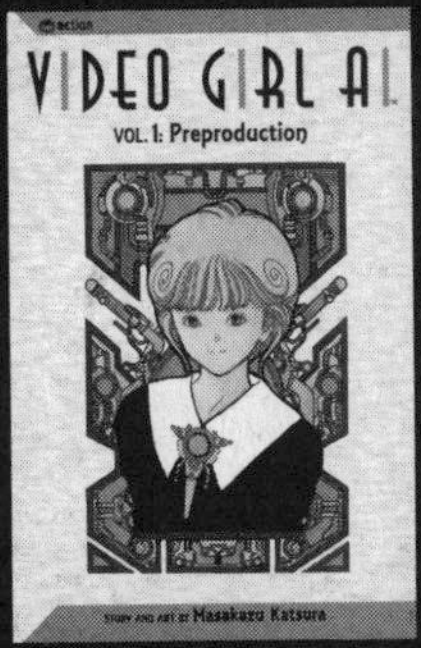
VIDEO GIRL AI
VOL. 1: Preproduction
Masakazu Katsura

VIDEO GIRL AI ©1989 by MASAKAZU KATSURA/SHUEISHA Inc.

VIDEO GIRL AI

When Moemi, the object of Yota's incurable crush, turns out to be in love with the dashing and popular Takashi, poor Yota is devastated. He rents a video to distract himself, but Ai, the cute idol featured on the tape, magically bursts out of the TV and into Yota's world. Ai's mission is to fix Yota's hopeless love life, but when Ai develops romantic feelings towards Yota, things get complicated. A true manga classic, sweet and hilarious!

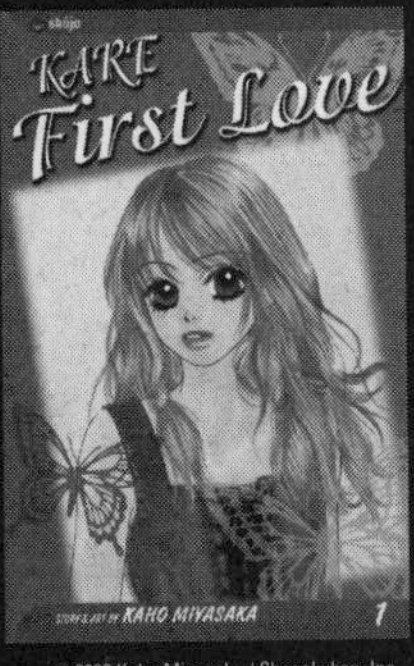
KARE
First Love
KAHO MIYASAKA
1

© 2002 Kaho Miyasaka / Shogakukan, Inc.

KARE FIRST LOVE

Sixteen-year-old plain-Jane Karin finds herself torn between keeping the friendship of her classmate Yuka and entertaining the advances of a boy named Kiriya, who also happens to be the object of Yuka's affections. Living happily ever after in high school isn't on the curriculum, as Karin soon finds herself the center of Kiriya's attention, as well as the bull's-eye in embittered pal Yuka's dartboard of hate. Experience the spine-tingling roller coaster ride of Karin's first experiences in love!

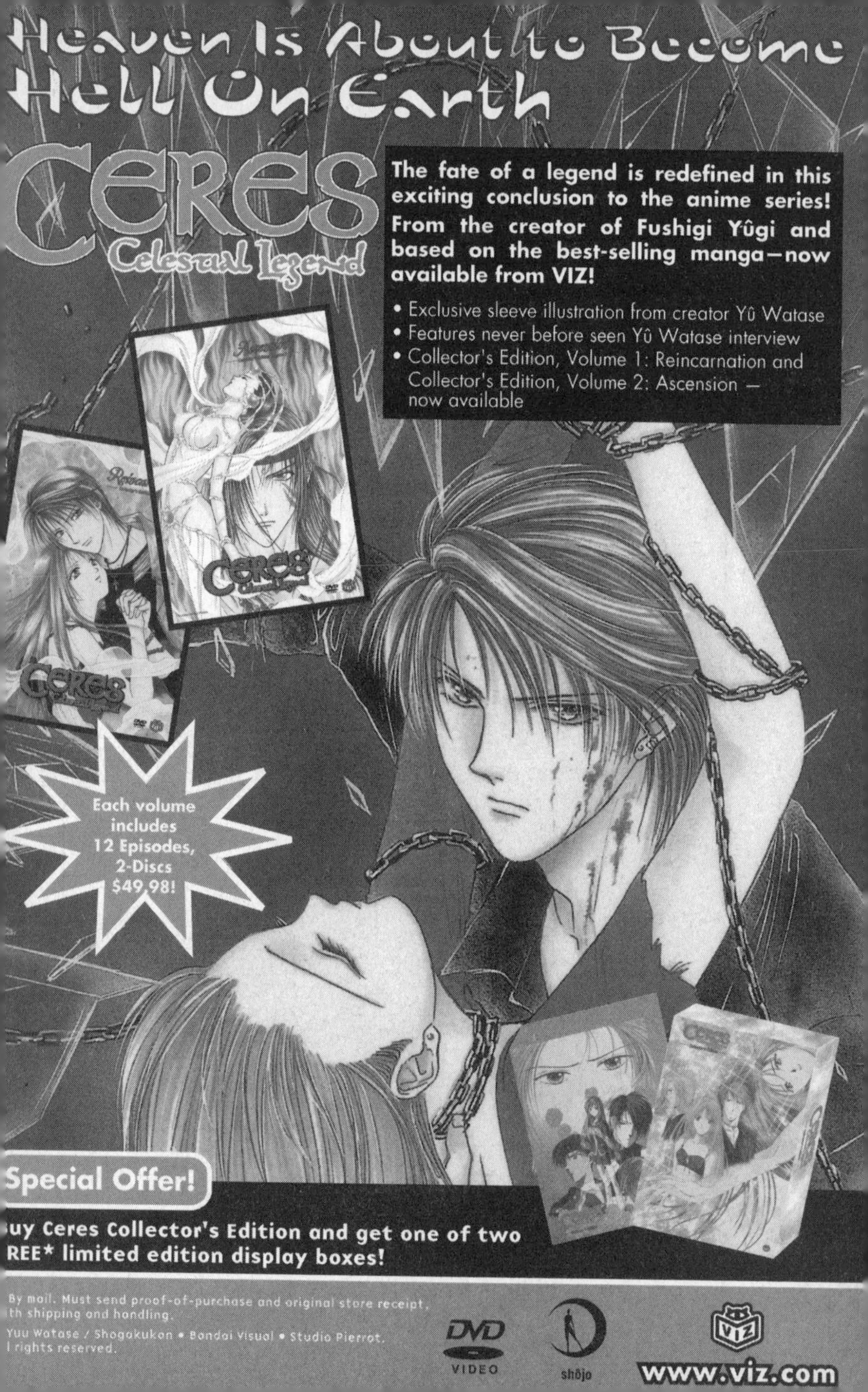

Heaven Is About to Become
Hell On Earth
Ceres
Celestial Legend
The fate of a legend is redefined in this exciting conclusion to the anime series! From the creator of Fushigi Yûgi and based on the best-selling manga—now available from VIZ!
• Exclusive sleeve illustration from creator Yû Watase
• Features never before seen Yû Watase interview
• Collector's Edition, Volume 1: Reincarnation and Collector's Edition, Volume 2: Ascension — now available
Each volume includes 12 Episodes, 2-Discs $49.98!
Special Offer!
uy Ceres Collector's Edition and get one of two
REE* limited edition display boxes!
By mail. Must send proof-of-purchase and original store receipt.
ith shipping and handling.
Yuu Watase / Shogakukan • Bandai Visual • Studio Pierrot.
l rights reserved.
DVD VIDEO
shôjo
VIZ
www.viz.com

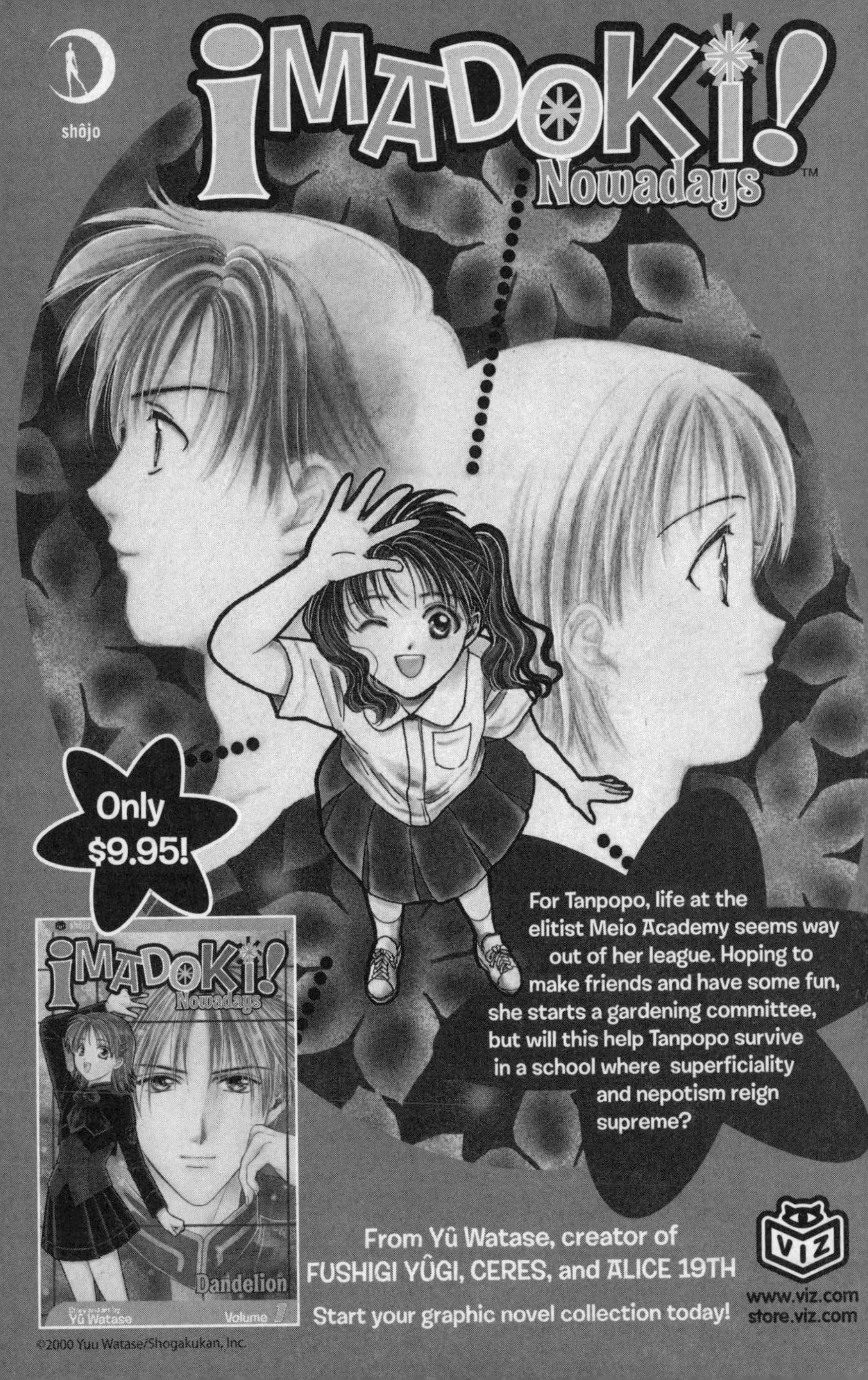
shôjo
iMADOKi! Nowadays™
Only $9.95!
shôjo
iMADOKi! Nowadays
Dandelion
Yû Watase
Volume 1
For Tanpopo, life at the elitist Meio Academy seems way out of her league. Hoping to make friends and have some fun, she starts a gardening committee, but will this help Tanpopo survive in a school where superficiality and nepotism reign supreme?
From Yû Watase, creator of FUSHIGI YÛGI, CERES, and ALICE 19TH
Start your graphic novel collection today!
VIZ
www.viz.com
store.viz.com
©2000 Yuu Watase/Shogakukan, Inc.

In Dorm Life, Anything Goes!

When Kazuya's brother marries his love interest – and takes her home to live with them – he escapes to a prestigious all-boys' school. Little did he know that life at Ryokuto Academy's dorm (a.k.a. Greenwood) would be nuttier than his already chaotic existence!

Only $9.99!

Here is Greenwood.

story and art by **Yukie Nasu** vol.1

Here is Greenwood

Start your graphic novel collection today!

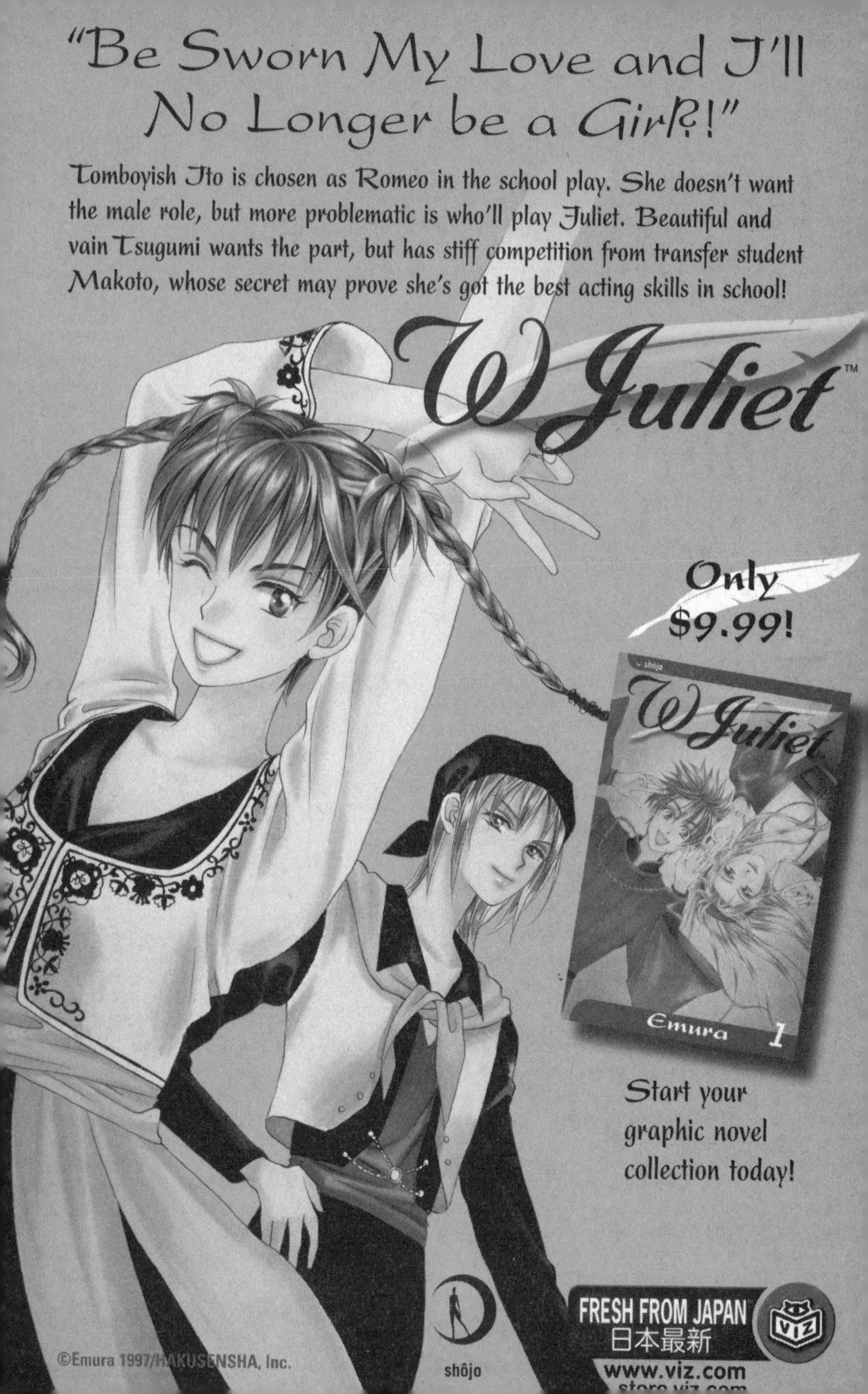
"Be Sworn My Love and I'll No Longer be a Girl?!"
Tomboyish Ito is chosen as Romeo in the school play. She doesn't want the male role, but more problematic is who'll play Juliet. Beautiful and vain Tsugumi wants the part, but has stiff competition from transfer student Makoto, whose secret may prove she's got the best acting skills in school!
W Juliet™
Only $9.99!
shôjo
W Juliet
Emura 1
Start your graphic novel collection today!
FRESH FROM JAPAN
日本最新
VIZ
www.viz.com
shôjo
©Emura 1997/HAKUSENSHA, Inc.

shôjo

AT THE HEART OF THE MATTER

- Alice 19th
- Angel Sanctuary
- Banana Fish
- Basara
- B.B. Explosion
- Boys Over Flowers *
- Ceres, Celestial Legend *
- Descendants of Darkness
- Dolls
- From Far Away
- Fushigi Yûgi
- Hana-Kimi
- Here Is Greenwood
- Hot Gimmick
- Imadoki
- Kare First Love
- Please Save My Earth *
- Red River
- Revolutionary Girl Utena
- Sensual Phrase
- W Juliet
- Wedding Peach
- Wild Com.
- X/1999

Start Your Shôjo Graphic Novel Collection Today!